Programming in ANSI C

— Third Edition —

About the Author

E Balagurusamy is the Vice Chancellor, Anna University, Chennai. He is a teacher, trainer, and consultant in the fields of Information Technology and Management. He holds an ME (Hons) in Electrical Engineering and Ph. D. in Systems Engineering from the Indian Institute of Technology, Roorkee. His areas of interest include Object-Oriented Software Engineering, Electronic Business, Technology Management, Business Process Re-engineering, and Total Quality Management.

A prolific writer, he has authored a large number of research papers and several books. His best selling books, among others include:

- Programming in C#
- Programming in Java, 2/e
- Object-oriented Programming with C++, 2/e
- Programming in BASIC, 3/e
- Numerical Methods, and
- Reliability Engineering

A recipient of numerous honours and awards, he has been listed in the Directory of Who's Who of Intellectuals and in the Directory of Distinguished Leaders in Education.

will output

I see,
I remember!

while the statement

```
printf( "I\n.. see,\n… … … I\n… … … remember !");
```

will print out

```
I
.. see
… … … I
… … … remember !
```

NOTE: Some authors recommend the inclusion of the statement

```
#include <stdio.h>
```

at the beginning of all programs that use any input/output library functions. However, this is not necessary for the functions *printf* and *scanf* which have been defined as a part of the C language. See Chapter 4 for more on input and output functions.

Before we proceed to discuss further examples, we must note one important point. C does make a distinction between *uppercase* and *lowercase* letters. For example, **printf** and **PRINTF** are not the same. In C, everything is written in lowercase letters. However, uppercase letters are used for symbolic names representing constants. We may also use uppercase letters in output strings like "I SEE" and "I REMEMBER"

The above example that printed **I see, I remember** is one of the simplest programs. Figure 1.3 highlights the general format of such simple programs. All C programs need a **main** function.

The main Function

The main is a part of every C program. C permits different forms of main statement. Following forms are allowed.

- main()
- int main()
- void main()
- main(void)
- void main(void)
- int main(void)

The empty pair of parentheses indicates that the function has no arguments. This may be explicitly indicated by using the keyword **void** inside the parentheses. We may also specify the keyword **int** or **void** before the word **main**. The keyword **void** means that the function does not return any information to the operating system and **int** means that the function returns an integer value to the operating system. When **int** is specified, the last statement in the program must be "return 0". For the sake of simplicity, we use the first form in our programs.

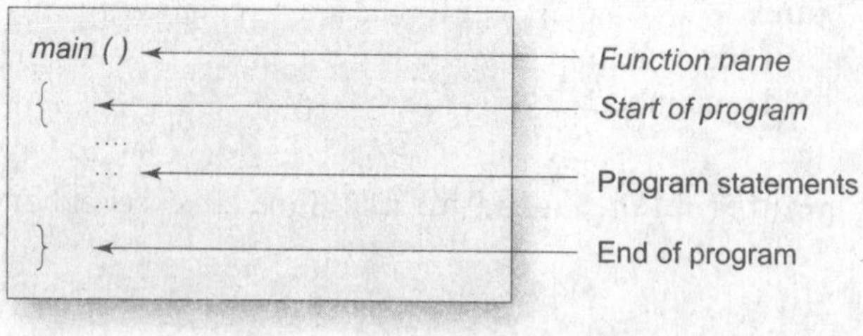

Fig. 1.3 *Format of simple C programs*

1.4 SAMPLE PROGRAM 2: ADDING TWO NUMBERS

Consider another program, which performs addition on two numbers and displays the result. The complete program is shown in Fig. 1.4.

```
/* Programm ADDITION                                  line-1 */
/* Written by EBG                                     line-2 */
main()                                             /* line-3 */
{                                                  /* line-4 */
        int number;                                /* line-5 */
        float amount;                              /* line-6 */
                                                   /* line-7 */
        number = 100;                              /* line-8 */
                                                   /* line-9 */
        amount = 30.75 + 75.35;                    /* line-10 */
        printf("%d\n",number);                     /* line-11 */
        printf("%5.2f",amount);                    /* line-12 */
}                                                  /* line-13 */
```

Fig. 1.4 *Program to add two numbers*

This program when executed will produce the following output:

```
100
106.10
```

The first two lines of the program are comment lines. It is a good practice to use comment lines in the beginning to give information such as name of the program, author, date, etc. Comment characters are also used in other lines to indicate line numbers.

The words **number** and **amount** are *variable names* that are used to store numeric data. The numeric data may be either in *integer* form or in *real* form. In C, *all variables should be declared* to tell the compiler what the ***variable names*** are and what ***type of data*** they hold. The variables must be declared before they are used. In lines 5 and 6, the declarations

```
int number;
float amount;
```

tell the compiler that **number** is an integer (**int** is the abbreviation for integer) and **amount** is a floating (**float**) point number. Declaration statements must appear at the beginning of the functions as shown in Fig.1.4. All declaration statements end with a semicolon. C supports many other data types and they are discussed in detail in Chapter 2.

The words such as **int** and **float** are called the *keywords* and cannot be used as *variable* names. A list of keywords is given in Chapter 2.

Data is stored in a variable by *assigning* a data value to it. This is done in lines 8 and 10. In line-8, an integer value 100 is assigned to the integer variable **number** and in line-10, the result of addition of two real numbers 30.75 and 75.35 is assigned to the floating point variable **amount.** The statements

```
number = 100;
amount = 30.75 + 75.35;
```

are called the *assignment* statements. Every assignment statement must have a semicolon at the end.

The next statement is an output statement that prints the value of **number**. The print statement

```
printf("%d\n", number);
```

contains two arguments. The first argument "%d" tells the compiler that the value of the second argument **number** should be printed as a *decimal integer*. Note that these arguments are separated by a comma. The newline character \n causes the next output to appear on a new line.

The last statement of the program

```
printf("%5.2f", amount);
```

prints out the value of **amount** in floating point format. The format specification *%5.2f* tells the compiler that the output must be in *floating point,* with five places in all and two places to the right of the decimal point.

1.5 SAMPLE PROGRAM 3: INTEREST CALCULATION

The program in Fig. 1.5 calculates the value of money at the end of each year of investment, assuming an interest rate of 11 percent and prints the year, and the corresponding amount, in two columns. The output is shown in Fig. 1.6 for a period of 10 years with an initial investment of 5000.00. The program uses the following formula:

Value at the end of year = Value at start of year (1 + interest rate)

In the program, the variable **value** represents the value of money at the end of the year while **amount** represents the value of money at the start of the year. The statement

```
amount = value ;
```

makes the value at the end of the *current* year as the value at start of the *next* year.

```
/*———————— INVESTMENT PROBLEM ————————*/
#define PERIOD  10
#define PRINCIPAL  5000.00
/*———————— MAIN PROGRAM BEGINS ————————*/
main()
```

```
{ /*________ DECLARATION STATEMENTS ________*/
    int year;
    float amount, value, inrate;
  /*________ ASSIGNMENT STATEMENTS ________*/
    amount = PRINCIPAL;
    inrate = 0.11;
    year = 0;
  /*________ COMPUTATION STATEMENTS ________*/
  /*________ COMPUTATION USING While LOOP ________*/
    while(year <= PERIOD)
    {  printf("%2d        %8.2f\n",year, amount);
       value  = amount + inrate * amount;
       year   = year + 1;
       amount = value;
    }
  /*________ while LOOP ENDS ________*/
}
  /*________ PROGRAM ENDS ________*/
```

Fig. 1.5 *Program for investment problem*

Let us consider the new features introduced in this program. The second and third lines begin with **#define** instructions. A **#define** instruction defines value to a *symbolic constant* for use in the program. Whenever a symbolic name is encountered, the compiler substitutes the value associated with the name automatically. To change the value, we have to simply change the definition. In this example, we have defined two symbolic constants **PERIOD** and **PRINCIPAL** and assigned values 10 and 5000.00 respectively. These values remain constant throughout the execution of the program.

```
 0      5000.00
 1      5550.00
 2      6160.50
 3      6838.15
 4      7590.35
 5      8425.29
 6      9352.07
 7     10380.00
 8     11522.69
 9     12790.00
10     14197.11
```

Fig. 1.6 *Output of the investment program*

The **#define** Directive

A **#define** is a preprocessor compiler directive and not a statement. Therefore **#define** lines should not end with a semicolon. Symbolic constants are generally written in uppercase so that they are easily distinguished from lowercase variable names. **#define** instructions are usually placed at the beginning before the **main()** function. Symbolic constants are not declared in declaration section. Preprocessor directions are discussed in Chapter 14.

We must note that the defined constants are not variables. We may not change their values within the program by using an assignment statement. For example, the statement

```
PRINCIPAL = 10000.00;
```

is illegal.

The declaration section declares **year** as integer and **amount, value** and **inrate** as floating point numbers. Note all the floating-point variables are declared in one statement. They can also be declared as

```
float amount;
float value;
float inrate;
```

When two or more variables are declared in one statement, they are separated by a comma.

All computations and printing are accomplished in a **while** loop. **while** is a mechanism for evaluating repeatedly a statement or a group of statements. In this case as long as the value of **year** is less than or equal to the value of **PERIOD**, the four statements that follow **while** are executed. Note that these four statements are grouped by braces. We exit the loop when **year** becomes greater than **PERIOD**. The concept and types of loops are discussed in Chapter 6.

C supports the basic four arithmetic operators (–, +, *, /) along with several others. They are discussed in Chapter 3.

1.6 SAMPLE PROGRAM 4: USE OF SUBROUTINES

So far, we have used only **printf** function that has been provided for us by the C system. The program shown in Fig. 1.7 uses a user-defined function. A function defined by the user is equivalent to a subroutine in FORTRAN or subprogram in BASIC.

```
/*———— PROGRAM USING FUNCTION ————*/
int mul (int a, int b); /*—— DECLARATION ———*/
/*———— MAIN PROGRAM BEGINS ————*/
    main ()
    {
        int a, b, c;

            a = 5;
```

```
        b = 10;
        c = mul (a,b);

        printf ("multiplication of %d and %d is %d",a,b,c);
    }
/* ———————————— MAIN PROGRAM ENDS
                MUL() FUNCTION STARTS ————————————*/
    int mul (int x, int y)
    int p;
    {
        p = x*y;
        return(p);
    }
/* ———————————— MUL () FUNCTION ENDS ————————————*/
```

Fig. 1.7 *A program using a user-defined function*

Figure 1.7 presents a very simple program that uses a **mul ( )** function. The program will print the following output.

Multiplication of 5 and 10 is 50

The **mul ( )** function multiplies the values of **x** and **y** and the result is returned to the **main ( )** function when it is called in the statement

```
c = mul (a, b);
```

The **mul ( )** has two *arguments* **x** and **y** that are declared as integers. The values of **a** and **b** are passed on to **x** and **y** respectively when the function **mul ( )** is called. User-defined functions are considered in detail in Chapter 9.

1.7 SAMPLE PROGRAM 5: USE OF MATH FUNCTIONS

We often use standard mathematical functions such as cos, sin, exp, etc. We shall see now the use of a mathematical function in a program. The standard mathematical functions are defined and kept as a part of C **math library**. If we want to use any of these mathematical functions, we must add an **#include** instruction in the program. Like **#define,** it is also a compiler directive that instructs the compiler to link the specified mathematical functions from the library. The instruction is of the form

```
#include <math.h>
```

math.h is the filename containing the required function. Figure 1.8 illustrates the use of cosine function. The program calculates cosine values for angles 0, 10, 20............180 and prints out the results with headings.

Another **#include** instruction that is often required is

```
#include <stdio.h>
```

stdio.h refers to the *standard* I/O header file containing standard input and output functions

```
/*———— PROGRAM USING COSINE FUNCTION ———— */
#include <math.h>
#define     PI      3.1416
#define     MAX     180

main ( )
{

        int angle;
        float x,y;

        angle = 0;
        printf("      Angle       Cos(angle)\n\n");

        while(angle <= MAX)
        {
            x = (PI/MAX)*angle:
            y = cos(x);
            printf("%15d %13.4f\n", angle, y);
            angle = angle + 10;
        }
}
```

Output

```
        Angle           Cos(angle)
        0                  1.0000
        10                 0.9848
        20                 0.9397
        30                 0.8660
        40                 0.7660
        50                 0.6428
        60                 0.5000
        70                 0.3420
        80                 0.1736
        90                -0.0000
        100               -0.1737
        110               -0.3420
        120               -0.5000
        130               -0.6428
        140               -0.7660
        150               -0.8660
        160               -0.9397
        170               -0.9848
        180               -1.0000
```

Fig. 1.8 *Program using a math function*

The #include Directive

As mentioned earlier, C programs are divided into modules or functions. Some functions are written by users like us and many others are stored in the C library. Library functions are grouped category-wise and stored in different files known as header files. If we want to access the functions stored in the library, it is necessary to tell the compiler about the files to be accessed.

This is achieved by using the preprocessor directive **#include** as follows:

#include<filename>

filename is the name of the library file that contains the required function definition. Preprocessor directives are placed at the beginning of a program.

A list of library functions and header files containing them are given in Appendix III.

1.8 BASIC STRUCTURE OF C PROGRAMS

The examples discussed so far illustrate that a C program can be viewed as a group of building blocks called *functions*. A function is a subroutine that may include one or more *statements* designed to perform a *specific task*. To write a C program, we first create functions and then put them together. A C program may contain one or more sections shown in Fig. 1.9.

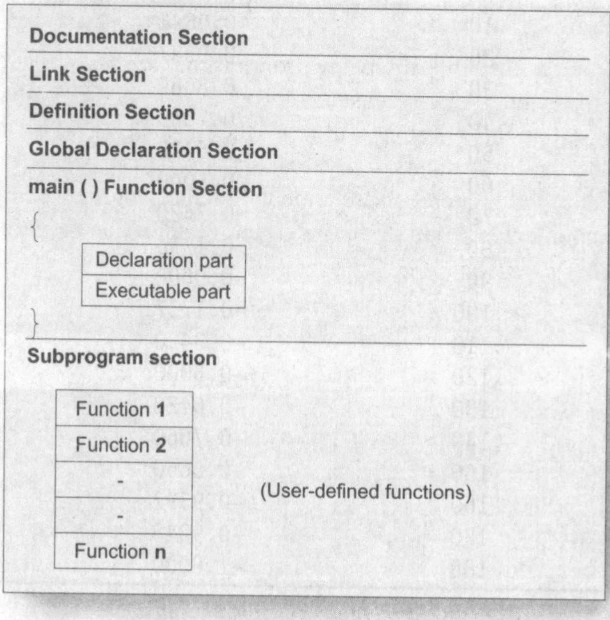

Fig. 1.9 *An overview of a C program*

The documentation section consists of a set of comment lines giving the name of the program, the author and other details, which the programmer would like to use later. The link section provides instructions to the compiler to link functions from the system library. The definition section defines all symbolic constants.

There are some variables that are used in more than one function. Such variables are called *global* variables and are declared in the *global* declaration section that is outside of all the functions. This section also declares all the user-defined functions.

Every C program must have one **main()** function section. This section contains two parts, declaration part and executable part. The declaration part declares all the variables used in the executable part. There is at least one statement in the executable part. These two parts must appear between the opening and the closing braces. The program execution begins at the opening brace and ends at the closing brace. The closing brace of the main function section is the logical end of the program. All statements in the declaration and executable parts end with a semicolon.

The subprogram section contains all the user-defined functions that are called in the **main** function. User-defined functions are generally placed immediately after the **main** function, although they may appear in any order.

All sections, except the **main** function section may be absent when they are not required.

1.9 PROGRAMMING STYLE

Unlike some other programming languages (COBOL, FORTRAN, etc.,) C is a *free-form* language. That is, the C compiler does not care, where on the line we begin typing. While this may be a licence for bad programming, we should try to use this fact to our advantage in developing readable programs. Although several alternative styles are possible, we should select one style and use it with total consistency.

First of all, we must develop the habit of writing programs in lowercase letters. C program statements are written in lowercase letters. Uppercase letters are used only for symbolic constants.

Braces group program statements together and mark the beginning and the end of functions. A proper indentation of braces and statements would make a program easier to read and debug. Note how the braces are aligned and the statements are indented in the program of Fig. 1.5.

Since C is a free-form language, we can group statements together on one line. The statements

```
a = b;
x = y + 1;
z = a + x;
```

can be written on one line as

```
a = b; x = y+1; z = a+x;
```

The program

```
main( )
{
        printf("hello C");
}
```

may be written in one line like

```
main( ) {printf("Hello C")};
```

However, this style make the program more difficult to understand and should not be used. In this book, each statement is written on a separate line.

The generous use of comments inside a program cannot be overemphasized. Judiciously inserted comments not only increase the readability but also help to understand the program logic. This is very important for debugging and testing the program.

1.10 EXECUTING A 'C' PROGRAM

Executing a program written in C involves a series of steps. These are:

1. Creating the program
2. Compiling the program
3. Linking the program with functions that are needed from the C library
4. Executing the program.

Figure 1.10 illustrates the process of creating, compiling and executing a C program. Although these steps remain the same irrespective of the *operating system,* system commands for implementing the steps and conventions for naming *files* may differ on different systems.

An operating system is a program that controls the entire operation of a computer system. All input/out operations are channeled through the operating system. The operating system, which is an interface between the hardware and the user, handles the execution of user programs.

The two most popular operating systems today are UNIX (for minicomputers) and MS-DOS (for microcomputers). We shall discuss briefly the procedure to be followed in executing C programs under both these operating systems in the following sections.

1.11 UNIX SYSTEM

Creating the program

Once we load the UNIX operating system into the memory, the computer is ready to receive program. The program must be entered into a file. The file name can consist of letters, digits and special characters, followed by a dot and a letter **c**. Examples of valid file names are:

```
hello.c
program.c
ebg1.c
```

The file is created with the help of a *text editor*, either **ed** or **vi.** The command for calling the editor and creating the file is

```
ed filename
```

If the file existed before, it is loaded. If it does not yet exist, the file has to be created so that it is ready to receive the new program. Any corrections in the program are done under the editor. (The name of your system's editor may be different. Check your system manual.)

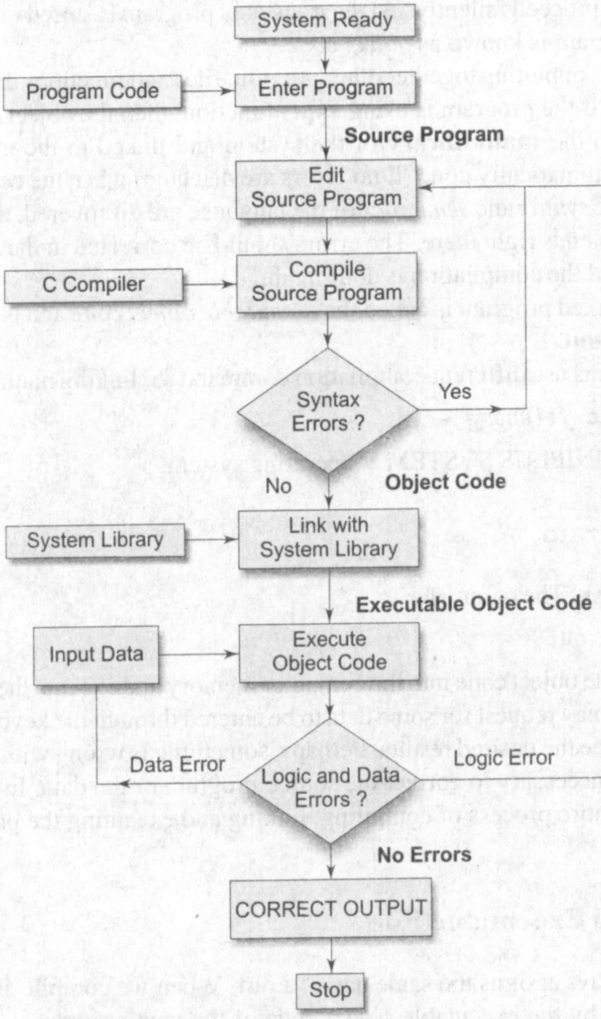

Fig. 1.10 *Process of compiling and running a C program*

When the editing is over, the file is saved on disk. It can then be referenced any time later by its file name. The program that is entered into the file is known as the *source program*, since it represents the original form of the program.

Compiling and Linking

Let us assume that the source program has been created in a file named *ebg1.c*. Now the program is ready for compilation. The compilation command to achieve this task under UNIX is

```
cc ebg1.c
```

The source program instructions are now translated into a form that is suitable for execution by the computer. The translation is done after examining each instruction for its correctness. If everything is alright, the compilation proceeds silently and the translated program is stored on another file with the name *ebg1.o*. This program is known as *object code*.

Linking is the process of putting together other program files and functions that are required by the program. For example, if the program is using **exp()** function, then the object code of this function should be brought from the **math library** of the system and linked to the main program. Under UNIX, the linking is automatically done (if no errors are detected) when the **cc** command is used.

If any mistakes in the *syntax* and *semantics* of the language are discovered, they are listed out and the compilation process ends right there. The errors should be corrected in the source program with the help of the editor and the compilation is done again.

The compiled and linked program is called the *executable object code* and is stored automatically in another file named **a.out.**

Note that some systems use different compilation command for linking mathematical functions.

```
cc filename - lm
```

is the command under UNIPLUS SYSTEM V operating system.

Executing the Program

Execution is a simple task. The command

```
a.out
```

would load the executable object code into the computer memory and execute the instructions. During execution, the program may request for some data to be entered through the keyboard. Sometimes the program does not produce the desired results. Perhaps, something is wrong with the program *logic* or *data*. Then it would be necessary to correct the source program or the data. In case the source program is modified, the entire process of compiling, linking and executing the program should be repeated.

Creating Your Own Executable File

Note that the linker always assigns the same name **a.out**. When we compile another program, this file will be overwritten by the executable object code of the new program. If we want to prevent from happening, we should rename the file immediately by using the command.

```
mv a.out name
```

We may also achieve this by specifying an option in the cc command as follows:

```
cc –o name source-file
```

This will store the executable object code in the file name and prevent the old file **a.out** from being destroyed.

Multiple Source Files

To compile and link multiple source program files, we must append all the files names to the **cc** command.

```
cc filename-1.c …. filename-n.c
```

These files will be separately compiled into object files called

```
filename-i.o
```

and then linked to produce an executable program file **a.out** as shown in Fig. 1.11.

It is also possible to compile each file separately and link them later. For example, the commands

```
cc -c mod1.c
cc -c mod2.c
```

will compile the source files *mod1.c* and *mod2.c* into objects files *mod1.o* and *mod2.o*. They can be linked together by the command

```
cc mod1.o mod2.o
```

we may also combine the source files and object files as follows:

```
cc mod1.c mod2.o
```

Only *mod1.c* is compiled and then linked with the object file mod2.o. This approach is useful when one of the multiple source files need to be changed and recompiled or an already existing object files is to be used along with the program to be compiled.

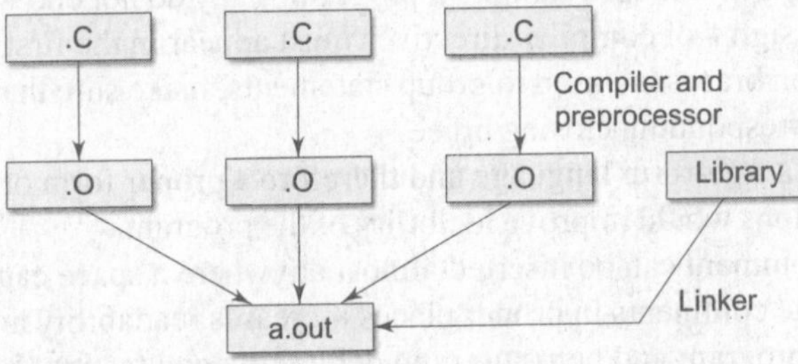

Fig. 1.11 *Compilation of multiple files*

1.12 MS-DOS SYSTEM

The program can be created using any word processing software in non-document mode. The file name should end with the characters ".c" like **program.c, pay.c,** etc. Then the command

```
MSC pay.c
```

under MS-DOS operating system would load the program stored in the file **pay.c** and generate the **object code.** This code is stored in another file under name **pay.obj**. In case any language errors are found, the compilation is not completed. The program should then be corrected and compiled again.

The linking is done by the command

```
LINK pay.obj
```

which generates the **executable code** with the filename **pay.exe**. Now the command

```
pay
```

would execute the program and give the results.

Just Remember

- Every C program requires a **main()** function (Use of more than one **main()** is illegal). The place **main** is where the program execution begins.
- The execution of a function begins at the opening brace of the function and ends at the corresponding closing brace.
- C programs are written in lowercase letters. However, uppercase letters are used for symbolic names and output strings.
- All the words in a program line must be separated from each other by at least one space, or a tab, or a punctuation mark.
- Every program statement in a C language must end with a semicolon.
- All variables must be declared for their types before they are used in the program.
- We must make sure to include header files using **#include** directive when the program refers to special names and functions that it does not define.
- Compiler directives such as **define** and **include** are special instructions to the compiler to help it compile a program. They do not end with a semicolon.
- The sign # of compiler directives must appear in the first column of the line.
- When braces are used to group statements, make sure that the opening brace has a corresponding closing brace.
- C is a free-form language and therefore a proper form of indentation of various sections would improve legibility of the program.
- A comment can be inserted almost anywhere a space can appear. Use of appropriate comments in proper places increases readability and understandability of the program and helps users in debugging and testing. Remember to match the symbols /* and */ appropriately.

REVIEW QUESTIONS

1.1 State whether the following statements are *true* or *false*.

(a) Every line in a C program should end with a semicolon.
(b) In C language lowercase letters are significant.
(c) Every C program ends with an END word.
(d) **main( )** is where the program begins its execution.
(e) A line in a program may have more than one statement.
(f) A **printf** statement can generate only one line of output.
(g) The closing brace of the **main( )** in a program is the logical end of the program.
(h) The purpose of the header file such as **stdio.h** is to store the source code of a program.
(i) Comments cause the computer to print the text enclosed between /* and */ when executed.
(j) Syntax errors will be detected by the compiler.

1.2 Which of the following statements are *true*?

(a) Every C program must have at least one user-defined function.

(b) Only one function may be named **main**( ).
(c) Declaration section contains instructions to the computer.

1.3 Which of the following statements about comments are *false*?
(a) Use of comments reduces the speed of execution of a program.
(b) Comments serve as internal documentation for programmers.
(c) A comment can be inserted in the middle of a statement.
(d) In C, we can have comments inside comments.

1.4 Fill in the blanks with appropriate words in each of the following statements.
(a) Every program statement in a C program must end with a ___________
(b) The ___________ Function is used to display the output on the screen.
(c) The ___________ header file contains mathematical functions.
(d) The escape sequence character ___________ causes the cursor to move to the next line on the screen.

1.5 Remove the semicolon at the end of the **printf** statement in the program of Fig. 1.2 and execute it. What is the output?

1.6 In the Sample Program 2, delete line-5 and execute the program. How helpful is the error message?

1.7 Modify the Sample Program 3 to display the following output:

Year	**Amount**
1	5500.00
2	6160.00
-	________
-	________
10	14197.11

1.8 Find errors, if any, in the following program:

```
/* A simple program
int main( )
{
    /* Does nothing */
}
```

1.9 Find errors, if any, in the following program:

```
#include (stdio.h)
void main(void)
{
    print("Hello C");
}
```

1.10 Find errors, if any, in the following program:

```
Include <math.h>
main { }
(
    FLOAT X;
    X = 2.5;
    Y = exp(x);
```

```
            Print(x,y);
        )
```

1.11 Why and when do we use the **#define** directive?
1.12 Why and when do we use the **#include** directive?
1.13 What does **void main(void)** mean?
1.14 Distinguish between the following pairs:
  (a) main( ) and void main(void)
  (b) int main( ) and void main( )
1.15 Why do we need to use comments in programs?
1.16 Why is the look of a program is important?
1.17 Where are blank spaces permitted in a C program?
1.18 Describe the structure of a C program.
1.19 Describe the process of creating and executing a C program under UNIX system.
1.20 How do we implement multiple source program files?

PROGRAMMING EXERCISES

1.1 Write a program that will print your mailing address in the following form:

First line	:	Name
Second line	:	Door No, Street
Third line	:	City, Pin code

1.2 Modify the above program to provide border lines to the address.
1.3 Write a program using one print statement to print the pattern of asterisks as shown below:

```
*
*   *
*   *   *
*   *   *   *
```

1.4 Write a program that will print the following figure using suitable characters.

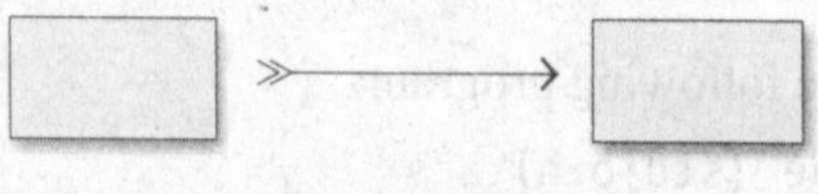

1.5 Given the radius of a circle, write a program to compute and display its area. Use a symbolic constant to define the π value and assume a suitable value for radius.
1.6 Write a program to output the following multiplication table:

$5 \times 1 = 5$

$5 \times 2 = 10$

$5 \times 3 = 15$

. .

. .

$5 \times 10 = 50$

1.7 Given two integers 20 and 10, write a program that uses a function add( ) to add these two numbers and sub( ) to find the difference of these two numbers and then display the sum and difference in the following form:

20 + 10 = 30

20 – 10 = 10

1.8 Given the values of three variables a, b and c, write a program to compute and display the value of x, where

$$x = \frac{a}{b - c}$$

Execute your program for the following values:

(a) a = 250, b = 85, c = 25

(b) a = 300, b = 70, c = 70

Comment on the output in each case.

Chapter 2

Constants, Variables, and Data Types

2.1 INTRODUCTION

A programming language is designed to help process certain kinds of *data* consisting of numbers, characters and strings and to provide useful output known as *information.* The task of processing of data is accomplished by executing a sequence of precise instructions called a *program.* These instructions are formed using certain symbols and words according to some rigid rules known as *syntax rules* (or *grammar*). Every program instruction must confirm precisely to the syntax rules of the language.

Like any other language, C has its own vocabulary and grammar. In this chapter, we will discuss the concepts of constants and variables and their types as they relate to C programming language.

2.2 CHARACTER SET

The characters that can be used to form words, numbers and expressions depend upon the computer on which the program is run. However, a subset of characters is available that can be used on most personal, micro, mini and mainframe computers. The characters in C are grouped into the following categories:

1. Letters
2. Digits
3. Special characters
4. White spaces

The entire character set is given in Table 2.1.

The compiler ignores white spaces unless they are a part of a string constant. White spaces may be used to separate words, but are prohibited between the characters of keywords and identifiers.

Trigraph Characters

Many non-English keyboards do not support all the characters mentioned in Table 2.1. ANSI C introduces the concept of "trigraph" sequences to provide a way to enter certain characters that are not available on some keyboards. Each trigraph sequence consists of three characters (two question marks followed by another character) as shown in Table 2.2. For example, if a keyboard does not support square brackets, we can still use them in a program using the trigraphs ??(and ??).

Table 2.1 *C Character Set*

Letters	*Digits*
Uppercase A.....Z	All decimal digits 0 9
Lowercase a.....z	
Special Characters	
, comma	& ampersand
. period	^ caret
; semicolon	* asterisk
: colon	– minus sign
? question mark	+ plus sign
' apostrophe	< opening angle bracket (or less than sign)
" quotation mark	> closing angle bracket (or greater than sign)
! exclamation mark	(left parenthesis
| vertical bar	) right parenthesis
/ slash	[left bracket
\ backslash	] right bracket
~ tilde	{ left brace
_ under score	} right brace
$ dollar sign	# number sign
% percent sign	
White Spaces	
Blank space	
Horizontal tab	
Carriage return	
New line	
Form feed	

Table 2.2 *ANSI C Trigraph Sequences*

Trigraph sequence	*Translation*
??=	# number sign
??(	[left bracket
??)	] right bracket
??<	{ left brace
??>	} right brace
??!	| vetical bar
??/	\ back slash
??/	^ caret
??-	~ tilde

2.3 C TOKENS

In a passage of text, individual words and punctuation marks are called *tokens*. Similarly, in a C program the smallest individual units are known as C tokens. C has six types of tokens as shown in Fig. 2.1. C programs are written using these tokens and the syntax of the language.

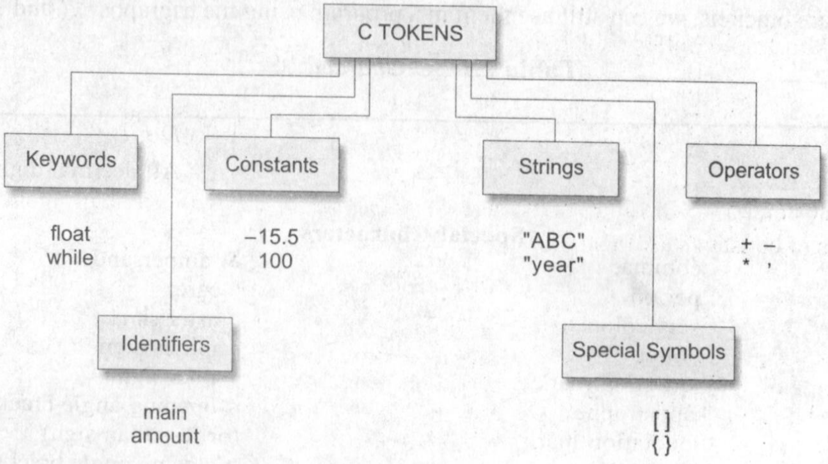

Fig. 2.1 *C tokens and examples*

2.4 KEYWORDS AND IDENTIFIERS

Every C word is classified as either a *keyword* or an *identifier*. All keywords have fixed meanings and these meanings cannot be changed. Keywords serve as basic building blocks for program statements. The list of all keywords of ANSI C are listed in Table 2.3. All keywords must be written in lowercase. Some compilers may use additional keywords that must be identified from the C manual.

Table 2.3 *ANSI C Keywords*

auto	double	int	struct
break	else	long	switch
case	enum	register	typedef
char	extern	return	union
const	float	short	unsigned
continue	for	signed	void
default	goto	sizeof	volatile
do	if	static	while

Identifiers refer to the names of variables, functions and arrays. These are user-defined names and consist of a sequence of letters and digits, with a letter as a first character. Both uppercase and lowercase letters are permitted, although lowercase letters are commonly used. The underscore character is also permitted in identifiers. It is usually used as a link between two words in long identifiers.

Rules for Identifiers

1. First character must be an alphabet (or underscore).
2. Must consist of only letters, digits or underscore.
3. Only first 31 characters are significant.
4. Cannot use a keyword.
5. Must not contain white space.

2.5 CONSTANTS

Constants in C refer to fixed values that do not change during the execution of a program. C supports several types of constants as illustrated in Fig. 2.2.

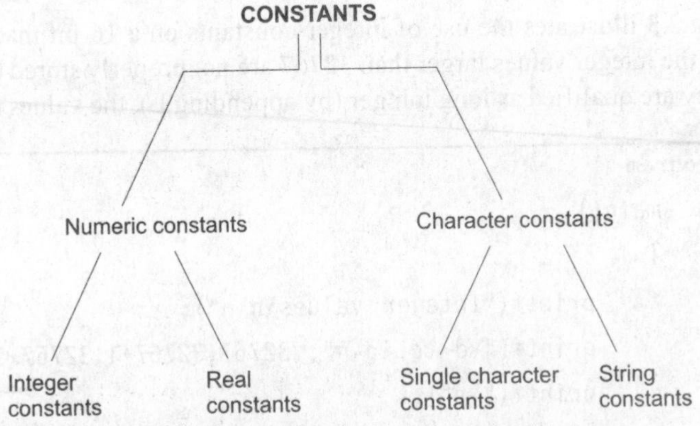

Fig. 2.2 *Basic types of C constants*

Integer Constants

An *integer* constant refers to a sequence of digits. There are three types of integers, namely, *decimal* integer, *octal* integer and *hexadecimal* integer.

Decimal integers consist of a set of digits, 0 through 9, preceded by an optional – or + sign. Valid examples of decimal integer constants are:

123 – 321 0 654321 +78

Embedded spaces, commas, and non-digit characters are not permitted between digits. For example,

15 750 20,000 $1000

are illegal numbers. Note that ANSI C supports *unary plus* which was not defined earlier.

An *octal* integer constant consists of any combination of digits from the set 0 through 7, with a leading 0. Some examples of octal integer are:

037 0 0435 0551

A sequence of digits preceded by 0x or 0X is considered as *hexadecimal* integer. They may also include alphabets A through F or a through f. The letter A through F represent the numbers 10 through 15. Following are the examples of valid hex integers.

0X2 0x9F 0Xbcd 0x

We rarely use octal and hexadecimal numbers in programming.

The largest integer value that can be stored is machine-dependent. It is 32767 on 16-bit machines and 2,147,483,647 on 32-bit machines. It is also possible to store larger integer constants on these machines by appending *qualifiers* such as U,L and UL to the constants. For examples:

56789U	or 56789u	(unsigned integer)
987612347UL	or 98761234ul	(unsigned long integer)
9876543L	or 98765431	(long integer)

The concept of unsigned and long integers are discussed in detail in Section 2.7.

Example 2.1 Representation of integer constants on a 16-bit computer.

The program in Fig.2.3 illustrates the use of integer constants on a 16-bit machine. The output in Fig. 2.3 shows that the integer values larger than 32767 are not properly stored on a 16-bit machine. However, when they are qualified as long integer (by appending L), the values are correctly stored.

Program

```
main()
{
    printf("Integer values\n\n");
    printf("%d %d %d\n", 32767,32767+1,32767+10);
    printf("\n");
    printf("Long integer values\n\n");
    printf("%ld %ld %ld\n", 32767L,32767L+1L,32767L+10L);
}
```

Output

```
Integer values
32767 -32768 -32759
Long integer values
32767 32768 32777
```

Fig. 2.3 *Representation of integer constants on 16-bit machine*

Real Constants

Integer numbers are inadequate to represent quantities that vary continuously, such as distances, heights, temperatures, prices, and so on. These quantities are represented by numbers containing fractional parts like 17.548. Such numbers are called *real* (or *floating point*) constants. Further examples of real constants are:

0.0083 –0.75 435.36 +247.0

These numbers are shown in *decimal notation*, having a whole number followed by a decimal point and the fractional part. It is possible to omit digits before the decimal point, or digits after the decimal point. That is,

215. .95 –.71 +.5

are all valid real numbers.

A real number may also be expressed in *exponential* (or *scientific) notation*. For example, the value 215.65 may be written as 2.1565e2 in exponential notation. e2 means multiply by 10^2. The general form is:

mantissa *e* exponent

The *mantissa* is either a real number expressed in *decimal notation* or an integer. The *exponent* is an integer number with an optional *plus* or *minus sign.* The letter **e** separating the mantissa and the exponent can be written in either lowercase or uppercase. Since the exponent causes the decimal point to "float", this notation is said to represent a real number in *floating point form.* Examples of legal floating-point constants are:

0.65e4 12e-2 1.5e+5 3.18E3 -1.2E-1

Embedded white space is not allowed.

Exponential notation is useful for representing numbers that are either very large or very small in magnitude. For example, 7500000000 may be written as 7.5E9 or 75E8. Similarly, -0.000000368 is equivalent to –3.68E-7.

Floating-point constants are normally represented as double-precision quantities. However, the suffixes f or F may be used to force single-precision and l or L to extend double precision further.

Some examples of valid and invalid numeric constants are given in Table 2.4.

Table 2.4 *Examples of Numeric Constants*

Constant	*Valid ?*	*Remarks*
698354L	Yes	Represents long integer
25,000	No	Comma is not allowed
+5.0E3	Yes	(ANSI C supports unary plus)
3.5e-5	Yes	
7.1e 4	No	No white space is permitted
-4.5e-2	Yes	
1.5E+2.5	No	Exponent must be an integer
$255	No	$ symbol is not permitted
0X7B	Yes	Hexadecimal integer

Single Character Constants

A single character constant (or simply character constant) contains a single character enclosed within a pair of *single* quote marks. Example of character constants are:

'5' 'X' ';' ' '

Note that the character constant '5' is not the same as the *number* 5. The last constant is a blank space.

Character constants have integer values known as ASCII values. For example, the statement

```
printf("%d", 'a');
```

would print the number 97, the ASCII value of the letter a. Similarly, the statement

```
printf("%c", '97');
```

would output the letter 'a'. ASCII values for all characters are given in Appendix II.

Since each character constant represents an integer value, it is also possible to perform arithmetic operations on character constants. They are discussed in Chapter 8.

String Constants

A string constant is a sequence of characters enclosed in *double* quotes. The characters may be letters, numbers, special characters and blank space. Examples are:

"Hello!" "1987" "WELL DONE" "?...!" "5+3" "X"

Remember that a character constant (e.g., 'X') is not equivalent to the single character string constant (e.g., "X"). Further, a single character string constant does not have an equivalent integer value while a character constant has an integer value. Character strings are often used in programs to build meaningful programs. Manipulation of character strings are considered in detail in Chapter 8.

Backslash Character Constants

C supports some special backslash character constants that are used in output functions. For example, the symbol '\n' stands for newline character. A list of such backslash character constants is given in Table 2.5. Note that each one of them represents one character, although they consist of two characters. These characters combinations are known as *escape sequences*.

Table 2.5 *Backslash Character Constants*

Constant	*Meaning*
'\a'	audible alert (bell)
'\b'	back space
'\f'	form feed
'\n'	new line
'\r'	carriage return
'\t'	horizontal tab

(Contd.)

Table 2.5 *(Contd.)*

Constant	*Meaning*
'\v'	vertical tab
'\''	single quote
'\"'	double quote
'\?'	question mark
'\\'	backslash
'\0'	null

2.6 VARIABLES

A *variable* is a data name that may be used to store a data value. Unlike constants that remain unchanged during the execution of a program, a variable may take different values at different times during execution. In Chapter 1, we used several variables. For instance, we used the variable **amount** in Sample Program 3 to store the value of money at the end of each year (after adding the interest earned during that year).

A variable name can be chosen by the programmer in a meaningful way so as to reflect its function or nature in the program. Some examples of such names are:

Average
height
Total
Counter_1
class_strength

As mentioned earlier, variable names may consist of letters, digits, and the underscore(_) character, subject to the following conditions:

1. They must begin with a letter. Some systems permit underscore as the first character.
2. ANSI standard recognizes a length of 31 characters. However, length should not be normally more than eight characters, since only the first eight characters are treated as significant by many compilers.
3. Uppercase and lowercase are significant. That is, the varible **Total** is not the same as **total** or **TOTAL**.
4. It should not be a keyword.
5. White space is not allowed.

Some examples of valid variable names are:

John	Value	T_raise
Delhi	x1	ph_value
mark	sum1	distance

Invalid examples include:

123	(area)
%	25th

Further examples of variable names and their correctness are given in Table 2.6.

Table 2.6 *Examples of Variable Names*

Variable name	*Valid ?*	*Remark*
First_tag	Valid	
char	Not valid	char is a keyword
Price$	Not valid	Dollar sign is illegal
group one	Not valid	Blank space is not permitted
average_number	Valid	First eight characters are significant
int_type	Valid	Keyword may be part of a name

If only the first eight characters are recognized by a compiler, then the two names

average_height
average_weight

mean the same thing to the computer. Such names can be rewritten as

avg_height and avg_weight

or

ht_average and wt_average

without changing their meanings.

2.7 DATA TYPES

C language is rich in its *data types.* Storage representations and machine instructions to handle constants differ from machine to machine. The variety of data types available allow the programmer to select the type appropriate to the needs of the application as well as the machine.

ANSI C supports three classes of data types:

1. Primary (or fundamental) data types
2. Derived data types
3. User-defined data types

The primary data types and their extensions are discussed in this section. The user-defined data types are defined in the next section while the derived data types such as arrays, functions, structures and pointers are discussed as and when they are encountered.

All C compilers support five fundamental data types, namely integer **(int),** character **(char)**, floating point (**float),** double-precision floating point **(double)** and **void.** Many of them also offer extended data types such as **long int** and **long double**. Various data types and the terminology used to describe them are given in Fig. 2.4. The range of the basic four types are given in Table 2.7. We discuss briefly each one of them in this section.

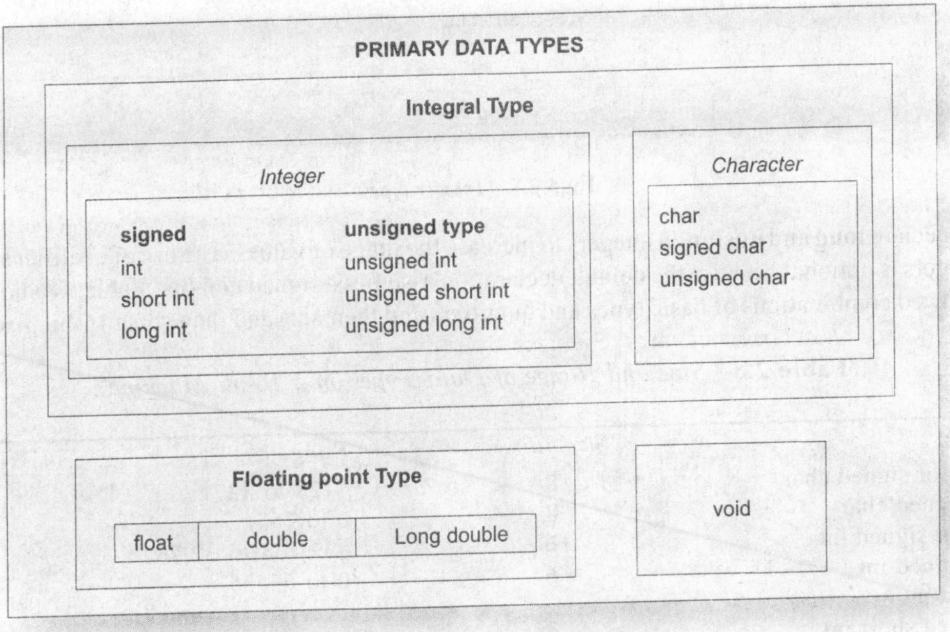

Fig. 2.4 *Primary data types in C*

Table 2.7 *Size and Range of Basic Data Types on 16-bit Machines*

Data type	*Range of values*
char	–128 to 127
int	–32,768 to 32,767
float	3.4e–38 to 3.4e+e38
double	1.7e–308 to 1.7e+308

Integer Types

Integers are whole numbers with a range of values supported by a particular machine. Generally, integers occupy one word of storage, and since the word sizes of machines vary (typically, 16 or 32 bits) the size of an integer that can be stored depends on the computer. If we use a 16 bit word length, the size of the integer value is limited to the range –32768 to +32767 (that is, -2^{15} to $+2^{15}-1$). A signed integer uses one bit for sign and 15 bits for the magnitude of the number. Similarly, a 32 bit word length can store an integer ranging from -2,147,483,648 to 2,147,483,647.

In order to provide some control over the range of numbers and storage space, C has three classes of integer storage, namely **short int, int,** and **long int,** in both **signed** and **unsigned** forms. ANSI C defines these types so that they can be organized from the smallest to the largest, as shown in Fig. 2.5. For example, **short int** represents fairly small integer values and requires half the amount of storage as a regular **int** number uses. Unlike signed integers, unsigned integers use all the bits for the magnitude of the number and are always positive. Therefore, for a 16 bit machine, the range of unsigned integer numbers will be from 0 to 65,535.

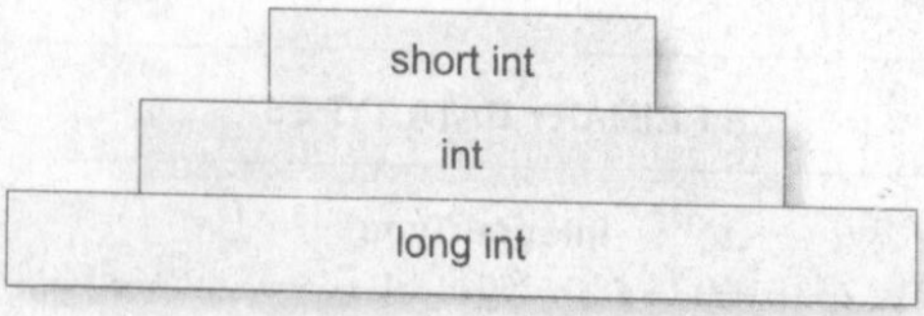

Fig. 2.5 *Integer types*

We declare **long** and **unsigned** integers to increase the range of values. The use of qualifier **signed** on integers is optional because the default declaration assumes a signed number. Table 2.8 shows all the allowed combinations of basic types and qualifiers and their size and range on a 16-bit machine.

Table 2.8 *Size and Range of Data Types on a 16-bit Machine*

Type	*Size (bits)*	*Range*
char or signed char	8	–128 to 127
unsigned char	8	0 to 255
int or signed int	16	–32,768 to 32,767
unsigned int	16	0 to 65535
short int or signed short int	8	–128 to 127
unsigned short int	8	0 to 255
long int or signed long int	32	–2,147,483,648 to 2,147,483,647
unsigned long int	32	0 to 4,294,967,295
float	32	3.4E – 38 to 3.4E + 38
double	64	1.7E – 308 to 1.7E + 308
long double	80	3.4E – 4932 to 1.1E + 4932

Floating Point Types

Floating point (or real) numbers are stored in 32 bits (on all 16 bit and 32 bit machines), with 6 digits of precision. Floating point numbers are defined in C by the keyword **float.** When the accuracy provided by a **float** number is not sufficient, the type **double** can be used to define the number. A **double** data type number uses 64 bits giving a precision of 14 digits. These are known as *double precision* numbers. Remember that double type represents the same data type that **float** represents, but with a greater precision. To extend the precision further, we may use **long double** which uses 80 bits. The relationship among floating types is illustrated in Fig. 2.6.

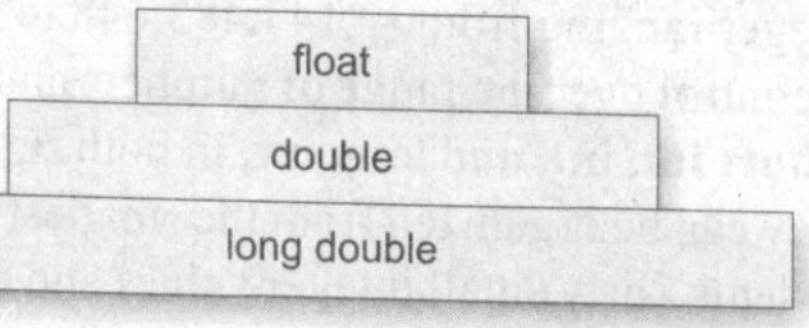

Fig. 2.6 *Floating-point types*

Void Types

The **void** type has no values. This is usually used to specify the type of functions. The type of a function is said to be **void** when it does not return any value to the calling function. It can also play the role of a generic type, meaning that it can represent any of the other standard types.

Character Types

A single character can be defined as a character(**char**) type data. Characters are usually stored in 8 bits (one byte) of internal storage. The qualifier **signed** or **unsigned** may be explicitly applied to char. While **unsigned chars** have values between 0 and 255, **signed chars** have values from –128 to 127.

2.8 DECLARATION OF VARIABLES

After designing suitable variable names, we must declare them to the compiler. Declaration does two things:

1. It tells the compiler what the variable name is.
2. It specifies what type of data the variable will hold.

The declaration of variables must be done before they are used in the program.

Primary Type Declaration

A variable can be used to store a value of any data type. That is, the name has nothing to do with its type. The syntax for declaring a variable is as follows:

data-type v1,v2,....vn ;

v1, v2, ...vn are the names of variables. Variables are separated by commas. A declaration statement must end with a semicolon. For example, valid declarations are:

```
int count;
int number, total;
double ratio;
```

int and **double** are the keywords to represent integer type and real type data values respectively. Table 2.9 shows various data types and their keyword equivalents.

Table 2.9 *Data Types and Their Keywords*

Data type	*Keyword equivalent*
Character	char
Unsigned character	unsigned char
Signed character	signed char
Signed integer	signed int (or int)

(Contd.)

Data type	*Keyword equivalent*
Signed short integer	signed short int (or short int or short)
Signed long integer	signed long int (or long int or long)
Unsigned integer	unsigned int (or unsigned)
Unsigned short integer	unsigned short int (or unsigned short)
Unsigned long integer	unsigned long int (or unsigned long)
Floating point	float
Double-precision floating point	double
Extended double-precision floating point	long double

The program segment given in Fig. 2.7 illustrates declaration of variables. **main()** is the beginning of the program. The opening brace { signals the execution of the program. Declaration of variables is usually done immediately after the opening brace of the program. The variables can also be declared outside (either before or after) the **main** function. The importance of place of declaration will be dealt in detail later while discussing functions.

```
main() /*.........Program Name........................ */
{
  /*...............Declaration.........................*/
     float       x, y;
     int         code;
     short int   count;
     long int    amount;
     double      deviation;
     unsigned    n;
     char        c;
  /*...............Computation.........................*/
     . . . .
     . . . .
     . . . .
} /*............Program ends...........................*/
```

Fig. 2.7 *Declaration of variables*

When an adjective (qualifier) **short, long, or unsigned** is used without a basic data type specifier, C compilers treat the data type as an **int.** If we want to declare a character variable as unsigned, then we must do so using both the terms like **unsigned char**.

Default values of Constants

Integer constants, by default, represent **int** type data. We can override this default by specifying unsigned or long after the number (by appending U or L) as shown below:

Literal	Type	Value
+111	int	111
–222	int	–222
45678U	unsigned int	45,678
–56789L	long int	–56,789
987654UL	unsigned long int	9,87,654

Similarly, floating point constants, by default represent **double** type data. If we want the resulting data type to be **float** or **long double**, we must append the letter f or F to the number for **float** and letter l or L for **long double** as shown below:

Literal	Type	Value
0.	double	0.0
.0	double	0.0
12.0	double	12.0
1.234	double	1.234
–1.2f	float	–1.2
1.23456789L	long double	1.23456789

User-Defined Type Declaration

C supports a feature known as "type definition" that allows users to define an identifier that would represent an existing data type. The user-defined data type identifier can later be used to declare variables . It takes the general form:

typedef *type* **identifier;**

Where *type* refers to an existing data type and "identifier" refers to the "new" name given to the data type. The existing data type may belong to any class of type, including the user-defined ones. Remember that the new type is 'new' only in name, but not the data type. **typedef** cannot create a new type. Some examples of type definition are:

```
typedef int units;
typedef float marks;
```

Here, **units** symbolizes **int** and **marks** symbolizes **float.** They can be later used to declare variables as follows:

```
units batch1, batch2;
marks name1[50], name2[50];
```

batch1 and batch2 are inclared as **int** variable and name1[50] and name2[50] are declared as 50 element floating point array variables. The main advantage of **typedef** is that we can create meaningful data type names for increasing the readability of the program.

Another user-defined data type is enumerated data type provided by ANSI standard. It is defined as follows:

enum **identifier** {*value1, value2, ... valuen*};

The "identifier" is a user-defined enumerated data type which can be used to declare variables that can have one of the values enclosed within the braces (known as *enumeration constants*). After this definition, we can declare variables to be of this 'new' type as below:

```
enum identifier v1, v2, ... vn;
```

The enumerated variables v1, v2, ... vn can only have one of the values *value1, value2, ... valuen.* The assignments of the following types are valid:

```
v1 = value3;
v5 = value1;
```

An example:

```
enum day {Monday,Tuesday, ... Sunday};
enum day week_st, week_end;
week_st = Monday;
week_end = Friday;
if(week_st == Tuesday)
   week_end = Saturday;
```

The compiler automatically assigns integer digits beginning with 0 to all the enumeration constants. That is, the enumeration constant value1 is assigned 0, value2 is assigned 1, and so on. However, the automatic assignments can be overridden by assigning values explicitly to the enumeration constants. For example:

```
enum day {Monday = 1, Tuesday, ... Sunday};
```

Here, the constant Monday is assigned the value of 1. The remaining constants are assigned values that increase successively by 1.

The definition and declaration of enumerated variables can be combined in one statement. Example:

```
enum day {Monday, ... Sunday} week_st, week_end;
```

2.9 DECLARATION OF STORAGE CLASS

Variables in C can have not only *data type* but also *storage class* that provides information about their location and visibility. The storage class decides the portion of the program within which the variables are recognized. Consider the following example:

```
    /* Example of storage classes */
int m;
main()
```

```
{
    int i;
    float balance;
    ....
    ....
    function1();
}
function1()
{
    int i;
    float sum;
    ....
    ....
}
```

The variable **m** which has been declared before the **main** is called *global* variable. It can be used in all the functions in the program. It need not be declared in other functions. A global variable is also known as an *external* variable.

The variables **i, balance** and **sum** are called *local* variables because they are declared inside a function. Local variables are visible and meaningful only inside the functions in which they are declared. They are not known to other functions. Note that the variable **i** has been declared in both the functions. Any change in the value of **i** in one function does not affect its value in the other.

C provides a variety of storage class specifiers that can be used to declare explicitly the scope and lifetime of variables. The concepts of scope and lifetime are important only in multifunction and multiple file programs and therefore the storage classes are considered in detail later when functions are discussed. For now, remember that there are four storage class specifiers **(auto, register, static**, and **extern**) whose meanings are given in Table 2.10.

The storage class is another qualifier (like **long** or **unsigned)** that can be added to a variable declaration as shown below:

```
auto int count;
register char ch;
static int x;
extern long total;
```

Static and external (**extern**) variables are automatically initialized to zero. Automatic (**auto**) variables contain undefined values (known as 'garbage') unless they are initialized explicitly.

Table 2.10 *Storage Classes and Their Meaning*

Storage class	*Meaning*
auto	Local variable known only to the function in which it is declared. *Default is auto.*
static	Local variable which exists and retains its value even after the control is transferred to the calling function.
extern	Global variable known to all functions in the file.
register	Local variable which is stored in the register.

2.10 ASSIGNING VALUES TO VARIABLES

Variables are created for use in program statements such as

```
value = amount + inrate * amount;
while (year <= PERIOD)
{
    ....
    ....
    year = year + 1;
}
```

In the first statement, the numeric value stored in the variable **inrate** is multiplied by the value stored in **amount** and the product is added to **amount**. The result is stored in the variable value. This process is possible only if the variables **amount** and inrate have already been given values. The variable **value** is called the *target variable*. While all the variables are declared for their type, the variables that are used in expressions (on the right side of equal (=) sign of a computational statement) *must* be assigned values before they are encountered in the program. Similarly, the variable **year** and the symbolic constant **PERIOD** in the **while** statement must be assigned values before this statement is encountered.

Assignment Statement

Values can be assigned to variables using the assignment operator = as follows:

variable_name = constant;

We have already used such statements in Chapter 1. Further examples are:

```
initial_value = 0;
final_value   = 100;
balance       = 75.84;
yes           = 'x';
```

C permits multiple assignments in one line. For example

```
initial_value = 0; final_value = 100;
```

are valid statements.

An assignment statement implies that the value of the variable on the left of the 'equal sign' is set equal to the value of the quantity (or the expression) on the right. The statement

```
year = year + 1;
```

means that the 'new value' of **year** is equal to the 'old value' of **year** plus 1.

During assignment operation, C converts the type of value on the right-hand side to the type on the left. This may involve truncation when real value is converted to an integer.

It is also possible to assign a value to a variable at the time the variable is declared. This takes the following form:

data-type variable_name = constant;

Some examples are:

```
int final_value  =  100;
char yes         =  'x';
double balance   =  75.84;
```

The process of giving initial values to variables is called *initialization*. C permits the *initialization* of more than one variables in one statement using multiple assignment operators. For example the statements

```
p = q = s = 0;
x = y = z = MAX;
```

are valid. The first statement initializes the variables **p, q,** and **s** to zero while the second initializes **x, y,** and **z** with **MAX.** Note that **MAX** is a symbolic constant defined at the beginning.

Remember that external and static variables are initialized to zero by *default*. Automatic variables that are not initialized explicitly will contain garbage.

Example 2.2 Program in Fig. 2.8 shows typical declarations, assignments and values stored in various types of variables.

The variables **x** and **p** have been declared as floating-point variables. Note that the way the value of 1.234567890000 that we assigned to **x** is displayed under different output formats. The value of **x** is displayed as 1.234567880630 under %.12lf format, while the actual value assigned is 1.234567890000. This is because the variable **x** has been declared as a **float** that can store values only up to six decimal places.

The variable **m** that has been declared as **int** is not able to store the value 54321 correctly. Instead, it contains some garbage. Since this program was run on a 16-bit machine, the maximum value that an **int** variable can store is only 32767. However, the variable **k** (declared as **unsigned**) has stored the value 54321 correctly. Similarly, the **long int** variable **n** has stored the value 1234567890 correctly.

The value 9.87654321 assigned to **y** declared as double has been stored correctly but the value is printed as 9.876543 under %lf format. Note that unless specified otherwise, the **printf** function will always display a **float** or **double** value to six decimal places. We will discuss later the output formats for displaying numbers.

Program

```
main()
{
/*..........DECLARATIONS.............................*/
    float    x, p ;
    double   y, q ;
    unsigned k ;
/*..........DECLARATIONS AND ASSIGNMENTS............*/
    int       m = 54321 ;
    long int n = 1234567890 ;
/*..........ASSIGNMENTS.............................*/
    x = 1.234567890000 ;
```

```
        y = 9.87654321 ;
        k = 54321 ;
        p = q = 1.0 ;
    /*..........PRINTING................................*/
        printf("m = %d\n", m) ;
        printf("n = %ld\n", n) ;
        printf("x = %.12lf\n", x) ;
        printf("x = %f\n", x) ;
        printf("y = %.12lf\n",y) ;
        printf("y = %lf\n", y) ;
        printf("k = %u p = %f q = %.12lf\n", k, p, q) ;
    }
```

Output

```
        m = -11215
        n = 1234567890
        x = 1.234567880630
        x = 1.234568
        y = 9.876543210000
        y = 9.876543
        k = 54321 p = 1.000000 q = 1.000000000000
```

Fig. 2.8 *Examples of assignments*

Reading Data from Keyboard

Another way of giving values to variables is to input data through keyboard using the **scanf** function. It is a general input function available in C and is very similar in concept to the **printf** function. It works much like an INPUT statement in BASIC. The general format of **scanf** is as follows:

scanf("**control string**", **&variable1,&variable2,....**);

The control string contains the format of data being received. The ampersand symbol **&** before each variable name is an operator that specifies the variable name's *address*. We must always use this operator, otherwise unexpected results may occur. Let us look at an example:

```
scanf("%d", &number);
```

When this statement is encountered by the computer, the execution stops and waits for the value of the variable **number** to be typed in. Since the control string "%d" specifies that an integer value is to be read from the terminal, we have to type in the value in integer form. Once the number is typed in and the 'Return' Key is pressed, the computer then proceeds to the next statement. Thus, the use of **scanf** provides an interactive feature and makes the program 'user friendly'. The value is assigned to the variable **number**.

Example 2.3 The program in Fig. 2.9 illustrates the use of **scanf** function.

The first executable statement in the program is a **printf,** requesting the user to enter an integer number. This is known as "prompt message" and appears on the screen like

Enter an integer number

As soon as the user types in an integer number, the computer proceeds to compare the value with 100. If the value typed in is less than 100, then a message

Your number is smaller than 100

is printed on the screen. Otherwise, the message

Your number contains more than two digits

is printed. Outputs of the program run for two different inputs are also shown in Fig. 2.9.

```
Program
 main()
 {
       int number;

       printf("Enter an integer number\n");
       scanf ("%d", &number);

       if ( number < 100 )
         printf("Your number is smaller than 100\n\n");
       else
         printf("Your number contains more than two digits\n");
 }

Output
 Enter an integer number
 54
 Your number is smaller than 100
 Enter an integer number
 108
 Your number contains more than two digits
```

Fig. 2.9 *Use of scanf function for interactive computing*

Some compilers permit the use of the 'prompt message' as a part of the control string in **scanf**, like

```
scanf("Enter a number %d",&number);
```

We discuss more about **scanf** in Chapter 4.

In Fig. 2.9 we have used a decision statement **if...else** to decide whether the number is less than 100. Decision statements are discussed in depth in Chapter 5.

Example 2.4 Sample program 3 discussed in Chapter 1 can be converted into a more flexible interactive program using **scanf** as shown in Fig. 2.10.

In this case, computer requests the user to input the values of the amount to be invested, interest rate and period of investment by printing a prompt message

Input amount, interest rate, and period

and then waits for input values. As soon as we finish entering the three values corresponding to the

Program

```
main()
{
        int year, period ;
        float amount, inrate, value ;

        printf("Input amount, interest rate, and period\n\n") ;
        scanf ("%f %f %d", &amount, &inrate, &period) ;
        printf("\n") ;
        year = 1 ;

        while( year <= period )
        {
              value = amount + inrate * amount ;
              printf("%2d Rs %8.2f\n", year, value) ;
              amount = value ;
              year = year + 1 ;
        }
}
```

Output

```
Input amount, interest rate, and period

  10000 0.14 5

    1 Rs 11400.00
    2 Rs 12996.00
    3 Rs 14815.44
    4 Rs 16889.60
    5 Rs 19254.15

  Input amount, interest rate, and period

  20000 0.12 7

    1 Rs 22400.00
    2 Rs 25088.00
    3 Rs 28098.56
    4 Rs 31470.39
    5 Rs 35246.84
    6 Rs 39476.46
    7 Rs 44213.63
```

Fig. 2.10 *Interactive investment program*

three variables **amount, inrate,** and **period,** the computer begins to calculate the amount at the end of each year, up to 'period' and produces output as shown in Fig. 2.10.

Note that the **scanf** function contains three variables. In such cases, care should be exercised to see that the values entered match the *order* and *type* of the variables in the list. Any mismatch might lead to unexpected results. The compiler may not detect such errors.

2.11 DEFINING SYMBOLIC CONSTANTS

We often use certain unique constants in a program. These constants may appear repeatedly in a number of places in the program. One example of such a constant is 3.142, representing the value of the mathematical constant **"pi"**. Another example is the total number of students whose mark-sheets are analysed by a 'test analysis program'. The number of students, say 50, may be used for calculating the class total, class average, standard deviation, etc. We face two problems in the subsequent use of such programs.

1. Problem in modification of the program.
2. Problem in understanding the program.

Modifiability

We may like to change the value of "pi" from 3.142 to 3.14159 to improve the accuracy of calculations or the number 50 to 100 to process the test results of another class. In both the cases, we will have to search throughout the program and explicitly change the value of the constant wherever it has been used. If any value is left unchanged, the program may produce disastrous outputs.

Understandability

When a numeric value appears in a program, its use is not always clear, especially when the same value means different things in different places. For example, the number 50 may mean the number of students at one place and the 'pass marks' at another place of the same program. We may forget what a certain number meant, when we read the program some days later.

Assignment of such constants to a *symbolic name* frees us from these problems. For example, we may use the name **STRENGTH** to define the number of students and **PASS_MARK** to define the pass marks required in a subject. Constant values are assigned to these names at the beginning of the program. Subsequent use of the names **STRENGTH** and **PASS_MARK** in the program has the effect of causing their defined values to be automatically substituted at the appropriate points. A constant is defined as follows:

#define ***symbolic-name value of constant***

Valid examples of constant definitions are:

```
#define STRENGTH 100
#define PASS_MARK 50
```

```
#define MAX 200
#define PI 3.14159
```

Symbolic names are sometimes called *constant identifiers.* Since the symbolic names are constants (not variables), they do not appear in declarations. The following rules apply to a **#define** statement which define a symbolic constant.

1. Symbolic names have the same form as variable names. (Symbolic names are written in CAPITALS to visually distinguish them from the normal variable names, which are written in lowercase letters. This is only a convention, not a rule.)
2. No blank space between the pound sign '#' and the word **define** is permitted.
3. '#' must be the first character in the line.
4. A blank space is required between **#define** and *symbolic name* and between the ***symbolic name*** and the *constant.*
5. **#define** statements must not end with a semicolon.
6. After definition, the *symbolic name* should not be assigned any other value within the program by using an assignment statement. For example, STRENGTH = 200; is illegal.
7. Symbolic names are NOT declared for data types. Its data type depends on the type of constant.
8. **#define** statements may appear *anywhere* in the program but before it is referenced in the program (the usual practice is to place them in the beginning of the program).

#define statement is a *preprocessor* compiler directive and is much more powerful than what has been mentioned here. More advanced types of definitions will be discussed later. Table 2.11 illustrates some invalid statements of **#define.**

Table 2.11 *Examples of Invalid #define Statements*

Statement	*Validity*	*Remark*
#define X = 2.5	Invalid	'=' sign is not allowed
# define MAX 10	Invalid	No white space between # and define
#define N 25;	Invalid	No semicolon at the end
#define N 5, M 10	Invalid	A statement can define only one name.
#Define ARRAY 11	Invalid	define should be in lowercase letters
#define PRICE$ 100	Invalid	$ symbol is not permitted in name

2.12 DECLARING A VARIABLE AS CONSTANT

We may like the value of certain variables to remain constant during the execution of a program. We can achieve this by declaring the variable with the qualifier **const** at the time of initialization. Example:

```
const int class_size = 40;
```

const is a new data type qualifier defined by ANSI standard. This tells the compiler that the value of the **int** variable **class_size** must not be modified by the program. However, it can be used on the right_hand side of an assignment statement like any other variable.

2.13 DECLARING A VARIABLE AS VOLATILE

ANSI standard defines another qualifier **volatile** that could be used to tell explicitly the compiler that a variable's value may be changed at any time by some external sources (from outside the program). For example:

```
volatile int date;
```

The value of **date** may be altered by some external factors even if it does not appear on the left-hand side of an assignment statement. When we declare a variable as **volatile**, the compiler will examine the value of the variable each time it is encountered to see whether any external alteration has changed the value.

Remember that the value of a variable declared as **volatile** can be modified by its own program as well. If we wish that the value must not be modified by the program while it may be altered by some other process, then we may declare the variable as both **const** and **volatile** as shown below:

```
volatile const int location = 100;
```

2.14 OVERFLOW AND UNDERFLOW OF DATA

Problem of data overflow occurs when the value of a variable is either too big or too small for the data type to hold. The largest value that a variable can hold also depends on the machine. Since floating-point values are rounded off to the number of significant digits allowed (or specified), an overflow normally results in the largest possible real value, whereas an underflow results in zero.

Integers are always exact within the limits of the range of the integral data types used. However, an overflow which is a serious problem may occur if the data type does not match the value of the constant. C does not provide any warning or indication of integer overflow. It simply gives incorrect results. (Overflow normally produces a negative number.) We should therefore exercise a greater care to define correct data types for handling the input/output values.

Just Remember

- Do not use the underscore as the first character of identifiers (or variable names) because many of the identifiers in the system library start with underscore.
- Use only 31 or less characters for identifiers. This helps ensure portability of programs.
- Do not use keywords or any system library names for identifiers.
- Use meaningful and intelligent variable names.
- Do not create variable names that differ only by one or two letters.
- Each variable used must be declared for its type at the beginning of the program or function.
- All variables must be initialized before they are used in the program.
- Integer constants, by default, assume **int** types. To make the numbers **long** or **unsigned**, we must append the letters L and U to them.
- Floating point constants default to **double**. To make them to denote **float** or **long double**, we must append the letters F or L to the numbers.

- Do not use lowercase l for long as it is usually confused with the number 1.
- Use single quote for character constants and double quotes for string constants.
- A character is stored as an integer. It is therefore possible to perform arithmetic operations on characters.
- Do not combine declarations with executable statements.
- A variable can be made constant either by using the preprocessor command **#define** at the beginning of the program or by declaring it with the qualifier **const** at the time of initialization.
- Do not use semicolon at the end of **#define** directive.
- The character # should be in the first column.
- Do not give any space between # and **define.**
- C does not provide any warning or indication of overflow. It simply gives incorrect results. Care should be exercised in defining correct data type.
- A variable defined before the main function is available to all the functions in the program.
- A variable defined inside a function is local to that function and not available to other functions.

CASE STUDIES

1. Calculation of Average of Numbers

A program to calculate the average of a set of N numbers is given in Fig. 2.11.

Program

```
    #define     N    10                 /* SYMBOLIC CONSTANT */
    main()
    {
        int    count ;                  /* DECLARATION OF */
        float  sum, average, number ;   /* VARIABLES */
        sum    = 0 ;                    /* INITIALIZATION */
        count  = 0 ;                    /* OF VARIABLES */
        while( count < N )
        {
              scanf("%f", &number) ;
              sum = sum + number ;
              count = count + 1 ;
        }
        average = sum/N ;
        printf("N = %d Sum = %f", N, sum);
        printf(" Average = %f", average);
    }
```

```
Output
1
2.3
4.67
1.42
7
3.67
4.08
2.2
4.25
8.21
N = 10    Sum = 38.799999 Average = 3.880000
```

Fig. 2.11 *Average of N numbers*

The variable **number** is declared as **float** and therefore it can take both integer and real numbers. Since the symbolic constant **N** is assigned the value of 10 using the **#define** statement, the program accepts ten values and calculates their sum using the **while** loop. The variable **count** counts the number of values and as soon as it becomes 11, the **while** loop is exited and then the average is calculated.

Notice that the actual value of sum is 38.8 but the value displayed is 38.799999. In fact, the actual value that is displayed is quite dependent on the computer system. Such an inaccuracy is due to the way the floating point numbers are internally represented inside the computer.

2. Temperature Conversion Problem

The program presented in Fig. 2.12 converts the given temperature in fahrenheit to celsius using the following conversion formula:

$$C = \frac{F - 32}{1.8}$$

```
Program
    #define F_LOW      0       /* --------------- */
    #define F_MAX    250       /* SYMBOLIC CONSTANTS */
    #define STEP      25       /* --------------- */

    main()
    {
          typedef float REAL ;          /* TYPE DEFINITION */
          REAL fahrenheit, celsius ; /* DECLARATION */

          fahrenheit = F_LOW ;          /* INITIALIZATION */
          printf("Fahrenheit Celsius\n\n") ;
          while( fahrenheit <= F_MAX )
          {
              celsius = ( fahrenheit - 32.0 ) / 1.8 ;
```

```
        printf(" %5.1f %7.2f\n", fahrenheit, celsius);
        fahrenheit = fahrenheit + STEP ;
    }
}
```

Output

```
Fahrenheit      Celsius

    0.0         -17.78
   25.0          -3.89
   50.0          10.00
   75.0          23.89
  100.0          37.78
  125.0          51.67
  150.0          65.56
  175.0          79.44
  200.0          93.33
  225.0         107.22
  250.0         121.11
```

Fig. 2.12 *Temperature conversion—fahrenheit-celsius*

The program prints a conversion table for reading temperature in celsius, given the fahrenheit values. The minimum and maximum values and step size are defined as symbolic constants. These values can be changed by redefining the **#define** statements. An user-defined data type name **REAL** is used to declare the variables **fahrenheit** and **celsius**.

The formation specifications %5.1f and %7.2 in the second **printf** statement produces two-column output as shown.

REVIEW QUESTIONS

2.1 State whether the following statements are *true* or *false*.

(a) Any valid printable ASCII character can be used in an identifier.
(b) All variables must be given a type when they are declared.
(c) Declarations can appear anywhere in a program.
(d) ANSI C treats the variables **name** and **Name** to be same.
(e) The underscore can be used anywhere in an identifier.
(f) The keyword **void** is a data type in C.
(g) Floating point constants, by default, denote **float** type values.
(h) Like variables, constants have a type.
(i) Character constants are coded using double quotes.
(j) Initialization is the process of assigning a value to a variable at the time of declaration.
(k) All **static** variables are automatically initialized to zero.
(l) The **scanf** function can be used to read only one value at a time.

2.2 Fill in the blanks with appropriate words.

(a) The keyword _____ can be used to create a data type identifier.
(b) _______ is the largest value that an unsigned short int type variable can store.

(c) A global variable is also known as ________ variable.
(d) A variable can be made constant by declaring it with the qualifier ________ at the time of initialization.

2.3 What are trigraph characters? How are they useful?
2.4 Describe the four basic data types. How could we extend the range of values they represent?
2.5 What is an unsigned integer constant? What is the significance of declaring a constant unsigned?
2.6 Describe the characteristics and purpose of escape sequence characters.
2.7 What is a variable and what is meant by the "value" of a variable?
2.8 How do variables and symbolic names differ?
2.9 State the differences between the declaration of a variable and the definition of a symbolic name.
2.10 What is initialization? Why is it important?
2.11 What are the qualifiers that an **int** can have at a time?
2.12 A programmer would like to use the word DPR to declare all the double-precision floating point values in his program. How could he achieve this?
2.13 What are enumeration variables? How are they declared? What is the advantage of using them in a program?
2.14 Describe the purpose of the qualifiers **const** and **volatile**.
2.15 When dealing with very small or very large numbers, what steps would you take to improve the accuracy of the calculations?
2.16 Which of the following are invalid constants and why?

0.0001	5x1.5	99999
+100	75.45 E-2	"15.75"
–45.6	–1.79 e + 4	0.00001234

2.17 Which of the following are invalid variable names and why?

Minimum	First.name	n1+n2	&name
doubles	3rd_row	n$	Row1
float	Sum Total	Row Total	Column-total

2.18 Find errors, if any, in the following declaration statements.

```
Int x;
float letter,DIGIT;
double = p,q
exponent alpha,beta;
m,n,z: INTEGER
short char c;
long int m; count;
long float temp;
```

2.19 What would be the value of x after execution of the following statements?

```
int x, y = 10;
char z = 'a';
x = y + z;
```

2.20 Identify syntax errors in the following program. After corrections, what output would you expect when you execute it?

```
#define PI 3.14159
main()
{
    int R,C;                /* R-Radius of circle
    float perimeter;        /* Circumference of circle */
    float area;             /* Area of circle */
    C = PI
    R = 5;
    Perimeter = 2.0 * C *R;
    Area    = C*R*R;
    printf("%f", "%d",&perimeter,&area)
    }
```

PROGRAMMING EXERCISES

2.1 Write a program to determine and print the sum of the following harmonic series for a given value of n:

1+ 1/2 +1/3 +....+ 1/n

The value of n should be given interactively through the terminal.

2.2 Write a program to read the price of an item in decimal form (like 15.95) and print the output in paise (like 1595 paise).

2.3 Write a program that prints the even numbers from 1 to 100.

2.4 Write a program that requests two float type numbers from the user and then divides the first number by the second and display the result along with the numbers.

2.5 The price of one kg of rice is Rs. 16.75 and one kg of sugar is Rs. 15. Write a program to get these values from the user and display the prices as follows:

*** LIST OF ITEMS ***

Item	Price
Rice	Rs 16.75
Sugar	Rs 15.00

Chapter 3

Operators and Expressions

3.1 INTRODUCTION

C supports a rich set of operators. We have already used several of them, such as =, +, –, *, & and <. An *operator* is a symbol that tells the computer to perform certain mathematical or logical manipulations. Operators are used in programs to manipulate data and variables. They usually form a part of the mathematical or logical *expressions.*

C operators can be classified into a number of categories. They include:

1. Arithmetic operators.
2. Relational operators.
3. Logical operators.
4. Assignment operators.
5. Increment and decrement operators.
6. Conditional operators.
7. Bitwise operators.
8. Special operators.

An expression is a sequence of operands and operators that reduces to a single value. For example,

10 + 15

is an expression whose value is 25. The value can be any type other than ***void***.

3.2 ARITHMETIC OPERATORS

C provides all the basic arithmetic operators. They are listed in Table 3.1. The operators +, –, *, and / all work the same way as they do in other languages. These can operate on any built-in data type allowed in C. The unary minus operator, in effect, multiplies its single operand by –1. Therefore, a number preceded by a minus sign changes its sign.

Table 3.1 *Arithmetic Operators*

Operator	*Meaning*
+	Addition or unary plus
–	Subtraction or unary minus
*	Multiplication
/	Division
%	Modulo division

Integer division truncates any fractional part. The modulo division operation produces the remainder of an integer division. Examples of use of arithmetic operators are:

```
a – b    a + b
a * b    a / b
a % b   –a * b
```

Here **a** and **b** are variables and are known as *operands*. The modulo division operator % cannot be used on floating point data. Note that C does not have an operator for *exponentiation*. Older versions of C does not support unary plus but ANSI C supports it.

Integer Arithmetic

When both the operands in a single arithmetic expression such as a+b are integers, the expression is called an *integer expression*, and the operation is called *integer arithmetic*. Integer arithmetic always yields an integer value. The largest integer value depends on the machine, as pointed out earlier. In the above examples, if **a** and **b** are integers, then for **a** = 14 and **b** = 4 we have the following results:

```
a – b = 10
a + b = 18
a * b = 56
a / b = 3 (decimal part truncated)
a % b = 2 (remainder of division)
```

During integer division, if both the operands are of the same sign, the result is truncated towards zero. If one of them is negative, the direction of trunction is implementation dependent. That is,

6/7 = 0 and –6/–7 = 0

but –6/7 may be zero or –1. (Machine dependent)

Similarly, during modulo division, the sign of the result is always the sign of the first operand (the dividend). That is

```
–14 % 3 = –2
–14 % –3 = –2
14 % –3 = 2
```

Example 3.1 The program in Fig. 3.1 shows the use of integer arithmetic to convert a given number of days into months and days.

```
Program
  main ()
  {
    int months, days ;

    printf("Enter days\n") ;
    scanf("%d", &days) ;

    months = days / 30 ;
    days = days % 30 ;
    printf("Months = %d Days = %d", months, days) ;
  }

Output
  Enter days
  265
  Months = 8 Days = 25
  Enter days
  364
  Months = 12 Days = 4
  Enter days
  45
  Months = 1 Days = 15
```

Fig. 3.1 *Illustration of integer arithmetic*

The variables months and days are declared as integers. Therefore, the statement

```
months = days/30;
```

truncates the decimal part and assigns the integer part to months. Similarly, the statement

```
days = days%30;
```

assigns the remainder part of the division to days. Thus the given number of days is converted into an equivalent number of months and days and the result is printed as shown in the output.

Real Arithmetic

An arithmetic operation involving only real operands is called *real arithmetic.* A real operand may assume values either in decimal or exponential notation. Since floating point values are rounded to the number of significant digits permissible, the final value is an approximation of the correct result. If **x, y,** and **z** are **floats**, then we will have:

$$x = 6.0/7.0 = 0.857143$$
$$y = 1.0/3.0 = 0.333333$$

z = –2.0/3.0 = –0.666667

The operator % cannot be used with real operands.

Mixed-mode Arithmetic

When one of the operands is real and the other is integer, the expression is called a *mixed-mode arithmetic* expression. If either operand is of the real type, then only the real operation is performed and the result is always a real number. Thus

15/10.0 = 1.5

whereas

15/10 = 1

More about mixed operations will be discussed later when we deal with the evaluation of expressions.

3.3 RELATIONAL OPERATORS

We often compare two quantities and depending on their relation, take certain decisions. For example, we may compare the age of two persons, or the price of two items, and so on. These comparisons can be done with the help of *relational operators.* We have already used the symbol '<', meaning 'less than'. An expression such as

a < b or 1 < 20

containing a relational operator is termed as a *relational expression*. The value of a relational expression is either *one* or *zero*. It is *one* if the specified relation is *true* and *zero* if the relation is *false*. For example

10 < 20 is true

but

20 < 10 is false

C supports six relational operators in all. These operators and their meanings are shown in Table 3.2.

Table 3.2 *Relational Operators*

Operator	*Meaning*
<	is less than
<=	is less than or equal to
>	is greater than
>=	is greater than or equal to
==	is equal to
!=	is not equal to

A simple relational expression contains only one relational operator and takes the following form:

ae-1 **relational operator** *ae-2*

ae-1 and *ae-2* are arithmetic expressions, which may be simple constants, variables or combination of them. Given below are some examples of simple relational expressions and their values:

4.5 <= 10 TRUE
4.5 < –10 FALSE
–35 >= 0 FALSE
10 < 7+5 TRUE
a+b = c+d TRUE only if the sum of values of a and b is equal to the sum of values of c and d.

When arithmetic expressions are used on either side of a relational operator, the arithmetic expressions will be evaluated first and then the results compared. That is, arithmetic operators have a higher priority over relational operators.

Relational expressions are used in *decision statements* such as **if** and **while** to decide the course of action of a running program. We have already used the **while** statement in Chapter 1. Decision statements are discussed in detail in Chapters 5 and 6.

Relational Operator Complements

Among the six relational operators, each one is a complement of another operator.

>	is complement of	<=
<	is complement of	>=
==	is complement of	!=

We can simplify an expression involving the *not* and the *less than* operators using the complements as shown below:

Actual one	*Simplified one*
!(x<y)	x >= y
!(x>y)	x <= y
!(x!=y)	x == y
!(x<=y)	x > y
!(x>=y)	x < y
!(x == y)	x != y

3.4 LOGICAL OPERATORS

In addition to the relational operators, C has the following three *logical operators*.

&&	meaning logical	AND
||	meaning logical	OR
!	meaning logical	NOT

The logical operators && and || are used when we want to test more than one condition and make decisions. An example is:

a > b && x == 10

An expression of this kind, which combines two or more relational expressions, is termed as a *logical expression* or a *compound relational expression*. Like the simple relational expressions, a logical expression also yields a value of *one* or *zero*, according to the truth table shown in Table 3.3. The logical expression given above is true only if **a > b** is *true* and **x == 10** is *true*. If either (or both) of them are false, the expression is *false*.

Table 3.3 *Truth Table*

op-1	*op-2*	*Value of the expression*	
		op-1 && op-2	*op-1 || op-2*
Non-zero	Non-zero	1	1
Non-zero	0	0	1
0	Non-zero	0	1
0	0	0	0

Some examples of the usage of logical expressions are:

1. if (age > 55 && salary < 1000)
2. if (number < 0 || number > 100)

We shall see more of them when we discuss decision statements.

3.5 ASSIGNMENT OPERATORS

Assignment operators are used to assign the result of an expression to a variable. We have seen the usual assignment operator, '='. In addition, C has a set of '*shorthand*' assignment operators of the form

v op= *exp*;

Where *v* is a variable, *exp* is an expression and *op* is a C binary arithmetic operator. The operator **op=** is known as the shorthand assignment operator.

The assignment statement

```
v op= exp;
```

is equivalent to

```
v = v op (exp);
```

with **v** evaluated only once. Consider an example

```
x += y+1;
```

This is same as the statement

```
x = x + (y+1);
```

The shorthand operator += means 'add y+1 to x' or 'increment x by y+1'. For y = 2, the above statement becomes

```
x += 3;
```

and when this statement is executed, 3 is added to x. If the old value of x is, say 5, then the new value of x is 8. Some of the commonly used shorthand assignment operators are illustrated in Table 3.4.

Table 3.4 *Shorthand Assignment Operators*

Statement with simple assignment operator	*Statement with shorthand operator*
a = a + 1	a += 1
a = a – 1	a –= 1
a = a * (n+1)	a *= n+1
a = a / (n+1)	a /= n+1
a = a % b	a %= b

The use of shorthand assignment operators has three advantages:

1. What appears on the left-hand side need not be repeated and therefore it becomes easier to write.
2. The statement is more concise and easier to read.
3. The statement is more efficient.

These advantages may be appreciated if we consider a slightly more involved statement like

```
value(5*j-2) = value(5*j-2) + delta;
```

With the help of the += operator, this can be written as follows:

```
value(5*j-2) += delta;
```

It is easier to read and understand and is more efficient because the expression 5*j–2 is evaluated only once.

Example 3.2 Program of Fig. 3.2 prints a sequence of squares of numbers. Note the use of the shorthand operator *= .

The program attempts to print a sequence of squares of numbers starting from 2. The statement

```
a *= a;
```

which is identical to

```
a = a*a;
```

replaces the current value of **a** by its square. When the value of **a** becomes equal or greater than **N** (=100) the **while** is terminated. Note that the output contains only three values 2, 4 and 16.

Program

```
#define  N 100
#define  A 2
main()
{
    int a;
    a = A;
    while( a < N )
    {
            printf("%d\n", a);
            a *= a;
    }
}
```

Output

```
2
4
16
```

Fig. 3.2 *Use of shorthand operator *=*

3.6 INCREMENT AND DECREMENT OPERATORS

C allows two very useful operators not generally found in other languages. These are the increment and decrement operators:

```
++ and --
```

The operator ++ adds 1 to the operand, while -- subtracts 1. Both are unary operators and takes the following form:

```
++m; or m++;
--m; or m--;

++m; is equivalent to m = m+1; (or m += 1;)
--m; is equivalent to m = m-1; (or m -= 1;)
```

We use the increment and decrement statements in **for** and **while** loops extensively.

While ++m and m++ mean the same thing when they form statements independently, they behave differently when they are used in expressions on the right-hand side of an assignment statement. Consider the following:

```
m = 5;
y = ++m;
```

In this case, the value of y and m would be 6. Suppose, if we rewrite the above statements as

```
m = 5;
y = m++;
```

then, the value of y would be 5 and m would be 6. *A prefix operator first adds 1 to the operand and then the result is assigned to the variable on left. On the other hand, a postfix operator first assigns the value to the variable on left and then increments the operand.*

Similar is the case, when we use ++ (or – –) in subscripted variables. That is, the statement

```
a[i++] = 10;
```

is equivalent to

```
a[i] = 10;
i = i+1;
```

The increment and decrement operators can be used in complex statements. Example:

```
m = n++ -j+10;
```

Old value of n is used in evaluating the expression. n is incremented after the evaluation. Some compilers require a space on either side of n++ or ++n.

Rules for ++ and – – Operators

- Increment and decrement operators are unary operators and they require variable as their operands.
- When postfix ++ (or – –) is used with a variable in an expression, the expression is evaluated first using the original value of the variable and then the variable is incremented (or decremented) by one.
- When prefix ++(or – –) is used in an expression, the variable is incremented (or decremented) first and then the expression is evaluated using the new value of the variable.
- The precedence and associatively of ++ and – – operators are the same as those of unary + and unary –.

3.7 CONDITIONAL OPERATOR

A ternary operator pair "? :" is available in C to construct conditional expressions of the form

exp1 ? exp2 : exp3

where *exp1*, *exp2*, and *exp3* are expressions.

The operator ? : works as follows: *exp1* is evaluated first. If it is nonzero (true), then the expression *exp2* is evaluated and becomes the value of the expression. If *exp1* is false, *exp3* is evaluated and its value becomes the value of the expression. Note that only one of the expressions (either *exp2* or *exp3*) is evaluated. For example, consider the following statements.

```
a = 10;
b = 15;
x = (a > b) ? a : b;
```

In this example, x will be assigned the value of b. This can be achieved using the **if..else** statements as follows:

```
if (a > b)
    x = a;
else
    x = b;
```

3.8 BITWISE OPERATORS

C has a distinction of supporting special operators known as *bitwise operators* for manipulation of data at bit level. These operators are used for testing the bits, or shifting them right or left. Bitwise operators may not be applied to **float** or **double**. Table 3.5 lists the bitwise operators and their meanings. They are discussed in detail in Appendix I.

Table 3.5 *Bitwise Operators*

Operator	*Meaning*
&	bitwise AND
|	bitwise OR
^	bitwise exclusive OR
<<	shift left
>>	shift right

3.9 SPECIAL OPERATORS

C supports some special operators of interest such as comma operator, **sizeof** operator, pointer operators (**&** and *****) and member selection operators (. and –>). The comma and **sizeof** operators are discussed in this section while the pointer operators are discussed in Chapter 11. Member selection operators which are used to select members of a structure are discussed in Chapters 10 and 11. ANSI committee has introduced two preprocessor operators known as "string-izing" and "token-pasting" operators (# and ##). They will be discussed in Chapter 14.

The Comma Operator

The comma operator can be used to link the related expressions together. A comma-linked list of expressions are evaluated *left to right* and the value of *right-most* expression is the value of the combined expression. For example, the statement

```
value = (x = 10, y = 5, x+y);
```

first assigns the value 10 to **x**, then assigns 5 to **y**, and finally assigns 15 (i.e. 10 + 5) to **value**. Since comma operator has the lowest precedence of all operators, the parentheses are necessary. Some applications of comma operator are:

In **for** loops:

```
for ( n = 1, m = 10, n <=m; n++, m++)
```

In **while** loops:

```
while (c = getchar( ), c != '10')
```

Exchanging values:

```
t = x, x = y, y = t;
```

The sizeof Operator

The **sizeof** is a compile time operator and, when used with an operand, it returns the number of bytes the operand occupies. The operand may be a variable, a constant or a data type qualifier.

Examples: m = **sizeof**(sum);
n = **sizeof**(long int);
k = **sizeof**(235L);

The **sizeof** operator is normally used to determine the lengths of arrays and structures when their sizes are not known to the programmer. It is also used to allocate memory space dynamically to variables during execution of a program.

Example 3.3 In Fig. 3.3, the program employs different kinds of operators. The results of their evaluation are also shown for comparison.

Notice the way the increment operator ++ works when used in an expression. In the statement

```
c = ++a - b;
```

new value of **a** (= 16) is used thus giving the value 6 to c. That is, a is incremented by 1 before it is used in the expression. However, in the statement

```
d = b++ + a;
```

the old value of **b** (=10) is used in the expression. Here, b is incremented by 1 after it is used in the expression.

We can print the character % by placing it immediately after another % character in the control string. This is illustrated by the statement

```
printf("a%%b = %d\n", a%b);
```

The program also illustrates that the expression

```
c > d ? 1 : 0
```

assumes the value 0 when c is less than d and 1 when c is greater than d.

```
Program

    main()
    {
        int a, b, c, d;

        a = 15;
        b = 10;
        c = ++a - b;

        printf("a = %d b = %d c = %d\n",a, b, c);
```

```
        d = b++ +a;

        printf("a = %d b = %d d = %d\n",a, b, d);
        printf("a/b = %d\n", a/b);
        printf("a%%b = %d\n", a%b);
        printf("a *= b = %d\n", a*=b);
        printf("%d\n", (c>d) ? 1 : 0);
        printf("%d\n", (c<d) ? 1 : 0);
    }
Output
    a = 16 b = 10 c = 6
    a = 16 b = 11 d = 26
    a/b = 1
    a%b = 5
    a *= b = 176
    0
    1
```

Fig. 3.3 *Further illustration of arithmetic operators*

3.10 ARITHMETIC EXPRESSIONS

An arithmetic expression is a combination of variables, constants, and operators arranged as per the syntax of the language. We have used a number of simple expressions in the examples discussed so far. C can handle any complex mathematical expressions. Some of the examples of C expressions are shown in Table 3.6. Remember that C does not have an operator for exponentiation.

Table 3.6 *Expressions*

Algebraic expression	*C expression*
a x b - c	a * b - c
(m+n) (x+y)	(m+n) * (x+y)
$\left(\frac{ab}{c}\right)$	a * b/c
$3x^2 + 2x + 1$	3 * x * x + 2 * x + 1
$\left(\frac{x}{y}\right) + c$	x/y+c

3.11 EVALUATION OF EXPRESSIONS

Expressions are evaluated using an assignment statement of the form variable = *expression*;

Variable is any valid C variable name. When the statement is encountered, the expression is evaluated first and the result then replaces the previous value of the variable on the left-hand side. All variables used in the expression must be assigned values before evaluation is attempted. Examples of evaluation statements are

```
x = a * b - c;
y = b / c * a;
z = a - b / c + d;
```

The blank space around an operator is optional and adds only to improve readability. When these statements are used in a program, the variables a, b, c, and d must be defined before they are used in the expressions.

Example 3.4 The program in Fig. 3.4 illustrates the use of variables in expressions and their evaluation.

Output of the program also illustrates the effect of presence of parentheses in expressions. This is discussed in the next section.

Program

```
main()
{
        float a, b, c, x, y, z;

        a = 9;
        b = 12;
        c = 3;

        x = a – b / 3 + c * 2 - 1;
        y = a – b / (3 + c)  * (2 - 1);
        z = a – (b / (3 + c) * 2) - 1;

        printf("x = %f\n", x);
        printf("y = %f\n", y);
        printf("z = %f\n", z);
}
```

Output

```
x = 10.000000
y = 7.000000
z = 4.000000
```

Fig. 3.4 *Illustrations of evaluation of expressions*

3.12 PRECEDENCE OF ARITHMETIC OPERATORS

An arithmetic expression without parentheses will be evaluated from *left to right* using the rules of precedence of operators. There are two distinct priority levels of arithmetic operators in C:

High priority * / %

Low priority + –

The basic evaluation procedure includes 'two' left-to-right passes through the expression. During the first pass, the high priority operators (if any) are applied as they are encountered. During the second pass, the low priority operators (if any) are applied as they are encountered. Consider the following evaluation statement that has been used in the program of Fig. 3.4.

x = a–b/3 + c*2–1

When a = 9, b = 12, and c = 3, the statement becomes

x = 9–12/3 + 3*2–1

and is evaluated as follows

First pass

Step1: x = 9–4+3*2–1
Step2: x = 9–4+6–1

Second pass

Step3: x = 5+6–1
Step4: x = 11–1
Step5: x = 10

These steps are illustrated in Fig. 3.5. The numbers inside parentheses refer to step numbers.

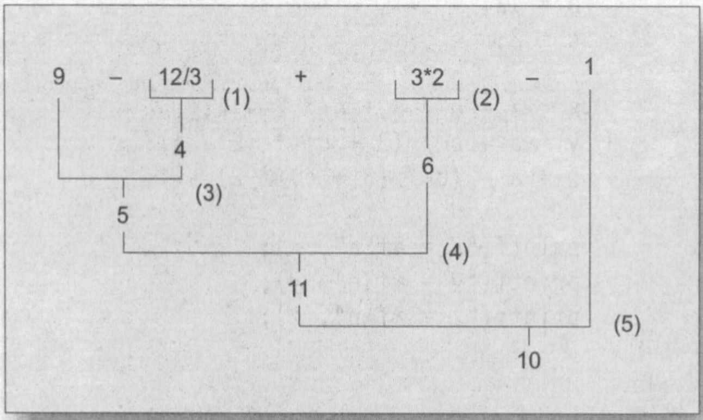

Fig. 3.5 *Illustration of hierarchy of operations*

However, the order of evaluation can be changed by introducing parentheses into an expression. Consider the same expression with parentheses as shown below:

9–12/(3+3)*(2–1)

Whenever parentheses are used, the expressions within parentheses assume highest priority. If two or more sets of parentheses appear one after another as shown above, the expression contained in the left-most set is evaluated first and the right-most in the last. Given below are the new steps.

First pass

Step1: 9-12/6 * (2-1)
Step2: 9-12/6 * 1

Second pass

Step3: 9-2 * 1
Step4: 9-2

Third pass

Step5: 7

This time, the procedure consists of three left-to-right passes. However, the number of evaluation steps remains the same as 5 (i.e equal to the number of arithmetic operators).

Parentheses may be nested, and in such cases, evaluation of the expression will proceed outward from the innermost set of parentheses. Just make sure that every opening parenthesis has a matching closing parenthesis. For example

$$9 - (12/(3+3) * 2) - 1 = 4$$

whereas

$$9 - ((12/3) + 3 * 2) - 1 = -2$$

While parentheses allow us to change the order of priority, we may also use them to improve understandability of the program. When in doubt, we can always add an extra pair just to make sure that the priority assumed is the one we require.

Rules for Evaluation of Expression

- First, parenthesized sub expression from left to right are evaluated.
- If parentheses are nested, the evaluation begins with the innermost sub-expression.
- The precedence rule is applied in determining the order of application of operators in evaluating sub-expressions
- The associativity rule is applied when two or more operators of the same precedence level appear in a sub-expression.
- Arithmetic expressions are evaluated from left to right using the rules of precedence.
- When parentheses are used, the expressions within parentheses assume highest priority.

3.13 SOME COMPUTATIONAL PROBLEMS

When expressions include real values, then it is important to take necessary precautions to guard against certain computational errors. We know that the computer gives approximate values for real numbers and the errors due to such approximations may lead to serious problems. For example, consider the following statements:

```
a = 1.0/3.0;
b = a * 3.0;
```

We know that (1.0/3.0) 3.0 is equal to 1. But there is no guarantee that the value of **b** computed in a program will equal 1.

Another problem is division by zero. On most computers, any attempt to divide a number by zero will result in abnormal termination of the program. In some cases such a division may produce meaningless results. Care should be taken to test the denominator that is likely to assume zero value and avoid any division by zero.

The third problem is to avoid overflow or underflow errors. It is our responsibility to guarantee that operands are of the correct type and range, and the result may not produce any overflow or underflow.

Example 3.5 Output of the program in Fig. 3.6 shows round-off errors that can occur in computation of floating point numbers.

```
Program
/*———————— Sum of n terms of 1/n ————————*/
main()
{
    float sum, n, term ;
    int count = 1 ;

    sum = 0 ;
    printf("Enter value of n\n") ;
      scanf("%f", &n) ;
    term = 1.0/n ;
    while( count <= n )
    {
        sum = sum + term ;
        count++ ;
    }
    printf("Sum = %f\n", sum) ;
}
Output

Enter value of n
99
Sum = 1.000001
Enter value of n
143
Sum = 0.999999
```

Fig. 3.6 *Round-off errors in floating point computations*

We know that the sum of n terms of 1/n is 1. However, due to errors in floating point representation, the result is not always 1.

3.14 TYPE CONVERSIONS IN EXPRESSIONS

Implicit Type Conversion

C permits mixing of constants and variables of different types in an expression. C automatically converts any intermediate values to the proper type so that the expression can be evaluated without loosing any significance. This automatic conversion is known as *implicit type conversion.*

During evaluation it adheres to very strict rules of type conversion. If the operands are of different types, the 'lower' type is automatically converted to the 'higher' type before the operation proceeds. The result is of the higher type. A typical type conversion process is illustrated in Fig. 3.7.

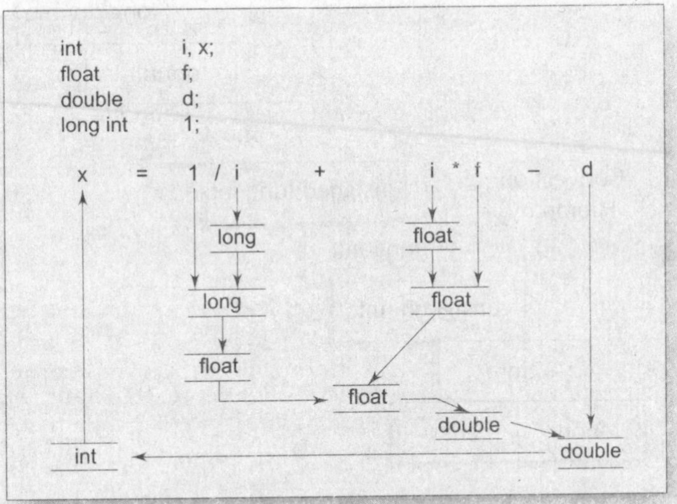

Fig. 3.7 *Process of implicit type conversion*

Given below is the sequence of rules that are applied while evaluating expressions.

All **short** and **char** are automatically converted to **int**; then

1. if one of the operands is **long double,** the other will be converted to **long double** and the result will be **long double**;
2. else, if one of the operands is **double,** the other will be converted to **double** and the result will be **double**;
3. else, if one of the operands is **float,** the other will be converted to **float** and the result will be **float**;
4. else, if one of the operands is **unsigned long int**, the other will be converted to **unsigned long int** and the result will be **unsigned long int**;
5. else, if one of the operands is **long int** and the other is **unsigned int,** then
   (a) if **unsigned int** can be converted to **long int**, the **unsigned int** operand will be converted as such and the result will be **long int**;

(b) else, both operands will be converted to **unsigned long int** and the result will be **unsigned long int**;

6. else, if one of the operands is **long int,** the other will be converted to **long int** and the result will be **long int**;
7. else, if one of the operands is **unsigned int,** the other will be converted to **unsigned int** and the result will be **unsigned int.**

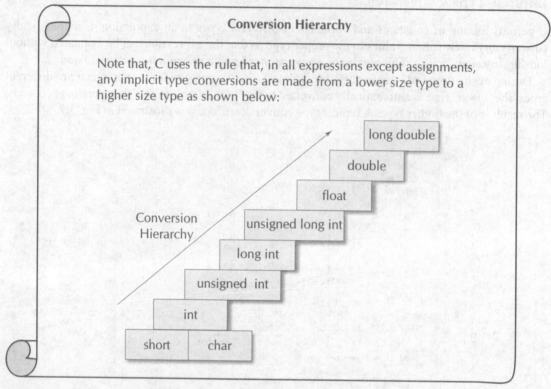

Conversion Hierarchy

Note that, C uses the rule that, in all expressions except assignments, any implicit type conversions are made from a lower size type to a higher size type as shown below:

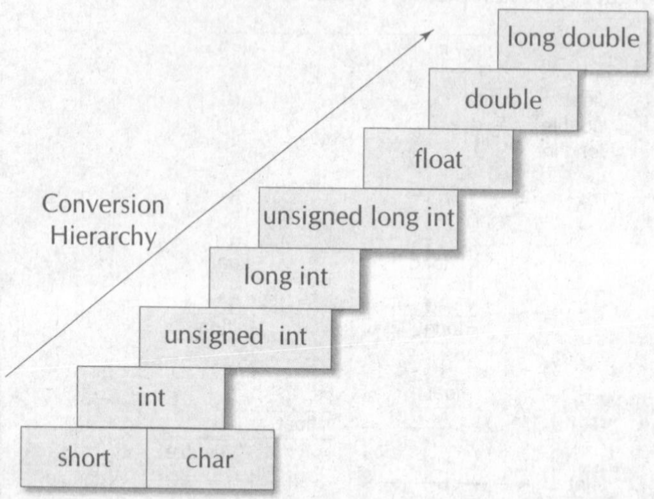

Note that some versions of C automatically convert all floating-point operands to double precision.

The final result of an expression is converted to the type of the variable on the left of the assignment sign before assigning the value to it. However, the following changes are introduced during the final assignment.

1. **float** to **int** causes truncation of the fractional part.
2. **double** to **float** causes rounding of digits.
3. **long int** to **int** causes dropping of the excess higher order bits.

Explicit Conversion

We have just discussed how C performs type conversion automatically. However, there are instances when we want to force a type conversion in a way that is different from the automatic conversion. Consider, for example, the calculation of ratio of females to males in a town.

ratio = female_number/male_number

Since **female_number** and **male_number** are declared as integers in the program, the decimal part of the result of the division would be lost and **ratio** would represent a wrong figure. This problem can be solved by converting locally one of the variables to the floating point as shown below:

ratio = **(float)** female_number/male_number

The operator (**float**) converts the **female_number** to floating point for the purpose of evaluation of the expression. Then using the rule of automatic conversion, the division is performed in floating point mode, thus retaining the fractional part of result.

Note that in no way does the operator (**float**) affect the value of the variable **female number.** And also, the type of **female number** remains as **int** in the other parts of the program.

The process of such a local conversion is known as *explicit conversion* or *casting a value.* The general form of a cast is:

(type-name) expression

Where *type-name* is one of the standard C data types. The expression may be a constant, variable or an expression. Some examples of casts and their actions are shown in Table 3.7.

Table 3.7 *Use of Casts*

Example	*Action*
x = **(int)** 7.5	7.5 is converted to integer by truncation.
a = **(int)** 21.3/(int)4.5	Evaluated as 21/4 and the result would be 5.
b = (**double**)sum/n	Division is done in floating point mode.
y = **(int)** (a+b)	The result of a+b is converted to integer.
z = (**int**)a+b	a is converted to integer and then added to b.
p = cos((**double**)x)	Converts x to double before using it.

Casting can be used to round-off a given value. Consider the following statement:

```
x = (int) (y+0.5);
```

If **y** is 27.6, **y**+0.5 is 28.1 and on casting, the result becomes 28, the value that is assigned to **x**. Of course, the expression, being cast is not changed.

Example 3.6 Figure 3.8 shows a program using a cast to evaluate the equation

$$sum = \sum_{i=1}^{n} (1/i)$$

```
Program

   main()
   {
        float  sum ;
        int     n ;

        sum = 0 ;
```

```
        for( n = 1 ; n <= 10 ; ++n )
        {
            sum = sum + 1/(float)n ;
            printf("%2d %6.4f\n", n, sum) ;
        }
    }
Output

     1 1.0000
     2 1.5000
     3 1.8333
     4 2.0833
     5 2.2833
     6 2.4500
     7 2.5929
     8 2.7179
     9 2.8290
    10 2.9290
```

Fig. 3.8 *Use of a cast*

3.15 OPERATOR PRECEDENCE AND ASSOCIATIVITY

Each operator in C has a precedence associated with it. This precedence is used to determine how an expression involving more than one operator is evaluated. There are distinct *levels of precedence* and an operator may belong to one of these levels. The operators at the higher level of precedence are evaluated first. The operators of the same precedence are evaluated either from 'left to right' or from 'right to left', depending on the level. This is known as the *associativity* property of an operator. Table 3.8 provides a complete list of operators, their precedence levels, and their rules of association. The groups are listed in the order of decreasing precedence. Rank 1 indicates the highest precedence level and 15 the lowest. The list also includes those operators, which we have not yet been discussed.

It is very important to note carefully, the order of precedence and associativity of operators. Consider the following conditional statement:

if (x == 10 + 15 && y < 10)

The precedence rules say that the ***addition*** operator has a higher priority than the logical operator (&&) and the relational operators (== and <). Therefore, the addition of 10 and 15 is executed first. This is equivalent to :

if (x == 25 && y < 10)

The next step is to determine whether **x** is equal to 25 and **y** is less than 10. If we assume a value of 20 for x and 5 for y, then

x == 25 is FALSE (0)

y < 10 is TRUE (1)

Note that since the operator < enjoys a higher priority compared to ==, y < 10 is tested first and then x == 25 is tested.

Finally we get:

if (FALSE && TRUE)

Because one of the conditions is FALSE, the complex condition is FALSE.

In the case of **&&**, it is guaranteed that the second operand will not be evaluated if the first is zero and in the case of ||, the second operand will not be evaluated if the first is non-zero.

Table 3.8 *Summary of C Operators*

Operator	*Description*	*Associativity*	*Rank*
( )	Function call	Left to right	1
[ ]	Aray element reference		
+	Unary plus	Right to left	2
–	Unary minus		
++	Increment		
– –	Decrement		
!	Logical negation		
~	Ones complement		
*	Pointer reference (indirection)		
&	Address		
sizeof	Size of an object		
(type)	Type cast (conversion)		
*	Multiplication	Left to right	3
/	Division		
%	Modulus		
+	Addition	Left to right	4
–	Subtraction		
<<	Left shift	Left to right	5
>>	Right shift		
<	Less than	Left to right	6
<=	Less than or equal to		
>	Greater than		
>=	Greater than or equal to		
==	Equality	Left to right	7
|=	Inequality		
&	Bitwise AND	Left to right	8
^	Bitwise XOR	Left to right	9
|	Bitwise OR	Left to right	10
&&	Logical AND	Left to right	11
||	Logical OR	Left to right	12
?:	Conditional expression	Right to left	13
=	Assignment operators	Right to left	14
* = /= %=			
+= –= &=			
^= |=			
<<= >>=			
,	Comma operator	Left to right	15

Rules of Precedence and Associativity

- Precedence rules decides the order in which different operators are applied
- Associativity rule decides the order in which multiple occurrences of the same level operator are applied

3.16 MATHEMATICAL FUNCTIONS

Mathematical functions such as cos, sqrt, log, etc. are frequently used in analysis of real-life problems. Most of the C compilers support these basic math functions. However, there are systems that have a more comprehensive math library and one should consult the reference manual to find out which functions are available. Table 3.9 lists some standard math functions.

Table 3.9 *Math functions*

Function	*Meaning*
Trigonometric	
acos(x)	Arc cosine of x
asin(x)	Arc sine of x
atan(x)	Arc tangent of x
atan 2(x,y)	Arc tangent of x/y
cos(x)	Cosine of x
sin(x)	Sine of x
tan(x)	Tangent of x
Hyperbolic	
cosh(x)	Hyperbolic cosine of x
sinh(x)	Hyperbolic sine of x
tanh(x)	Hyperbolic tangent of x
Other functions	
ceil(x)	x rounded up to the nearest integer
exp(x)	e to the x power (e^x)
fabs(x)	Absolute value of x.
floor(x)	x rounded down to the nearest integer
fmod(x,y)	Remainder of x/y
log(x)	Natural log of x, x > 0
log10(x)	Base 10 log of x, x > 0
pow(x,y)	x to the power y (x^y)
sqrt(x)	Square root of x, x > = 0

Note:
1. **x** and **y** should be declared as **double.**
2. In trigonometric and hyperbolic functions, **x** and **y** are in radians.
3. All the functions return a **double**.

As pointed out earlier in Chapter 1, to use any of these functions in a program, we should include the line:

```
#include <math.h>
```

in the beginning of the program.

Just Remember

- Use *decrement* and *increment* operators carefully. Understand the difference between **postfix** and **prefix** operations before using them.
- Add parentheses wherever you feel they would help to make the evaluation order clear.
- Be aware of side effects produced by some expressions.
- Avoid any attempt to divide by zero. It is normally undefined. It will either result in a fatal error or in incorrect results.
- Do not forget a semicolon at the end of an expression.
- Understand clearly the precedence of operators in an expression. Use parentheses, if necessary.
- Associativity is applied when more than one operator of the same precedence are used in an expression. Understand which operators associate from right to left and which associate from left to right.
- Do not use *increment* or *decrement* operators with any expression other than a *variable identifier*.
- It is illegal to apply modules operator % with anything other than integers.
- Do not use a variable in an expression before it has been assigned a value.
- Integer division always truncates the decimal part of the result. Use it carefully. Use casting where necessary.
- The result of an expression is converted to the type of the variable on the left of the assignment before assigning the value to it. Be careful about the loss of information during the conversion.
- All mathematical functions implement *double* type parameters and return *double* type values.
- It is an error if any space appears between the two symbols of the operators ==, !=, <= and >=.
- It is an error if the two symbols of the operators !=, <= and >= are reversed.
- Use spaces on either side of binary operator to improve the readability of the code.
- Do not use increment and decrement operators to floating point variables.
- Do not confuse the equality operator == with the assignment operator =.

CASE STUDIES

1. Salesman's Salary

A computer manufacturing company has the following monthly compensation policy to their sales-persons:

Minimum base salary : 1500.00

Bonus for every computer sold : 200.00
Commission on the total monthly sales : 2 per cent

Since the prices of computers are changing, the sales price of each computer is fixed at the beginning of every month. A program to compute a sales-person's gross salary is given in Fig. 3.9.

```
Program
    #define BASE_SALARY 1500.00
    #define BONUS_RATE   200.00
    #define COMMISSION     0.02

    main()
    {
        int quantity ;
        float gross_salary, price ;
        float bonus, commission ;

        printf("Input number sold and price\n") ;
        scanf("%d %f", &quantity, &price) ;

        bonus        = BONUS_RATE * quantity ;
        commission   = COMMISSION * quantity * price ;
        gross_salary = BASE_SALARY + bonus + commission ;

        printf("\n");
        printf("Bonus        = %6.2f\n", bonus) ;
        printf("Commission   = %6.2f\n", commission) ;
        printf("Gross salary = %6.2f\n", gross_salary) ;
    }
Output
    Input number sold and price
    5 20450.00
    Bonus          = 1000.00
    Commission     = 2045.00
    Gross salary   = 4545.00
```

Fig. 3.9 *Program of salesman's salary*

Given the base salary, bonus, and commission rate, the inputs necessary to calculate the gross salary are, the price of each computer and the number sold during the month.

The gross salary is given by the equation:

$$\text{Gross salary} = \text{base salary} + (\text{quantity} * \text{bonus rate}) + (\text{quantity} * \text{Price}) * \text{commission rate}$$

2. Solution of the quadratic equation

An equation of the form

$$ax^2 + bx + c = 0$$

is known as the *quadratic equation*. The values of x that satisfy the equation are known as the *roots* of the equation. A quadratic equation has two roots which are given by the following two formulae:

$$\text{root 1} = \frac{-b + \text{sqrt}(b^2 - 4ac)}{2a}$$

$$\text{root 2} = \frac{-b - \text{sqrt}(b^2 - 4ac)}{2a}$$

A program to evaluate these roots is given in Fig. 3.10. The program requests the user to input the values of **a**, **b** and **c** and outputs **root 1** and **root 2**.

Program

```
#include <math.h>

main()
{
    float a, b, c, discriminant,
          root1, root2;

    printf("Input values of a, b, and c\n");
    scanf("%f %f %f", &a, &b, &c);

    discriminant = b*b - 4*a*c ;
    if(discriminant < 0)
      printf("\n\nROOTS ARE IMAGINARY\n");
    else
    {
      root1 = (-b + sqrt(discriminant))/(2.0*a);
      root2 = (-b - sqrt(discriminant))/(2.0*a);
      printf("\n\nRoot1 = %5.2f\n\nRoot2 = %5.2f\n",
                  root1,root2 );
    }
}
```

Output

```
Input values of a, b, and c
2 4 -16

Root1 = 2.00

Root2 = -4.00

Input values of a, b, and c
1 2 3
```

```
ROOTS ARE IMAGINARY
```

Fig. 3.10 *Solution of a quadratic equation*

The term (b^2–4ac) is called the *discriminant*. If the discriminant is less than zero, its square roots cannot be evaluated. In such cases, the roots are said to be imaginary numbers and the program outputs an appropriate message.

REVIEW QUESTIONS

3.1 State whether the following statements are *true* or *false*.

(a) All arithmetic operators have the same level of precedence.

(b) The modulus operator % can be used only with integers.

(c) The operators <=, >= and != all enjoy the same level of priority.

(d) During modulo division, the sign of the result is positive, if both the operands are of the same sign.

(e) In C, if a data item is zero, it is considered false.

(f) The expression *!(x<=y)* is same as the expression *x>y*.

(g) A unary expression consists of only one operand with no operators.

(h) Associativity is used to decide which of several different expressions is evaluated first.

(i) An expression statement is terminated with a period.

(j) During the evaluation of mixed expressions, an implicit cast is generated automatically.

(k) An explicit cast can be used to change the expression.

(l) Parentheses can be used to change the order of evaluation expressions.

3.2 Fill in the blanks with appropriate words.

(a) The expression containing all the integer operands is called________ expression.

(b) The operator ________cannot be used with real operands.

(c) C supports as many as _______relational operators.

(d) An expression that combines two or more relational expressions is termed as __________expression.

(e) The ___________operator returns the number of bytes the operand occupies.

(f) The order of evaluation can be changed by using ______ in an expression.

(g) The use of ________ on a variable can change its type in the memory.

(h) __________is used to determine the order in which different operators in an expression are evaluated.

3.3 Given the statement

int a = 10, b = 20, c;

determine whether each of the following statements are true or false.

(a) The statement a = + 10, is valid.

(b) The expression a + 4/6 * 6/2 evaluates to 11.

(c) The expression b + 3/2 * 2/3 evaluates to 20.

(d) The statement a + = b; gives the values 30 to a and 20 to b.

(e) The statement ++a++; gives the value 12 to a

(f) The statement a = 1/b; assigns the value 0.5 to a

3.4 Declared **a** as *int* and **b** as *float*, state whether the following statements are true or false.

(a) The statement a = 1/3 + 1/3 + 1/3; assigns the value 1 to a.

(b) The statement b = 1.0/3.0 + 1.0/3.0 + 1.0/3.0; assigns a value 1.0 to b.

(c) The statement b = 1.0/3.0 * 3.0 gives a value 1.0 to b.

(d) The statement b = 1.0/3.0 + 2.0/3.0 assigns a value 1.0 to b.

(e) The statement a = 15/10.0 + 3/2; assigns a value 3 to a.

3.5 Which of the following expressions are true?

(a) !(5 + 5 >=10)

(b) 5 + 5 = = 10 || 1 + 3 = = 5

(c) 5 > 10 || 10 < 20 && 3 < 5

(d) 10 ! = 15 && !(10<20) || 15 > 30

3.6 Which of the following arithmetic expressions are valid ? If valid, give the value of the expression; otherwise give reason.

(a) 25/3 % 2 (e) –14 % 3

(b) +9/4 + 5 (f) 15.25 + – 5.0

(c) 7.5 % 3 (g) (5/3) * 3 + 5 % 3

(d) 14 % 3 + 7 % 2 (h) 21 % (int)4.5

3.7 Write C assignment statements to evaluate the following equations:

(a) $\text{Area} = \pi r^2 + 2\pi rh$

(b) $\text{Torque} = \dfrac{2m_1m_2}{m_1 + m_2} \cdot g$

(c) $\text{Side} = \sqrt{a^2 + b^2 - 2ab\cos(x)}$

(d) $\text{Energy} = \text{mass}\left[\text{acceleration} \times \text{height} + \dfrac{(\text{velocity})^2}{2}\right]$

3.8 Identify unnecessary parentheses in the following arithmetic expressions.

(a) ((x–(y/5)+z)%8) + 25

(b) ((x–y) * p)+q

(c) (m*n) + (–x/y)

(d) x/(3*y)

3.9 Find errors, if any, in the following assignment statements and rectify them.

(a) `x = y = z = 0.5, 2.0. –5.75;`

(b) `m = ++a * 5;`

(c) `y = sqrt(100);`

(d) `p * = x/y;`

(e) `s = /5;`

(f) `a = b++ –c*2`

3.10 Determine the value of each of the following logical expressions if a = 5, b = 10 and c = –6

(a) a > b && a < c

(b) a < b && a > c

(c) a == c || b > a

(d) b > 15 && c < 0 || a > 0

(e) (a/2.0 == 0.0 && b/2.0 != 0.0) || c < 0.0

PROGRAMMING EXERCISES

3.1 Given the values of the variables x, y and z, write a program to rotate their values such that x has the value of y, y has the value of z, and z has the value of x.

3.2 Write a program that reads a floating-point number and then displays the right-most digit of the integral part of the number.

3.3 Modify the above program to display the two right-most digits of the integral part of the number.

3.4 Write a program that will obtain the length and width of a rectangle from the user and compute its area and perimeter.

3.5 Given an integer number, write a program that displays the number as follows:

First line : all digits
Second line : all except first digit
Third line : all except first two digits
....
Last line : The last digit

For example, the number 5678 will be displayed as:

5 6 7 8
6 7 8
7 8
8

3.6 The straight-line method of computing the yearly depreciation of the value of an item is given by

$$\text{Depreciation} = \frac{\text{Purchase Price} - \text{Salvage Value}}{\text{Years of Service}}$$

Write a program to determine the salvage value of an item when the purchase price, years of service, and the annual depreciation are given.

3.7 Write a program that will read a real number from the keyboard and print the following output in one line:

Smallest integer not less than the number	The given number	Largest integer not greater than the number

3.8 The total distance travelled by a vehicle in t seconds is given by

$$\text{distance} = ut + (at^2)/2$$

Where u is the initial velocity (metres per second), a is the acceleration (metres per second^2). Write a program to evaluate the distance travelled at regular intervals of time, given the values of u and a. The program should provide the flexibility to the user to select his own time intervals and repeat the calculations for different values of u and a.

3.9 In inventory management, the Economic Order Quantity for a single item is given by

$$\text{EOQ} = \sqrt{\frac{2 \times \text{demand rate} \times \text{setup costs}}{\text{holding cost per item per unit time}}}$$

and the optimal Time Between Orders

$$\text{TBO} = \sqrt{\frac{2 \times \text{setup costs}}{\text{demand rate} \times \text{holding cost per item per unit time}}}$$

Write a program to compute EOQ and TBO, given demand rate (items per unit time), setup costs (per order), and the holding cost (per item per unit time).

3.10 For a certain electrical circuit with an inductance L and resistance R, the damped natural frequency is given by

$$\text{Frequency} = \sqrt{\frac{1}{LC} - \frac{R^2}{4C^2}}$$

It is desired to study the variation of this frequency with C (capacitance). Write a program to calculate the frequency for different values of C starting from 0.01 to 0.1 in steps of 0.01.

Chapter 4

Managing Input and Output Operations

4.1 INTRODUCTION

Reading, processing, and writing of data are the three essential functions of a computer program. Most programs take some data as input and display the processed data, often known as *information* or *results*, on a suitable medium. So far we have seen two methods of providing data to the program variables. One method is to assign values to variables through the assignment statements such as **x = 5; a = 0;** and so on. Another method is to use the input function **scanf** which can read data from a keyboard. We have used both the methods in most of our earlier example programs. For outputting results we have used extensively the function **printf** which sends results out to a terminal.

Unlike other high-level languages, C does not have any built-in input/output statements as part of its syntax. All input/output operations are carried out through function calls such as **printf** and **scanf**. There exist several functions that have more or less become standard for input and output operations in C. These functions are collectively known as the standard I/O library. In this chapter we shall discuss some common I/O functions that can be used on many machines without any change. However, one should consult the system reference manual for exact details of these functions and also to see what other functions are available.

It may be recalled that we have included a statement

```
#include <math.h>
```

in the Sample Program 5 in Chapter 1, where a math library function cos(x) has been used. This is to instruct the compiler to fetch the function cos(x) from the math library, and that it is not a part of C language. Similarly, each program that uses a standard input/output function must contain the statement

```
#include <stdio.h>
```

at the beginning. However, there might be exceptions. For example, this is not necessary for the functions **printf** and **scanf** which have been defined as a part of the C language.

The file name **stdio.h** is an abbrevation for *standard input-output header* file. The instruction **#include** *<stdio.h>* tells the compiler 'to search for a file named **stdio.h** and place its contents at this point in the program'. The contents of the header file become part of the source code when it is compiled.

4.2 READING A CHARACTER

The simplest of all input/output operations is reading a character from the 'standard input' unit (usually the keyboard) and writing it to the 'standard output' unit (usually the screen). Reading a single character can be done by using the function **getchar.** (This can also be done with the help of the **scanf** function which is discussed in Section 4.4.) The **getchar** takes the following form:

variable_name = **getchar( );**

variable_name is a valid C name that has been declared as **char** type. When this statement is encountered, the computer waits until a key is pressed and then assigns this character as a value to **getchar** function. Since **getchar** is used on the right-hand side of an assignment statement, the character value of **getchar** is in turn assigned to the variable name on the left. For example

```
char name;
name = getchar();
```

will assign the character 'H' to the variable **name** when we press the key H on the keyboard. Since **getchar** is a function, it requires a set of parentheses as shown.

Example 4.1 The program in Fig. 4.1 shows the use of **getchar** function in an interactive environment.

The program displays a question of YES/NO type to the user and reads the user's response in a single character (Y or N). If the response is Y, it outputs the message

My name is BUSY BEE

otherwise, outputs.

You are good for nothing

Note: There is one line space between the input text and output message.

```
Program
    #include <stdio.h>
    main()
    {
      char answer;
      printf("Would you like to know my name?\n");
      printf("Type Y for YES and N for NO: ");
      answer = getchar(); /* .... Reading a character...*/
      if(answer == 'Y' || answer == 'y')
        printf("\n\nMy name is BUSY BEE\n");
      else
```

```
        printf("\n\nYou are good for nothing\n");
}
Output
        Would you like to know my name?
        Type Y for YES and N for NO: Y
        My name is BUSY BEE
        Would you like to know my name?
        Type Y for YES and N for NO: n
        You are good for nothing
```

Fig. 4.1 *Use of **getchar** function to read a **character** from keyboard*

The **getchar** function may be called successively to read the characters contained in a line of text. For example, the following program segment reads characters from keyboard one after another until the 'Return' key is pressed.

```
---------
---------
char character;
character = ' ';
while(character != '\n')
{
    character = getchar();
}
---------
---------
```

WARNING

The **getchar()** function accepts any character keyed in. This includes RETURN and TAB. This means when we enter single character input, the newline character is waiting in the input queue after **getchar()** returns. This could create problems when we use **getchar()** in a loop interactively. A dummy **getchar()** may be used to 'eat' the unwanted newline character. We can also use the **fflush** function to flush out the unwanted characters.

Note: We shall be using decision statements like **if, if...else** and **while** extensively in this chapter. They are discussed in detail in Chapters 5 and 6.

Example 4.2 The program of Fig. 4.2 requests the user to enter a character and displays a message on the screen telling the user whether the character is an alphabet or digit, or any other special character.

This program receives a character from the keyboard and tests whether it is a letter or digit and prints out a message accordingly. These tests are done with the help of the following functions:

```
isalpha(character)
isdigit(character)
```

For example, **isalpha** assumes a value non-zero (TRUE) if the argument **character** contains an alphabet; otherwise it assumes 0 (FALSE). Similar is the case with the function **isdigit**.

```
Program:
        #include <stdio.h>
        #include <ctype.h>
        main()
        {
           char character;
           printf("Press any key\n");
           character = getchar();
           if (isalpha(character) > 0)
              printf("The character is a letter.");
           else
             if (isdigit (character) > 0)
                printf("The character is a digit.");
             else
                printf("The character is not alphanumeric.");
        }
Output
           Press any key
           h
           The character is a letter.
           Press any key
           5
           The character is a digit.
           Press any key
           *
           The character is not alphanumeric.
```

Fig. 4.2 *Program to test the* ***character*** *type*

C supports many other similar functions, which are given in Table 4.1. These character functions are contained in the file **ctype.h** and therefore the statement

```
        #include <ctype.h>
```

must be included in the program.

Table 4.1 *Character Test Functions*

Function	*Test*
isalnum(c)	Is c an alphanumeric character?
isalpha(c)	Is c an alphabetic character?
isdigit(c)	Is c a digit?
islower(c)	Is c lower case letter?
isprint(c)	Is c a printable character?

(Contd.)

Table 4.1 *(Contd.)*

Function	*Test*
ispunct(c)	Is c a punctuation mark?
isspace(c)	Is c a white space character?
isupper(c)	Is c an upper case letter?

4.3 WRITING A CHARACTER

Like **getchar**, there is an analogous function **putchar** for writing characters one at a time to the terminal. It takes the form as shown below:

putchar (*variable_name*);

where ***variable_name*** is a type **char** variable containing a character. This statement displays the character contained in the ***variable_name*** at the terminal. For example, the statements

```
answer = 'Y';
putchar (answer);
```

will display the character Y on the screen. The statement

```
putchar ('\n');
```

would cause the cursor on the screen to move to the beginning of the next line.

Example 4.3 A program that reads a character from keyboard and then prints it in reverse case is given in Fig. 4.3. That is, if the input is upper case, the output will be lower case and vice versa.

The program uses three new functions: **islower, toupper**, and **tolower**. The function **islower** is a conditional function and takes the value TRUE if the argument is a lowercase alphabet; otherwise takes the value FALSE. The function **toupper** converts the lowercase argument into an uppercase alphabet while the function **tolower** does the reverse.

```
Program
    #include <stdio.h>
    #include <ctype.h>
    main()
    {
      char alphabet;
      printf("Enter an alphabet");
      putchar('\n'); /* move to next line */
      alphabet = getchar();
      if (islower(alphabet))
        putchar(toupper(alphabet));
      else
        putchar(tolower(alphabet));
    }
Output
        Enter an alphabet
```

```
a
A
Enter an alphabet
Q
q
Enter an alphabet
z
Z
```

Fig. 4.3 *Reading and writing of alphabets in reverse case*

4.4 FORMATTED INPUT

Formatted input refers to an input data that has been arranged in a particular format. For example, consider the following data:

```
15.75 123 John
```

This line contains three pieces of data, arranged in a particular form. Such data has to be read conforming to the format of its appearance. For example, the first part of the data should be read into a variable **float**, the second into **int**, and the third part into **char**. This is possible in C using the **scanf** function. (**scanf** means *scan* formatted.)

We have already used this input function in a number of examples. Here, we shall explore all of the options that are available for reading the formatted data with **scanf** function. The general form of **scanf** is

scanf ("*control string*", *arg1*, *arg2*, ... *argn*);

The *control string* specifies the field format in which the data is to be entered and the arguments *arg*1, *arg2*, ..., *argn* specify the address of locations where the data is stored. Control string and arguments are separated by commas.

Control string (also known as *format string*) contains field specifications, which direct the interpretation of input data. It may include:

- Field (or format) specifications, consisting of the conversion character %, a data type character (or type specifier), and an *optional* number, specifying the field width.
- Blanks, tabs, or newlines.

Blanks, tabs and newlines are ignored. The data type character indicates the type of data that is to be assigned to the variable associated with the corresponding argument. The field width specifier is optional. The discussions that follow will clarify these concepts.

Inputting Integer Numbers

The field specification for reading an integer number is:

```
% w d
```

The percent sign (**%**) indicates that a conversion specification follows. *w* is an integer number that specifies the *field width* of the number to be read and d, known as data type character, indicates that the number to be read is in integer mode. Consider the following example:

```
scanf ("%2d %5d", &num1, &num2);
```

Data line:

```
50  31426
```

The value 50 is assigned to **num1** and 31426 to **num2**. Suppose the input data is as follows:

```
31426 50
```

The variable **num1** will be assigned 31 (because of %2d) and **num2** will be assigned 426 (unread part of 31426). The value 50 that is unread will be assigned to the first variable in the next **scanf** call. This kind of errors may be eliminated if we use the field specifications without the field width specifications. That is, the statement

```
scanf("%d %d", &num1, &num2);
```

will read the data

```
31426 50
```

correctly and assign 31426 to **num1** and 50 to **num2.**

Input data items must be separated by spaces, tabs or newlines. Punctuation marks do not count as separators. When the **scanf** function searches the input data line for a value to be read, it will always bypass any white space characters.

What happens if we enter a floating point number instead of an integer? The fractional part may be stripped away! Also, **scanf** may skip reading further input.

When the **scanf** reads a particular value, reading of the value will be terminated as soon as the number of characters specified by the field width is reached (if specified) or until a character that is not valid for the value being read is encountered. In the case of integers, valid characters are an optionally signed sequence of digits.

An input field may be skipped by specifying * in the place of field width. For example, the statement

```
scanf("%d %*d %d", &a, &b)
```

will assign the data

```
123 456 789
```

as follows:

```
123 to a
456 skipped (because of *)
789 to b
```

The data type character **d** may be preceded by 'l' (letter ell) to read long integers and **h** to read short integers.

Note: We have provided white space between the field specifications. These spaces are not necessary with the numeric input, but it is a good practice to include them.

Example 4.4 Various input formatting options for reading integers are experimented in the program shown in Fig. 4.4.

Program

```
main()
{
    int a,b,c,x,y,z;
    int p,q,r;
    printf("Enter three integer numbers\n");
    scanf("%d %*d %d",&a,&b,&c);
    printf("%d %d %d \n\n",a,b,c);
    printf("Enter two 4-digit numbers\n");
    scanf("%2d %4d",&x,&y);
    printf("%d %d\n\n", x,y);
    printf("Enter two integers\n");
    scanf("%d %d", &a,&x);
    printf("%d %d \n\n",a,x);
    printf("Enter a nine digit number\n");
    scanf("%3d %4d %3d",&p,&q,&r);
    printf("%d %d %d \n\n",p,q,r);
    printf("Enter two three digit numbers\n");
    scanf("%d %d",&x,&y);
    printf("%d %d",x,y);
}
```

Output

```
Enter three integer numbers
1 2 3
1 3 -3577
Enter two 4-digit numbers
6789 4321
67 89
Enter two integers
44 66
4321 44
Enter a nine-digit number
123456789
66 1234 567
Enter two three-digit numbers
123 456
89 123
```

Fig. 4.4 *Reading integers using scanf*

The first **scanf** requests input data for three integer values **a, b,** and **c,** and accordingly three values 1, 2, and 3 are keyed in. Because of the specification %*d the value 2 has been skipped and 3 is assigned to the variable **b**. Notice that since no data is available for **c**, it contains garbage.

The second **scanf** specifies the format %2d and %4d for the variables **x** and **y** respectively. Whenever we specify field width for reading integer numbers, the input numbers should not contain more digits that the specified size. Otherwise, the extra digits on the right-hand side will be truncated and assigned to the next variable in the list. Thus, the second **scanf** has truncated the four digit number 6789 and assigned 67 to **x** and 89 to **y**. The value 4321 has been assigned to the first variable in the immediately following **scanf** statement.

Note: It is legal to use a non-whitespace character between field specifications. However, the **scanf** expects a matching character in the given location. For example,

```
scanf"%d-%d", &a, &b);
```

accepts input like

```
123-456
```

to assign 123 to **a** and 456 to **b**.

Inputting Real Numbers

Unlike integer numbers, the field width of real numbers is not to be specified and therefore **scanf** reads real numbers using the simple specification **%f** for both the notations, namely, decimal point notation and exponential notation. For example, the statement

```
scanf("%f %f %f", &x, &y, &z);
```

with the input data

```
475.89 43.21E-1 678
```

will assign the value 475.89 to **x**, 4.321 to **y**, and 678.0 to **z**. The input field specifications may be separated by any arbitrary blank spaces.

If the number to be read is of **double** type, then the specification should be **%lf** instead of simple **%f.** A number may be skipped using **%*f** specification.

Example 4.5 Reading of real numbers (in both decimal point and exponential notation) is illustrated in Fig. 4.5.

```
Program
    main()
    {
        float x,y;
        double p,q;

        printf("Values of x and y:");
        scanf("%f %e", &x, &y);
        printf("\n");
        printf("x = %f\ny = %f\n\n", x, y);
```

```
        printf("Values of p and q:");
        scanf("%lf %lf", &p, &q);
        printf("\n\np = %.12lf\np = %.12e", p,q);
    }
Output
        Values of x and y:12.3456 17.5e-2
        x = 12.345600
        y = 0.175000

        Values of p and q:4.142857142857 18.5678901234567890

        p = 4.142857142857
        q = 1.856789012346e+001
```

Fig. 4.5 *Reading of real numbers*

Inputting Character Strings

We have already seen how a single character can be read from the terminal using the **getchar** function. The same can be achieved using the **scanf** function also. In addition, a **scanf** function can input strings containing more than one character. Following are the specifications for reading character strings:

%*ws* **or** %*wc*

The corresponding argument should be a pointer to a character array. However, %c may be used to read a single character when the argument is a pointer to a **char** variable.

Example 4.6 Reading of strings using **%wc** and **%ws** is illustrated in Fig. 4.6.

The program in Fig. 4.6 illustrates the use of various field specifications for reading strings. When we use **%wc** for reading a string, the system will wait until the wth character is keyed in.
Note that the specification **%s** terminates reading at the encounter of a blank space. Therefore, **name2** has read only the first part of "New York" and the second part is automatically assigned to **name3**. However, during the second run, the string "New-York" is correctly assigned to **name2**.

```
Program
    main()
    {
        int no;
        char name1[15], name2[15], name3[15];

        printf("Enter serial number and name one\n");
        scanf("%d %15c", &no, name1);
        printf("%d %15s\n\n", no, name1);
```

```
        printf("Enter serial number and name two\n");
        scanf("%d %s", &no, name2);
        printf("%d %15s\n\n", no, name2);

        printf("Enter serial number and name three\n");
        scanf("%d %15s", &no, name3);
        printf("%d %15s\n\n", no, name3);
    }
Output
        Enter serial number and name one
        1 123456789012345
        1 123456789012345r
        Enter serial number and name two
        2 New York
        2           New
        Enter serial number and name three
        2           York
        Enter serial number and name one
        1 123456789012
        1 123456789012r
        Enter serial number and name two
        2 New-York
        2         New-York
        Enter serial number and name three
        3 London
        3         London
```

Fig. 4.6 *Reading of strings*

Some versions of **scanf** support the following conversion specifications for strings:

%[characters]

%[^characters]

The specification **%[characters]** means that only the characters specified within the brackets are permissible in the input string. If the input string contains any other character, the string will be terminated at the first encounter of such a character. The specification **%[^characters]** does exactly the reverse. That is, the characters specified after the circumflex (^) are not permitted in the input string. The reading of the string will be terminated at the encounter of one of these characters.

Example 4.7 The program in Fig. 4.7 illustrates the function of %[ ] specification.

```
Program-A
    main()
    {
        char address[80];
```

```
        printf("Enter address\n");
        scanf("%[a-z]", address);
        printf("%-80s\n\n", address);
    }
```

Output

```
        Enter address
        new delhi 110002
        new delhi
```

Program-B

```
    main()
    {
        char address[80];

        printf("Enter address\n");
        scanf("%[^\n]", address);
        printf("%-80s", address);
    }
```

Output

```
        Enter address
        New Delhi 110 002
        New Delhi 110 002
```

Fig. 4.7 *Illustration of conversion specification%[] for strings*

Reading Blank Spaces

We have earlier seen that %s specifier cannot be used to read strings with blank spaces. But, this can be done with the help of %[ ] specification. Blank spaces may be included within the brackets, thus enabling the ***scanf*** to read strings with spaces. Remember that the lowercase and uppercase letters are distinct. See Fig. 4.7.

Reading Mixed Data Types

It is possible to use one **scanf** statement to input a data line containing mixed mode data. In such cases, care should be exercised to ensure that the input data items match the control specifications *in order* and *type*. When an attempt is made to read an item that does not match the type expected, the **scanf** function does not read any further and immediately returns the values read. The statement

```
scanf ("%d %c %f %s", &count, &code, &ratio, name);
```

will read the data

```
15 p 1.575 coffee
```

correctly and assign the values to the variables in the order in which they appear. Some systems accept integers in the place of real numbers and vice versa, and the input data is converted to the type specified in the control string.

Note: A space before the *%c* specification in the format string is necessary to skip the white space before p.

Detection of Errors in Input

When a **scanf** function completes reading its list, it returns the value of number of items that are successfully read. This value can be used to test whether any errors occurred in reading the input. For example, the statement

```
scanf("%d %f %s, &a, &b, name);
```

will return the value 3 if the following data is typed in:

```
20 150.25 motor
```

and will return the value 1 if the following line is entered

```
20 motor 150.25
```

This is because the function would encounter a string when it was expecting a floating-point value, and would therefore terminate its scan after reading the first value.

Example 4.8 The program presented in Fig.4.8 illustrates the testing for correctness of reading of data by **scanf** function.

The function **scanf** is expected to read three items of data and therefore, when the values for all the three variables are read correctly, the program prints out their values. During the third run, the second item does not match with the type of variable and therefore the reading is terminated and the error message is printed. Same is the case with the fourth run.

In the last run, although data items do not match the variables, no error message has been printed. When we attempt to read a real number for an **int** variable, the integer part is assigned to the variable, and the truncated decimal part is assigned to the next variable.

Note that the character '2' is assigned to the character variable c.

Program

```
main()
{
    int a;
    float b;
    char c;
    printf("Enter values of a, b and c\n");
    if (scanf("%d %f %c", &a, &b, &c) == 3)
        printf("a = %d b = %f c = %c\n" , a, b, c);
    else
        printf("Error in input.\n");
}
```

Output

```
Enter values of a, b and c
     12 3.45 A
```

```
a = 12    b = 3.450000      c = A
Enter values of a, b and c
23 78 9
a = 23    b = 78.000000     c = 9
Enter values of a, b and c
8 A 5.25
Error in input.
Enter values of a, b and c
Y 12 67
Error in input.
Enter values of a, b and c
15.75 23 X
a = 15    b = 0.750000      c = 2
```

Fig. 4.8 *Detection of errors in* ***scanf*** *input*

Commonly used **scanf** format codes are given in Table 4.2

Table 4.2 *Commonly used scanf Format Codes*

Code	*Meaning*
%c	read a single character
%d	read a decimal integer
%e	read a floating point value
%f	read a floating point value
%g	read a floating point value
%h	read a short integer
%i	read a decimal, hexadecimal or octal integer
%o	read an octal integer
%s	read a string
%u	read an unsigned decimal integer
%x	read a hexadecimal integer
%[..]	read a string of word(s)

The following letters may be used as prefix for certain conversion characters.

h for short integers
l for long integers or double
L for long double

Points to Remember While Using scanf

If we do not plan carefully, some 'crazy' things can happen with **scanf**. Since the I/O routines are not a part of C language, they are made available either as a separate module of the C library or as a part of the operating system (like UNIX). New features are added to these routines from time to time as new versions of systems are released. We should consult the system reference manual before using these routines. Given below are some of the general points to keep in mind while writing a **scanf** statement.

1. All function arguments, except the control string, *must* be pointers to variables.
2. Format specifications contained in the control string should match the arguments in order.
3. Input data items must be separated by spaces and must match the variables receiving the input in the same order.
4. The reading will be terminated, when **scanf** encounters a 'mismatch' of data or a character that is not valid for the value being read.
5. When searching for a value, **scanf** ignores line boundaries and simply looks for the next appropriate character.
6. Any unread data items in a line will be considered as part of the data input line to the next **scanf** call.
7. When the field width specifier *w* is used, it should be large enough to contain the input data size.

Rules for scanf

- Each variable to be read must have a filed specification.
- For each field specification, there must be a variable address of proper type.
- Any non-whitespace character used in the format string must have a matching character in the user input.
- Never end the format string with whitespace. It is a fatal error!
- The scanf reads until:
  - A whitespace character is found in a numberic specification, or
  - The maximum number of characters have been read or
  - An error is detected, or
  - The end of file is reached

4.5 FORMATTED OUTPUT

We have seen the use of **printf** function for printing captions and numerical results. It is highly desirable that the outputs are produced in such a way that they are understandable and are in an easy-to-use form. It is therefore necessary for the programmer to give careful consideration to the appearance and clarity of the output produced by his program.

The **printf** statement provides certain features that can be effectively exploited to control the alignment and spacing of print-outs on the terminals. The general form of **printf** statement is

printf("*control string*", ***arg1, arg2, ..., argn***);

Control string consists of three types of items:

1. Characters that will be printed on the screen as they appear.

2. Format specifications that define the output format for display of each item.
3. *Escape sequence* characters such as \n, \t, and \b.

The control string indicates how many arguments follow and what their types are. The arguments *arg1, arg2, ..., argn* are the variables whose values are formatted and printed according to the specifications of the control string. The arguments should match in number, order and type with the format specifications.

A simple format specification has the following form:

% w.p type-specifier

where *w* is an integer number that specifies the total number of columns for the output value and *p* is another integer number that specifies the number of digits to the right of the decimal point (of a real number) or the number of characters to be printed from a string. Both ***w*** and *p* are optional. Some examples of formatted **printf** statement are:

```
printf("Programming in C");
printf(" ");
printf("\n");
printf("%d", x);
printf("a = %f\n b = %f", a, b);
printf("sum = %d", 1234);
printf("\n\n");
```

printf never supplies a *newline* automatically and therefore multiple **printf** statements may be used to build one line of output. A *newline* can be introduced by the help of a newline character '\n' as shown in some of the examples above.

Output of Integer Numbers

The format specification for printing an integer number is

% *w* **d**

where ***w*** specifies the minimum field width for the output. However, if a number is greater than the specified field width, it will be printed in full, overriding the minimum specification. ***d*** specifies that the value to be printed is an integer. The number is written *right-justified* in the given field width. Leading blanks will appear as necessary. The following examples illustrate the output of the number 9876 under different formats:

Format	Output
printf("%d", 9876)	| 9 | 8 | 7 | 6 |
printf("%6d", 9876)	| | | 9 | 8 | 7 | 6 |
printf("%2d", 9876)	| 9 | 8 | 7 | 6 |

printf("%-6d", 9876)

9	8	7	6		

printf("%06d", 9876)

0	0	9	8	7	6

It is possible to force the printing to be left-*justified* by placing a *minus* sign directly after the % character, as shown in the fourth example above. It is also possible to pad with zeros the leading blanks by placing a 0 (zero) before the field width specifier as shown in the last item above. The minus (–) and zero (0) are known as *flags*.

Long integers may be printed by specifying **ld** in the place of **d** in the format specification. Similarly, we may use **hd** for printing short integers.

Example 4.9 The program in Fig. 4.9 illustrates the output of integer numbers under various formats.

Program

```
main()
{
    int m = 12345;
    long n = 987654;
    printf("%d\n",m);
    printf("%10d\n",m);
    printf("%010d\n",m);
    printf("%-10d\n",m);
    printf("%10ld\n",n);
    printf("%10ld\n",-n);
}
```

Output

```
12345
     12345
0000012345
12345
    987654
  - 987654
```

Fig. 4.9 *Formatted output of integers*

Output of Real Numbers

The output of a real number may be displayed in decimal notation using the following format specification:

% *w*.p f

The integer ***w*** indicates the minimum number of positions that are to be used for the display of the value and the integer ***p*** indicates the number of digits to be displayed after the decimal point (*preci-*

sion). The value, when displayed, is *rounded to p decimal places* and printed *right-justified* in the field of *w* columns. Leading blanks and trailing zeros will appear as necessary. The default precision is 6 decimal places. The negative numbers will be printed with the minus sign. The number will be displayed in the form [–] mmm-nnn.

We can also display a real number in exponential notation by using the specification

% *w.p* e

The display takes the form

[-] m.nnnne[±]xx

where the length of the string of n's is specified by the precision *p*. The default precision is 6. The field width **w** should satisfy the condition.

$$w \geq p+7$$

The value will be rounded off and printed right justified in the field of **w** columns.

Padding the leading blanks with zeros and printing with *left-justification* are also possible by using flags 0 or – before the field width specifier **w**.

The following examples illustrate the output of the number y = 98.7654 under different format specifications:

Format	*Output*
printf("%7.4f",y)	`98.7654`
printf("%7.2f",y)	`  98.77`
printf("%-7.2f",y)	`98.77  `
printf("%f",y)	`98.7654`
printf("%10.2e",y)	`  9.88e+01`
printf("%11.4e",-y)	`-9.8765e+01`
printf("%-10.2e",y)	`9.88e+01  `
printf("%e",y)	`9.876540e+01`

Some systems also support a special field specification character that lets the user define the field size at run time. This takes the following form:

```
printf("%*.*f", width, precision, number);
```

In this case, both the field width and the precision are given as arguments which will supply the values for **w** and **p**. For example,

```
printf("%*.*f",7,2,number);
```

is equivalent to

```
printf("%7.2f",number);
```

The advantage of this format is that the values for *width* and *precision* may be supplied at run time, thus making the format a *dynamic* one. For example, the above statement can be used as follows:

```
int width = 7;
int precision = 2;
........
........
printf("%*.*f", width, precision, number);
```

Example 4.10 All the options of printing a real number are illustrated in Fig. 4.10.

```
Program
    main()
    {
      float y = 98.7654;
      printf("%7.4f\n", y);
      printf("%f\n", y);
      printf("%7.2f\n", y);
      printf("%-7.2f\n", y);
      printf("%07.2f\n", y);
      printf("%*.*f", 7, 2, y);
      printf("\n");
      printf("%10.2e\n", y);
      printf("%12.4e\n", -y);
      printf("%-10.2e\n", y);
      printf("%e\n", y);
    }
Output
      98.7654
      98.765404
      98.77
      98.77
      0098.77
      98.77
      9.88e+001
      -9.8765e+001
      9.88e+001
      9.876540e+001
```

Fig. 4.10 *Formatted output of real numbers*

Printing of a Single Character

A single character can be displayed in a desired position using the format

%*wc*

The character will be displayed *right-justified* in the field of *w* columns. We can make the display *left-justified* by placing a minus sign before the integer w. The default value for w is 1.

Printing of Strings

The format specification for outputting strings is similar to that of real numbers. It is of the form

%*w.ps*

where *w* specifies the field width for display and *p* instructs that only the first p characters of the string are to be displayed. The display is *right-justified*.

The following examples show the effect of variety of specifications in printing a string "NEW DELHI 110001", containing 16 characters (including blanks).

Specification	1	2	3	4	5	6	7	8	9	0	1	2	3	4	5	6	7	8	9	0
%s	N	E	W		D	E	L	H	I		1	1	0	0	0	1				
%20s					N	E	W		D	E	L	H	I		1	1	0	0	0	1
%20.10s											N	E	W		D	E	L	H	I	
%.5s	N	E	W		D															
%-20.10s	N	E	W		D	E	L	H	I											
%5s	N	E	W		D	E	L	H	I		1	1	0	0	0	1				

Example 4.11 Printing of characters and strings is illustrated in Fig. 4.11.

```
Program
    main()
    {
        char x = 'A';
        char name[20] = "ANIL KUMAR GUPTA";
```

```
            printf("OUTPUT OF CHARACTERS\n\n");
            printf("%c\n%3c\n%5c\n", x,x,x);
            printf("%3c\n%c\n", x,x);
            printf("\n");
            printf("OUTPUT OF STRINGS\n\n");
            printf("%s\n", name);
            printf("%20s\n", name);
            printf("%20.10s\n", name);
            printf("%.5s\n", name);
            printf("%-20.10s\n", name);
            printf("%5s\n", name);
        }
```

Output

```
OUTPUT OF CHARACTERS
A
  A
    A
  A
A
OUTPUT OF STRINGS
ANIL KUMAR GUPTA
    ANIL KUMAR GUPTA
          ANIL KUMAR
ANIL
ANIL KUMAR
ANIL KUMAR GUPTA
```

Fig. 4.11 *Printing of characters and strings*

Mixed Data Output

It is permitted to mix data types in one **printf** statement. For example, the statement of the type

```
printf("%d %f %s %c", a, b, c, d);
```

is valid. As pointed out earlier, **printf** uses its control string to decide how many variables to be printed and what their types are. Therefore, the format specifications should match the variables in number, order, and type. If there are not enough variables or if they are of the wrong type, the output results will be incorrect.

Table 4.3 *Commonly used printf Format Codes*

Code	*Meaning*
%c	print a single character
%d	print a decimal integer
%e	print a floating point value in exponent form

Code	Meaning
%f	print a floating point value without exponent
%g	print a floating point value either e-type or f-type depending on value
%i	print a signed decimal integer
%o	print an octal integer, without leading zero
%s	print a string
%u	print an unsigned decimal integer
%x	print a hexadecimal integer, without leading Ox

The following letters may be used as prefix for certain conversion characters.

- h for short integers
- l for long integers or double
- L for long double.

Table 4.4 *Commonly used **Output** Format Flags*

Flag	Meaning
–	Output is left-justified within the field. Remaining field will be blank.
+	+ or – will precede the signed numeric item.
0	Causes leading zeros to appear.
#(with o or x)	Causes octal and hex items to be preceded by O and Ox, respectively.
#(with e, f or g)	Causes a decimal point to be present in all floating point numbers, even if it is whole number. Also prevents the truncation of trailing zeros in g-type conversion.

Enhancing the Readability of Output

Computer outputs are used as information for analysing certain relationships between variables and for making decisions. Therefore the correctness and clarity of outputs are of utmost importance. While the correctness depends on the solution procedure, the clarity depends on the way the output is presented. Following are some of the steps we can take to improve the clarity and hence the readability and understandability of outputs.

1. Provide enough blank space between two numbers.
2. Introduce appropriate headings and variable names in the output.
3. Print special messages whenever a peculiar condition occurs in the output.
4. Introduce blank lines between the important sections of the output.

The system usually provides two blank spaces between the numbers. However, this can be increased by selecting a suitable field width for the numbers or by introducing a 'tab' character between the specifications. For example, the statement

```
printf("a = %d\t b = %d", a, b);
```

will provide four blank spaces between the two fields. We can also print them on two separate lines by using the statement

```
printf("a = %d\n b = %d", a, b);
```

Messages and headings can be printed by using the character strings directly in the **printf** statement. Examples:

```
printf("\n OUTPUT RESULTS \n");
printf("Code\t Name\t Age\n");
printf("Error in input data\n");
printf("Enter your name\n");
```

Just Remember

- While using **getchar** function, care should be exercised to clear any unwanted characters in the input stream.
- Do not forget to include <**stdio.h**> headerfiles when using functions from standard input/output library.
- Do not forget to include <**ctype.h**> header file when using functions from character handling library.
- Provide proper field specifications for every variable to be read or printed.
- Enclose format control strings in double quotes.
- Do not forget to use address operator & for basic type variables in the input list of **scanf**.
- Use double quotes for character string constants.
- Use single quotes for single character constants.
- Provide sufficient field with to handle a value to be printed.
- Be aware of the situations where output may be imprecise due to formatting.
- Do not specify any precision in input field specifications.
- Do not provide any white-space at the end of format string of a **scanf** statement.
- Do not forget to close the format string in the **scanf** or **printf** statement with double quotes.
- Using an incorrect conversion code for data type being read or written will result in runtime error.
- Do not forget the comma after the format string in **scanf** and **printf** statements.
- Not separating read and write arguments is an error.
- Do not use commas in the format string of a **scanf** statement.
- Using an address operator & with a variable in the **printf** statement will result in runtime error.

CASE STUDIES

1. Inventory Report

Problem: The ABC Electric Company manufactures four consumer products. Their inventory position on a particular day is given below:

Code	*Quantity*	*Rate (Rs)*
F105	275	575.00
H220	107	99.95
I019	321	215.50
M315	89	725.00

It is required to prepare the inventory report table in the following format:

INVENTORY REPORT

Code	*Quantity*	*Rate*	*Value*
____	____	____	____
____	____	____	____
____	____	____	____
____			____
		Total Value:	______

The value of each item is given by the product of quantity and rate.

Program: The program given in Fig. 4.12 reads the data from the terminal and generates the required output. The program uses subscripted variables which are discussed in Chapter 7.

```
Program
    #define ITEMS 4
    main()
    { /* BEGIN */
      int i, quantity[5];
      float rate[5], value, total_value;
      char code[5][5];
      /* READING VALUES */
      i = 1;
      while ( i <= ITEMS)
      {
         printf("Enter code, quantity, and rate:");
         scanf("%s %d %f", code[i], &quantity[i],&rate[i]);
         i++;
      }
    /*.......Printing of Table and Column Headings.......*/
      printf("\n\n");
```

```
        printf("        INVENTORY REPORT       \n");
        printf("-------------------------------\n");
        printf("  Code Quantity Rate Value    \n");
        printf("-------------------------------\n");
      /*.......Preparation of Inventory Position.........*/
        total_value = 0;
        i = 1;
        while ( i <= ITEMS)
        {
           value = quantity[i] * rate[i];
           printf("%5s %10d %10.2f %e\n",code[i],quantity[i],
              rate[i],value);
           total_value += value;
           i++;
        }
      /*.......Printing of End of Table.................*/
        printf("-----------------------\n");
        printf("        Total Value = %e\n",total_value);
        printf("-----------------------\n");
      } /* END */
Output
        Enter code, quantity, and rate:F105 275 575.00
        Enter code, quantity, and rate:H220 107  99.95
        Enter code, quantity, and rate:I019 321 215.50
        Enter code, quantity, and rate:M315 89  725.00
                    INVENTORY REPORT
        Code    Quantity  Rate          Value
        F105      275    575.00    1.581250e+005
        H220      107     99.95    1.069465e+004
        I019      321    215.50    6.917550e+004
        M315       89    725.00    6.452500e+004
                      Total Value = 3.025202e+005
```

Fig. 4.12 *Program for inventory report*

2. Reliability Graph

Problem: The reliability of an electronic component is given by

reliability (r) = $e^{-\lambda t}$

where λ is the component failure rate per hour and t is the time of operation in hours. A graph is required to determine the reliability at various operating times, from 0 to 3000 hours. The failure rate λ (lambda) is 0.001.

Problem

```
#include <math.h>
#define LAMBDA 0.001
main()
{
   double t;
   float r;
   int i, R;
   for (i=1; i<=27; ++i)
   {
      printf("--");
   }
   printf("\n");
   for (t=0; t<=3000; t+=150)
   {
      r = exp(-LAMBDA*t);
      R = (int)(50*r+0.5);
      printf(" |");
      for (i=1; i<=R; ++i)
      {
         printf("*");
      }
      printf("#\n");
   }
   for (i=1; i<3; ++i)
   {
      printf(" |\n");
   }
}
```

Output

```
------------------------------------------------------
 |**************************************************#
 |*******************************************#
 |*************************************#
 |********************************#
 |***************************#
 |************************#
 |********************#
 |*****************#
 |***************#
 |*************#
 |***********#
 |**********#
 |********#
 |*******#
 |******#
```

```
|*****#
|*****#
|****#
|***#
|***#
|**#
```

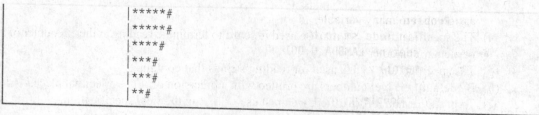

Fig. 4.13 *Program to draw reliability graph*

Program: The program given in Fig. 4.13 produces a shaded graph. The values of t are self-generated by the **for** statement

```
for (t=0; t <= 3000; t = t+150)
```

in steps of 150. The integer 50 in the statement

```
R = (int)(50*r+0.5)
```

is a scale factor which converts r to a large value where an integer is used for plotting the curve. Remember r is always less than 1.

REVIEW QUESTIONS

4.1 State whether the following statements are *true* or *false*.

(a) The purpose of the header file <studio.h> is to store the programs created by the users.

(b) The C standard function that receives a single character from the keyboard is **getchar**.

(c) The **getchar** cannot be used to read a line of text from the keyboard.

(d) The input list in a **scanf** statement can contain one or more variables.

(e) When an input stream contains more data items than the number of specifications in a **scanf** statement, the unused items will be used by the next **scanf** call in the program.

(f) Format specifiers for output convert internal representations for data to readable characters.

(g) Variables form a legal element of the format control string of a **printf** statement.

(h) The **scanf** function cannot be used to read a single character from the keyboard.

(i) The format specification %+−8d prints an integer left-justified in a field width of 8 with a plus sign, if the number is positive.

(j) If the field width of a format specifier is larger than the actual width of the value, the value is printed right-justified in the field.

(k) The print list in a **printf** statement can contain function calls.

(l) The format specification %5s will print only the first 5 characters of a given string to be printed.

4.2 Fill in the blanks in the following statements.

(a) The _________ specification is used to read or write a short integer.

(b) The conversion specifier _________ is used to print integers in hexadecimal form.

(c) For using character functions, we must include the header file _________ in the program.

(d) For reading a double type value, we must use the specification _________.

(e) The specification _______ is used to read a data from input list and discard it without assigning it to many variable.

(f) The specification _____ may be used in **scanf** to terminate reading at the encounter of a particular character.

(g) The specification %[ ] is used for reading strings that contain ________.

(h) By default, the real numbers are printed with a precision of ______ decimal places.

(i) To print the data left-justified, we must use ______ in the field specification.

(j) The specifier _______ prints floating-point values in the scientific notation.

4.3 Distinguish between the following pairs:

(a) ***getchar*** and ***scanf*** functions.

(b) %s and %c specifications for reading.

(c) %s and %[ ] specifications for reading.

(d) %g and %f specification for printing.

(e) %f and %e specifications for printing.

4.4 Write **scanf** statements to read the following data lists:

(a) 78 B 45

(b) 123 1.23 45A

(c) 15-10-2002

(d) 10 TRUE 20

4.5 State the outputs produced by the following **printf** statements.

```
(a) printf ("%d%c%f", 10, 'x', 1.23);
(b) printf ("%2d %c %4.2f", 1234,, 'x', 1.23);
(c) printf ("%d\t%4.2f", 1234, 456);
(d) printf ("\"%08.2f\"", 123.4);
(e) printf ("%d%d %d", 10, 20);
```

For questions 4.6 to 4.10 assume that the following declarations have been made in the program:

```
int year, count;
float amount, price;
char code, city[10];
double root;
```

4.6 State errors, if any, in the following input statements.

```
(a) scanf("%c%f%d", city, &price, &year);
(b) scanf("%s%d", city, amount);
(c) scanf("%f, %d, &amount, &year);
(d) scanf(\n"%f", root);
(e) scanf("%c %d %ld", *code, &count, Root);
```

4.7 What will be the values stored in the variables **year** and **code** when the data

1988, x

is keyed in as a response to the following statements:

```
(a) scanf("%d %c", &year, &code);
(b) scanf("%c %d", &year, &code);
(c) scanf("%d %c", &code, &year);
(d) scanf("%s %c", &year, &code);
```

4.8 The variables **count, price**, and **city** have the following values:

count <—— 1275

price <—— –235.74

city <—— Cambridge

Show the exact output that the following output statements will produce:

(a) `printf("%d %f", count, price);`
(b) `printf("%2d\n%f", count, price);`
(c) `printf("%d %f", price, count);`
(d) `printf("%10dxxxx%5.2f",count, price);`
(e) `printf("%s", city);`
(f) `printf(%-10d %-15s", count, city);`

4.9 State what (if anything) is wrong with each of the following output statements:

(a) `printf(%d 7.2%f, year, amount);`
(b) `printf("%-s, %c"\n, city, code);`
(c) `printf("%f, %d, %s, price, count, city);`
(d) `printf("%c%d%f\n", amount, code, year);`

4.10 In response to the input statement
scanf("%4d%*%d", &year, &code, &count);
the following data is keyed in:

19883745

What values does the computer assign to the variables **year, code,** and **count**?

PROGRAMMING EXERCISES

4.1 Given the string "WORDPROCESSING", write a program to read the string from the terminal and display the same in the following formats:

(a) WORD PROCESSING
(b) WORD
PROCESSING
(c) W.P.

4.2 Write a program to read the values of x and y and print the results of the following expressions in one line:

(a) $\dfrac{x+y}{x-y}$ (b) $\dfrac{x+y}{2}$ (c) $(x+y)(x-y)$

4.3 Write a program to read the following numbers, round them off to the nearest integers and print out the results in integer form:

35.7 50.21 – 23.73 – 46.45

4.4 Write a program that reads 4 floating point values in the range, 0.0 to 20.0, and prints a horizontal bar chart to represent these values using the character * as the fill character. For the purpose of the chart, the values may be rounded off to the nearest integer. For example, the value 4.36 should be represented as follows.

```
*   *   *   *
*   *   *   *   4.36
*   *   *   *
```

Note that the actual values are shown at the end of each bar.

4.5 Write an interactive program to demonstrate the process of multiplication. The program should ask the user to enter two two-digit integers and print the product of integers as shown below.

		45
	×	37
7 × 45 is		315
3 × 45 is		135
Add them		1665

Chapter 5

Decision Making and Branching

5.1 INTRODUCTION

We have seen that a C program is a set of statements which are normally executed sequentially in the order in which they appear. This happens when no options or no repetitions of certain calculations are necessary. However, in practice, we have a number of situations where we may have to change the order of execution of statements based on certain conditions, or repeat a group of statements until certain specified conditions are met. This involves a kind of decision making to see whether a particular condition has occurred or not and then direct the computer to execute certain statements accordingly.

C language possesses such decision-making capabilities by supporting the following statements:

1. **if** statement
2. **switch** statement
3. Conditional operator statement
4. **goto** statement

These statements are popularly known as *decision-making statements*. Since these statements 'control' the flow of execution, they are also known as *control statements*.

We have already used some of these statements in the earlier examples. Here, we shall discuss their features, capabilities and applications in more detail.

5.2 DECISION MAKING WITH IF STATEMENT

The **if** statement is a powerful decision-making statement and is used to control the flow of execution of statements. It is basically a two-way decision statement and is used in conjunction with an expression. It takes the following form:

if *(test expression)*

It allows the computer to evaluate the expression first and then, depending on whether the value of the expression (relation or condition) is 'true' (or non-zero) or 'false' (zero), it transfers the control to a particular statement. This point of program has two *paths* to follow, one for the *true* condition and the other for the *false* condition as shown in Fig. 5.1.

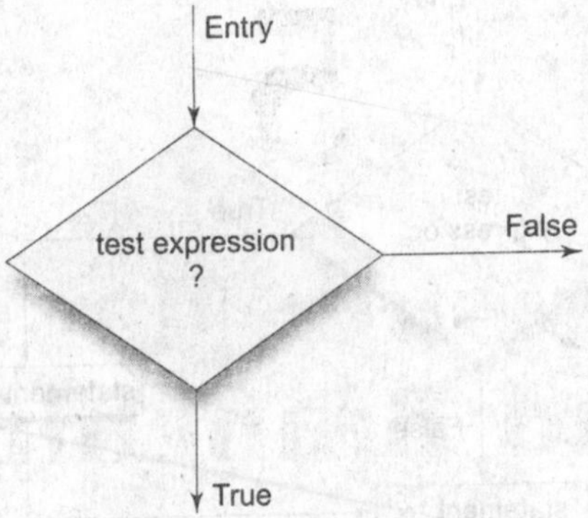

Fig. 5.1 *Two-way branching*

Some examples of decision making, using **if** statements are:

1. **if** (bank balance is zero)
   borrow money
2. **if** (room is dark)
   put on lights
3. **if** (code is 1)
   person is male
4. **if** (age is more than 55)
   person is retired

The **if** statement may be implemented in different forms depending on the complexity of conditions to be tested. The different forms are:

1. Simple **if** statement
2. **if.....else** statement
3. Nested **if....else** statement
4. **else if** ladder.

We shall discuss each one of them in the next few sections.

5.3 SIMPLE IF STATEMENT

The general form of a simple **if** statement is

```
if (test expression)
{
     statement-block;
}
statement-x;
```

The 'statement-block' may be a single statement or a group of statements. If the *test expression* is true, the *statement-block* will be executed; otherwise the statement-block will be skipped and the execution will jump to the *statement-x*. Remember, when the condition is true both the statement-block and the statement-x are executed in sequence. This is illustrated in Fig. 5.2.

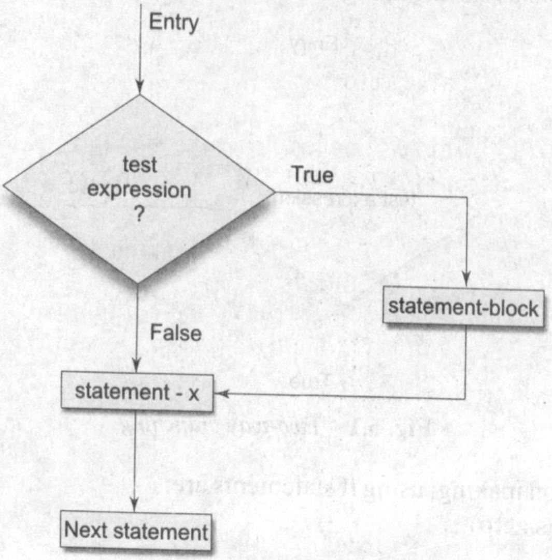

Fig. 5.2 *Flowchart of simple if Control*

Consider the following segment of a program that is written for processing of marks obtained in an entrance examination.

```
.........
.........
if (category == SPORTS)
{
    marks = marks + bonus_marks;
}
printf("%f", marks);
.........
.........
```

The program tests the type of category of the student. If the student belongs to the SPORTS category, then additional bonus_marks are added to his marks before they are printed. For others, bonus_marks are not added.

Example 5.1 The program in Fig. 5.3 reads four values a, b, c, and d from the terminal and evaluates the ratio of (a+b) to (c–d) and prints the result, if c–d is not equal to zero.

The program given in Fig. 5.3 has been run for two sets of data to see that the paths function properly. The result of the first run is printed as

Ratio = –3.181818

```
Program
  main()
  {
      int a, b, c, d;
      float ratio;

      printf("Enter four integer values\n");
      scanf("%d %d %d %d", &a, &b, &c, &d);

      if (c-d != 0) /* Execute statement block */
      {
          ratio = (float)(a+b)/(float)(c-d);
          printf("Ratio = %f\n", ratio);
      }
  }

Output

  Enter four integer values
  12 23 34 45
  Ratio = -3.181818

  Enter four integer values
  12  23  34  34
```

Fig. 5.3 *Illustration of simple* ***if*** *statement*

The second run has neither produced any results nor any message. During the second run, the value of (c–d) is equal to zero and therefore the statements contained in the statement-block are skipped. Since no other statement follows the statement-block, program stops without producing any output.

Note the use of **float** conversion in the statement evaluating the **ratio.** This is necessary to avoid truncation due to integer division. Remember, the output of the first run –3.181818 is printed correct to six decimal places. The answer contains a round off error. If we wish to have higher accuracy, we must use **double** or **long double** data type.

The simple **if** is often used for counting purposes. The Example 5.2 illustrates this.

Example 5.2 The program in Fig. 5.4 counts the number of boys whose weight is less than 50 kg and height is greater than 170 cm.

The program has to test two conditions, one for weight and another for height. This is done using the compound relation

if (weight < 50 && height > 170)

This would have been equivalently done using two **if** statements as follows:

```
if (weight < 50)
    if (height > 170)
        count = count +1;
```

If the value of **weight** is less than 50, then the following statement is executed, which in turn is another **if** statement. This **if** statement tests **height** and if the **height** is greater than 170, then the **count** is incremented by 1.

Program

```
main()
{
        int count, i;
        float weight, height;

        count = 0;
        printf("Enter weight and height for 10 boys\n");

        for (i =1; i <= 10; i++)
        {
            scanf("%f %f", &weight, &height);
            if (weight < 50 && height > 170)
                count = count + 1;
        }
        printf("Number of boys with weight < 50 kg\n");
        printf("and height > 170 cm = %d\n", count);
}
```

Output

```
Enter weight and height for 10 boys
45   176.5
55   174.2
47   168.0
49   170.7
54   169.0
53   170.5
49   167.0
48   175.0
47   167
51   170
Number of boys with weight < 50 kg
and height > 170 cm = 3
```

Fig. 5.4 *Use of **if** for counting*

Applying De Morgan's Rule

While designing decision statements, we often come across a situation where the logical NOT operator is applied to a compound logical expression, like !(x&&y||!z). However, a positive logic is always easy to read and comprehend than a negative logic. In such cases, we may apply what is known as **De Morgan's** rule to make the total expression positive. This rule is as follows:

"Remove the parentheses by applying the NOT operator to every logical expression component, while complementing the relational operators"

That is,

x becomes !x
!x becomes x
&& becomes ||
|| becomes &&

Examples:

!(x && y || !z) becomes !x || !y && z

!(x <=0 || !condition) becomes x >0&& condition

5.4 THE IF.....ELSE STATEMENT

The **if...else** statement is an extension of the simple **if** statement. The general form is

```
If (test expression)
    {
        True-block statement(s)
    }
else
    {
        False-block statement(s)
    }
statement-x
```

If the *test expression* is true, then the *true-block statement(s),* immediately following the **if** statements are executed; otherwise, the *false-block statement(s)* are executed. In either case, either *true-block* or *false-block* will be executed, not both. This is illustrated in Fig. 5.5. In both the cases, the control is transferred subsequently to the statement-x.

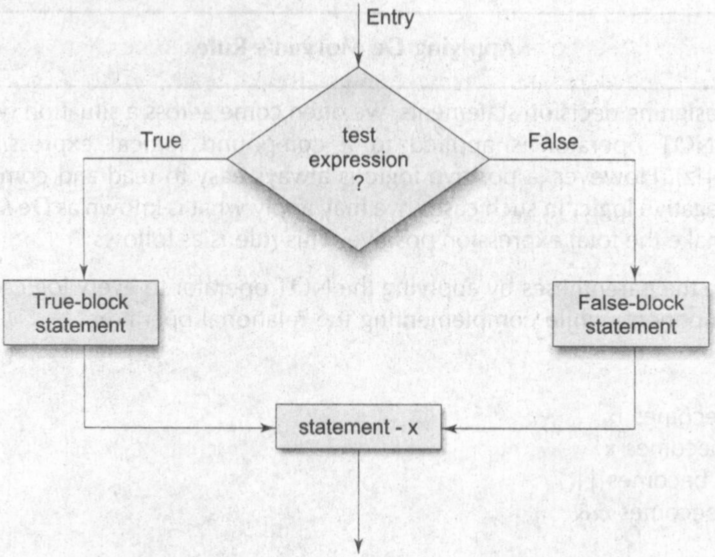

Fig. 5.5 *Flowchart of if......else control*

Let us consider an example of counting the number of boys and girls in a class. We use code 1 for a boy and 2 for a girl. The program statement to do this may be written as follows:

```
.........
.........
if (code == 1)
   boy = boy + 1;
if (code == 2)
   girl = girl+1;
.........
.........
```

The first test determines whether or not the student is a boy. If yes, the number of boys is increased by 1 and the program continues to the second test. The second test again determines whether the student is a girl. This is unnecessary. Once a student is identified as a boy, there is no need to test again for a girl. A student can be either a boy or a girl, not both. The above program segment can be modified using the **else** clause as follows:

```
..........
..........
if (code == 1)
   boy = boy + 1;
else
   girl = girl + 1;
xxxxxxxxxx
..........
```

Here, if the code is equal to 1, the statement **boy = boy + 1**; is executed and the control is transferred to the statement **xxxxxx**, after skipping the else part. If the code is not equal to 1, the statement **boy = boy + 1**; is skipped and the statement in the **else** part **girl = girl + 1**; is executed before the control reaches the statement **xxxxxxxx.**

Consider the program given in Fig. 5.3. When the value (c–d) is zero, the ratio is not calculated and the program stops without any message. In such cases we may not know whether the program stopped due to a zero value or some other error. This program can be improved by adding the **else** clause as follows:

```
..........
..........
if (c-d != 0)
   {
     ratio = (float)(a+b)/(float)(c-d);
     printf("Ratio = %f\n", ratio);
   }
else
   printf("c-d is zero\n");
..........
..........
```

Example 5.3 A program to evaluate the power series

$$e^x = 1 + x + \frac{x^2}{2!} + \frac{x^3}{3!} + \ldots + \frac{x^n}{n!}, \quad 0 < x < 1$$

is given in Fig. 5.6. It uses **if......else** to test the accuracy.

The power series contains the recurrence relationship of the type

$$T_n = T_{n-1}\left(\frac{x}{n}\right) \text{ for } n > 1$$

$$T_1 = x \text{ for } n = 1$$

$$T_0 = 1$$

If T_{n-1} (usually known as *previous term*) is known, then T_n (known as *present term*) can be easily found by multiplying the previous term by x/n. Then

$$e^x = T_0 + T_1 + T_2 + \ldots\ldots + T_n = \text{sum}$$

```
Program
   #define ACCURACY 0.0001
   main()
   {
     int n, count;
     float x, term, sum;
     printf("Enter value of x:");
```

```
        scanf("%f", &x);
        n = term = sum = count = 1;
        while (n <= 100)
        {
          term = term * x/n;
          sum = sum + term;
          count = count + 1;
          if (term < ACCURACY)
            n = 999;
          else
            n = n + 1;
        }
        printf("Terms = %d Sum = %f\n", count, sum);
    }
```

Output

```
Enter value of x:0
Terms = 2 Sum = 1.000000

Enter value of x:0.1
Terms = 5 Sum = 1.105171

Enter value of x:0.5
Terms = 7 Sum = 1.648720

Enter value of x:0.75
Terms = 8 Sum = 2.116997

Enter value of x:0.99
Terms = 9 Sum = 2.691232

Enter value of x:1
Terms = 9 Sum = 2.718279
```

Fig. 5.6 *Illustration of if...else statement*

The program uses **count** to count the number of terms added. The program stops when the value of the term is less than 0.0001 (**ACCURACY**). Note that when a term is less than **ACCURACY**, the value of n is set equal to 999 (a number higher than 100) and therefore the **while** loop terminates. The results are printed outside the **while** loop.

5.5 NESTING OF IF....ELSE STATEMENTS

When a series of decisions are involved, we may have to use more than one **if...else** statement in *nested* form as shown below:

```
if    (test condition-1)
     {
      if  (test condition-2);
         {
          statement -1;
         }
      else
         {
          statement -2;
         }
     }
else
     {
      statement -3;
     }
statement -x;
```

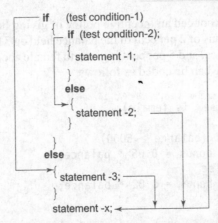

The logic of execution is illustrated in Fig. 5.7. If the *condition-1* is false, the statement-3 will be executed; otherwise it continues to perform the second test. If the *condition-2* is true, the statement-1 will be evaluated; otherwise the statement-2 will be evaluated and then the control is transferred to the statement-x.

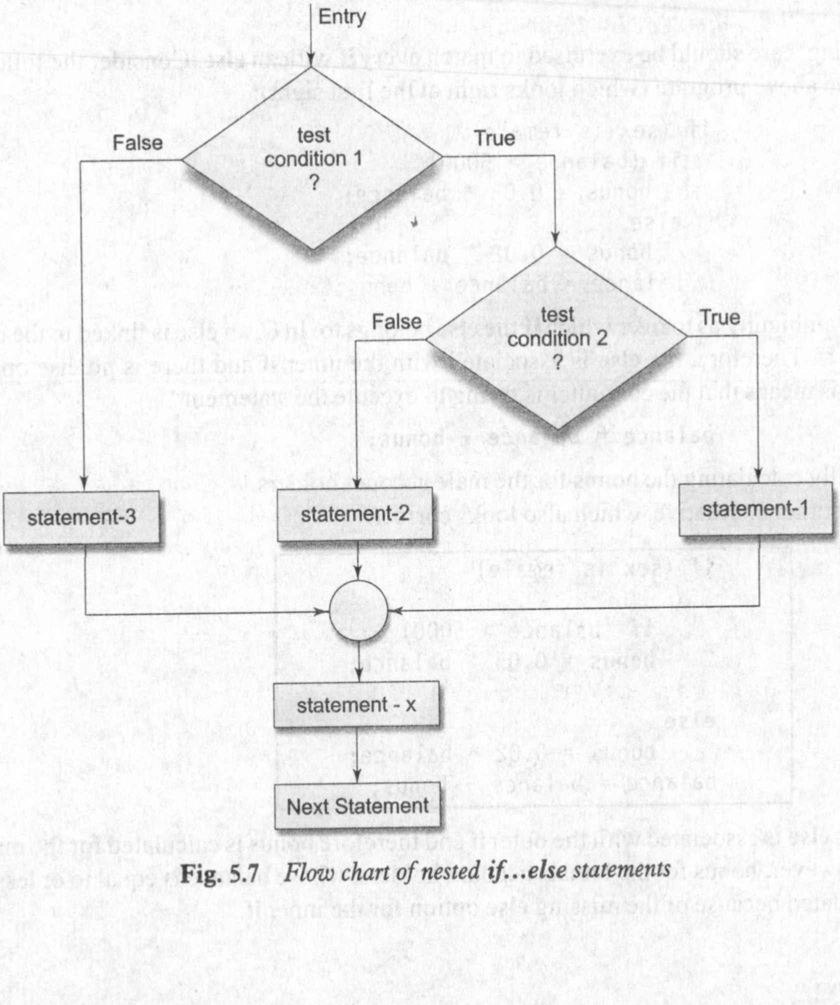

Fig. 5.7 *Flow chart of nested if...else statements*

A commercial bank has introduced an incentive policy of giving bonus to all its deposit holders. The policy is as follows: A bonus of 2 per cent of the balance held on 31st December is given to every one, irrespective of their balance, and 5 per cent is given to female account holders if their balance is more than Rs. 5000. This logic can be coded as follows:

```
.........
 if (sex is female)
 {
   if (balance > 5000)
     bonus = 0.05 * balance;
   else
     bonus = 0.02 * balance;
 }
 else
 {
     bonus = 0.02 * balance;
 }
 balance = balance + bonus;
 .........
 .........
```

When nesting, care should be exercised to match every **if** with an **else**. Consider the following alternative to the above program (which looks right at the first sight):

```
if (sex is female)
  if (balance > 5000)
    bonus = 0.05 * balance;
  else
    bonus = 0.02 * balance;
  balance = balance + bonus;
```

There is an ambiguity as to over which **if** the **else** belongs to. In C, an else is linked to the closest non-terminated **if.** Therefore, the **else** is associated with the inner **if** and there is no else option for the outer **if**. This means that the computer is trying to execute the statement

```
balance = balance + bonus;
```

without really calculating the bonus for the male account holders.
Consider another alternative, which also looks correct:

```
if (sex is female)
  {
    if (balance > 5000)
    bonus = 0.05 * balance;
  }
else
    bonus = 0.02 * balance;
balance = balance + bonus;
```

In this case, **else** is associated with the outer **if** and therefore bonus is calculated for the male account holders. However, bonus for the female account holders, whose balance is equal to or less than 5000 is not calculated because of the missing **else** option for the inner **if**.

Example 5.4 The program in Fig. 5.8 selects and prints the largest of the three numbers using nested **if....else** statements.

Program

```
main()
{
float A, B, C;
printf("Enter three values\n");
scanf("%f %f %f", &A, &B, &C);
printf("\nLargest value is ");
if (A>B)
{
  if (A>C)
    printf("%f\n", A);
  else
    printf("%f\n", C);
}
else
{
  if (C>B)
    printf("%f\n", C);
  else
    printf("%f\n", B);
}
}
```

Output

```
Enter three values
23445 67379 88843
Largest value is 88843.000000
```

Fig 5.8 *Selecting the largest of three numbers*

Dangling Else Problem

One of the classic problems encountered when we start using nested **if....else** statements is the dangling else. This occurs when a matching **else** is not available for an **if**. The answer to this problem is very simple. Always match an **else** to the most recent unmatched **if** in the current block. In some cases, it is possible that the false condition is not required. In such situations, **else** statement may be omitted

"**else** is always paired with the most recent unpaired **if**"

5.6 THE ELSE IF LADDER

There is another way of putting **if**s together when multipath decisions are involved. A multipath decision is a chain of **if**s in which the statement associated with each **else** is an **if**. It takes the following general form:

```
if ( condition 1)
    statement-1;
else if ( condition 2)
        statement-2;
    else if ( condition 3)
            statement-3;
        else if ( condition n)
                statement-n;
            else
                default-statement;
statement-x;
```

This construct is known as the **else if** ladder. The conditions are evaluated from the top (of the ladder), downwards. As soon as a true condition is found, the statement associated with it is executed and the control is transferred to the statement-x (skipping the rest of the ladder). When all the n conditions become false, then the final **else** containing the *default-statement* will be executed. Fig. 5.9 shows the logic of execution of **else if** ladder statements.

Let us consider an example of grading the students in an academic institution. The grading is done according to the following rules:

Average marks	Grade
80 to 100	Honours
60 to 79	First Division
50 to 59	Second Division
40 to 49	Third Division
0 to 39	Fail

This grading can be done using the **else if** ladder as follows:

```
if (marks > 79)
    grade = "Honours";
  else if (marks > 59)
      grade = "First Division";
    else if (marks > 49)
        grade = "Second Division";
      else if (marks > 39)
```

```
                grade = "Third Division";
            else
                grade = "Fail";
        printf ("%s\n", grade);
```

Consider another example given below:

```
----
----
if (code == 1)
  colour = "RED";
else if (code == 2)
    colour = "GREEN";
  else if (code == 3)
        colour = "WHITE";
      else
        colour = "YELLOW";
---
---
```

Code numbers other than 1, 2 or 3 are considered to represent YELLOW colour. The same results can be obtained by using nested **if...else** statements.

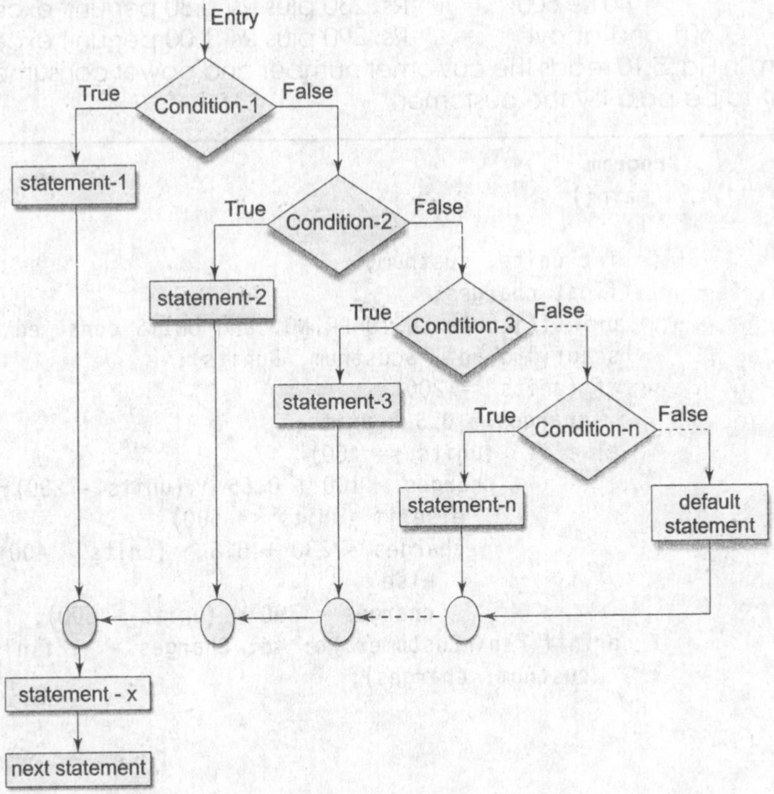

Fig. 5.9 *Flow chart of else..if ladder*

```
if (code != 1)
  if (code != 2)
    if (code != 3)
      colour = "YELLOW";
    else
      colour = "WHITE";
  else
      colour = "GREEN";
else
      colour = "RED";
```

In such situations, the choice is left to the programmer. However, in order to choose an **if** structure that is both effective and efficient, it is important that the programmer is fully aware of the various forms of an **if** statement and the rules governing their nesting.

Example 5.5 An electric power distribution company charges its domestic consumers as follows:

Consumption Units	*Rate of Charge*
0 – 200	Rs. 0.50 per unit
201 – 400	Rs. 100 plus Rs. 0.65 per unit excess of 200
401 – 600	Rs. 230 plus Rs. 0.80 per unit excess of 400
601 and above	Rs. 390 plus Rs. 1.00 per unit excess of 600

The program in Fig. 5.10 reads the customer number and power consumed and prints the amount to be paid by the customer.

```
Program
  main()
  {
    int units, custnum;
    float charges;
    printf("Enter CUSTOMER NO. and UNITS consumed\n");
    scanf("%d %d", &custnum, &units);
    if (units <= 200)
      charges = 0.5 * units;
    else if  (units <= 400)
            charges = 100 + 0.65 * (units - 200);
              else if (units <= 600)
              charges = 230 + 0.8 * (units - 400);
                else
                charges = 390 + (units - 600);
    printf("\n\nCustomer No: %d: Charges = %.2f\n",
      custnum, charges);
  }
```

Output

```
Enter CUSTOMER NO. and UNITS consumed 101 150
Customer No:101 Charges = 75.00
Enter CUSTOMER NO. and UNITS consumed 202 225
Customer No:202 Charges = 116.25
Enter CUSTOMER NO. and UNITS consumed 303 375
Customer No:303 Charges = 213.75
Enter CUSTOMER NO. and UNITS consumed 404 520
Customer No:404 Charges = 326.00
Enter CUSTOMER NO. and UNITS consumed 505 625
Customer No:505 Charges = 415.00
```

Fig. 5.10 *Illustration of else..if ladder*

Rules for Indentation

When using control structures, a statement often controls many other statements that follow it. In such situations it is a good practice to use *indentation* to show that the indented statements are dependent on the preceding controlling statement. Some guidelines that could be followed while using indentation are listed below:

- Indent statements that are dependent on the previous statements; provide at least three spaces of indentation.
- Align vertically else clause with their matching if clause.
- Use braces on separate lines to identify a block of statements.
- Indent the statements in the block by at least three spaces to the right of the braces.
- Align the opening and closing braces.
- Use appropriate comments to signify the beginning and end of blocks.
- Indent the nested statements as per the above rules.
- Code only one clause or statement on each line.

5.7 THE SWITCH STATEMENT

We have seen that when one of the many alternatives is to be selected, we can use an **if** statement to control the selection. However, the complexity of such a program increases dramatically when the number of alternatives increases. The program becomes difficult to read and follow. At times, it may confuse even the person who designed it. Fortunately, C has a built-in multiway decision statement known as a **switch.** The **switch** statement tests the value of a given variable (or expression) against a list of **case** values and when a match is found, a block of statements associated with that **case** is executed. The general form of the **switch** statement is as shown below:

```
switch (expression)
{
    case value-1:
                block-1
                break;
    case value-2:
                block-2
                break;
    ......
    ......
    default:
                default-block
                break;
}
statement-x;
```

The *expression* is an integer expression or characters. *Value-1, value-2* ..... are constants or constant expressions (evaluable to an integral constant) and are known as *case labels*. Each of these values should be unique within a **switch** statement. **block-1, block-2** .... are statement lists and may contain zero or more statements. There is no need to put braces around these blocks. Note that **case** labels end with a colon (:).

When the **switch** is executed, the value of the expression is successfully compared against the values *value-1, value-2,*.... If a case is found whose value matches with the value of the expression, then the block of statements that follows the case are executed.

The **break** statement at the end of each block signals the end of a particular case and causes an exit from the **switch** statement, transferring the control to the **statement-x** following the **switch.**

The **default** is an optional case. When present, it will be executed if the value of the *expression* does not match with any of the case values. If not present, no action takes place if all matches fail and the control goes to the **statement-x**. (ANSI C permits the use of as many as 257 case labels).

The selection process of **switch** statement is illustrated in the flow chart shown in Fig. 5.11.

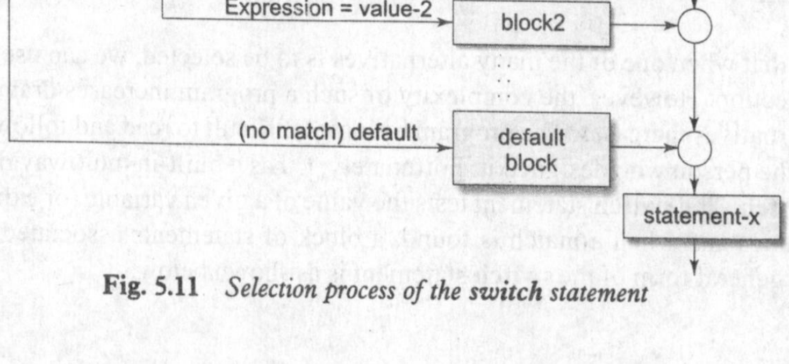

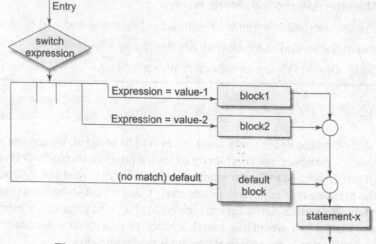

Fig. 5.11 *Selection process of the switch statement*

The **switch** statement can be used to grade the students as discussed in the last section. This is illustrated below:

```
---
---
index = marks/10
switch (index)
{
  case 10:
  case  9:
  case  8:
            grade = "Honours";
            break;
  case  7:
  case  6:
            grade = "First Division";
            break;
  case  5:
            grade = "Second Division";
            break;
  case  4:
            grade = "Third Division";
            break;
   default:
            grade = "Fail";
            break;
}
printf("%s\n", grade);
---
---
```

Note that we have used a conversion statement

```
index = marks / 10;
```

where, index is defined as an integer. The variable index takes the following integer values.

Marks	Index
100	10
90 - 99	9
80 - 89	8
70 - 79	7
60 - 69	6
50 - 59	5
40 - 49	4
.	.
.	.
0	0

This segment of the program illustrates two important features. First, it uses empty cases. The first three cases will execute the same statements

```
grade = "Honours";
break;
```

Same is the case with case 7 and case 6. Second, default condition is used for all other cases where marks is less than 40.

The **switch** statement is often used for menu selection. For example:

```
----
----
printf(" TRAVEL GUIDE\n\n");
printf(" A Air Timings\n" );
printf(" T Train Timings\n");
printf(" B Bus Service\n" );
printf(" X To skip\n" );
printf("\n Enter your choice\n");
character = getchar();
switch (character)
{
  case 'A' :
            air-display();
            break;
  case 'B' :
            bus-display();
            break;
  case 'T' :
            train-display();
            break;
default :
            printf(" No choice\n");
}
  ----
  ----
```

It is possible to nest the **switch** statements. That is, a **switch** may be part of a **case** statement. ANSI C permits 15 levels of nesting.

Rules for switch statement

- The **switch** expression must be an integral type.
- Case labels must be constants or constant expressions.
- Case labels must be unique. No two labels can have the same value.
- Case labels must end with semicolon.

- The **break** statement transfers the control out of the **switch** statement.
- The **break** statement is optional. That is, two or more case labels may belong to the same statements.
- The **default** label is optional. If present, it will be executed when the expression does not find a matching case label.
- There can be at most one **default** label.
- The **default** may be placed anywhere but usually placed at the end.
- It is permitted to nest **switch** statements.

5.8 THE ? : OPERATOR

The C language has an unusual operator, useful for making two-way decisions. This operator is a combination of ? and :, and takes three operands. This operator is popularly known as the *conditional operator*. The general form of use of the conditional operator is as follows:

conditional expression ? expression1 : expression2

The *conditional expression* is evaluated first. If the result is nonzero, *expression1* is evaluated and is returned as the value of the conditional expression. Otherwise, *expression2* is evaluated and its value is returned. For example, the segment

```
if (x < 0)
    flag = 0;
else
    flag = 1;
```

can be written as

```
flag = ( x < 0 ) ? 0 : 1;
```

Consider the evaluation of the following function:

$y = 1.5x + 3$ for $x \le 2$

$y = 2x + 5$ for $x > 2$

This can be evaluated using the conditional operator as follows:

```
y = ( x > 2 ) ? (2 * x + 5) : (1.5 * x + 3);
```

The conditional operator may be nested for evaluating more complex assignment decisions. For example, consider the weekly salary of a salesgirl who is selling some domestic products. If x is the number of products sold in a week, her weekly salary is given by

$$\text{salary} = \begin{cases} 4x + 100 & \text{for } x < 40 \\ 300 & \text{for } x = 40 \\ 4.5x + 150 & \text{for } x > 40 \end{cases}$$

This complex equation can be written as

```
salary = (x != 40) ? ((x < 40) ? (4*x+100) : (4.5*x+150)) : 300;
```

The same can be evaluated using **if...else** statements as follows:

```
if (x <= 40)
    if (x < 40)
        salary = 4 * x+100;
    else
        salary = 300;
else
        salary = 4.5 * x+150;
```

When the conditional operator is used, the code becomes more concise and perhaps, more efficient. However, the readability is poor. It is better to use **if** statements when more than a single nesting of conditional operator is required.

Example 5.6 An employee can apply for a loan at the beginning of every six months, but he will be sanctioned the amount according to the following company rules:

Rule 1 : An employee cannot enjoy more than two loans at any point of time.

Rule 2 : Maximum permissible total loan is limited and depends upon the category of the employee.

A program to process loan applications and to sanction loans is given in Fig. 5.12.

Program

```
#define MAXLOAN 50000
main()
{
    long int loan1, loan2, loan3, sancloan, sum23;
    printf("Enter the values of previous two loans:\n");
    scanf(" %ld %ld", &loan1, &loan2);
    printf("\nEnter the value of new loan:\n");
    scanf(" %ld", &loan3);
    sum23 = loan2 + loan3;
    sancloan = (loan1>0)? 0 : ((sum23>MAXLOAN)?
                    MAXLOAN - loan2 : loan3);
    printf("\n\n");
    printf("Previous loans pending:\n%ld %ld\n",loan1,loan2);
    printf("Loan requested = %ld\n", loan3);
    printf("Loan sanctioned = %ld\n", sancloan);
}
```

Output

```
Enter the values of previous two loans:
0 20000
Enter the value of new loan:
45000
Previous loans pending:
0 20000
Loan requested = 45000
Loan sanctioned = 30000
```

```
Enter the values of previous two loans:
1000 15000
Enter the value of new loan:
25000
Previous loans pending:
1000 15000
Loan requested   = 25000
Loan sanctioned = 0
```

Fig. 5.12 *Illustration of the conditional operator*

The program uses the following variables:

loan3 - present loan amount requested
loan2 - previous loan amount pending
loan1 - previous to previous loan pending
sum23 - sum of loan2 and loan3
sancloan - loan sanctioned

The rules for sanctioning new loan are:

1. loan1 should be zero.
2. loan2 + loan3 should not be more than MAXLOAN.

Note the use of **long int** type to declare variables.

Some Guidelines for Writing Multiway Selection Statements

Complex multiway selection statements require special attention. The readers should be able to understand the logic easily. Given below are some guidelines that would help improve readability and facilitate maintenance.

- Avoid compound negative statements. Use positive statements wherever possible.
- Keep logical expressions simple. We can achieve this using nested if statements, if necessary (KISS - Keep It Simple and Short).
- Try to code the normal/anticipated condition first.
- Use the most probable condition first. This will eliminate unnecessary tests, thus improving the efficiency of the program.
- The choice between the nested if and switch statements is a matter of individual's preference. A good rule of thumb is to use the switch when alternative paths are three to ten.
- Use proper indentations (See Rules for Indentation).
- Have the habit of using default clause in switch statements.
- Group the case labels that have similar actions.

5.9 THE GOTO STATEMENT

So far we have discussed ways of controlling the flow of execution based on certain specified conditions. Like many other languages, C supports the **goto** statement to branch unconditionally from one point to another in the program. Although it may not be essential to use the **goto** statement in a highly structured language like C, there may be occasions when the use of **goto** might be desirable.

The **goto** requires a *label* in order to identify the place where the branch is to be made. A *label* is any valid variable name, and must be followed by a colon. The *label* is placed immediately before the statement where the control is to be transferred. The general forms of **goto** and *label* statements are shown below:

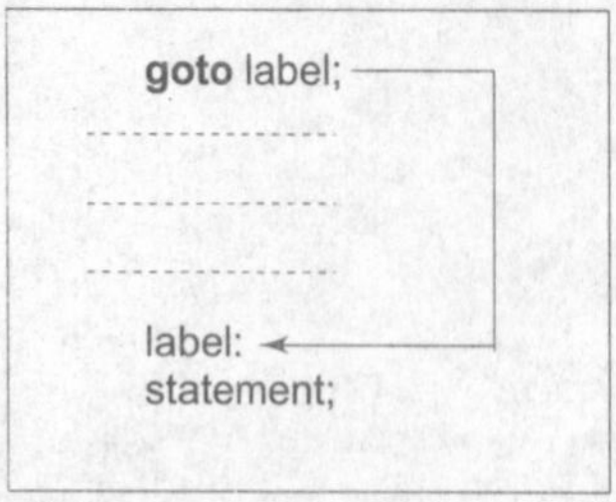

Forward jump

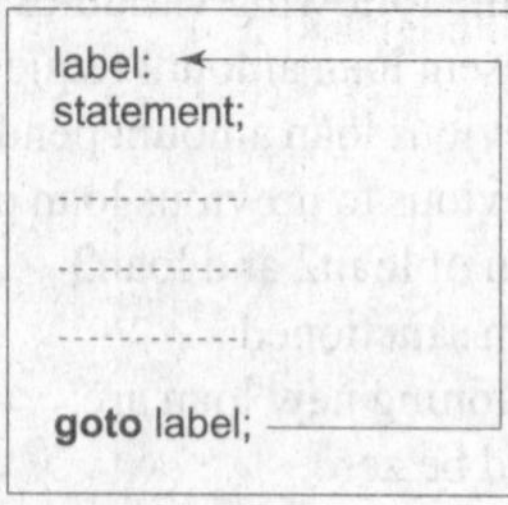

Backward jump

The *label*: can be anywhere in the program either before or after the **goto** label; statement.
During running of a program when a statement like

goto begin;

is met, the flow of control will jump to the statement immediately following the label **begin**:. This happens unconditionally.

Note that a **goto** breaks the normal sequential execution of the program. If the *label:* is before the statement **goto** *label*; a *loop* will be formed and some statements will be executed repeatedly. Such a jump is known as a *backward jump*. On the other hand, if the *label:* is placed after the **goto** *label*; some statements will be skipped and the jump is known as a *forward jump*.

A **goto** is often used at the end of a program to direct the control to go to the input statement, to read further data. Consider the following example:

```
main()
{
    double x, y;
    read:
    scanf("%f", &x);
    if (x < 0) goto read;
    y = sqrt(x);
    printf("%f %f\n", x, y);
    goto read;
}
```

This program is written to evaluate the square root of a series of numbers read from the terminal. The program uses two **goto** statements, one at the end, after printing the results to transfer the control back to the input statement and the other to skip any further computation when the number is negative.

Due to the unconditional **goto** statement at the end, the control is always transferred back to the input statement. In fact, this program puts the computer in a permanent loop known as an *infinite loop*. The computer goes round and round until we take some special steps to terminate the loop. Such infinite loops should be avoided. Example 5.7 illustrates how such infinite loops can be eliminated.

Example 5.7 Program presented in Fig. 5.13 illustrates the use of the **goto** statement. The program evaluates the square root for five numbers. The variable count keeps the count of numbers read. When count is less than or equal to 5, **goto read**; directs the control to the label **read**; otherwise, the program prints a message and stops.

Program

```
#include <math.h>
main()
{
    double x, y;
    int count;
    count = 1;
    printf("Enter FIVE real values in a LINE \n");
read:
    scanf("%lf", &x);
    printf("\n");
    if (x < 0)
      printf("Value - %d is negative\n",count);
    else
    {
      y = sqrt(x);
      printf("%lf\t %lf\n", x, y);
    }
    count = count + 1;
    if (count <= 5)
goto read;
    printf("\nEnd of computation");
}
```

Output

```
Enter FIVE real values in a LINE
50.70 40 -36 75 11.25
50.750000      7.123903
40.000000      6.324555
Value -3 is negative
75.000000      8.660254
11.250000      3.354102
End of computation
```

Fig. 5.13 *Use of the goto statement*

Another use of the **goto** statement is to transfer the control out of a loop (or nested loops) when certain peculiar conditions are encountered. Example:

```
----
----
while (----)
{
    for (----)
    {
    ----
    ----
    if (----)goto end_of_program;──┐
    ----                           │
    }                              │  Jumping
----                               │  out of
----                               │  loops
}                                  │
end_of_program: <──────────────────┘
```

We should try to avoid using **goto** as far as possible. But there is nothing wrong, if we use it to enhance the readability of the program or to improve the execution speed.

Just Remember

- Be aware of dangling **else** statements.
- Be aware of any side effects in the control expression such as if(x++).
- Use braces to encapsulate the statements in **if** and **else** clauses of an if.... else statement.
- Check the use of =operator in place of the equal operator = =.
- Do not give any spaces between the two symbols of relational operators = =, !=, >= and <=.
- Writing !=, >= and <= operators like =!, => and =< is an error.
- Remember to use two ampersands (&&) and two bars (||) for logical operators. Use of single operators will result in logical errors.
- Do not forget to place parentheses for the if expression.
- It is an error to place a semicolon after the if expression.
- Do not use the equal operator to compare two floating-point values. They are seldom exactly equal.
- Do not forget to use a break statement when the cases in a switch statement are exclusive.
- Although it is optional, it is a good programming practice to use the default clause in a switch statement.
- It is an error to use a variable as the value in a case label of a switch statement. (Only integral constants are allowed.)
- Do not use the same constant in two case labels in a switch statement.

✍ Avoid using operands that have side effects in a logical binary expression such as (x−−&&++y). The second operand may not be evaluated at all.

✍ Try to use simple logical expressions.

CASE STUDIES

1. Range of Numbers

Problem: A survey of the computer market shows that personal computers are sold at varying costs by the vendors. The following is the list of costs (in hundreds) quoted by some vendors:

35.00,	40.50,	25.00,	31.25,	68.15,
47.00,	26.65,	29.00	53.45,	62.50

Determine the average cost and the range of values.

Problem analysis: Range is one of the measures of dispersion used in statistical analysis of a series of values. The range of any series is the difference between the highest and the lowest values in the series. That is

Range = highest value – lowest value

It is therefore necessary to find the highest and the lowest values in the series.

Program: A program to determine the range of values and the average cost of a personal computer in the market is given in Fig. 5.14.

```
Program
main()
{
    int count;
    float value, high, low, sum, average, range;
    sum = 0;
    count = 0;
    printf("Enter numbers in a line :
      input a NEGATIVE number to end\n");
input:
    scanf("%f", &value);
    if (value < 0) goto output;
      count = count + 1;
    if (count == 1)
      high = low = value;
    else if (value > high)
        high = value;
      else if (value < low)
          low = value;
    sum = sum + value;
    goto input;
```

```
Output:
        average = sum/count;
        range = high - low;
        printf("\n\n");
        printf("Total values : %d\n", count);
        printf("Highest-value: %f\nLowest-value : %f\n",
               high, low);
        printf("Range          : %f\nAverage : %f\n",
               range, average);
    }
Output
    Enter numbers in a line : input a NEGATIVE number to end
    35 40.50 25 31.25 68.15 47 26.65 29 53.45 62.50 -1

    Total values   : 10
    Highest-value : 68.150002
    Lowest-value   : 25.000000
    Range          : 43.150002
    Average        : 41.849998
```

Fig. 5.14 *Calculation of range of values*

When the value is read the first time, it is assigned to two buckets, **high** and **low**, through the statement

```
high = low = value;
```

For subsequent values, the value read is compared with high; if it is larger, the value is assigned to high. Otherwise, the value is compared with low; if it is smaller, the value is assigned to low. Note that at a given point, the buckets high and low hold the highest and the lowest values read so far.

The values are read in an input loop created by the **goto** input; statement. The control is transferred out of the loop by inputting a negative number. This is caused by the statement

```
if (value < 0) goto output;
```

Note that this program can be written without using **goto** statements. Try.

2. Pay-Bill Calculations

Problem: A manufacturing company has classified its executives into four levels for the benefit of certain perks. The levels and corresponding perks are shown below:

Level	Perks	
	Conveyance allowance	Entertainment allowance
1	1000	500
2	750	200
3	500	100
4	250	–

An executive's gross salary includes basic pay, house rent allowance at 25% of basic pay and other perks. Income tax is withheld from the salary on a percentage basis as follows:

Gross salary	*Tax rate*
Gross <= 2000	No tax deduction
2000 < Gross <= 4000	3%
4000 < Gross <= 5000	5%
Gross > 5000	8%

Write a program that will read an executive's job number, level number, and basic pay and then compute the net salary after withholding income tax.

Problem analysis:

Gross salary = basic pay + house rent allowance + perks

Net salary = Gross salary – income tax.

The computation of perks depends on the level, while the income tax depends on the gross salary. The major steps are:

1. Read data.
2. Decide level number and calculate perks.
3. Calculate gross salary.
4. Calculate income tax.
5. Compute net salary.
6. Print the results.

Program: A program and the results of the test data are given in Fig. 5.15. Note that the last statement should be an executable statement. That is, the label **stop:** cannot be the last line.

```
Program
  #define CA1 1000
  #define CA2 750
  #define CA3 500
  #define CA4 250
  #define EA1 500
  #define EA2 200
  #define EA3 100
  #define EA4 0
  main()
  {
    int level, jobnumber;
    float gross,
          basic,
          house_rent,
          perks,
          net,
          incometax;
    input:
    printf("\nEnter level, job number, and basic pay\n");
    printf("Enter 0 (zero) for level to END\n\n");
    scanf("%d", &level);
```

```
        if (level == 0) goto stop;
        scanf("%d %f", &jobnumber, &basic);
        switch (level)
        {
          case 1:
                  perks = CA1 + EA1;
                  break;
          case 2:
                  perks = CA2 + EA2;
                  break;
          case 3:
                  perks = CA3 + EA3;
                  break;
          case 4:
                  perks = CA4 + EA4;
                  break;
          default:
                  printf("Error in level code\n");
                  goto stop;
        }
        house_rent = 0.25 * basic;
        gross = basic + house_rent + perks;
        if (gross <= 2000)
          incometax = 0;
        else if (gross <= 4000)
              incometax = 0.03 * gross;
            else if (gross <= 5000)
                incometax = 0.05 * gross;
              else
                incometax = 0.08 * gross;
        net = gross - incometax;
        printf("%d %d %.2f\n", level, jobnumber, net);
        goto input;
        stop: printf("\n\nEND OF THE PROGRAM");
      }
```

Output

```
Enter level, job number, and basic pay
Enter 0 (zero) for level to END
1 1111 4000
1 1111 5980.00
Enter level, job number, and basic pay
Enter 0 (zero) for level to END
2 2222 3000
2 2222 4465.00
```

```
Enter level, job number, and basic pay
Enter 0 (zero) for level to END
3 3333 2000
3 3333 3007.00
Enter level, job number, and basic pay
Enter 0 (zero) for level to END
4 4444 1000
4 4444 1500.00
Enter level, job number, and basic pay
Enter 0 (zero) for level to END
0
END OF THE PROGRAM
```

Fig. 5.15 *Pay-bill calculations*

REVIEW QUESTIONS

5.1 State whether the following are *true* or *false*:

(a) When **if** statements are nested, the last **else** gets associated with the nearest **if** without an **else**.

(b) One **if** can have more than one **else** clause.

(c) A **switch** statement can always be replaced by a series of **if..else** statements.

(d) A **switch** expression can be of any type.

(e) A program stops its execution when a **break** statement is encountered.

(f) Each expression in the **else if** must test the same variable.

(g) Any expression can be used for the **if** expression.

(h) Each case label can have only one statement.

(i) The **default** case is required in the **switch** statement.

(j) The predicate !((x >= 10)¦(y = = 5)) is equivalent to (x < 10) && (y !=5).

5.2 Fill in the blanks in the following statements.

(a) The ________ operator is true only when both the operands are true.

(b) Multiway selection can be accomplished using an **else if** statement or the __________ statement.

(c) The ______ statement when executed in a **switch** statement causes immediate exit from the structure.

(d) The ternary conditional expression using the operator ?: could be easily coded using ______statement.

(e) The expression ! (x ! = y) can be replaced by the expression ________.

5.3 Find errors, if any, in each of the following segments:

(a)
```
if (x + y = z && y > 0)
    printf(" ");
```

(b)
```
if (code > 1);
    a = b + c
```

```
    else
        a = 0
(c) if (p < 0) || (q < 0)
        printf (" sign is negative");
```

5.4 The following is a segment of a program:

```
x = 1;
y = 1;
if (n > 0)
    x = x + 1;
    y = y - 1;
printf(" %d %d", x, y);
```

What will be the values of x and y if n assumes a value of (a) 1 and (b) 0.

5.5 Rewrite each of the following without using compound relations:

```
(a) if (grade <= 59 && grade >= 50)
        second = second + 1;
(b) if (number > 100 || number < 0)
        printf(" Out of range");
    else
        sum = sum + number;
(c) if ((M1 > 60 && M2 > 60) || T > 200)
        printf(" Admitted\n");
    else
        printf(" Not admitted\n");
```

5.6 Assuming x = 10, state whether the following logical expressions are true or false.

(a) x = = 10 && x > 10 && !x (b) x = = 10 || x > 10 && ! x

(c) x = = 10 && x > 10 || ! x (d) x = = 10 || x > 10 || !x

5.7 Find errors, if any, in the following switch related statements. Assume that the variables x and y are of int type and x = 1 and y = 2

```
(a) switch (y);
(b) case 10;
(c) switch (x + y)
(d) switch (x) {case 2: y = x + y; break};
```

5.8 Simplify the following compound logical expressions

(a) !(x <=10) (b) !(x = = 10) ||! ((y = = 5) || (z < 0))

(c) ! ((x +y = = z) && !(z > 5) (d) !((x <=5) && (y = = 10) & & (z < 5))

5.9 Assuming that x = 5, y = 0, and z = 1 initially, what will be their values after executing the following code segments?

```
(a) if (x && y)
        x = 10;
    else
        y = 10;
(b) if (x || y || z)
        y = 10;
    else
```

```
z = 0;
```

(c)
```
if (x)
    if (y)
        z = 10;
    else
        z = 0;
```

(d)
```
if (x = = 0 || x & & y)
    if (!y)
        z = 0;
    else
        y = 1;
```

5.10 Assuming that x = 2, y = 1 and z = 0 initially, what will be their values after executing the following code segments?

(a)
```
switch (x)
{
    case 2:
        x = 1;
        y = x + 1;
    case 1:
        x = 0;
        break;
    default:
        x = 1;
        y = 0;
}
```

(b)
```
switch (y)
{
    case 0:
        x = 0;
        y = 0;
    case 2:
        x = 2;
        z = 2;
    default:
        x = 1;
        y = 2;
}
```

PROGRAMMING EXERCISES

5.1 Write a program to determine whether a given number is 'odd' or 'even' and print the message
NUMBER IS EVEN
or
NUMBER IS ODD
(a) without using **else** option, and (b) with **else** option.

5.2 Write a program to find the number of and sum of all integers greater than 100 and less than 200 that are divisible by 7.

5.3 A set of two linear equations with two unknowns x1 and x2 is given below:

$$ax_1 + bx_2 = m$$

$$cx_1 + dx_2 = n$$

The set has a unique solution

$$x1 = \frac{md - bn}{ad - cb}$$

$$x2 = \frac{na - mc}{ad - cb}$$

provided the denominator ad – cb is not equal to zero.
Write a program that will read the values of constants a, b, c, d, m, and n and compute the values of x_1 and x_2. An appropriate message should be printed if ad – cb = 0.

5.4 Given a list of marks ranging from 0 to 100, write a program to compute and print the number of students:
(a) who have obtained more than 80 marks,
(b) who have obtained more than 60 marks,
(c) who have obtained more than 40 marks,
(d) who have obtained 40 or less marks,
(e) in the range 81 to 100,
(f) in the range 61 to 80,
(g) in the range 41 to 60, and
(h) in the range 0 to 40.
The program should use a minimum number of if statements.

5.5 Admission to a professional course is subject to the following conditions:
(a) Marks in Mathematics >= 60
(b) Marks in Physics >= 50
(c) Marks in Chemistry >= 40
(d) Total in all three subjects >= 200
or
Total in Mathematics and Physics >= 150
Given the marks in the three subjects, write a program to process the applications to list the eligible candidates.

5.6 Write a program to print a two-dimensional Square Root Table as shown below, to provide the square root of any number from 0 to 9.9. For example, the value x will give the square root of 3.2 and y the square root of 3.9.

Square Root Table

Number	0.0	0.1	0.2	....	0.9
0.0					
1.0					
2.0					
3.0		x			y
9.0					

5.7 Shown below is a Floyd's triangle.

1
2 3
4 5 6
7 8 9 10
11 15
.
.
.
79 91

(a) Write a program to print this triangle.

(b) Modify the program to produce the following form of Floyd's triangle.

1
0 1
1 0 1
0 1 0 1
1 0 1 0 1

5.8 A cloth showroom has announced the following seasonal discounts on purchase of items:

Purchase amount	*Discount*	
	Mill cloth	*Handloom items*
0 – 100	–	5%
101 – 200	5%	7.5%
201 – 300	7.5%	10.0%
Above 300	10.0%	15.0%

Write a program using **switch** and **if** statements to compute the net amount to be paid by a customer.

5.9 Write a program that will read the value of x and evaluate the following function

$$y = \begin{cases} 1 & \text{for } x < 0 \\ 0 & \text{for } x = 0 \\ -1 & \text{for } x < 0 \end{cases}$$

using

(a) nested **if** statements,
(b) **else if** statements, and
(c) conditional operator ? :

5.10 Write a program to compute the real roots of a quadratic equation

$$ax^2 + bx + c = 0$$

The roots are given by the equations

$$x_1 = -b + \frac{\sqrt{b^2 - 4ac}}{2a}$$

$$x_2 = -b - \frac{\sqrt{b^2 - 4ac}}{2a}$$

The program should request for the values of the constants a, b and c and print the values of x_1 and x_2. Use the following rules:

(a) No solution, if both a and b are zero
(b) There is only one root, if a = 0 (x = – c/b)
(c) There are no real roots, if b^2 – 4 ac is negative
(d) Otherwise, there are two real roots

Test your program with appropriate data so that all logical paths are working as per your design. Incorporate appropriate output messages.

Chapter

6

Decision Making and Looping

6.1 INTRODUCTION

We have seen in the previous chapter that it is possible to execute a segment of a program repeatedly by introducing a counter and later testing it using the **if** statement. While this method is quite satisfactory for all practical purposes, we need to initialize and increment a counter and test its value at an appropriate place in the program for the completion of the loop. For example, suppose we want to calculate the sum of squares of all integers between 1 and 10. We can write a program using the **if** statement as follows:

```
      -----------
      -----------
      sum = 0;
      n = 1;
  --> loop:
L     sum = sum + n*n;
      if (n == 10)
o          goto print;--
      else
o     {                       n = 10,
p          n = n+1;           end of loop
           goto loop;
      }
      print: <--
      -----------
      -----------
```

This program does the following things:

1. Initializes the variable **n**.
2. Computes the square of **n** and adds it to **sum**.
3. Tests the value of **n** to see whether it is equal to 10 or not. If it is equal to 10, then the program prints the results.

4. If n is less than 10, then it is incremented by one and the control goes back to compute the **sum** again.

The program evaluates the statement

```
sum = sum + n*n;
```

10 times. That is, the loop is executed 10 times. This number can be decreased or increased easily by modifying the relational expression appropriately in the statement **if** (n == 10). On such occasions where the exact number of repetitions are known, there are more convenient methods of looping in C. These looping capabilities enable us to develop concise programs containing repetitive processes without the use of **goto** statements.

In looping, a sequence of statements are executed until some conditions for termination of the loop are satisfied. A *program loop* therefore consists of two segments, one known as the *body of the loop* and the other known as the *control statement*. The control statement tests certain conditions and then directs the repeated execution of the statements contained in the body of the loop.

Depending on the position of the control statement in the loop, a control structure may be classified either as the *entry-controlled loop* or as the *exit-controlled loop*. The flow charts in Fig. 6.1 illustrate these structures. In the entry-controlled loop, the control conditions are tested before the start of the loop execution. If the conditions are not satisfied, then the body of the loop will not be executed. In the case of an exit-controlled loop, the test is performed at the end of the body of the loop and therefore the body is executed unconditionally for the first time. The entry-controlled and exit-controlled loops are also known as *pre-test* and *post-test* loops respectively.

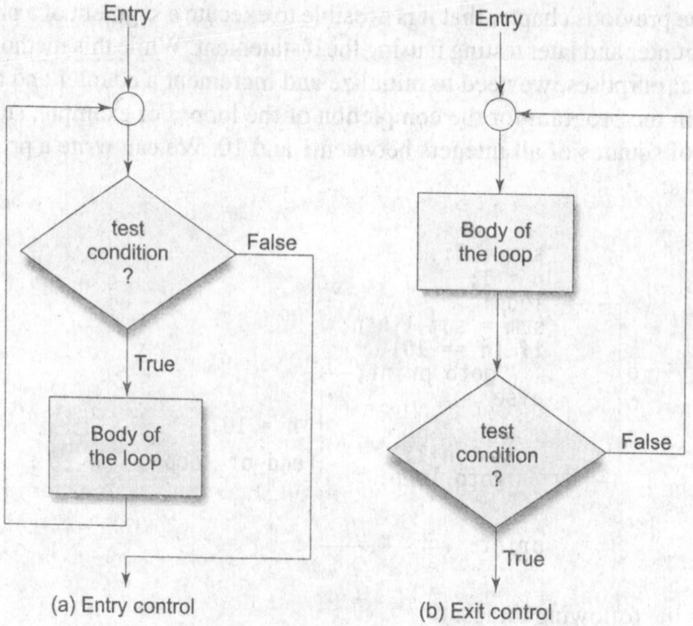

Fig. 6.1 *Loop control structures*

The test conditions should be carefully stated in order to perform the desired number of loop executions. It is assumed that the test condition will eventually transfer the control out of the loop. In case, due to some reason it does not do so, the control sets up an *infinite loop* and the body is executed over and over again.

A looping process, in general, would include the following four steps:

1. Setting and initialization of a condition variable.
2. Execution of the statements in the loop.
3. Test for a specified value of the condition variable for execution of the loop.
4. Incrementing or updating the condition variable.

The test may be either to determine whether the loop has been repeated the specified number of times or to determine whether a particular condition has been met.

The C language provides for three *constructs* for performing *loop* operations. They are:

1. The **while** statement.
2. The **do** statement.
3. The **for** statement.

We shall discuss the features and applications of each of these statements in this chapter.

Sentinel Loops

Based on the nature of control variable and the kind of value assigned to it for testing the control expression, the loops may be classified into two general categories:

1. Counter-controlled loops
2. Sentinel-controlled loops

When we know in advance exactly how many times the loop will be executed, we use a *counter-controlled loop*. We use a control variable known *as counter*. The counter must be initialized, tested and updated properly for the desired loop operations. The number of times we want to execute the loop may be a constant or a variable that is assigned a value. A counter-controlled loop is sometimes called *definite repetition loop*.

In a *sentinel-controlled loop*, a special value called a *sentinel* value is used to change the loop control expression from true to false. For example, when reading data we may indicate the "end of data" by a special value, like – 1 and 999. The control variable is called **sentinel** variable. A sentinel-controlled loop is often called *indefinite repetition loop* because the number of repetitions is not known before the loop begins executing.

6.2 THE WHILE STATEMENT

The simplest of all the looping structures in C is the **while** statement. We have used **while** in many of our earlier programs. The basic format of the **while** statement is

```
while (test condition)
  {
     body of the loop
  }
```

The **while** is an *entry-controlled* loop statement. The *test-condition* is evaluated and if the condition is *true*, then the body of the loop is executed. After execution of the body, the test-condition is once again evaluated and if it is true, the body is executed once again. This process of repeated execution of the body continues until the test-condition finally becomes *false* and the control is transferred out of the loop. On exit, the program continues with the statement immediately after the body of the loop.

The body of the loop may have one or more statements. The braces are needed only if the body contains two or more statements. However, it is a good practice to use braces even if the body has only one statement.

We can rewrite the program loop discussed in Section 6.1 as follows:

```
            ========
            sum = 0;
            n = 1;                         /* Initialization */
         ┌─ while(n <= 10)                 /* Testing */
         │  {
  loop   │     sum = sum + n * n;
         └─    n = n+1;                     /* Incrementing */
            }
            printf("sum = %d\n", sum);
            ========
```

The body of the loop is executed 10 times for n = 1, 2, ..., 10, each time adding the square of the value of n, which is incremented inside the loop. The test condition may also be written as **n < 11**; the result would be the same. This is a typical example of counter-controlled loops. The variable n is called ***counter*** or ***control variable***.

Another example of **while** statement, which uses the keyboard input is shown below:

```
=========
character = ' ';
while (character != 'Y')
        character = getchar();
xxxxxxx;
=========
```

First the **character** is initialized to ' '. The **while** statement then begins by testing whether **character** is not equal to Y. Since the **character** was initialized to ' ', the test is true and the loop statement

```
character = getchar();
```

is executed. Each time a letter is keyed in, the test is carried out and the loop statement is executed until the letter Y is pressed. When Y is pressed, the condition becomes false because **character** equals Y, and the loop terminates, thus transferring the control to the statement xxxxxxx;. This is a typical example of sentinel-controlled loops. The character constant 'y' is called *sentinel* value and the variable **character** is the condition variable, which often referred to as the *sentinel variable*.

Example 6.1 A program to evaluate the equation

$$y = x^n$$

when n is a non-negative integer, is given in Fig. 6.2

The variable **y** is initialized to 1 and then multiplied by **x**, n times using the **while** loop. The loop control variable **count** is initialized outside the loop and incremented inside the loop. When the value of **count** becomes greater than **n**, the control exists the loop.

Program

```
main()
{
   int count, n;
   float x, y;
   printf("Enter the values of x and n : ");
   scanf("%f %d", &x, &n);
   y = 1.0;
   count = 1;              /* Initialisation */
   /* LOOP BEGINs */
   while ( count <= n) /* Testing */
   {
      y = y*x;
      count++;             /* Incrementing */
   }
   /* END OF LOOP */
   printf("\nx = %f; n = %d; x to power n = %f\n",x,n,y);
}
```

Output

```
Enter the values of x and n : 2.5 4
x = 2.500000; n = 4; x to power n = 39.062500
Enter the values of x and n : 0.5 4
x = 0.500000; n = 4; x to power n = 0.062500
```

Fig. 6.2 *Program to compute **x** to the power n using while loop*

6.3 THE DO STATEMENT

The **while** loop construct that we have discussed in the previous section makes a test of condition *before* the loop is executed. Therefore, the body of the loop may not be executed at all if the condition is not satisfied at the very first attempt. On some occasions it might be necessary to execute the body of the loop before the test is performed. Such situations can be handled with the help of the do statement. This takes the form:

```
do
{
      body of the loop
}
while (test-condition);
```

On reaching the **do** statement, the program proceeds to evaluate the body of the loop first. At the end of the loop, the *test-condition* in the **while** statement is evaluated. If the condition is true, the program continues to evaluate the body of the *loop* once again. This process continues as long as the *condition* is true. When the condition becomes false, the loop will be terminated and the control goes to the statement that appears immediately after the **while** statement.

Since the *test-condition* is evaluated at the bottom of the loop, the **do...while** construct provides an *exit-controlled* loop and therefore the body of the loop is *always executed at least once.*

A simple example of a **do...while** loop is:

```
          -----------
          do
      ┌─> {
      │         printf ("Input a number\n");
loop  │         number = getnum ( );
      │   }
      └── while (number > 0);
          -----------
```

This segment of a program reads a number from the keyboard until a zero or a negative number is keyed in, and assigned to the sentinel variable **number**.

The test conditions may have compound relations as well. For instance, the statement

```
while (number > 0 && number < 100);
```

in the above example would cause the loop to be executed as long as the number keyed in lies between 0 and 100.

Consider another example:

```
          -------
          I = 1;                         /* Initializing */
          sum = 0;
          do
      ┌─> {
      │     sum = sum + I;
loop  │     I = I+2;                     /* Incrementing */
      └── }
          while(sum < 40 || I < 10);     /* Testing */
          printf("%d %d\n", I, sum);
          -------
```

The loop will be executed as long as one of the two relations is true.

Example 6.2 A program to print the multiplication table from 1 x 1 to 12 x 10 as shown below is given in Fig. 6.3.

1	2	3	4	....	10
2	4	6	8	....	20
3	6	9	12	....	30
4				....	40
-					
-					
-					
12		.	.	....	120

This program contains two **do.... while** loops in nested form. The outer loop is controlled by the variable **row** and executed 12 times. The inner loop is controlled by the variable **column** and is executed 10 times, each time the outer loop is executed. That is, the inner loop is executed a total of 120 times, each time printing a value in the table.

```
Program:
    #define COLMAX 10
    #define ROWMAX 12
    main()
    {
        int row,column, y;
        row = 1;
        printf("     MULTIPLICATION TABLE      \n");
        printf("-----------------------------\n");
        do /*......OUTER LOOP BEGINS........*/
        {
            column = 1;
            do /*.......INNER LOOP BEGINS.......*/
            {
              y = row * column;
              printf("%4d", y);
              column = column + 1;
            }
            while (column <= COLMAX); /*... INNER LOOP ENDS...*/
            printf("\n");
            row = row + 1;
        }
        while (row <= ROWMAX);/*..... OUTER LOOP ENDS .....*/
        printf("-------------------------------------\n");
    }
```

```
Output
                    MULTIPLICATION TABLE
 1    2    3    4    5    6    7    8    9    10
 2    4    6    8    10   12   14   16   18   20
 3    6    9    12   15   18   21   24   27   30
 4    8    12   16   20   24   28   32   36   40
 5    10   15   20   25   30   35   40   45   50
 6    12   18   24   30   36   42   48   54   60
 7    14   21   28   35   42   49   56   63   70
 8    16   24   32   40   48   56   64   72   80
 9    18   27   36   45   54   63   72   81   90
 10   20   30   40   50   60   70   80   90   100
 11   22   33   44   55   66   77   88   99   110
 12   24   36   48   60   72   84   96   108  120
```

Fig. 6.3 *Printing of a multiplication table using* ***do...while*** *loop*

Notice that the **printf** of the inner loop does not contain any new line character (\n). This allows the printing of all row values in one line. The empty **printf** in the outer loop initiates a new line to print the next row.

6.4 THE FOR STATEMENT

Simple 'for' Loops

The **for** loop is another *entry-controlled* loop that provides a more concise loop control structure. The general form of the **for** loop is

```
for ( initialization ; test-condition ; increment)
{
    body of the loop
}
```

The execution of the **for** statement is as follows:

1. *Initialization* of the *control variables* is done first, using assignment statements such as i = 1 and count = 0. The variables **i** and **count** are known as loop-control variables.
2. The value of the control variable is tested using the test-condition. The *test-condition* is a relational expression, such as i < 10 that determines when the loop will exit. If the condition is *true,* the body of the loop is executed; otherwise the loop is terminated and the execution continues with the statement that immediately follows the loop.
3. When the body of the loop is executed, the control is transferred back to the **for** statement after evaluating the last statement in the loop. Now, the control variable is *incremented* using an assignment statement such as i = i+1 and the new value of the control variable is again tested to see whether it satisfies the loop condition. If the condition is satisfied, the body of the loop is again executed. This process continues till the value of the control variable fails to satisfy the test-condition.

Consider the following segment of a program:

```
        for ( x = 0 ; x <= 9 ; x = x+1)
loop    {
            printf("%d", x);
        }
        printf("\n");
```

This **for** loop is executed 10 times and prints the digits 0 to 9 in one line. The three sections enclosed within parentheses must be separated by semicolons. Note that there is no semicolon at the end of the *increment* section, x = x+1.

The **for** statement allows for *negative increments*. For example, the loop discussed above can be written as follows:

```
for ( x = 9 ; x >= 0 ; x = x-1 )
    printf("%d", x);
printf("\n");
```

This loop is also executed 10 times, but the output would be from 9 to 0 instead of 0 to 9. Note that braces are optional when the body of the loop contains only one statement.

Since the conditional test is always performed at the beginning of the loop, the body of the loop may not be executed at all, if the condition fails at the start. For example,

```
for (x = 9; x < 9; x = x-1)
    printf("%d", x);
```

will never be executed because the test condition fails at the very beginning itself.

Let us again consider the problem of sum of squares of integers discussed in Section 6.1. This problem can be coded using the **for** statement as follows:

```
-----------------
sum = 0;
for (n = 1; n <= 10; n = n+1)
{
      sum = sum+ n*n;
}
printf("sum = %d\n", sum);
-----------------
```

The body of the loop

```
sum = sum + n*n;
```

is executed 10 times for n = 1, 2, ..., 10 each time incrementing the **sum** by the square of the value of n.

One of the important points about the **for** loop is that all the three actions, namely *initialization, testing*, and *incrementing*, are placed in the **for** statement itself, thus making them visible to the programmers and users, in one place. The **for** statement and its equivalent of **while** and **do** statements are shown in Table 6.1.

Table 6.1 *Comparison of the Three Loops*

for	*while*	*do*

for (n=1; n<=10; ++n)
{
____
____
}
	n = 1;
	while (n<=10)
	{
	________
	________
	n = n+1;
	}
		n = 1;
		do
		{
		________
		________
		n = n+1;
		}
		while(n<=10);

Example 6.3 The program in Fig. 6.4 uses a **for** loop to print the "Powers of 2" table for the power 0 to 20, both positive and negative.

The program evaluates the value

$$p = 2^{n}$$

successively by multiplying 2 by itself n times.

$$q = 2^{-n} = \frac{1}{p}$$

Note that we have declared **p** as a ***long int*** and **q** as a **double**.

Additional Features of for Loop

The **for** loop in C has several capabilities that are not found in other loop constructs. For example, more than one variable can be initialized at a time in the **for** statement. The statements

```
p = 1;
for (n=0; n<17; ++n)
```

can be rewritten as

```
for (p=1, n=0; n<17; ++n)
```

```
Program
main()
{
    long int p;
    int n;
    double q;
    printf("--------------------------------------\n");
    printf(" 2 to power n          n          2 to power -n\n");
    printf("--------------------------------------\n");
    p = 1;
    for (n = 0; n < 21 ; ++n) /* LOOP BEGINS */
```

```
        {
          if (n == 0)
            p = 1;
          else
            p = p * 2;
          q = 1.0/(double)p ;
          printf("%10ld %10d %20.12lf\n", p, n, q);
        }                                /* LOOP ENDS */
        printf("---------------------------------------\n");
}
Output
        ----------------------------------------------
        2 to power n        n        2 to power -n
        ----------------------------------------------
                  1         0        1.000000000000
                  2         1        0.500000000000
                  4         2        0.250000000000
                  8         3        0.125000000000
                 16         4        0.062500000000
                 32         5        0.031250000000
                 64         6        0.015625000000
                128         7        0.007812500000
                256         8        0.003906250000
                512         9        0.001953125000
               1024        10        0.000976562500
               2048        11        0.000488281250
               4096        12        0.000244140625
               8192        13        0.000122070313
              16384        14        0.000061035156
              32768        15        0.000030517578
              65536        16        0.000015258789
             131072        17        0.000007629395
             262144        18        0.000003814697
             524288        19        0.000001907349
            1048576        20        0.000000953674
        ----------------------------------------------
```

Fig. 6.4 *Program to print 'Power of 2' table using for loop*

Notice that the initialization section has two parts p = 1 and n = 1 separated by a *comma*.

Like the initialization section, the increment section may also have more than one part. For example, the loop

```
for (n=1, m=50; n<=m; n=n+1, m=m-1)
{
    p = m/n;
    printf("%d %d %d\n", n, m, p);
}
```

is perfectly valid. The multiple arguments in the increment section are separated by *commas*.

The third feature is that the test-condition may have any compound relation and the testing need not be limited only to the loop control variable. Consider the example below:

```
sum = 0;
for (i = 1; i < 20 && sum < 100; ++i)
{
    sum = sum+i;
    printf("%d %d\n", i, sum);
}
```

The loop uses a compound test condition with the counter variable **i** and sentinel variable **sum**. The loop is executed as long as both the conditions i < 20 and sum < 100 are true. The **sum** is evaluated inside the loop.

It is also permissible to use expressions in the assignment statements of initialization and increment sections. For example, a statement of the type

```
for (x = (m+n)/2; x > 0; x = x/2)
```

is perfectly valid.

Another unique aspect of **for** loop is that one or more sections can be omitted, if necessary. Consider the following statements:

```
-------
m = 5;
for ( ; m != 100 ; )
{
    printf("%d\n", m);
    m = m+5;
}
-------
```

Both the initialization and increment sections are omitted in the **for** statement. The initialization has been done before the **for** statement and the control variable is incremented inside the loop. In such cases, the sections are left 'blank'. However, the semicolons separating the sections must remain. If the test-condition is not present, the **for** statement sets up an *'infinite'* loop. Such loops can be broken using **break** or **goto** statements in the loop.

We can set up *time delay loops* using the null statement as follows:

```
for  ( j = 1000; j > 0; j = j-1)
     ;
```

This loop is executed 1000 times without producing any output; it simply causes a time delay. Notice that the body of the loop contains only a semicolon, known as a *null* statement. This can also be written as

```
for (j=1000; j > 0; j = j-1)
```

This implies that the C compiler will not give an error message if we place a semicolon by mistake at the end of a **for** statement. The semicolon will be considered as a *null statement* and the program may produce some nonsense.

Nesting of for Loops

Nesting of loops, that is, one **for** statement within another **for** statement, is allowed in C. For example, two loops can be nested as follows:

```
------------
------------
for (i = 1; i < 10; ++i)
{
   ------------
   ------------
   for ( j = 1; j != 5; ++j)
   {                                Inner    Outer
      ------------                  loop     loop
      ------------
   }
   ------------
   ------------
}
------------
------------
```

The nesting may continue up to any desired level. The loops should be properly indented so as to enable the reader to easily determine which statements are contained within each **for** statement. (ANSI C allows up to 15 levels of nesting. However, some compilers permit more).

The program to print the multiplication table discussed in Example 6.2 can be written more concisely using nested for statements as follows:

```
-------------
for (row = 1; row <= ROWMAX ; ++row)
{
  for (column = 1; column <= COLMAX ; ++column)
  {
      y = row * column;
      printf("%4d", y);
  }
  printf("\n");
}
-------------
```

The outer loop controls the rows while the inner loop controls the columns.

Example 6.4 A class of **n** students take an annual examination in **m** subjects. A program to read the marks obtained by each student in various subjects and to compute and print the total marks obtained by each of them is given in Fig. 6.5.

The program uses two **for** loops, one for controlling the number of students and the other for controlling the number of subjects. Since both the number of students and the number of subjects are requested by the program, the program may be used for a class of any size and any number of subjects. The outer loop includes three parts:

(1) reading of roll-numbers of students, one after another,
(2) inner loop, where the marks are read and totalled for each student, and
(3) printing of total marks and declaration of grades.

Program

```
#define FIRST 360
#define SECOND 240
main()
{
    int n, m, i, j,
        roll_number, marks, total;
    printf("Enter number of students and subjects\n");
    scanf("%d %d", &n, &m);
    printf("\n");
    for (i = 1; i <= n ; ++i)
    {
        printf("Enter roll_number : ");
        scanf("%d", &roll_number);
        total = 0 ;
        printf("\nEnter marks of %d subjects for ROLL NO %d\n",
                m,roll_number);
        for (j = 1; j <= m; j++)
        {
            scanf("%d", &marks);
            total = total + marks;
        }
        printf("TOTAL MARKS = %d ", total);
        if (total >= FIRST)
            printf("( First Division )\n\n");
        else if (total >= SECOND)
                printf("( Second Division )\n\n");
            else
                printf("( *** F A I L *** )\n\n");
    }
}
```

Output

```
Enter number of students and subjects
3 6
Enter roll_number : 8701
Enter marks of 6 subjects for ROLL NO 8701
81 75 83 45 61 59
TOTAL MARKS = 404 ( First Division )
Enter roll_number : 8702
Enter marks of 6 subjects for ROLL NO 8702
51 49 55 47 65 41
TOTAL MARKS = 308 ( Second Division )
Enter roll_number : 8704
Enter marks of 6 subjects for ROLL NO 8704
40 19 31 47 39 25
TOTAL MARKS = 201 ( *** F A I L *** )
```

Fig. 6.5 *Illustration of nested for loops*

Selecting a Loop

Given a problem, the programmer's first concern is to decide the type of loop structure to be used. To choose one of the three loop supported by C, we may use the following strategy:

- Analyse the problem and see whether it required a pre-test or post-test loop.
- If it requires a post-test loop, then we can use only one loop, **do while**.
- If it requires a pre-test loop, then we have two choices: **for** and **while**.
- Decide whether the loop termination requires counter-based control or sentinel-based control.
- Use **for** loop if the counter-based control is necessary.
- Use **while** loop if the sentinel-based control is required.
- Note that both the counter-controlled and sentinel-controlled loops can be implemented by all the three control structures.

6.5 JUMPS IN LOOPS

Loops perform a set of operations repeatedly until the control variable fails to satisfy the test-condition. The number of times a loop is repeated is decided in advance and the test condition is written to achieve this. Sometimes, when executing a loop it becomes desirable to skip a part of the loop or to leave the loop as soon as a certain condition occurs. For example, consider the case of searching for a particular name in a list containing, say, 100 names. A program loop written for reading and testing the names 100 times must be terminated as soon as the desired name is found. C permits a jump from one statement to another within a loop as well as a jump out of a loop.

Jumping Out of a Loop

An early exiting from a loop can be accomplished by using the **break** statement or the **goto** statement. We have already seen the use of the **break** in the **switch** statement and the **goto** in the **if...else** construct. These statements can also be used within **while, do**, or **for** loops. They are illustrated in Fig. 6.6 and Fig. 6.7.

When a **break** statement is encountered inside a loop, the loop is immediately exited and the program continues with the statement immediately following the loop. When the loops are nested, the **break** would only exit from the loop containing it. That is, the **break** will exit only a single loop.

Since a **goto** statement can transfer the control to any place in a program, it is useful to provide branching within a loop. Another important use of **goto** is to exit from deeply nested loops when an error occurs. A simple **break** statement would not work here.

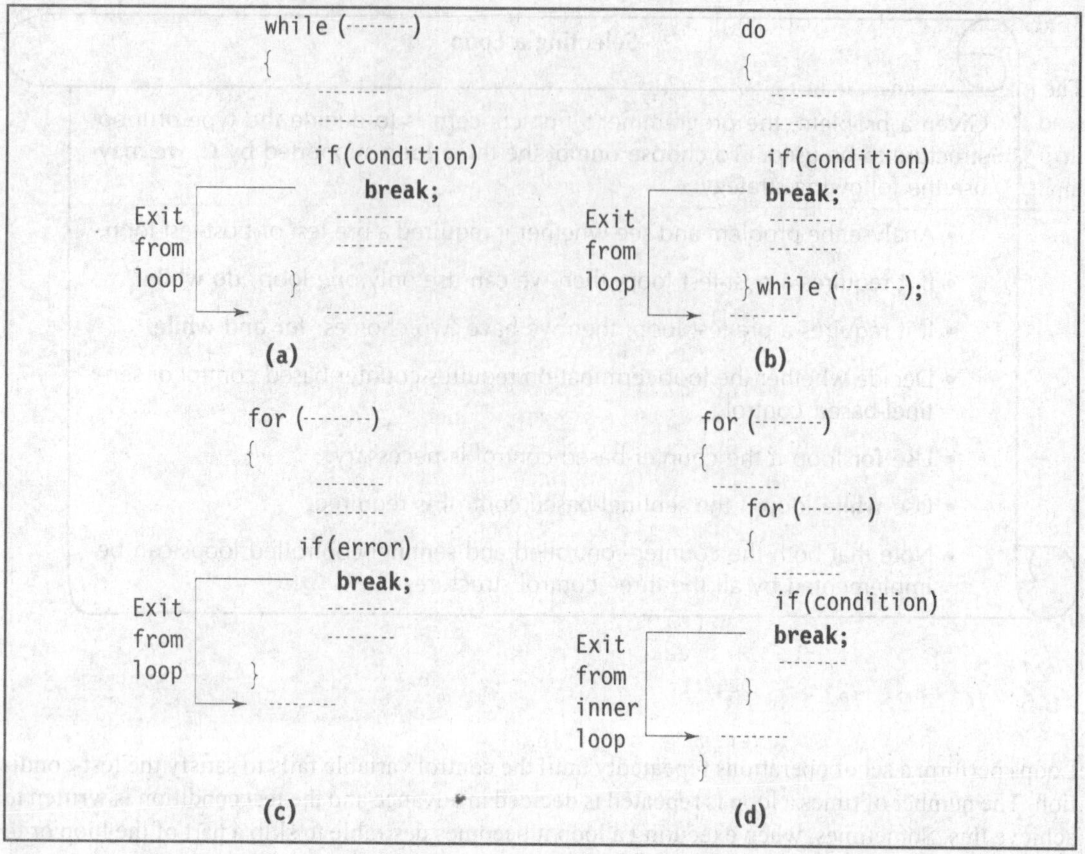

Fig. 6.6 *Exiting a loop with **break** statement*

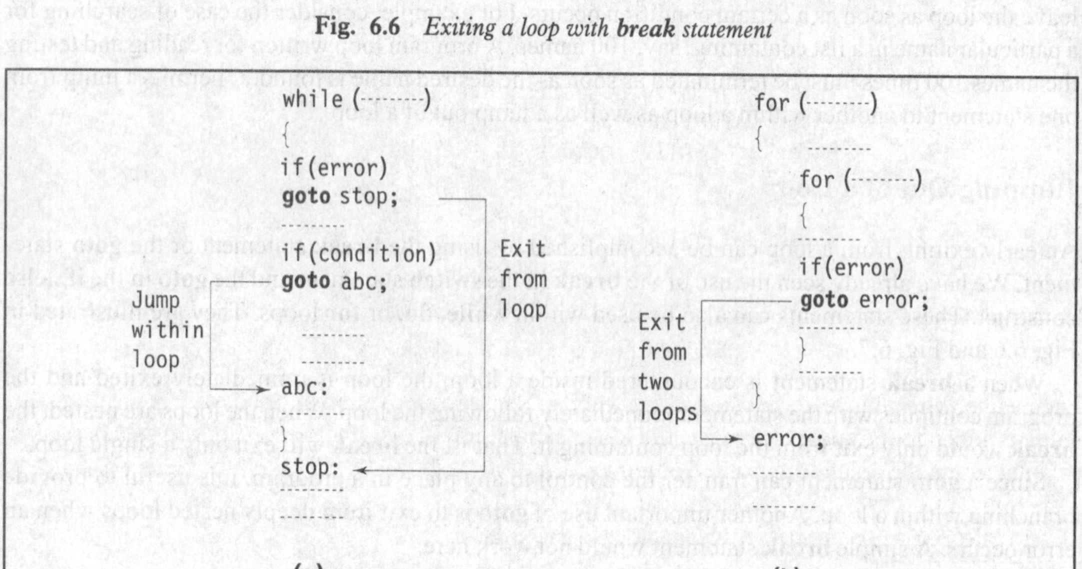

Fig. 6.7 *Jumping within and exiting from the loops with **goto** statement*

Example 6.5 The program in Fig. 6.8 illustrates the use of the break statement in a C program.

The program reads a list of positive values and calculates their average. The **for** loop is written to read 1000 values. However, if we want the program to calculate the average of any set of values less than 1000, then we must enter a 'negative' number after the last value in the list, to mark the end of input.

Program

```
main()
{
        int m;
        float x, sum, average;

        printf("This  program computes the average of a
                      set of numbers\n");
        printf("Enter values one after another\n");
        printf("Enter a NEGATIVE number at the end.\n\n");
        sum = 0;
        for (m = 1 ; m < = 1000 ; ++m)
        {
          scanf("%f", &x);
          if (x < 0)
            break;
          sum += x ;
        }
        average = sum/(float)(m-1);
        printf("\n");
        printf("Number of values  = %d\n", m-1);
        printf("Sum               = %f\n", sum);
        printf("Average           = %f\n", average);
}
```

Output

```
This program computes the average of a set of numbers
Enter values one after another
Enter a NEGATIVE number at the end.

21 23 24 22 26 22 -1

Number of values = 6
Sum              = 138.000000
Average          = 23.000000
```

Fig. 6.8 *Use of **break** in a program*

Each value, when it is read, is tested to see whether it is a positive number or not. If it is positive, the value is added to the **sum;** otherwise, the loop terminates. On exit, the average of the values read is calculated and the results are printed out.

Example 6.6 A program to evaluate the series

$$\frac{1}{1-x} = 1 + x + x^2 + x^3 + ... + x^n$$

for –1 < x < 1 with 0.01 per cent accuracy is given in Fig. 6.9. The **goto** statement is used to exit the loop on achieving the desired accuracy.

We have used the **for** statement to perform the repeated addition of each of the terms in the series. Since it is an infinite series, the evaluation of the function is terminated when the term x^n reaches the desired accuracy. The value of n that decides the number of loop operations is not known and therefore we have decided arbitrarily a value of 100, which may or may not result in the desired level of accuracy.

Program

```
#define  LOOP       100
#define  ACCURACY   0.0001
main()
{
    int n;
    float x, term, sum;
    printf("Input value of x : ");
    scanf("%f", &x);
    sum = 0 ;
    for (term = 1, n = 1 ; n <= LOOP ; ++n)
    {
        sum += term ;
        if (term <= ACCURACY)
          goto output; /* EXIT FROM THE LOOP */
        term *= x ;
    }
    printf("\nFINAL VALUE OF N IS NOT SUFFICIENT\n");
    printf("TO ACHIEVE DESIRED ACCURACY\n");
    goto end;
    output:
    printf("\nEXIT FROM LOOP\n");
    printf("Sum = %f; No.of terms = %d\n", sum, n);
    end:
    ;          /* Null Statement */
}
```

Output

```
Input value of x : .21
EXIT FROM LOOP
Sum = 1.265800; No.of terms = 7

Input value of x : .75
EXIT FROM LOOP
Sum = 3.999774; No.of terms = 34

Input value of x : .99
FINAL VALUE OF N IS NOT SUFFICIENT
TO ACHIEVE DESIRED ACCURACY
```

Fig. 6.9 *Use of goto to exit from a loop*

The test of accuracy is made using an **if** statement and the **goto** statement exits the loop as soon as the accuracy condition is satisfied. If the number of loop repetitions is not large enough to produce the desired accuracy, the program prints an appropriate message.

Note that the **break** statement is not very convenient to use here. Both the normal exit and the **break** exit will transfer the control to the same statement that appears next to the loop. But, in the present problem, the normal exit prints the message

"FINAL VALUE OF N IS NOT SUFFICIENT
TO ACHIEVE DESIRED ACCURACY"

and the *forced exit* prints the results of evaluation. Notice the use of a *null* statement at the end. This is necessary because a program should not end with a label.

Structured Programming

Structured programming is an approach to the design and development of programs. It is a discipline of making a program's logic easy to understand by using only the basic three control structures:

- Sequence (straight line) structure
- Selection (branching) structure
- Repetition (looping) structure

While sequence and loop structures are sufficient to meet all the requirements of programming, the selection structure proves to be more convenient in some situations.

The use of structured programming techniques helps ensure well-designed programs that are easier to write, read, debug and maintain compared to those that are unstructured.

Structured programming discourages the implementation of unconditional branching using jump statements such as **goto**, **break** and **continue**. In its purest form, structured programming is synonymous with *"goto less programming"*.

Do not go to **goto** statement!

Skipping a Part of a Loop

During the loop operations, it may be necessary to skip a part of the body of the loop under certain conditions. For example, in processing of applications for some job, we might like to exclude the processing of data of applicants belonging to a certain category. On reading the category code of an applicant, a test is made to see whether his application should be considered or not. If it is not to be considered, the part of the program loop that processes the application details is skipped and the execution continues with the next loop operation.

Like the **break** statement, C supports another similar statement called the **continue** statement. However, unlike the break which causes the loop to be terminated, the **continue**, as the name implies, causes the loop to be continued with the next iteration after skipping any statements in between. The **continue** statement tells the compiler, "SKIP THE FOLLOWING STATEMENTS AND CONTINUE WITH THE NEXT ITERATION". The format of the **continue** statement is simply

```
continue;
```

The use of the **continue** statement in loops is illustrated in Fig. 6.10. In **while** and **do** loops, **continue** causes the control to go directly to the test-condition and then to continue the iteration process. In the case of **for** loop, the increment section of the loop is executed before the test-condition is evaluated.

```
while (test-condition)
{
    ---------
    if (---------)
        continue;
    ---------
    ---------
}
(a)
```

```
do
{
    ---------
    if (---------)
        continue;
    ---------
    ---------
} while (test-condition);
(b)
```

```
for (initialization; test condition; increment)
{
    ---------
    if (---------)
        continue;
    ---------
}
(c)
```

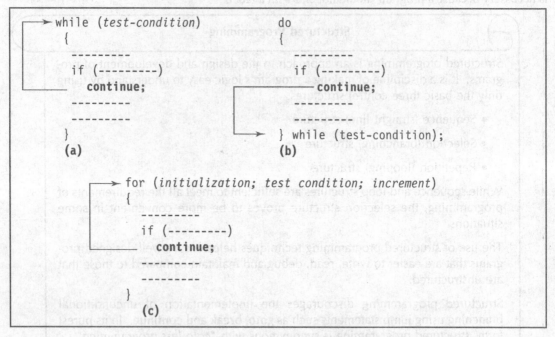

Fig. 6.10 *Bypassing and continuing in loops*

Example 6.7 The program in Fig. 6.11 illustrates the use of **continue** statement.

The program evaluates the square root of a series of numbers and prints the results. The process stops when the number 9999 is typed in.

In case, the series contains any negative numbers, the process of evaluation of square root should be bypassed for such numbers because the square root of a negative number is not defined. The **continue** statement is used to achieve this. The program also prints a message saying that the number is negative and keeps an account of negative numbers.

The final output includes the number of positive values evaluated and the number of negative items encountered.

Program:

```
#include <math.h>
main()
{
    int count, negative;
    double number, sqroot;
    printf("Enter 9999 to STOP\n");
    count = 0 ;
    negative = 0 ;
    while (count < = 100)
    {
        printf("Enter a number : ");
        scanf("%lf", &number);
        if (number == 9999)
            break;         /* EXIT FROM THE LOOP */
        if (number < 0)
        {
            printf("Number is negative\n\n");
            negative++ ;
            continue; /* SKIP REST OF THE LOOP */
        }
        sqroot = sqrt(number);
        printf("Number      = %lf\n Square root = %lf\n\n",
                                number, sqroot);

        count++ ;
    }
    printf("Number of items done = %d\n", count);
    printf("\n\nNegative items = %d\n", negative);
    printf("END OF DATA\n");
}
```

Output

```
Enter 9999 to STOP
Enter a number : 25.0
Number        = 25.000000
Square root   = 5.000000
Enter a number : 40.5
Number        = 40.500000
Square root   = 6.363961
Enter a number : -9
Number is negative
Enter a number : 16
Number        = 16.000000
Square root   = 4.000000
Enter a number : -14.75
```

```
Number is negative
Enter a number : 80
Number          = 80.000000
Square root     = 8.944272
Enter a number : 9999
Number of items done = 4
Negative items       = 2
END OF DATA
```

Fig. 6.11 *Use of **continue** statement*

Avoiding goto

As mentioned earlier, it is a good practice to avoid using **gotos**. There are many reasons for this. When **goto** is used, many compilers generate a less efficient code. In addition, using many of them makes a program logic complicated and renders the program unreadable. It is possible to avoid using **goto** by careful program design. In case any **goto** is absolutely necessary, it should be documented. The following **goto** jumps would cause problems and therefore must be avoided.

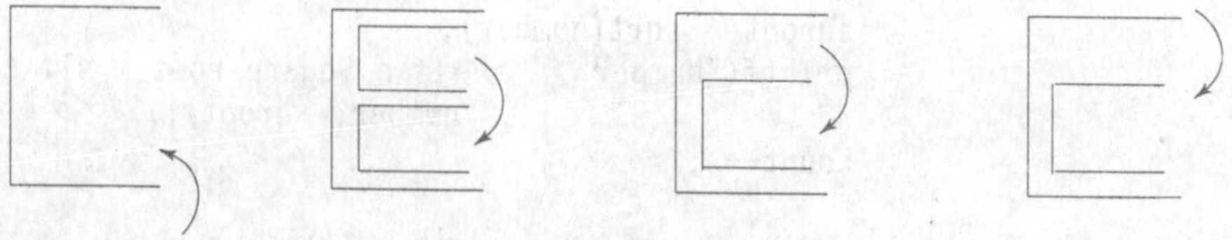

Concise Test Expressions

We often use test expressions in the **if, for, while** and **do** statements that are evaluated and compared with zero for making branching decisions. Since every integer expression has a true/false value, we need not make explicit comparisons with zero. For instance, the expression x is true whenever x is not zero, and false when x is zero. Applying! operator, we can write concise test expressions without using any relational operators.

if (expression ==0)

is equivalent to

if(!expression)

Similarly,

if (expression! = 0)

is equivalent to

if (expression)

For example,

if (m%5==0 && n%5==0) is same as **if (!(m%5)&&!(n%5))**

Just Remember

- Do not forget to place the semicolon at the end of **do ....while** statement.
- Placing a semicolon after the control expression in a **while** or **for** statement is not a syntax error but it is most likely a logic error.
- Using commas rather than semicolon in the header of a **for** statement is an error.
- Do not forget to place the *increment* statement in the body of a **while** or **do...while** loop.
- It is a common error to use wrong relational operator in test expressions. Ensure that the loop is evaluated exactly the required number of times.
- Avoid a common error using = in place of = = operator.
- Do not change the control variable in both the **for** statement and the body of the loop. It is a logic error.
- Do not compare floating-point values for equality.
- Avoid using **while** and **for** statements for implementing exit-controlled (post-test) loops. Use **do...while** statement. Similarly, do not use **do...while** for pre-test loops.
- When performing an operation on a variable repeatedly in the body of a loop, make sure that the variable is initialized properly before entering the loop.
- Although it is legally allowed to place the initialization, testing and increment sections outside the header of a **for** statement, avoid them as far as possible.
- Although it is permissible to use arithmetic expressions in initialization and increment section, be aware of round off and truncation errors during their evaluation.
- Although statements preceding a **for** and statements in the body can be placed in the **for** header, avoid doing so as it makes the program more difficult to read.
- The use of **break** and **continue** statements in any of the loops is considered unstructured programming. Try to eliminate the use of these jump statements, as far as possible.
- Avoid the use of **goto** anywhere in the program.
- Indent the statements in the body of loops properly to enhance readability and understandability.
- Use of blank spaces before and after the loops and terminating remarks are highly recommended.

CASE STUDIES

1. Table of Binomial Coefficients

Problem: Binomial coefficients are used in the study of binomial distributions and reliability of multicomponent redundant systems. It is given by

$$B(m,x) = \binom{m}{x} = \frac{m!}{x!(m-x)!}, \quad m >= x$$

A table of binomial coefficients is required to determine the binomial coefficient for any set of m and x.

Problem Analysis: The binomial coefficient can be recursively calculated as follows:

$$B(m,o) = 1$$

$$B(m,x) = B(m,x-1)\left[\frac{m-x+1}{x}\right], x = 1,2,3,...,m$$

Further,

$$B(o,o) = 1$$

That is, the binomial coefficient is one when either x is zero or m is zero. The program in Fig. 6.12 prints the table of binomial coefficients for m = 10. The program employs one **do** loop and one **while** loop.

```
Program
    #define MAX 10
    main()
    {
            int m, x, binom;
            printf(" m x");
            for (m = 0; m <= 10 ; ++m)
                printf("%4d", m);
            printf("\n--------------------------------------------\n");
            m = 0;
            do
            {
                printf("%2d ", m);
                x = 0; binom = 1;
                while (x <= m)
                {
                    if(m == 0 || x == 0)
                      printf("%4d", binom);
                    else
                      {
                          binom = binom * (m - x + 1)/x;
                          printf("%4d", binom);
                      }
                    x = x + 1;
```

```
            }
            printf("\n");
            m = m + 1;
        }
        while (m <= MAX);
        printf("---------------------------------------------------\n");
    }
```

Output

```
     mx    0   1   2   3   4   5   6   7   8   9  10
---------------------------------------------------------
      0    1
      1    1   1
      2    1   2   1
      3    1   3   3   1
      4    1   4   6   4   1
      5    1   5  10  10   5   1
      6    1   6  15  20  15   6   1
      7    1   7  21  35  35  21   7   1
      8    1   8  28  56  70  56  28   8   1
      9    1   9  36  84 126 126  84  36   9   1
     10    1  10  45 120 210 252 210 120  45  10   1
---------------------------------------------------------
```

Fig. 6.12 *Program to print **binomial coefficient** table*

2. Histogram

Problem: In an organization, the employees are grouped according to their basic pay for the purpose of certain perks. The pay-range and the number of employees in each group are as follows:

Group	Pay-Range	Number of Employees
1	750 – 1500	12
2	1501 – 3000	23
3	3001 – 4500	35
4	4501 – 6000	20
5	above 6000	11

Draw a histogram to highlight the group sizes.

Problem Analysis: Given the size of groups, it is required to draw bars representing the sizes of various groups. For each bar, its group number and size are to be written.

Program in Fig. 6.13 reads the number of employees belonging to each group and draws a histogram. The program uses four **for** loops and two **if.....else** statements.

Program:

```
#define   N 5
main()
{
    int value[N];
    int i, j, n, x;
```

```
        for (n=0; n < N; ++n)
        {
          printf("Enter employees in Group - %d : ",n+1);
          scanf("%d", &x);
          value[n] = x;
          printf("%d\n", value[n]);
        }
        printf("\n");
        printf("|\n");
        for (n = 0 ; n < N ; ++n)
        {
          for (i = 1 ; i <= 3 ; i++)
          {
              if ( i == 2)
                  printf("Group-%1d |",n+1);
              else
                  printf("|");
              for (j = 1 ; j <= value[n]; ++j)
                  printf("*");
              if (i == 2)
                  printf("(%d)\n", value[n]);
              else
                  printf("\n");
          }
          printf("|\n");
        }
    }
```

Output

```
Enter employees in Group - 1 : 12
12
Enter employees in Group - 2 : 23
23
Enter employees in Group - 3 : 35
35
Enter employees in Group - 4 : 20
20
Enter Employees in Group - 5 : 11
11
          |
          |************
Group-1   |************(12)
          |************
          |
          |***********************
Group-2   |***********************(23)
          |***********************
```

```
               |
               |************************************
    Group-3    |************************************(35)
               |************************************
               |
               |********************
    Group-4    |********************(20)
               |********************
               |
               |***********
    Group-5    |***********(11)
               |***********
               |
```

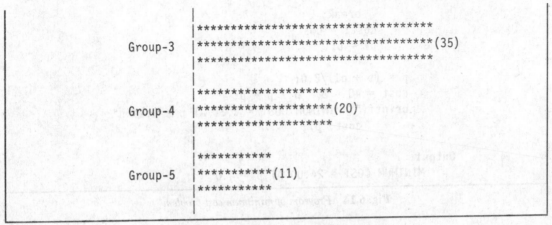

Fig. 6.13 *Program to draw a* ***histogram***

3. Minimum Cost

Problem: The cost of operation of a unit consists of two components C1 and C2 which can be expressed as functions of a parameter p as follows:

$$C1 = 30 - 8p$$

$$C2 = 10 + p^2$$

The parameter p ranges from 0 to 10. Determine the value of p with an accuracy of + 0.1 where the cost of operation would be minimum.

Problem Analysis:

$$\text{Total cost} = C_1 + C_2 = 40 - 8p + p^2$$

The cost is 40 when p = 0, and 33 when p = 1 and 60 when p = 10. The cost, therefore, decreases first and then increases. The program in Fig. 6.14 evaluates the cost at successive intervals of p (in steps of 0.1) and stops when the cost begins to increase. The program employs **break** and **continue** statements to exit the loop.

```
Program
    main()
    {
      float p, cost, p1, cost1;
      for (p = 0; p <= 10; p = p + 0.1)
      {
        cost = 40 - 8 * p + p * p;
        if(p == 0)
        {
          cost1 = cost;
          continue;
        }
        if (cost >= cost1)
```

```
            break;
          cost1 = cost;
          p1 = p;
        }
      p = (p + p1)/2.0;
      cost = 40 - 8 * p + p * p;
      printf("\nMINIMUM COST = %.2f AT p = %.1f\n",
            cost, p);
    }
Output
    MINIMUM COST = 24.00 AT p = 4.0
```

Fig. 6.14 *Program of minimum cost problem*

4. Plotting of Two Functions

Problem: We have two functions of the type

$$y1 = \exp(-ax)$$
$$y2 = \exp(-ax^2/2)$$

Plot the graphs of these functions for x varying from 0 to 5.0.

Problem Analysis: Initially when x = 0, y1 = y2 =1 and the graphs start from the same point. The curves cross when they are again equal at x = 2.0. The program should have appropriate branch statements to print the graph points at the following three conditions:

1. y1 > y2
2. y1 < y2
3. y1 = y2

The functions y1 and y2 are normalized and converted to integers as follows:

$$y1 = 50\exp(-ax) + 0.5$$
$$y2 = 50\exp(-ax^2/2) + 0.5$$

The program in Fig. 6.15 plots these two functions simultaneously. (0 for y1, * for y2, and # for the common point).

```
Program
    #include <math.h>
    main()
    {
      int i;
      float a, x, y1, y2;
      a = 0.4;
      printf("                        Y ---->                   \n");
      printf(" 0 ---------------------------------------------------\n");
      for ( x = 0; x < 5; x = x+0.25)
      { /* BEGINNING OF FOR LOOP */
```

```
        /*......Evaluation of functions .......*/
          y1 = (int) ( 50 * exp( -a * x ) + 0.5 );
          y2 = (int) ( 50 * exp( -a * x * x/2 ) + 0.5 );
        /*......Plotting when y1 = y2.........*/
          if ( y1 == y2)
          {
            if ( x == 2.5)
               printf(" X   |");
            else
               printf("|");
            for ( i = 1; i <= y1 - 1; ++i)
               printf(" ");
            printf("#\n");
            continue;
          }
        /*...... Plotting when y1 > y2 .....*/
          if ( y1 > y2)
          {
            if ( x == 2.5 )
              printf(" X |");
            else
              printf("    |");
            for ( i = 1; i <= y2 -1 ; ++i)
              printf(" ");
            printf("*");
            for ( i = 1; i <= (y1 - y2 - 1); ++i)
              printf("-");
            printf("0\n");
            continue;
          }
        /*........ Plotting when y2 > y1.........*/
          if ( x == 2.5)
            printf(" X |");
          else
            printf("    |");
          for ( i = 1 ; i <= (y1 - 1); ++i )
            printf(" ");
          printf("0");
          for ( i = 1; i <= ( y2 - y1 - 1 ); ++i)
            printf("-");
          printf("*\n");
        } /*.......END OF FOR LOOP........*/
          printf("    |\n");
      }
```

```
Output
                                  Y ------->
0 -------------------------------------------------------------------------
  |                                                                  #
  |                                                            0 --- *
  |                                                       0------ *
  |                                                  0-------- *
  |                                              0------ *
  |                                         0------ *
  |                                     0---- *
  |                                  0-*
  |                               #
  |                        *-0
X |                   *--- 0
  |               *----- 0
  |           *------0
  |        *-------0
  |      *-------0
  |     *--------0
  |    *-------0
  |  *-------0
  |  *------0
  |  *-----0
  |
```

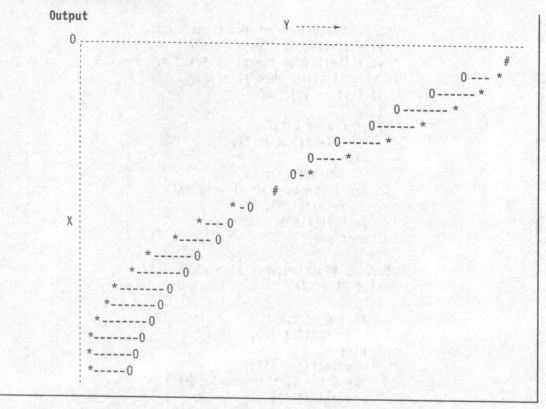

Fig. 6.15 *Plotting of two functions*

REVIEW QUESTIONS

6.1 State whether the following statements are *true* or *false*.

(a) The **do...while** statement first executes the loop body and then evaluate the loop control expression.

(b) In a pretest loop, if the body is executed n times, the test expression is executed n + 1 times.

(c) The number of times a control variable is updated always equals the number of loop iterations.

(d) Both the pretest loops include initialization within the statement.

(e) In a **for** loop expression, the starting value of the control variable must be less than its ending value.

(f) The initialization, test condition and increment parts may be missing in a **for** statement.

(g) **while** loops can be used to replace **for** loops without any change in the body of the loop.

(h) An exit-controlled loop is executed a minimum of one time.

(i) The use of **continue** statement is considered as unstructured programming.

(j) The three loop expressions used in a **for** loop header must be separated by commas.

6.2 Fill in the blanks in the following statements.

(a) In an exit-controlled loop, if the body is executed n times, the test condition is evaluated ________ times.

(b) The ________ statement is used to skip a part of the statements in a loop.

(c) A **for** loop with the no test condition is known as ______ loop.

(d) The sentinel-controlled loop is also known as _______ loop.

(e) In a counter-controlled loop, variable known as _____ is used to count the loop operations.

6.3 Can we change the value of the control variable in **for** statements? If yes, explain its consequences.

6.4 What is a null statement? Explain a typical use of it.

6.5 Use of **goto** should be avoided. Explain a typical example where we find the application of **goto** becomes necessary.

6.6 How would you decide the use of one of the three loops in C for a given problem?

6.7 How can we use **for** loops when the number of iterations are not known?

6.8 Explain the operation of each of the following **for** loops.

(a)
```
for ( n = 1; n != 10; n += 2)
sum = sum + n;
```
(b)
```
for (n = 5; n <= m; n -=1)
sum = sum + n;
```
(c)
```
for (n = 1; n <= 5;)
sum = sum + n;
```
(d)
```
for ( n = 1; ; n = n + 1)
sum = sum + n;
```
(e)
```
for (n = 1; n < 5; n ++)
n = n -1
```

6.9 What would be the output of each of the following code segments?

(a)
```
count = 5;
while (count -- > 0)
printf(count);
```
(b)
```
count = 5;
while ( -- count > 0)
printf(count);
```
(c)
```
count = 5;
do printf(count);
while (count > 0);
```
(d)
```
for (m = 10; m > 7, m -=2)
printf(m);
```

6.10 Compare, in terms of their functions, the following pairs of statements:

(a) while and do...while

(b) while and for

(c) break and goto

(d) break and continue

(e) continue and goto

6.11 Analyse each of the program segments that follow and determine how many times the body of each loop will be executed.

(a)
```
x = 5;
y = 50;
while ( x <= y)
{
    x = y/x;
    ---
    ---
}
```
(b)
```
m = 1;
do
{
    ---
    ---
    m = m+2;
}
while (m < 10);
```
(c)
```
int i;
for (i = 0; i <= 5; i = i+2/3)
{
    ---
    ---
    ---
}
```
(d)
```
int m = 10;
int n = 7;
while ( m % n >= 0)
{
    ---
    m = m + 1;
    n = n + 2;
    ---
}
```

6.12 Find errors, if any, in each of the following looping segments. Assume that all the variables have been declared and assigned values.

(a)
```
while (count != 10);
{
    count = 1;
    sum = sum + x;
    count = count + 1;
}
```
(b)
```
name = 0;
do { name = name + 1;
```

```
    printf("My name is John\n");}
    while (name = 1)
(c) do;
    total = total + value;
    scanf("%f", &value);
    while (value != 999);
(d) for (x = 1, x > 10; x = x + 1)
    {
        ---
        ---
        ---
    }
(e) m = 1;
    n = 0;
    for ( ; m+n < 10; ++n);
    printf("Hello\n");
    m = m+10
(f) for (p = 10; p > 0;)
    p = p - 1;
    printf("%f", p);
```

6.13 Write a **for** statement to print each of the following sequences of integers:

(a) 1, 2, 4, 8, 16, 32

(b) 1, 3, 9, 27, 81, 243

(c) – 4, –2, 0, 2, 4

(d) –10, –12, –14, –18, –26, – 42

6.14 Change the following **for** loops to **while** loops:

```
(a) for (m = 1; m < 10; m = m + 1)
    printf(m);
(b) for ( ; scanf("%d", & m) != -1;)
    printf(m);
```

6.15 Change the **for** loops in Exercise 6.14 to **do** loops.

PROGRAMMING EXERCISES

6.1 Given a number, write a program using **while** loop to reverse the digits of the number. For example, the number

12345

should be written as

54321

(**Hint:** Use modulus operator to extract the last digit and the integer division by 10 to get the n–1 digit number from the n digit number.)

6.2 The factorial of an integer m is the product of consecutive integers from 1 to m. That is,

factorial m = m! = m x (m–1) x ...... x 1.

Write a program that computes and prints a table of factorials for any given m.

6.3 Write a program to compute the sum of the digits of a given integer number.

6.4 The numbers in the sequence

1 1 2 3 5 8 13 21 ....

are called Fibonacci numbers. Write a program using a **do....while** loop to calculate and print the first m Fibonacci numbers.

(**Hint:** After the first two numbers in the series, each number is the sum of the two preceding numbers.)

6.5 Rewrite the program of the Example 6.1 using the **for** statement.

6.6 Write a program to evaluate the following investment equation

$V = P(1+r)^n$

and print the tables which would give the value of V for various combination of the following values of P, r, and n.

P : 1000, 2000, 3000,........, 10,000
r : 0.10, 0.11, 0.12, ..., 0.20
n : 1, 2, 3, ..., 10

(**Hint:** P is the principal amount and V is the value of money at the end of n years. This equation can be recursively written as

$V = P(1+r)$
$P = V$

That is, the value of money at the end of first year becomes the principal amount for the next year and so on.)

6.7 Write programs to print the following outputs using **for** loops.

```
(a) 1              (b) * * * * *
    2 2                 * * * *
    3 3 3                 * * *
    4 4 4 4                 * *
    5 5 5 5 5                 *
```

6.8 Write a program to read the age of 100 persons and count the number of persons in the age group 50 to 60. Use **for** and **continue** statements.

6.9 Rewrite the program of case study 6.4 (plotting of two curves) using **else...if** constructs instead of **continue** statements.

6.10 Write a program to print a table of values of the function

$y = \exp(-x)$

for x varying from 0.0 to 10.0 in steps of 0.10. The table should appear as follows:

Table for Y = EXP(–X)

x	*0.1*	*0.2*	*0.3*	....	*0.9*
0.0					
1.0					
2.0					
3.0					
.					

(Contd.)

x	0.1	0.2	0.3	....	0.9
.					
.					
9.0					

6.11 Write a program that will read a positive integer and determine and print its binary equivalent.
(**Hint:** The bits of the binary representation of an integer can be generated by repeatedly dividing the number and the successive quotients by 2 and saving the remainder, which is either 0 or 1, after each division.)

6.12 Write a program using **for** and **if** statement to display the capital letter S in a grid of 15 rows and 18 columns as shown below.

```
* * * * * * * * * * * * * * * * * *
* * - - - - - - - - - - - - - - - - * *
* * * * * * * * * - - - - - - - - - * *
* * * *
* * * *
* * * *
* * * * - - - - - - - - - - - - * * * *
- - - - - - - - - - - - - - - - - * * * *
- - - - - - - - - - - - - - - - - * * * *
                                  * * * *
                                  * * * *
                                  * * * *
* * * * - - - - - - - - - - - - * * * *
* * * - - - - - - - - - - - - - * * * *
* * - - - - - - - - - - - - - - * * * *
```

6.13 Write a program to compute the value of Euler's number e, that is used as the base of natural logarithms. Use the following formula.

$$e = 1 + 1/1! + 1/2! + 1/3! + \ldots + 1/n!$$

Use a suitable loop construct. The loop must terminate when the difference between two successive values of e is less than 0.00001.

6.14 Write programs to evaluate the following functions to 0.0001% accuracy.

(a) $\sin x = x - x^3/3! + x^5/5! - x^7/7! + \ldots$

(b) $\cos x = 1 - x^2/2! + x^4/4! - x^6/6! + \ldots$

(c) $SUM = 1 + (1/2)^2 + (1/3)^3 + (1/4)^4 + \ldots$

6.15 The present value (popularly known as book value) of an item is given by the relationship.

$$P = c\,(1-d)^n$$

where
c = original cost
d = rate of depreciation (per year)
n = number of years
p = present value after y years.

If P is considered the scrap value at the end of useful life of the item, write a program to compute the useful life in years given the original cost, depreciation rate, and the scrap value. The program should request the user to input the data interactively.

Chapter

7

Arrays

7.1 INTRODUCTION

So far we have used only the fundamental data types, namely **char, int, float, double** and variations of **int** and **double**. Although these types are very useful, they are constrained by the fact that a variable of these types can store only one value at any given time. Therefore, they can be used only to handle limited amounts of data. In many applications, however, we need to handle a large volume of data in terms of reading, processing and printing. To process such large amounts of data, we need a powerful data type that would facilitate efficient storing, accessing and manipulation of data items. C supports a derived data type known as *array* that can be used for such applications.

An array is a *fixed-size* sequenced collection of elements of the same data type. It is simply a grouping of like-type data. In its simplest form, an array can be used to represent a list of numbers, or a list of names. Some examples where the concept of an array can be used:

- List of temperatures recorded every hour in a day, or a month, or a year.
- List of employees in an organization.
- List of products and their cost sold by a store.
- Test scores of a class of students.
- List of customers and their telephone numbers.
- Table of daily rainfall data.

and so on.

Since an array provides a convenient structure for representing data, it is classified as one of the *data structures* in C. Other data structures include structures, lists, queues and trees. A complete discussion of all data structures is beyond the scope of this text. However, we shall consider structures in Chapter 10 and lists in Chapter 13.

As we mentioned earlier, an array is a sequenced collection of related data items that share a common name. For instance, we can use an array name *salary* to represent a *set of salaries* of a group of employees in an organization. We can refer to the individual salaries by writing a number called *index* or *subscript* in brackets after the array name. For example,

```
salary [10]
```

represents the salary of 10th employee. While the complete set of values is referred to as an array, individual values are called *elements*.

The ability to use a single name to represent a collection of items and to refer to an item by specifying the item number enables us to develop concise and efficient programs. For example, we can use a loop construct discussed earlier with the subscript as the control variable to read the entire array, perform calculations, and print out the results.

We can use arrays to represent not only simple lists of values but also tables of data in two or three or more dimensions. In this chapter, we introduce the concept of an array and discuss how to use it to create and apply the following types of arrays.

- One-dimensional arrays
- Two-dimensional arrays
- Multidimensional arrays

Data Structures

C supports a rich set of derived and user-defined data types in addition to a variety of fundamental types as shown below:

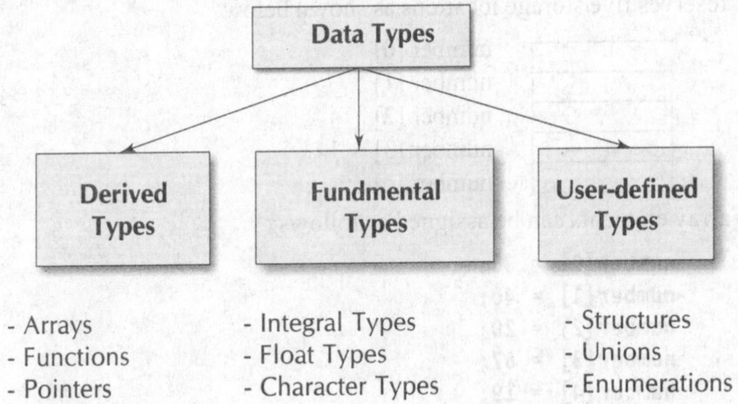

Arrays and structures are referred to as *structured data types* because they can be used to represent data values that have a structure of some sort. Structured data types provide an organizational scheme that shows the relationships among the individual elements and facilitate efficient data manipulations. In programming parlance, such data types are known as *data structures*.

In addition to arrays and structures, C supports creation and manipulation of the following data structures:

- Linked Lists
- Stacks
- Queues
- Trees

7.2 ONE-DIMENSIONAL ARRAYS

A list of items can be given one variable name using only one subscript and such a variable is called a *single-subscripted variable* or a *one-dimensional* array. In mathematics, we often deal with variables that are single-subscripted. For instance, we use the equation.

$$A = \frac{\sum_{i=1}^{n} x_i}{n}$$

to calculate the average of n values of x. The subscripted variable x_i refers to the ith element of x. In C, single-subscripted variable x_i can be expressed as

x[1], x[2], x[3],.........x[n]

The subscript can begin with number 0. That is

x[0]

is allowed. For example, if we want to represent a set of five numbers, say (35,40,20,57,19), by an array variable **number**, then we may declare the variable **number** as follows

```
int number[5];
```

and the computer reserves five storage locations as shown below:

	number [0]
	number [1]
	number [2]
	number [3]
	number [4]

The values to the array elements can be assigned as follows:

```
number[0] = 35;
number[1] = 40;
number[2] = 20;
number[3] = 57;
number[4] = 19;
```

This would cause the array **number** to store the values as shown below:

number [0]	35
number [1]	40
number [2]	20
number [3]	57
number [4]	19

These elements may be used in programs just like any other C variable. For example, the following are valid statements:

```
a = number[0] + 10;
number[4] = number[0] + number [2];
number[2] = x[5] + y[10];
value[6] = number[i] * 3;
```

The subscripts of an array can be integer constants, integer variables like i, or expressions that yield integers. *C performs no bounds checking and, therefore, care should be exercised to ensure that the array indices are within the declared limits.*

7.3 DECLARATION OF ONE-DIMENSIONAL ARRAYS

Like any other variable, arrays must be declared before they are used. The general form of array declaration is

type *variable-name[* size*];*

The *type* specifies the type of element that will be contained in the array, such as **int, float,** or **char** and the *size* indicates the maximum number of elements that can be stored inside the array. For example,

```
float height[50];
```

declares the **height** to be an array containing 50 real elements. Any subscripts 0 to 49 are valid. Similarly,

```
int group[10];
```

declares the **group** as an array to contain a maximum of 10 integer constants. Remember:

- Any reference to the arrays outside the declared limits would not necessarily cause an error. Rather, it might result in unpredictable program results.
- The size should be either a numeric constant or a symbolic constant.

The C language treats character strings, simply as arrays of characters. The *size* in a character string represents the maximum number of characters that the string can hold. For instance,

```
char name[10];
```

declares the **name** as a character array (string) variable that can hold a maximum of 10 characters. Suppose we read the following string constant into the string variable **name.**

"WELL DONE"

Each character of the string is treated as an element of the array **name** and is stored in the memory as follows:

'W'
'E'
'L'
'L'
' '
'D'
'O'
'N'
'E'
'\0'

When the compiler sees a character string, it terminates it with an additional null character. Thus, the element **name[10]** holds the null character '\0'. *When declaring character arrays, we must allow one extra element space for the null terminator.*

Example 7.1 Write a program using a single-subscripted variable to evaluate the following expressions:

$$\text{Total} = \sum_{i=1}^{10} x_i^2$$

The values of x1,x2,....are read from the terminal.

Program in Fig. 7.1 uses a one-dimensional array **x** to read the values and compute the sum of their squares.

```
Program
    main()
    {
        int i ;
        float x[10], value, total ;
    /*. . . . . .READING VALUES INTO ARRAY . . . . . . */
        printf("ENTER 10 REAL NUMBERS\n") ;
        for( i = 0 ; i < 10 ; i++ )
        {
            scanf("%f", &value) ;
            x[i] = value ;
        }
    /* . . . . . . .COMPUTATION OF TOTAL . . . . . . .*/
        total = 0.0 ;
        for( i = 0 ; i < 10 ; i++ )
            total = total + x[i] * x[i] ;

    /*. . . . PRINTING OF x[i] VALUES AND TOTAL . . . */

        printf("\n");
        for( i = 0 ; i < 10 ; i++ )
            printf("x[%2d] = %5.2f\n", i+1, x[i]) ;

        printf("\ntotal = %.2f\n", total) ;
    }
```

Output

```
ENTER 10 REAL NUMBERS
1.1 2.2 3.3 4.4 5.5 6.6 7.7 8.8 9.9 10.10

x[ 1] = 1.10
x[ 2] = 2.20
x[ 3] = 3.30
x[ 4] = 4.40
x[ 5] = 5.50
x[ 6] = 6.60
x[ 7] = 7.70
x[ 8] = 8.80
x[ 9] = 9.90
x[10] = 10.10

Total = 446.86
```

Fig. 7.1 *Program to illustrate **one-dimensional array***

7.4 INITIALIZATION OF ONE-DIMENSIONAL ARRAYS

After an array is declared, its elements must be initialized. Otherwise, they will contain "garbage". An array can be initialized at either of the following stages

- At compile time
- At run time

Compile Time Initialization

We can initialize the elements of arrays in the same way as the ordinary variables when they are declared. The general form of initialization of arrays is:

type array-name[size] = { list of values };

The values in the list are separated by commas. For example, the statement

```
int number[3] = { 0,0,0 };
```

will declare the variable **number** as an array of size 3 and will assign zero to each element. If the number of values in the list is less than the number of elements, then only that many elements will be initialized. The remaining elements will be set to zero automatically. For instance,

```
float total[5] = {0.0,15.75,-10};
```

will initialize the first three elements to 0.0, 15.75, and –10.0 and the remaining two elements to zero.

The *size* may be omitted. In such cases, the compiler allocates enough space for all initialized elements. For example, the statement

```
int counter[ ] = {1,1,1,1};
```

will declare the **counter** array to contain four elements with initial values 1. This approach works fine as long as we initialize every element in the array.

Character arrays may be initialized in a similar manner. Thus, the statement

```
char name[ ] = {'J','o', 'h', 'n', '\0'};
```

declares the **name** to be an array of five characters, initialized with the string "John" ending with the null character. Alternatively, we can assign the string literal directly as under:

```
char name [ ] = "John";
```

(Character arrays and strings are discussed in detail in Chapter 8.)

Compile time initialization may be partial. That is, the number of initializers may be less than the declared size. In such cases, the remaining elements are inilialized to *zero*, if the array type is numeric and *NULL* if the type is char. For example,

```
int number [5] = {10, 20};
```

will initialize the first two elements to 10 and 20 respectively, and the remaining elements to 0. Similarly, the declaration.

```
char city [5] = {'B'};
```

will initialize the first element to 'B' and the remaining four to NULL. It is a good idea, however, to declare the size explicitly, as it allows the compiler to do some error checking.

Remember, however, if we have more initializers than the declared size, the compiler will produce an error. That is, the statement

```
int number [3] = {10, 20, 30, 40};
```

will not work. It is illegal in C.

Run Time Initialization

An array can be explicitly initialized at run time. This approach is usually applied for initializing large arrays For example; consider the following segment of a C program.

```
--------
--------
for (i = 0; i < 100; i = i+1)
{
    if   i < 50
        sum[i] = 0.0;               /*assignment statement */
    else
        sum[i] = 1.0;
}
--------
--------
```

The first 50 elements of the array **sum** are initialized to zero while the remaining 50 elements are initialized to 1.0 at run time.

We can also use a read function such as **scanf** to initialize an array. For example, the statements

```
int x [3];
scanf("%d%d%d", &x[0], &[1], &x[2]);
```

will initialize array elements with the values entered through the keyboard.

Example 7.2 Given below is the list of marks obtained by a class of 50 students in an annual examination.

43 65 51 27 79 11 56 61 82 09 25 36 07 49 55 63 74 81 49 37
40 49 16 75 87 91 33 24 58 78 65 56 76 67 45 54 36 63 12 21
73 49 51 19 39 49 68 93 85 59

Write a program to count the number of students belonging to each of following groups of marks: 0-9, 10-19, 20-29,.....,100.

The program coded in Fig. 7.2 uses the array **group** containing 11 elements, one for each range of marks. Each element counts those values falling within the range of values it represents.

For any value, we can determine the correct group element by dividing the value by 10. For example, consider the value 59. The integer division of 59 by 10 yields 5. This is the element into which 59 is counted.

```
Program
  #define  MAXVAL   50
  #define  COUNTER  11
  main()
  {
      float       value[MAXVAL];
      int         i, low, high;
      int  group[COUNTER] = {0,0,0,0,0,0,0,0,0,0,0};
      /* . . . . . . . .READING AND COUNTING . . . . . .*/
      for( i = 0 ; i < MAXVAL ; i++)
      {
      /*. . . . . . . . .READING OF VALUES . . . . . . . . . */
        scanf("%f", &value[i]) ;
      /*. . . . . . .COUNTING FREQUENCY OF GROUPS. . . . . */
        ++ group[ (int) ( value[i]) / 10] ;
      }
      /* . . . .PRINTING OF FREQUENCY TABLE . . . . . . .*/
      printf("\n");
      printf(" GROUP     RANGE     FREQUENCY\n\n") ;
      for( i = 0 ; i< COUNTER ; i++ )
      {
          low = i * 10 ;
          if(i == 10)
            high = 100 ;
          else
```

```
                high = low + 9 ;
                printf(" %2d %3d to %3d %d\n",
                        i+1, low, high, group[i] ) ;
        }
    }
```

```
Output
    43 65 51 27 79 11 56 61 82 09 25 36 07 49 55 63 74
    81 49 37 40 49 16 75 87 91 33 24 58 78 65 56 76 67 (Input data)
    45 54 36 63 12 21 73 49 51 19 39 49 68 93 85 59
     GROUP              RANGE              FREQUENCY
       1              0   to   9              2
       2             10   to  19              4
       3             20   to  29              4
       4             30   to  39              5
       5             40   to  49              8
       6             50   to  59              8
       7             60   to  69              7
       8             70   to  79              6
       9             80   to  89              4
      10             90   to  99              2
      11            100   to  100             0
```

Fig. 7.2 *Program for frequency counting*

Note that we have used an initialization statement.

```
int group [COUNTER] = {0,0,0,0,0,0,0,0,0,0,0};
```

which can be replaced by

```
int group [COUNTER] = {0};
```

This will initialize all the elements to zero.

Searching and Sorting

Searching and sorting are the two most frequent operations performed on arrays. Computer Scientists have devised several data structures and searching and sorting techniques that facilitate rapid access to data stored in lists.

Sorting is the process of arranging elements in the list according to their values, in ascending or descending order. A sorted list is called an *ordered list*. Sorted lists are especially important in list searching because they facilitate rapid search operations. Many sorting techniques are available. The three simple and most important among them are:

- Bubble sort
- Selection sort
- Insertion sort

Other sorting techniques include Shell sort, Merge sort and Quick sort.

Searching is the process of finding the location of the specified element in a list. The specified element is often called the *search key*. If the process of searching finds a match of the search key with a list element value, the search said to be successful; otherwise, it is unsuccessful. The two most commonly used search techniques are:

- Sequential search
- Binary search

A detailed discussion on these techniques is beyond the scope of this text. Consult any good book on data structures and algorithms.

7.5 TWO-DIMENSIONAL ARRAYS

So far we have discussed the array variables that can store a list of values. There could be situations where a table of values will have to be stored. Consider the following data table, which shows the value of sales of three items by four sales girls:

	Item1	*Item2*	*Item3*
Salesgirl #1	310	275	365
Salesgirl #2	210	190	325
Salesgirl #3	405	235	240
Salesgirl #4	260	300	380

The table contains a total of 12 values, three in each line. We can think of this table as a matrix consisting of four *rows* and three *columns*. Each row represents the values of sales by a particular salesgirl and each column represents the values of sales of a particular item.

In mathematics, we represent a particular value in a matrix by using two subscripts such as $\mathbf{v}_{ij}$. Here **v** denotes the entire matrix and $\mathbf{v}_{ij}$ refers to the value in the ith row and j^{th} column. For example, in the above table v_{23} refers to the value 325.

C allows us to define such tables of items by using two-dimensional arrays. The table discussed above can be defined in C as

v[4][3]

Two-dimensional arrays are declared as follows:

type array_name **[row_size][column_size];**

Note that unlike most other languages, which use one pair of parentheses with commas to separate array sizes, C places each size in its own set of brackets.

Two-dimensional arrays are stored in memory as shown in Fig.7.3. As with the single-dimensional arrays, each dimension of the array is indexed from zero to its maximum size minus one; the first index selects the row and the second index selects the column within that row.

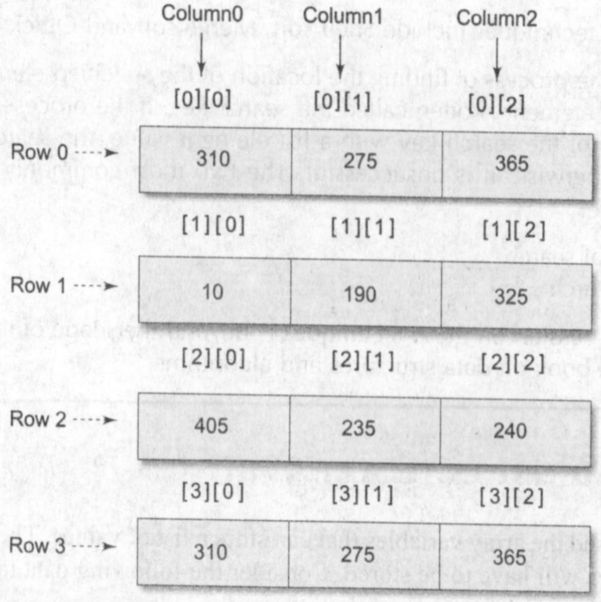

Fig. 7.3 *Representation of a* ***two-dimensional*** *array in memory*

Example 7.3 Write a program using a two-dimensional array to compute and print the following information from the table of data discussed above:
(a) Total value of sales by each girl.
(b) Total value of each item sold.
(c) Grand total of sales of all items by all girls.

The program and its output are shown in Fig. 7.4. The program uses the variable **value** in two-dimensions with the index i representing girls and j representing items. The following equations are used in computing the results:

(a) Total sales by m^{th} girl $= \sum_{j=0}^{2} \text{value}[m][j]$ (girl_total[m])

(b) Total value of nth item $= \sum_{i=0}^{3} \text{value}[i][n]$ (item_total[n])

(c) Grand total $= \sum_{i=0}^{3} \sum_{j=0}^{2} \text{value}[i][j]$

$= \sum_{i=0}^{3} \text{girl\_total}[i]$

$= \sum_{j=0}^{2} \text{item\_total}[j]$

Program

```
#define  MAXGIRLS 4
#define  MAXITEMS 3
main()
{
    int  value[MAXGIRLS][MAXITEMS];
    int  girl_total[MAXGIRLS] , item_total[MAXITEMS];
    int  i, j, grand_total;
/*.......READING OF VALUES AND COMPUTING girl_total ...*/

    printf("Input data\n");
    printf("Enter values, one at a time, row-wise\n\n");

    for( i = 0 ; i < MAXGIRLS ; i++ )
    {
        girl_total[i] = 0;
        for( j = 0 ; j < MAXITEMS ; j++ )
        {
            scanf("%d", &value[i][j]);
            girl_total[i] = girl_total[i] + value[i][j];
        }
    }
/*.......COMPUTING item_total..........................*/

    for( j = 0 ; j < MAXITEMS ; j++ )
    {
        item_total[j] = 0;
        for( i =0 ; i < MAXGIRLS ; i++ )
            item_total[j] = item_total[j] + value[i][j];
    }
/*.......COMPUTING grand_total.........................*/

    grand_total = 0;
    for( i =0 ; i < MAXGIRLS ; i++ )
      grand_total = grand_total + girl_total[i];
/* .......PRINTING OF RESULTS...........................*/

    printf("\n GIRLS TOTALS\n\n");
    for( i = 0 ; i < MAXGIRLS ; i++ )
        printf("Salesgirl[%d] = %d\n", i+1, girl_total[i] );
    printf("\n ITEM TOTALS\n\n");
    for( j = 0 ; j < MAXITEMS ; j++ )
        printf("Item[%d] = %d\n", j+1 , item_total[j] );
    printf("\nGrand Total = %d\n", grand_total);
}
```

```
Output
   Input data
   Enter values, one at a time, row_wise

   310 257 365
   210 190 325
   405 235 240
   260 300 380

   GIRLS TOTALS

   Salesgirl[1]  = 950
   Salesgirl[2]  = 725
   Salesgirl[3]  = 880
   Salesgirl[4]  = 940

   ITEM TOTALS

   Item[1]  = 1185
   Item[2]  = 1000
   Item[3]  = 1310

   Grand Total = 3495
```

Fig. 7.4 *Illustration of two-dimensional arrays*

Example 7.4 Write a program to compute and print a multiplication table for numbers 1 to 5 as shown below:

	1	2	3	4	5
1	1	2	3	4	5
2	2	4	6	8	10
3	3	6	.	.	.
4	4	8	.	.	.
5	5	10	.	.	25

The program shown in Fig. 7.5 uses a two-dimensional array to store the table values. Each value is calculated using the control variables of the nested for loops as follows:

product[i] [j] = row * column

where i denotes rows and j denotes columns of the product table. Since the indices i and j range from 0 to 4, we have introduced the following transformation:

row = i+1
column = j+1

```
Program
   #define  ROWS      5
   #define  COLUMNS   5
   main()
```

```
{
        int row, column, product[ROWS][COLUMNS] ;
        int i, j ;
        printf(" MULTIPLICATION TABLE\n\n") ;
        printf(" ") ;
        for( j = 1 ; j <= COLUMNS ; j++ )
          printf("%4d" , j ) ;
        printf("\n") ;
        printf("-------------------------------------------\n");
        for( i = 0 ; i < ROWS ; i++ )
        {
            row = i + 1 ;
            printf("%2d |", row) ;
            for( j = 1 ; j <= COLUMNS ; j++ )
            {
              column = j ;
              product[i][j] = row * column ;
              printf("%4d", product[i][j] ) ;
            }
            printf("\n") ;
        }
}
```

Output

```
    MULTIPLICATION TABLE
      1   2   3   4   5
    ---------------------
 1 |  1   2   3   4   5
 2 |  2   4   6   8  10
 3 |  3   6   9  12  15
 4 |  4   8  12  16  20
 5 |  5  10  15  20  25
```

Fig. 7.5 *Program to print multiplication table using two-dimensional array*

7.6 INITIALIZING TWO-DIMENSIONAL ARRAYS

Like the one-dimensional arrays, two-dimensional arrays may be initialized by following their declaration with a list of initial values enclosed in braces. For example,

```
int table[2][3] = { 0,0,0,1,1,1};
```

initializes the elements of the first row to zero and the second row to one. The initialization is done row by row. The above statement can be equivalently written as

```
int table[2][3] = {{0,0,0}, {1,1,1}};
```

by surrounding the elements of the each row by braces.

We can also initialize a two-dimensional array in the form of a matrix as shown below:

```
int table[2][3] = {
                  {0,0,0},
                  {1,1,1}
                 };
```

Note the syntax of the above statements. Commas are required after each brace that closes off a row, except in the case of the last row.

When the array is completely initialized with all values, explicitly, we need not specify the size of the first dimension. That is, the statement

```
int table [ ] [3] = {
                    { 0, 0, 0},
                    { 1, 1, 1}
                   };
```

is permitted

If the values are missing in an initializer, they are automatically set to zero. For instance, the statement

```
int table[2][3] = {
                  {1,1},
                  {2}
                 };
```

will initialize the first two elements of the first row to one, the first element of the second row to two, and all other elements to zero.

When all the elements are to be initialized to zero, the following short-cut method may be used.

```
int m[3][5] = { {0}, {0}, {0}};
```

The first element of each row is explicitly initialized to zero while other elements are automatically initialized to zero. The following statement will also achieve the same result:

```
int m [3] [5] = { 0, 0};
```

Example 7.5 A survey to know the popularity of four cars (Ambassador, Fiat, Dolphin and Maruti) was conducted in four cities (Bombay, Calcutta, Delhi and Madras). Each person surveyed was asked to give his city and the type of car he was using. The results, in coded form, are tabulated as follows:

M	1	C	2	B	1	D	3	M	2	B	4
C	1	D	3	M	4	B	2	D	1	C	3
D	4	D	4	M	1	M	1	B	3	B	3
C	1	C	1	C	2	M	4	M	4	C	2
D	1	C	2	B	3	M	1	B	1	C	2
D	3	M	4	C	1	D	2	M	3	B	4

Codes represent the following information:

M – Madras	1 – Ambassador
D – Delhi	2 – Fiat
C – Calcutta	3 – Dolphin
B – Bombay	4 – Maruti

Write a program to produce a table showing popularity of various cars in four cities.

A two-dimensional array **frequency** is used as an accumulator to store the number of cars used, under various categories in each city. For example, the element **frequency** [i][j] denotes the number of cars of type j used in city i. The **frequency** is declared as an array of size 5 × 5 and all the elements are initialized to zero.

The program shown in Fig. 7.6 reads the city code and the car code, one set after another, from the terminal. Tabulation ends when the letter X is read in place of a city code.

Program

```
main()
{
   int i, j, car;
   int frequency[5][5] = { {0},{0},{0},{0},{0} };
   char city;
   printf("For each person, enter the city code \n");
   printf("followed by the car code.\n");
   printf("Enter the letter X to indicate end.\n");
  /*. . . . . . TABULATION BEGINS . . . . . */
   for( i = 1 ; i < 100 ; i++ )
   {
     scanf("%c", &city );
     if( city == 'X' )
        break;
     scanf("%d", &car );
     switch(city)
     {
            case 'B' :  frequency[1][car]++;
                        break;
            case 'C' :  frequency[2][car]++;
                        break;
            case 'D' :  frequency[3][car]++;
                        break;
            case 'M' :  frequency[4][car]++;
                        break;
     }
   }
 /*. . . . .TABULATION COMPLETED AND PRINTING BEGINS. . . .*/
   printf("\n\n");
   printf(" POPULARITY TABLE\n\n");
   printf("___________________________________\n");
   printf("City Ambassador Fiat Dolphin Maruti \n");
   printf("___________________________________\n");
   for( i = 1 ; i <= 4 ; i++ )
   {
       switch(i)
       {
             case 1 : printf("Bombay   ") ;
```

```
                    break ;
            case 2 : printf("Calcutta ") ;
                    break ;
            case 3 : printf("Delhi    ") ;
                    break ;
            case 4 : printf("Madras   ") ;
                    break ;
        }
        for( j = 1 ; j <= 4 ; j++ )
           printf("%7d", frequency[i][j] ) ;
        printf("\n") ;
    }
    printf("————————————————————————————————\n");
 /*. . . . . . . . . . PRINTING ENDS. . . . . . . . . . . .*/
}
```

Output

```
For each person, enter the city code
followed by the car code.
Enter the letter X to indicate end.
M 1  C 2  B 1  D 3  M 2  B 4
C 1  D 3  M 4  B 2  D 1  C 3
D 4  D 4  M 1  M 1  B 3  B 3
C 1  C 1  C 2  M 4  M 4  C 2
D 1  C 2  B 3  M 1  B 1  C 2
D 3  M 4  C 1  D 2  M 3  B 4    X
```

POPULARITY TABLE

City	Ambassador	Fiat	Dolphin	Maruti
Bombay	2	1	3	2
Calcutta	4	5	1	0
Delhi	2	1	3	2
Madras	4	1	1	4

Fig. 7.6 *Program to tabulate a survey data*

Memory Layout

The subscripts in the definition of a two-dimensional array represent rows and columns. This format maps the way that data elements are laid out in the memory. The elements of all arrays are stored contiguously in increasing memory locations, essentially in a single list. If we consider the memory as a row of bytes, with the lowest address on the left and the highest address on the right, a simple array will be stored in memory with the first element at the left end and the last element at the right end. Similarly, a two-dimensional array is stored "row-wise, starting from the first row and ending with the last row, treating each row like a simple array. This is illustrated below.

Column

		0	1	2
	0	10	20	30
row	1	40	50	60
	2	70	80	90

3 × 3 array

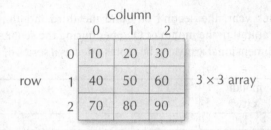

row 0			row 1			row 2		
10	20	30	40	50	60	70	80	90
[0][0]	[0][1]	[0][2]	[1][0]	[1][1]	[1][2]	[2][0]	[2][1]	[2][2]
1	2	3	4	5	6	7	8	9

Memory Layout

For a multidimensional array, the order of storage is that the first element stored has 0 in all its subscripts, the second has all of its subscripts 0 except the far right which has a value of 1 and so on.

The elements of a 2 x 3 x 3 array will be stored as under

1	2	3	4	5	6	7	8	9
000	001	002	010	011	012	020	021	022

..

10	11	12	13	14	15	16	17	18
100	101	102	110	111	112	120	121	122

The far right subscript increments first and the other subscripts increment in order from right to left. The sequence numbers 1, 2,......, 18 represents the location of that element in the list

7.7 MULTI-DIMENSIONAL ARRAYS

C allows arrays of three or more dimensions. The exact limit is determined by the compiler. The general form of a multi-dimensional array is

```
type array_name[s1][s2][s3]....[sm];
```

where s_i is the size of the ith dimension. Some example are:

```
int survey[3][5][12];
float table[5][4][5][3];
```

survey is a three-dimensional array declared to contain 180 integer type elements. Similarly **table** is a four-dimensional array containing 300 elements of floating-point type.

The array **survey** may represent a survey data of rainfall during the last three years from January to December in five cities.

If the first index denotes year, the second city and the third month, then the element **survey[2][3][10]** denotes the rainfall in the month of October during the second year in city-3.

Remember that a three-dimensional array can be represented as a series of two-dimensional arrays as shown below:

Year 1

month city	1	2	....	12
1				
. . . 5				

Year 2

month city	1	2	....	12
1				
. . . 5				

ANSI C does not specify any limit for array dimension. However, most compilers permit seven to ten dimensions. Some allow even more.

7.8 DYNAMIC ARRAYS

So far, we created arrays at compile time. An array created at compile time by specifying size in the source code has a fixed size and cannot be modified at run time. The process of allocating memory at compile time is known as *static memory allocation* and the arrays that receive static memory allocation are called *static arrays*. This approach works fine as long as we know exactly what our data requirements are.

Consider a situation where we want to use an array that can vary greatly in size. We must guess what will be the largest size ever needed and create the array accordingly. A difficult task in fact! Modern languages like C do not have this limitation. In C it is possible to allocate memory to arrays at run time. This feature is known as *dynamic memory allocation* and the arrays created at run time are called *dynamic* arrays. This effectively postpones the array definition to run time.

Dynamic arrays are created using what are known as *pointer variables* and *memory management functions* **malloc**, **calloc** and **realloc**. These functions are included in the header file **<stdlib.h>.** The concept of dynamic arrays is used in creating and manipulating data structures such as linked lists, stacks and queues. We discuss in detail pointers and pointer variables in Chapter 11 and creating and managing linked lists in Chapter 13.

7.9 MORE ABOUT ARRAYS

What we have discussed in this chapter are the basic concepts of arrays and their applications to a limited extent. There are some more important aspects of application of arrays. They include:

- Using printers for accessing arrays
- Passing arrays as function parameters
- Arrays as members of structures
- Using structure type data as array elements
- Arrays as dynamic data structures
- Manipulating character arrays and strings

These aspects of arrays are covered later in the following chapters:

Chapter 8 : Strings

Chapter 9 : Functions

Chapter 10 : Structures

Chapter 11 : Pointers

Chapter 13 : Linked Lists

Just Remember

- We need to specify three things, namely, name, type and size, when we declare an array.
- Always remember that subscripts begin at 0 (not 1) and end at size –1.
- Defining the size of an array as a symbolic constant makes a program more scalable.
- Be aware of the difference between the "kth element" and the "element k". The kth element has a subscript k-1, whereas the element k has a subscript of k itself.
- Do not forget to initialize the elements; otherwise they will contain "garbage".
- Supplying more initializers in the initializer list is a compile time error.
- Use of invalid subscript is one of the common errors. An incorrect or invalid index may cause unexpected results.
- When using expressions for subscripts, make sure that their results do not go outside the permissible range of 0 to size –1. Referring to an element outside the array bounds is an error.
- When using control structures for looping through an array, use proper relational expressions to eliminate "off-by-one" errors. For example, for an array of size 5, the following **for** statements are wrong:

```
for (i = 1; i < =5; i+ +)
for (i = 0; i < =5; i+ +)
for (i = 0; i = =5; i+ +)
for (i = 0; i < 4;  i+ +)
```

- Referring a two-dimensional array element like x[i,j] instead of x[i][j] is a compile time error.
- When initializing character arrays, provide enough space for the terminating null character.

- Make sure that the subscript variables have been properly initialized before they are used.
- Leaving out the subscript reference operator [ ] in an assignment operation is compile time error.
- During initialization of multidimensional arrays, it is an error to omit the array size for any dimension other than the first.

CASE STUDIES

7.1 Median of a List of Numbers

When all the items in a list are arranged in order, the middle value which divides the items into two parts with equal number of items on either side is called the *median*. Odd number of items have just one middle value while even number of items have two middle values. The median for even number of items is therefore designated as the average of the two middle values.

The major steps for finding the median are as follows:

1. Read the items into an array while keeping a count of the items.
2. Sort the items in increasing order.
3. Compute median.

The program and sample output are shown in Fig. 7.7. The sorting algorithm used is as follows:

1. Compare the first two elements in the list, say a[1], and a[2]. If a[2] is smaller than a[1], then interchange their values.
2. Compare a[2] and a[3]; interchange them if a[3] is smaller than a[2].
3. Continue this process till the last two elements are compared and interchanged.
4. Repeat the above steps n–1 times.

In repeated trips through the array, the smallest elements 'bubble up' to the top. Because of this bubbling up effect, this algorithm is called *bubble sorting*. The bubbling effect is illustrated below for four items.

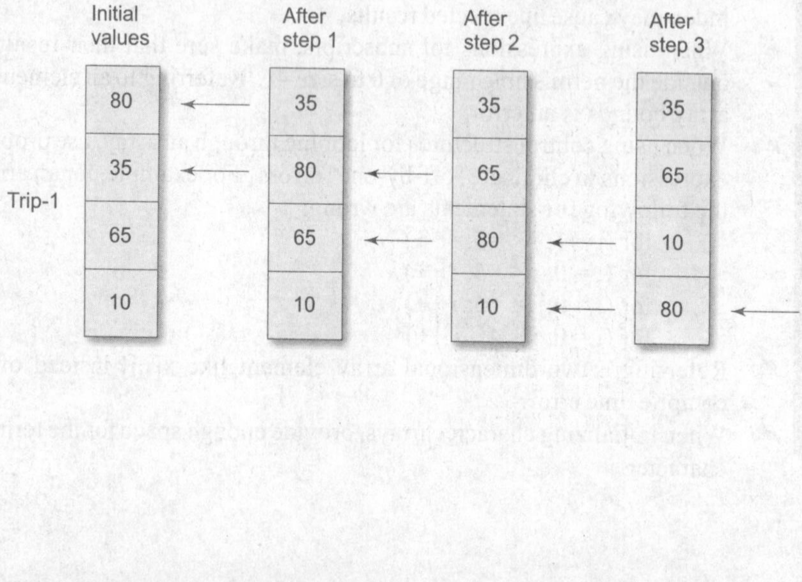

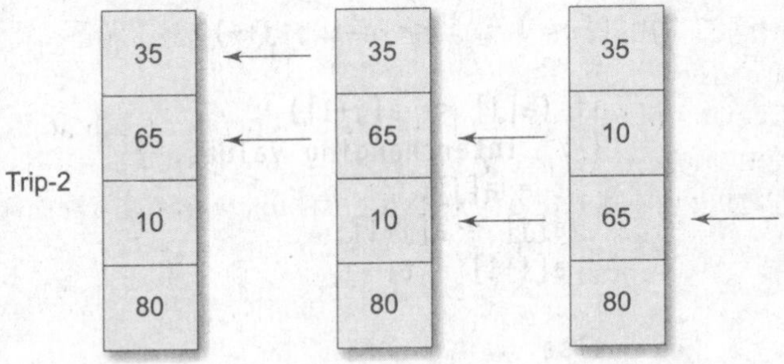

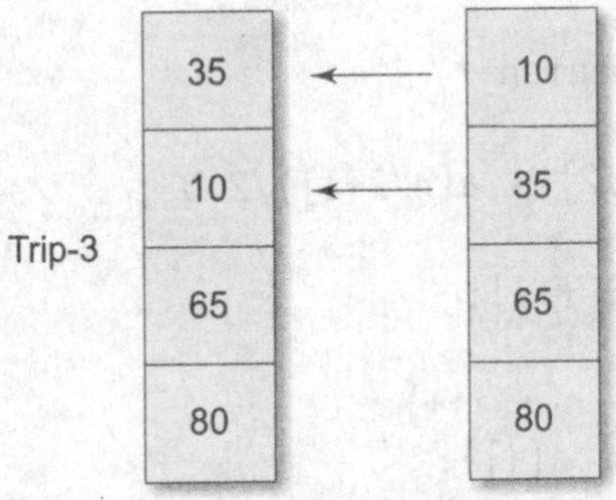

During the first trip, three pairs of items are compared and interchanged whenever needed. It should be noted that the number 80, the largest among the items, has been moved to the bottom at the end of the first trip. This means that the element 80 (the last item in the new list) need not be considered any further. Therefore, trip-2 requires only two pairs to be compared. This time, the number 65 (the second largest value) has been moved down the list. Notice that each trip brings the smallest value 10 up by one level.

The number of steps required in a trip is reduced by one for each trip made. The entire process will be over when a trip contains only one step. If the list contains n elements, then the number of comparisons involved would be n(n–1)/2.

Program

```
#define N 10
main( )
{
   int i,j,n;
   float median,a[N],t;
   printf("Enter the number of items\n");
   scanf("%d", &n);
/* Reading items into array a */
   printf("Input %d values \n",n);
   for (i = 1; i <= n ;  i++)
      scanf("%f", &a[i]);
/* Sorting begins */
   for (i = 1 ; i <= n-1 ; i++)
   {    /* Trip-i begins */
```

```
            for (j = 1 ; j <= n-i ; j++)
            {
                if (a[j] <= a[j+1])
                { /* Interchanging values */
                  t = a[j];
                  a[j] = a[j+1];
                  a[j+1] = t;
                }
                else
                  continue ;
            }
          } /* sorting ends */
        /* calculation of median */
          if ( n % 2 == 0)
             median = (a[n/2] + a[n/2+1])/2.0 ;
          else
             median = a[n/2 + 1];
        /* Printing */
          for (i = 1 ; i <= n ; i++)
               printf("%f ", a[i]);
          printf("\n\nMedian is %f\n", median);
        }
```

Output

```
Enter the number of items
5
Input 5 values
1.111 2.222 3.333 4.444 5.555
5.555000 4.444000 3.333000 2.222000 1.111000
Median is 3.333000
Enter the number of items
6
Input 6 values
3 5 8 9 4 6
9.000000 8.000000 6.000000 5.000000 4.000000 3.000000

Median is 5.500000
```

Fig. 7.7 *Program to sort a list of numbers and to determine median*

2. Calculation of Standard Deviation

In statistics, standard deviation is used to measure deviation of data from its mean. The formula for calculating standard deviation of n items is

$$s = \sqrt{\text{variance}}$$

where

$$\text{variance} = \frac{1}{n}\sum_{i=1}^{n}(x_i - m)^2$$

and

$$m = \text{mean} = \frac{1}{n}\sum_{i=1}^{n} x_i$$

The algorithm for calculating the standard deviation is as follows:

1. Read n items.
2. Calculate sum and mean of the items.
3. Calculate variance.
4. Calculate standard deviation.

Complete program with sample output is shown in Fig. 7.8.

Program

```
#include <math.h>
#define MAXSIZE 100
main( )
{
    int i,n;
    float value [MAXSIZE], deviation,
          sum,sumsqr,mean,variance,stddeviation;
    sum = sumsqr = n = 0 ;
    printf("Input values: input -1 to end \n");
    for (i=1; i< MAXSIZE ; i++)
    {
      scanf("%f", &value[i]);
      if (value[i] == -1)
        break;
      sum += value[i];
      n += 1;
    }
    mean = sum/(float)n;
    for (i = 1 ; i<= n; i++)
    {
      deviation = value[i] - mean;
      sumsqr += deviation * deviation;
    }
    variance = sumsqr/(float)n ;
    stddeviation = sqrt(variance) ;
    printf("\nNumber of items : %d\n",n);
```

```
        printf("Mean : %f\n", mean);
        printf("Standard deviation : %f\n", stddeviation);
    }
Output
    Input values: input -1 to end
    65 9 27 78 12 20 33 49 -1

    Number of items : 8
    Mean : 36.625000
    Standard deviation : 23.510303
```

Fig. 7.8 *Program to calculate standard deviation*

3. Evaluating a Test

A test consisting of 25 multiple-choice items is administered to a batch of 3 students. Correct answers and student responses are tabulated as shown below:

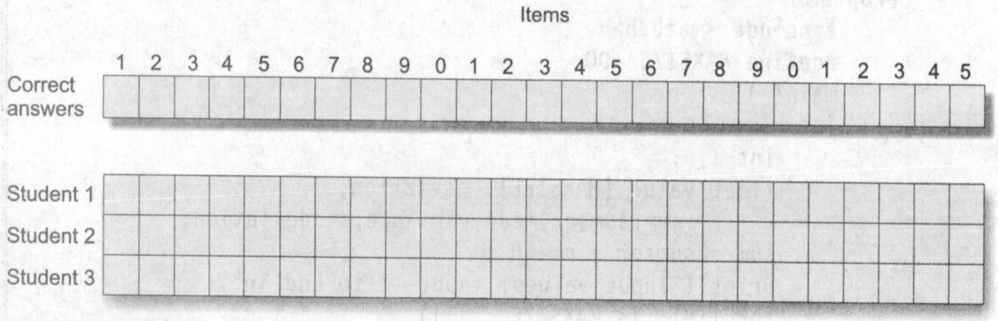

The algorithm for evaluating the answers of students is as follows:

1. Read correct answers into an array.
2. Read the responses of a student and count the correct ones.
3. Repeat step-2 for each student.
4. Print the results.

A program to implement this algorithm is given in Fig. 7.9. The program uses the following arrays:

key[i] - To store correct answers of items

response[i] - To store responses of students

correct[i] - To identify items that are answered correctly.

```
Program
    #define STUDENTS 3
    #define ITEMS    25
    main( )
    {
```

```
    char key[ITEMS+1],response[ITEMS+1];
    int count, i, student,n,
        correct[ITEMS+1];
  /*Reading of Correct answers */
    printf("Input key to the items\n");
    for(i=0; i < ITEMS; i++)
      scanf("%c",&key[i]);
    scanf("%c",&key[i]);
    key[i] = '\0';
  /*Evaluation begins */
    for(student = 1; student <= STUDENTS ; student++)
    {
  /*Reading student responses and counting correct ones*/
      count = 0;
      printf("\n");
      printf("Input responses of student-%d\n",student);
      for(i=0; i < ITEMS ; i++)
        scanf("%c",&response[i]);
      scanf("%c",&response[i]);
      response[i] = '\0';
      for(i=0; i < ITEMS; i++)
        correct[i] = 0;
      for(i=0; i < ITEMS ; i++)
        if(response[i] == key[i])
        {
          count = count +1 ;
          correct[i] = 1 ;
        }
      /* printing of results */
      printf("\n");
      printf("Student-%d\n", student);
      printf("Score is %d out of %d\n",count, ITEMS);
      printf("Response to the items below are wrong\n");
      n = 0;
      for(i=0; i < ITEMS ; i++)
        if(correct[i] == 0)
        {
            printf("%d ",i+1);
            n = n+1;
        }
      if(n == 0)
        printf("NIL\n");
      printf("\n");
      } /* Go to next student */
```

```
        /* Evaluation and printing ends */
        }
Output
        Input key to the items
        abcdabcdabcdabcdabcdabcda

        Input responses of student-1
        abcdabcdabcdabcdabcdabcda

        Student-1
        Score is 25 out of 25
        Response to the following items are wrong
        NIL

        Input responses of student-2
        abcddcbaabcdabcdddddddddd

        Student-2
        Score is 14 out of 25
        Response to the following items are wrong
        5 6 7 8 17 18 19 21 22 23 25

        Input responses of student-3
        aaaaaaaaaaaaaaaaaaaaaaaaa

        Student-3
        Score is 7 out of 25
        Response to the following items are wrong
        2 3 4 6 7 8 10 11 12 14 15 16 18 19 20 22 23 24
```

Fig. 7.9 *Program to evaluate responses to a multiple-choice test*

4. Production and Sales Analysis

A company manufactures five categories of products and the number of items manufactured and sold are recorded product-wise every week in a month. The company reviews its production schedule at every month-end. The review may require one or more of the following information:

(a) Value of weekly production and sales.
(b) Total value of all the products manufactured.
(c) Total value of all the products sold.
(d) Total value of each product, manufactured and sold.

Let us represent the products manufactured and sold by two two-dimensional arrays M and S respectively. Then,

M =

M11	M12	M13	M14	M15
M21	M22	M23	M24	M25
M31	M32	M33	M34	M35
M41	M42	M43	M44	M45

S =

S11	S12	S13	S14	S15
S21	S22	S23	S24	S25
S31	S32	S33	S34	S35
S41	S42	S43	S44	S45

where Mij represents the number of jth type product manufactured in ith week and Sij the number of jth product sold in ith week. We may also represent the cost of each product by a single dimensional array C as follows:

C =

C1	C2	C3	C4	C5

where Cj is the cost of jth type product.

We shall represent the value of products manufactured and sold by two value arrays, namely, **Mvalue** and **Svalue**. Then,

Mvalue[i][j] = Mij x Cj

Svalue[i][j] = Sij x Cj

A program to generate the required outputs for the review meeting is shown in Fig. 7.10. The following additional variables are used:

Mweek[i] = Value of all the products manufactured in week i.

$$= \sum_{J=1}^{5} \text{Mvalue[i][j]}$$

Sweek[i] = Value of all the products in week i.

$$= \sum_{J=1}^{5} \text{Svalue[i][j]}$$

Mproduct[j] = Value of jth type product manufactured during the month

$$= \sum_{i=1}^{4} \text{Mvalue[i][j]}$$

Sproduct[j] = Value of jth type product sold during the month

$$= \sum_{i=1}^{4} \text{Svalue[i][j]}$$

Mtotal = Total value of all the products manufactured during the month

$$= \sum_{i=1}^{4} \text{Mweek[i]} = \sum_{j=1}^{5} \text{Mproduct[j]}$$

Stotal = Total value of all the products sold during the month

$$= \sum_{i=1}^{4} \text{Sweek[i]} = \sum_{j=1}^{5} \text{Sproduct[j]}$$

Program

```
main( )
{
  int M[5][6],S[5][6],C[6],
    Mvalue[5][6],Svalue[5][6],
    Mweek[5], Sweek[5],
    Mproduct[6], Sproduct[6],
    Mtotal, Stotal, i,j,number;
/*  Input data    */
  printf (" Enter products manufactured week_wise \n");
  printf (" M11,M12,—, M21,M22,— etc\n");
  for(i=1; i<=4; i++)
    for(j=1;j<=5; j++)
      scanf("%d",&M[i][j]);
  printf (" Enter products sold week_wise\n");
  printf (" S11,S12,—, S21,S22,— etc\n");
  for(i=1; i<=4; i++)
    for(j=1; j<=5; j++)
      scanf("%d", &S[i][j]);
  printf(" Enter cost of each product\n");
    for(j=1; j <=5; j++)
      scanf("%d",&C[j]);
/*Value matrices of production and sales */
  for(i=1; i<=4; i++)
    for(j=1; j<=5; j++)
    {
      Mvalue[i][j] = M[i][j] * C[j];
      Svalue[i][j] = S[i][j] * C[j];
    }
/*Total value of weekly production and sales */
  for(i=1; i<=4; i++)
  {
    Mweek[i] = 0 ;
    Sweek[i] = 0 ;
    for(j=1; j<=5; j++)
    {
      Mweek[i] += Mvalue[i][j];
      Sweek[i] += Svalue[i][j];
    }
  }
/*Monthly value of product_wise production and sales */
  for(j=1; j<=5; j++)
  {
    Mproduct[j] = 0 ;
    Sproduct[j] = 0 ;
    for(i=1; i<=4; i++)
```

```
            {
              Mproduct[j] += Mvalue[i][j];
              Sproduct[j] += Svalue[i][j];
            }
         }
      /*Grand total of production and sales values */
         Mtotal = Stotal = 0;
         for(i=1; i<=4; i++)
         {
           Mtotal += Mweek[i];
           Stotal += Sweek[i];
         }
         /*******************************************
           Selection and printing of information required
         *******************************************/
         printf("\n\n");
         printf(" Following is the list of things you can\n");
         printf(" request for. Enter appropriate item number\n");
         printf(" and press RETURN Key\n\n");
         printf(" 1.Value matrices of production & sales\n");
         printf(" 2.Total value of weekly production & sales\n");
         printf(" 3.Product wise monthly value of production &");
         printf(" sales\n");
         printf(" 4.Grand total value of production & sales\n");
         printf(" 5.Exit\n");
         number = 0;
         while(1)
         {    /* Beginning of while loop */
           printf("\n\n ENTER YOUR CHOICE:");
           scanf("%d",&number);
           printf("\n");
           if(number == 5)
           {
             printf(" G O O D  B Y E\n\n");
             break;
           }
           switch(number)
           { /* Beginning of switch */
      /* V A L U E  M A T R I C E S */
           case 1:
             printf(" VALUE MATRIX OF PRODUCTION\n\n");
             for(i=1; i<=4; i++)
             {
               printf(" Week(%d)\t",i);
               for(j=1; j <=5; j++)
                 printf("%7d", Mvalue[i][j]);
```

```
            printf("\n");
          }
          printf("\n VALUE MATRIX OF SALES\n\n");
          for(i=1; i <=4; i++)
          {
            printf(" Week(%d)\t",i);
            for(j=1; j <=5; j++)
              printf("%7d", Svalue[i][j]);
            printf("\n");
          }
          break;
    /* W E E K L Y   A N A L Y S I S */
        case 2:
          printf(" TOTAL WEEKLY  PRODUCTION &  SALES\n\n");
          printf("               PRODUCTION    SALES\n");
          printf("               -----         --  \n");
          for(i=1; i <=4; i++)
          {
            printf(" Week(%d)\t", i);
            printf("%7d\t%7d\n", Mweek[i], Sweek[i]);
          }
          break;
    /* P R O D U C T   W I S E   A N A L Y S I S */
        case 3:
          printf(" PRODUCT_WISE TOTAL PRODUCTION &");
          printf(" SALES\n\n");
          printf("               PRODUCTION SALES\n");
          printf("               -----      --  \n");
          for(j=1; j <=5; j++)
          {
            printf(" Product(%d)\t", j);
            printf("%7d\t%7d\n",Mproduct[j],Sproduct[j]);
          }
          break;
    /* G R A N D   T O T A L S */
        case 4:
          printf(" GRAND TOTAL OF PRODUCTION & SALES\n");
          printf("\n Total production = %d\n", Mtotal);
          printf(" Total sales = %d\n", Stotal);
          break;
    /* D E F A U L T */
        default :
          printf(" Wrong choice, select again\n\n");
          break;
        } /* End of switch */
      } /* End of while loop */
```

```
    printf(" Exit from the program\n\n");
  } /* End of main */
```

Output

```
  Enter products manufactured week_wise
    M11, M12, ----, M21, M22, ---- etc
    11   15   12   14   13
    13   13   14   15   12
    12   16   10   15   14
    14   11   15   13   12

  Enter products sold week_wise
  S11,S12,----, S21,S22,---- etc
  10   13   9    12   11
  12   10   12   14   10
  11   14   10   14   12
  12   10   13   11   10
  Enter cost of each product
  10 20 30 15 25

  Following is the list of things you can
  request for. Enter appropriate item number
  and press RETURN key
  1.Value matrices of production & sales
  2.Total value of weekly production & sales
  3.Product_wise monthly value of production & sales
  4.Grand total value of production & sales
  5.Exit
  ENTER YOUR CHOICE:1
  VALUE MATRIX OF PRODUCTION
      Week(1)     110    300    360    210    325
      Week(2)     130    260    420    225    300
      Week(3)     120    320    300    225    350
      Week(4)     140    220    450    185    300
  VALUE MATRIX OF SALES
      Week(1)     100    260    270    180    275
      Week(2)     120    200    360    210    250
      Week(3)     110    280    300    210    300
      Week(4)     120    200    390    165    250
  ENTER YOUR CHOICE:2
  TOTAL WEEKLY  PRODUCTION &  SALES
                PRODUCTION    SALES
                __________    _____
    Week(1)         1305      1085
    Week(2)         1335      1140
    Week(3)         1315      1200
    Week(4)         1305      1125
```

```
ENTER YOUR CHOICE:3
PRODUCT_WISE TOTAL PRODUCTION & SALES
                    PRODUCTION    SALES
                    ----------    -----
     Product(1)        500         450
     Product(2)       1100         940
     Product(3)       1530        1320
     Product(4)        855         765
     Product(5)       1275        1075
ENTER YOUR CHOICE:4

GRAND TOTAL OF PRODUCTION & SALES

 Total production = 5260
 Total sales      = 4550
ENTER YOUR CHOICE:5
G O O D  B Y E
Exit from the program
```

Fig. 7.10 *Program for production and sales analysis*

REVIEW QUESTIONS

7.1 State whether the following statements are *true* or *false*.

(a) The type of all elements in an array must be the same.

(b) When an array is declared, C automatically initializes its elements to zero.

(c) An expression that evaluates to an integral value may be used as a subscript.

(d) Accessing an array outside its range is a compile time error.

(e) A **char** type variable cannot be used as a subscript in an array.

(f) An unsigned long int type can be used as a subscript in an array.

(g) In C, by default, the first subscript is zero.

(h) When initializing a multidimensional array, not specifying all its dimensions is an error.

(i) When we use expressions as a subscript, its result should be always greater than zero.

(j) In C, we can use a maximum of 4 dimensions for an array.

(k) In declaring an array, the array size can be a constant or variable or an expression.

(l) The declaration int x[2] = {1,2,3}; is illegal.

7.2 Fill in the blanks in the following statements.

(a) The variable used as a subscript in an array is popularly known as ______ variable.

(b) An array can be initialized either at compile time or at ______.

(c) An array created using **malloc** function at run time is referred to as ______ array.

(d) An array that uses more than two subscript is referred to as ______ array.

(e) ______ is the process of arranging the elements of an array in order.

7.3 Identify errors, if any, in each of the following array declaration statements, assuming that ROW and COLUMN are declared as symbolic constants:

(a) `int score (100);`

(b) `float values [10,15];`

(c) `float average[ROW],[COLUMN];`
(d) `char name[15];`
(e) `int sum[ ];`
(f) `double salary [i + ROW]`
(g) `long int number [ROW]`
(h) `int array x[COLUMN];`

7.4 Identify errors, if any, in each of the following initialization statements.

(a) `int number[ ] = {0,0,0,0,0};`
(b) `float item[3][2] = {0,1,2,3,4,5};`
(c) `char word[ ] = {'A','R', 'R', 'A', 'Y'};`
(d) `int m[2,4] = {(0,0,0,0)(1,1,1,1)};`
(e) `float result[10] = 0;`

7.5 Assume that the arrays A and B are declared as follows:

```
int A[5][4];
float B[4];
```

Find the errors (if any) in the following program segments.

(a)
```
for (i=1; i<=5; i++)
for(j=1; j<=4; j++)
A[i][j] = 0;
```
(b)
```
for (i=1; i<4; i++)
scanf("%f", B[i]);
```
(c)
```
for (i=0; i<=4; i++)
B[i] = B[i]+i;
```
(d)
```
for (i=4; i>=0; i--)
for (j=0; j<4; j++)
A[i][j] = B[j] + 1.0;
```

7.6 Write a **for** loop statement that initializes all the diagonal elements of an array to one and others to zero as shown below. Assume 5 rows and 5 columns.

1	0	0	0	0	.....	0
0	1	0	0	0	.....	0
0	0	1	0	0	.....	0
.	.	.	.	.		.
.	.	.	.	.		.
.	.	.	.	.		.
.	.	.	.	.		.
.	.	.	.	.		.
0	0	0	0	0		1

7.7 We want to declare a two-dimensional integer type array called **matrix** for 3 rows and 5 columns. Which of the following declarations are correct?

(a) `int maxtrix [3],[5];`
(b) `int matrix [5] [3];`

(c) `int matrix [1+2] [2+3];`
(d) `int matrix [3,5];`
(e) `int matrix [3] [5];`

7.8 Which of the following initialization statements are correct?
(a) `char str1[4] = "GOOD";`
(b) `char str2[ ] = "C";`
(c) `char str3[5] = "Moon";`
(d) `char str4[ ] = {'S', 'U', 'N'};`
(e) `char str5[10] = "Sun";`

7.9 What is a data structure? Why is an array called a data structure?

7.10 What is a dynamic array? How is it created? Give a typical example of use of a dynamic array.

PROGRAMMING EXERCISES

7.1 Write a program for fitting a straight line through a set of points (x_i, y_i), $i = 1, \ldots, n$. The straight line equation is

$$y = mx + c$$

and the values of m and c are given by

$$m = \frac{n\,\Sigma(x_1 y_i) - (\Sigma x_1)(\Sigma y_i)}{n(\Sigma x_i^2) - (\Sigma x_i)^2}$$

$$c = \frac{1}{n}\,(\Sigma\, y_i - m\,\Sigma\, x_i)$$

All summations are from 1 to n.

7.2 The daily maximum temperatures recorded in 10 cities during the month of January (for all 31 days) have been tabulated as follows:

Day \ City	1	2	3 - - -	10
1				
2				
3				
-				
-				
-				
-				
31				

Write a program to read the table elements into a two-dimensional array **temperature**, and to find the city and day corresponding to
(a) the highest temperature and
(b) the lowest temperature.

7.3 An election is contested by 5 candidates. The candidates are numbered 1 to 5 and the voting is done by marking the candidate number on the ballot paper. Write a program to read the ballots and count the votes cast for each candidate using an array variable **count**. In case, a number read is outside the range 1 to 5, the ballot should be considered as a 'spoilt ballot' and the program should also count the number of spoilt ballots.

7.4 The following set of numbers is popularly known as Pascal's triangle.

```
1
1   1
1   2   1
1   3   3   1
1   4   6   4   1
1   5   10  10  5   1
-   -   -   -   -   -   -

-   -   -   -   -   -   -   -
```

If we denote rows by i and columns by j, then any element (except the boundary elements) in the triangle is given by

$$p_{ij} = p_{i-1, j-1} + p_{i-1, j}$$

Write a program to calculate the elements of the Pascal triangle for 10 rows and print the results.

7.5 The annual examination results of 100 students are tabulated as follows:

Roll No.	Subject 1	Subject 2	Subject 3
.			
.			
.			

Write a program to read the data and determine the following:

(a) Total marks obtained by each student.
(b) The highest marks in each subject and the Roll No. of the student who secured it.
(c) The student who obtained the highest total marks.

7.6 Given are two one-dimensional arrays A and B which are sorted in ascending order. Write a program to **merge** them into a single sorted array C that contains every item from arrays A and B, in ascending order.

7.7 Two matrices that have the same number of rows and columns can be multiplied to produce a third matrix. Consider the following two matrices.

$$A = \begin{bmatrix} a_{11}\, a_{12} \ldots\ldots a_{1n} \\ a_{12}\, a_{22} \ldots\ldots a_{2n} \\ \cdot \qquad\qquad \cdot \\ \cdot \qquad\qquad \cdot \\ \cdot \qquad\qquad \cdot \\ a_{n1} \ldots\ldots a_{nn} \end{bmatrix}$$

$$B = \begin{bmatrix} b_{11} & b_{12} \dots & b_{1n} \\ b_{12} & b_{22} \dots & b_{2n} \\ . & & . \\ . & & . \\ b_{n1} & \dots & b_{nn} \end{bmatrix}$$

The product of **A** and **B** is a third matrix C of size nxn where each element of C is given by the following equation.

$$\mathbf{C}_{ij} = \sum_{k=1}^{n} a_{ik} b_{kj}$$

Write a program that will read the values of elements of A and B and produce the product matrix **C**.

7.8 Write a program that fills a five-by-five matrix as follows.
- Upper left triangle with +1s
- Lower right triangle with –1s
- Right to left diagonal with zeros

Display the contents of the matrix using not more than two **printf** statements

7.9 Selection sort is based on the following idea:
Selecting the largest array element and swapping it with the last array element leaves an unsorted list whose size is 1 less than the size of the original list. If we repeat this step again on the unsorted list we will have an ordered list of size 2 and an unordered list size n–2. When we repeat this until the size of the unsorted list becomes one, the result will be a sorted list.
Write a program to implement this algorithm.

7.10 Develop a program to implement the binary search algorithm. This technique compares the search key value with the value of the element that is midway in a "sorted" list. Then;
(a) If they match, the search is over.
(b) If the search key value is less than the middle value, then the first half of the list contains the key value.
(c) If the search key value is greater than the middle value, then the second half contains the key value.

Repeat this "divide-and-conquer" strategy until we have a match. If the list is reduced to one non-matching element, then the list does not contain the key value.
Use the sorted list created in Exercise 7.9 or use any other sorted list.

Chapter 8

Character Arrays and Strings

8.1 INTRODUCTION

A string is a sequence of characters that is treated as a single data item. We have used strings in a number of examples in the past. Any group of characters (except double quote sign) defined between double quotation marks is a string constant. Example:

"Man is obviously made to think."

If we want to include a double quote in the string to be printed, then we may use it with a back slash as shown below.

"\" Man is obviously made to think,\" said Pascal."

For example,

```
printf ("\" Well Done !"\");
```

will output the string

" Well Done !"

while the statement

```
printf(" Well Done !");
```

will output the string

Well Done !

Character strings are often used to build meaningful and readable programs. The common operations performed on character strings include:

- Reading and writing strings
- Combining strings together
- Copying one string to another

- Comparing strings for equality
- Extracting a portion of a string

In this chapter we shall discuss these operations in detail and examine library functions that implement them.

8.2 DECLARING AND INITIALIZING STRING VARIABLES

C does not support strings as a data type. However, it allows us to represent strings as character arrays. In C, therefore, a string variable is any valid C variable name and is always declared as an array of characters. The general form of declaration of a string variable is

char **string_name[** *size* **]**;

The *size* determines the number of characters in the string_ name. Some examples are:

```
char city[10];
char name[30];
```

When the compiler assigns a character string to a character array, it automatically supplies a *null* character ('\0 ') at the end of the string. Therefore, the *size* should be equal to the maximum number of characters in the string *plus* one.

Like numeric arrays, character arrays may be initialized when they are declared. C permits a character array to be initialized in either of the following two forms:

```
char city [9] = " NEW YORK ";
char city [9]={'N','E','W',' ','Y','O','R','K','\0'};
```

The reason that **city** had to be 9 elements long is that the string NEW YORK contains 8 characters and one element space is provided for the null terminator. Note that when we initialize a character array by listing its elements, we must supply explicitly the null terminator.

C also permits us to initialize a character array without specifying the number of elements. In such cases, the size of the array will be determined automatically, based on the number of elements initialized. For example, the statement

```
char string [ ] = {'G','O','O','D','\0'};
```

defines the array **string** as a five element array.

We can also declare the size much larger than the string size in the initializer. That is, the statement.

```
char str[10] = "GOOD";
```

is permitted. In this case, the computer creates a character array of size 10, places the value "GOOD" in it, terminates with the null character, and initializes all other elements to NULL. The storage will look like:

G	O	O	D	\0	\0	\0	\0	\0	\0

However, the following declaration is illegal.

```
char str2[3] = "GOOD";
```

This will result in a compile time error. Also note that we cannot separate the initialization from declaration. That is,

```
char str3[5];
str3 = "GOOD";
```

is not allowed. Similarly,

```
char s1[4] = "abc";
char s2[4];
s2 = s1; /* Error */
```

is not allowed. An array name cannot be used as the left operand of an assignment operator.

Terminating Null Character

You must be wondering, "why do we need a terminating null character?" As we know, a string is not a data type in C, but it is considered a data structure stored in an array. The string is a variable-length structure and is stored in a fixed-length array. The array size is not always the size of the string and most often it is much larger than the string stored in it. Therefore, the last element of the array need not represent the end of the string. We need some way to determine the end of the string data and the null character serves as the "end-of-string" marker.

8.3 READING STRINGS FROM TERMINAL

Using **scanf** Function

The familiar input function **scanf** can be used with **%s** format specification to read in a string of characters. Example:

```
char address[10]
scanf("%s", address);
```

The problem with the **scanf** function is that it terminates its input on the first white space it finds. (A white space includes blanks, tabs, carriage returns, form feeds, and new lines.) Therefore, if the following line of text is typed in at the terminal,

NEW YORK

then only the string "NEW" will be read into the array **address**, since the blank space after the word 'NEW' will terminate the string reading.

The **scanf** function automatically terminates the string that is read with a null character and therefore the character array should be large enough to hold the input string plus the null character. Note that unlike previous **scanf** calls, in the case of character arrays, the ampersand (&) is not required before the variable name.

The **address** array is created in the memory as shown below:

0	1	2	3	4	5	6	7	8	9
N	E	W	\0	?	?	?	?	?	?

Note that the unused locations are filled with garbage.

If we want to read the entire line "NEW YORK", then we may use two character arrays of appropriate sizes. That is,

```
char adr1[5], adr2[5];
scanf("%s %s", adr1, adr2);
```

with the line of text

NEW YORK

will assign the string "NEW" to **adr1** and "YORK" to **adr2.**

Example 8.1 Write a program to read a series of words from a terminal using **scanf** function.

The program shown in Fig. 8.1 reads four words and displays them on the screen. Note that the string 'Oxford Road' is treated as *two words* while the string 'Oxford-Road' as *one word*.

```
Program
main( )
{
        char word1[40], word2[40], word3[40], word4[40];

        printf("Enter text : \n");
        scanf("%s %s", word1, word2);
        scanf("%s", word3);
        scanf("%s", word4);

        printf("\n");
        printf("word1 = %s\nword2 = %s\n", word1, word2);
        printf("word3 = %s\nword4 = %s\n", word3, word4);
}
Output
 Enter text :
 Oxford Road, London M17ED

 word1 = Oxford
 word2 = Road,
 word3 = London
 word4 = M17ED
```

```
Enter text :
Oxford-Road, London-M17ED United Kingdom
word1 = Oxford-Road
word2 = London-M17ED
word3 = United
word4 = Kingdom
```

Fig. 8.1 *Reading a series of words using* ***scanf*** *function*

We can also specify the field width using the form %ws in the **scanf** statement for reading a specified number of characters from the input string . Example:

```
scanf("%ws", name);
```

Here, two things may happen.

1. The width w is equal to or greater than the number of characters typed in. The entire string will be stored in the string variable.
2. The width w is less than the number of characters in the string. The excess characters will be truncated and left unread.

Consider the following statements:

```
char name[10];
scanf("%5s", name);
```

The input string RAM will be stored as:

R	A	M	\0	?	?	?	?	?	?
0	1	2	3	4	5	6	7	8	9

The input string KRISHNA will be stored as:

K	R	I	S	H	\0	?	?	?	?
0	1	2	3	4	5	6	7	8	9

Reading a Line of Text

We have seen just now that **scanf** with %s or %ws can read only strings without whitespaces. That is, they cannot be used for reading a text containing more than one word. However, C supports a format specification known as the *edit set conversion code* %[..] that can be used to read a line containing a variety of characters, including whitespaces. Recall that we have used this conversion code in Chapter 4. For example,
the program segment

```
char line [80];
scanf("%[^\n]", line);
printf("%s", line);
```

will read a line of input from the keyboard and display the same on the screen. We would very rarely use this method, as C supports an intrinsic string function to do this job. This is discussed in the next section.

Using *getchar* and *gets* Functions

We have discussed in Chapter 4 as to how to read a single character from the terminal, using the function **getchar.** We can use this function repeatedly to read successive single characters from the input and place them into a character array. Thus, an entire line of text can be read and stored in an array. The reading is terminated when the newline character ('\n') is entered and the null character is then inserted at the end of the string. The **getchar** function call takes the form:

```
char ch;
ch = getchar( );
```

Note that the **getchar** function has no parameters.

Example 8.2 Write a program to read a line of text containing a series of words from the terminal.

The program shown in Fig. 8.2 can read a line of text (up to a maximum of 80 characters) into the string **line** using **getchar** function. Every time a character is read, it is assigned to its location in the string **line** and then tested for *newline* character. When the *newline* character is read (signalling the end of line), the reading loop is terminated and the *newline* character is replaced by the null character to indicate the end of character string.

When the loop is exited, the value of the index **c** is one number higher than the last character position in the string (since it has been incremented after assigning the new character to the string). Therefore the index value **c-1** gives the position where the *null* character is to be stored.

```
Program
    #include <stdio.h>
    main( )
    {
      char line[81], character;
      int c;
      c = 0;
      printf("Enter text. Press <Return> at end\n");
      do
      {
        character = getchar();
        line[c] = character;
        c++;
      }
      while(character != '\n');
      c = c - 1;
      line[c] = '\0';
      printf("\n%s\n", line);
    }
Output
    Enter text. Press <Return> at end
    Programming in C is interesting.
    Programming in C is interesting.
```

```
Enter text. Press <Return> at end
National Centre for Expert Systems, Hyderabad.
National Centre for Expert Systems, Hyderabad.
```

Fig. 8.2 *Program to* ***read a line of text*** *from terminal*

Another and more convenient method of reading a string of text containing whitespaces is to use the library function **gets** available in the *<stdio.h>* header file. This is a simple function with one string parameter and called as under:

```
gets (str);
```

str is a string variable declared properly. It reads characters into **str** from the keyboard until a new-line character is encountered and then appends a null character to the string. Unlike **scanf,** it does not skip whitespaces. For example the code segment

```
char line [80];
gets (line);
printf ("%s", line);
```

reads a line of text from the keyboard and displays it on the screen. The last two statements may be combined as follows:

```
printf("%s", gets(line));
```

(Be careful not to input more character that can be stored in the string variable used. Since C does not check array-bounds, it may cause problems.)

C does not provide operators that work on strings directly. For instance we cannot assign one string to another directly. For example, the assignment statements.

```
string = "ABC";
string1 = string2;
```

are not valid. If we really want to copy the characters in **string2** into **string1**, we may do so on a character-by-character basis.

Example 8.3 Write a program to copy one string into another and count the number of characters copied.

The program is shown in Fig. 8.3. We use a **for** loop to copy the characters contained inside **string2** into the **string1**. The loop is terminated when the *null* character is reached. Note that we are again assigning a null character to the **string1**.

```
Program
main( )
{
    char string1[80], string2[80];
    int i;

    printf("Enter a string \n");
    printf("?");
    scanf("%s", string2);
    for( i=0 ; string2[i] != '\0'; i++)
        string1[i] = string2[i];
```

```
        string1[i] = '\0';
        printf("\n");
        printf("%s\n", string1);
        printf("Number of characters = %d\n", i );
    }
Output
    Enter a string
    ?Manchester

    Manchester
    Number of characters = 10
    Enter a string
    ?Westminster

    Westminster
    Number of characters = 11
```

Fig. 8.3 *Copying one string into another*

8.4 WRITING STRINGS TO SCREEN

Using printf Function

We have used extensively the **printf** function with %s format to print strings to the screen. The format %s can be used to display an array of characters that is terminated by the null character. For example, the statement

```
printf("%s", name);
```

can be used to display the entire contents of the array **name**.

We can also specify the precision with which the array is displayed. For instance, the specification

```
%10.4
```

indicates that the *first four* characters are to be printed in a field width of 10 columns.

However, if we include the minus sign in the specification (e.g., %-10.4s), the string will be printed left-justified. The Example 8.4 illustrates the effect of various %s specifications.

Example 8.4 Write a program to store the string "United Kingdom" in the array **country** and display the string under various format specifications.

The program and its output are shown in Fig. 8.4. The output illustrates the following features of the **%s** specifications.

1. When the field width is less than the length of the string, the entire string is printed.
2. The integer value on the right side of the decimal point specifies the number of characters to be printed.
3. When the number of characters to be printed is specified as zero, nothing is printed.

4. The minus sign in the specification causes the string to be printed left-justified.
5. The specification % .ns prints the first n characters of the string.

```
Program
      main()
      {
        char country[15] = "United Kingdom";
        printf("\n\n");
        printf("*123456789012345*\n");
        printf(" -----\n");
        printf("%15s\n", country);
        printf("%5s\n", country);
        printf("%15.6s\n", country);
        printf("%-15.6s\n", country);
        printf("%15.0s\n", country);
        printf("%.3s\n", country);
        printf("%s\n", country);
        printf("----- \n");
      }
Output
      *123456789012345*
      -----
      United Kingdom
      United Kingdom
            United
      United

      Uni
      United Kingdom
      -----
```

Fig. 8.4 *Writing strings using %s format*

The **printf** on UNIX supports another nice feature that allows for variable field width or precision. For instance

```
printf("%*.*s\n", w, d, string);
```

prints the first **d** characters of the string in the field width of **w**.
This feature comes in handy for printing a sequence of characters. Example 8.5 illustrates this.

Example 8.5 Write a program using **for loop** to print the following output.

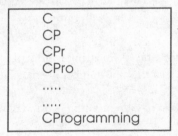

```
C
CP
CPr
CPro
.....
.....
CProgramming
```

```
CProgramming
.....
.....
CPro
CPr
CP
C
```

The outputs of the program in Fig. 8.5, for variable specifications **%12.*s, %.*s,** and **%*.1s** are shown in Fig. 8.6, which further illustrates the variable field width and the precision specifications.

Program

```
main()
{
    int c, d;
    char string[] = "CProgramming";
    printf("\n\n");
    printf("------------\n");
    for( c = 0 ; c <= 11 ; c++ )
    {
        d = c + 1;
        printf("|%-12.*s|\n", d, string);
    }
    printf("|------------|\n");
    for( c = 11 ; c >= 0 ; c-- )
    {
        d = c + 1;
        printf("|%-12.*s|\n", d, string);
    }
    printf("------------\n");
}
```

Output

```
C
CP
CPr
CPro
CProg
CProgr
CProgra
CProgram
CProgramm
CProgrammi
CProgrammin
CProgramming
```

```
CProgramming
CProgrammin
CProgrammi
CProgramm
CProgram
CProgra
CProgr
CProg
CPro
CPr
CP
C
```

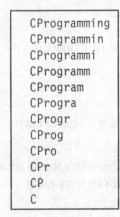

Fig. 8.5 *Illustration of variable field specifications by printing sequences of characters*

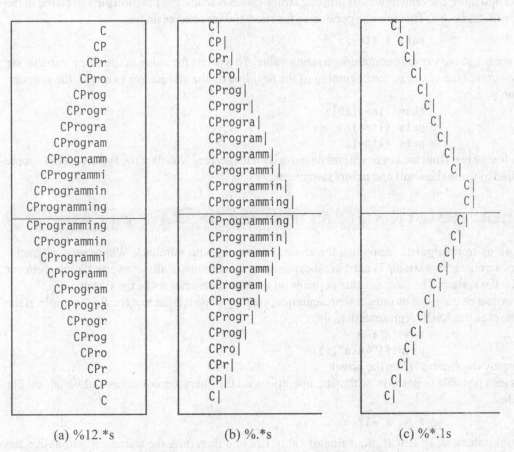

```
           C
          CP
         CPr
        CPro
       CProg
      CProgr
     CProgra
    CProgram
   CProgramm
  CProgrammi
 CProgrammin
CProgramming
CProgramming
 CProgrammin
  CProgrammi
   CProgramm
    CProgram
     CProgra
      CProgr
       CProg
        CPro
         CPr
          CP
           C
```

(a) %12.*s

```
C|
CP|
CPr|
CPro|
CProg|
CProgr|
CProgra|
CProgram|
CProgramm|
CProgrammi|
CProgrammin|
CProgramming|
CProgramming|
CProgrammin|
CProgrammi|
CProgramm|
CProgram|
CProgra|
CProgr|
CProg|
CPro|
CPr|
CP|
C|
```

(b) %.*s

```
C|
 C|
  C|
   C|
    C|
     C|
      C|
       C|
        C|
         C|
          C|
           C|
           C|
          C|
         C|
        C|
       C|
      C|
     C|
    C|
   C|
  C|
 C|
C|
```

(c) %*.1s

Fig. 8.6 *Further illustrations of variable specifications*

Using putchar and puts Functions

Like **getchar**, C supports another character handling function **putchar** to output the values of character variables. It takes the following form:

```
char ch = 'A';
putchar (ch);
```

The function **putchar** requires one parameter. This statement is equivalent to:

```
printf("%c", ch);
```

We have used **putchar** function in Chapter 4 to write characters to the screen. We can use this function repeatedly to output a string of characters stored in an array using a loop: Example:

```
char name[6] = "PARIS"
for (i=0, i<5; i++)
        putchar(name[i];
putchar('\n');
```

Another and more convenient way of printing string values is to use the function **puts** declared in the header file <*stdio.h*>. This is a one parameter function and invoked as under:

```
puts ( str );
```

where **str** is a string variable containing a string value. This prints the value of the string variable **str** and then moves the cursor to the beginning of the next line on the screen. For example, the program segment

```
char line [80];
gets (line);
puts (line);
```

reads a line of text from the keyboard and displays it on the screen. Note that the syntax is very simple compared to using the **scanf** and **printf** statements.

8.5 ARITHMETIC OPERATIONS ON CHARACTERS

C allows us to manipulate characters the same way we do with numbers. Whenever a character constant or character variable is used in an expression, it is automatically converted into an integer value by the system. The integer value depends on the local character set of the system.

To write a character in its integer representation, we may write it as an integer. For example, if the machine uses the ASCII representation, then,

```
x = 'a';
printf("%d\n",x);
```

will display the number 97 on the screen.

It is also possible to perform arithmetic operations on the character constants and variables. For example,

```
x = 'z'-1;
```

is a valid statement. In ASCII, the value of **'z'** is 122 and therefore, the statement will assign the value 121 to the variable **x.**

We may also use character constants in relational expressions. For example, the expression

```
ch >= 'A' && ch <= 'Z'
```

would test whether the character contained in the variable **ch** is an upper-case letter.

We can convert a character digit to its equivalent integer value using the following relationship:

```
x = character - '0';
```

where **x** is defined as an integer variable and **character** contains the character digit. For example, let us assume that the **character** contains the digit '7',

Then,

x = ASCII value of '7' - ASCII value of '0'
= 55 - 48
= 7

The C library supports a function that converts a string of digits into their integer values. The function takes the form

x = atoi(string);

x is an integer variable and **string** is a character array containing a string of digits. Consider the following segment of a program:

```
number = "1988";
year = atoi(number);
```

number is a string variable which is assigned the string constant "1988". The function **atoi** converts the string "1988" (contained in **number)** to its numeric equivalent 1988 and assigns it to the integer variable **year.** String conversion functions are stored in the header file <std.lib.h>.

Example 8.6 Write a program which would print the alphabet set a to z and A to Z in decimal and character form.

The program is shown in Fig. 8.7. In ASCII character set, the decimal numbers 65 to 90 represent uppercase alphabets and 97 to 122 represent lowercase alphabets. The values from 91 to 96 are excluded using an **if** statement in the **for** loop.

Program

```
main()
{
   char c;
   printf("\n\n");
   for( c = 65 ; c <= 122 ; c = c + 1 )
   {
      if( c > 90 && c < 97 )
         continue;
      printf("|%4d - %c ", c, c);
   }
   printf("|\n");
}
```

Output

```
| 65 - A | 66 - B | 67 - C | 68 - D | 69 - E | 70 - F
| 71 - G | 72 - H | 73 - I | 74 - J | 75 - K | 76 - L
```

```
|77 - M| 78 - N| 79 - O| 80 - P| 81 - Q| 82 - R
| 83 - S| 84 - T| 85 - U| 86 - V| 87 - W| 88 - X
| 89 - Y| 90 - Z| 97 - a| 98 - b| 99 - c| 100 - d
|101 - e| 102 - f| 103 - g| 104 - h| 105 - i| 106 - j
|107 - k| 108 - l| 109 - m| 110 - n| 111 - o| 112 - p
|113 - q| 114 - r| 115 - s| 116 - t| 117 - u| 118 - v
|119 - w| 120 - x| 121 - y| 122 - z|
```

Fig. 8.7 *Printing of the alphabet set in decimal and character form*

8.6 PUTTING STRINGS TOGETHER

Just as we cannot assign one string to another directly, we cannot join two strings together by the simple arithmetic addition. That is, the statements such as

```
string3 = string1 + string2;
string2 = string1 + "hello";
```

are not valid. The characters from **string1** and **string2** should be copied into the **string3** one after the other. The size of the array **string3** should be large enough to hold the total characters.

The process of combining two strings together is called *concatenation*. Example 8.7 illustrates the concatenation of three strings.

Example 8.7 The names of employees of an organization are stored in three arrays, namely **first_name, second_name,** and **last_name**. Write a program to concatenate the three parts into one string to be called **name**.

The program is given in Fig. 8.8. Three **for** loops are used to copy the three strings. In the first loop, the characters contained in the **first_name** are copied into the variable **name** until the *null* character is reached. The *null* character is not copied; instead it is replaced by a *space* by the assignment statement

```
name[i] = ' ' ;
```

Similarly, the **second_name** is copied into **name**, starting from the column just after the space created by the above statement. This is achieved by the assignment statement

```
name[i+j+1] = second_name[j];
```

If **first_name** contains 4 characters, then the value of i at this point will be 4 and therefore the first character from **second_name** will be placed in the *fifth cell* of **name.** Note that we have stored a space in the *fourth cell.*

In the same way, the statement

```
name[i+j+k+2] = last_name[k];
```

is used to copy the characters from **last_name** into the proper locations of **name.**

At the end, we place a null character to terminate the concatenated string **name**. In this example, it is important to note the use of the expressions **i+j+1** and **i+j+k+2.**

```
Program
        main()
        {
          int i, j, k ;
          char first_name[10] = {"VISWANATH"} ;
          char second_name[10] = {"PRATAP"} ;
          char last_name[10] = {"SINGH"} ;
          char name[30] ;
        /* Copy first_name into name */
          for( i = 0 ; first_name[i] != '\0' ; i++ )
            name[i] = first_name[i] ;
        /* End first_name with a space */
          name[i] = ' ' ;
        /* Copy second_name into name */
          for( j = 0 ; second_name[j] != '\0' ; j++ )
            name[i+j+1] = second_name[j] ;
        /* End second_name with a space */
          name[i+j+1] = ' ' ;
        /* Copy last_name into name */
          for( k = 0 ; last_name[k] != '\0'; k++ )
            name[i+j+k+2] = last_name[k] ;
        /* End name with a null character */
          name[i+j+k+2] = '\0' ;
          printf("\n\n") ;
          printf("%s\n", name) ;
        }
Output
        VISWANATH PRATAP SINGH
```

Fig. 8.8 *Concatenation of strings*

8.7 COMPARISON OF TWO STRINGS

Once again, C does not permit the comparison of two strings directly. That is, the statements such as

```
if(name1 == name2)
if(name == "ABC")
```

are not permitted. It is therefore necessary to compare the two strings to be tested, character by character. The comparison is done until there is a mismatch or one of the strings terminates into a null character, whichever occurs first. The following segment of a program illustrates this.

```
i=0;
while(str1[i] == str2[i] && str1[i] != '\0'
      && str2[i] != '\0')
   i = i+1;
if (str1[i] == '\0' && str2[i] == '\0')
     printf("strings are equal\n");
   else
     printf("strings are not equal\n");
```

8.8 STRING-HANDLING FUNCTIONS

Fortunately, the C library supports a large number of string-handling functions that can be used to carry out many of the string manipulations discussed so far. Following are the most commonly used string-handling functions.

Function	*Action*
strcat()	concatenates two strings
strcmp()	compares two strings
strcpy()	copies one string over another
strlen()	finds the length of a string

We shall discuss briefly how each of these functions can be used in the processing of strings.

strcat() Function

The **strcat** function joins two strings together. It takes the following form:

strcat(string1, string2);

string1 and **string2** are character arrays. When the function **strcat** is executed, **string2** is appended to **string1**. It does so by removing the null character at the end of **string1** and placing **string2** from there. The string at **string2** remains unchanged. For example, consider the following three strings:

Part 1 =

0	1	2	3	4	5	6	7	8	9	0	1
V	E	R	Y		\0						

Part 2 =

0	1	2	3	4	5	6
G	O	O	D	\0		

Part 3 =

0	1	2	3	4	5	6
B	A	D	\0			

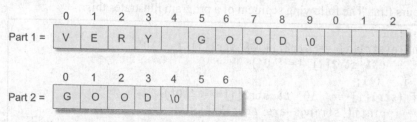

Execution of the statement

```
strcat(part1, part2);
```

will result in:

Part 1 =

0	1	2	3	4	5	6	7	8	9	0	1	2
V	E	R	Y		G	O	O	D	\0			

Part 2 =

0	1	2	3	4	5	6
G	O	O	D	\0		

while the statement

strcat(part 1, part 3);

will result in:

	0	1	2	3	4	5	6	7	8	9	0	1	2
Part 1 =	V	E	R	Y		B	A	D	\0				

	0	1	2	3	4	5	6
Part 3 =	B	A	D	\0			

We must make sure that the size of **string1** (to which **string2** is appended) is large enough to accommodate the final string.
strcat function may also append a string constant to a string variable. The following is valid:

```
strcat(part1,"GOOD");
```

C permits nesting of **strcat** functions. For example, the statement

```
strcat(strcat(string1,string2), string3);
```

is allowed and concatenates all the three strings together. The resultant string is stored in **string1.**

STRCMP() FUNCTION

The **strcmp** function compares two strings identified by the arguments and has a value 0 if they are equal. If they are not, it has the numeric difference between the first nonmatching characters in the strings. It takes the form:

strcmp(string1, string2);

string1 and **string2** may be string variables or string constants. Examples are:

```
strcmp(name1, name2);
strcmp(name1, "John");
strcmp("Rom", "Ram");
```

Our major concern is to determine whether the strings are equal; if not, which is alphabetically above. The value of the mismatch is rarely important. For example, the statement

```
strcmp("their", "there");
```

will return a value of –9 which is the numeric difference between ASCII "i" and ASCII "r". That is, "i" minus "r" in ASCII code is –9. If the value is negative, **string1** is alphabetically above **string2**.

strcpy() Function

The **strcpy** function works almost like a string-assignment operator. It takes the form

strcpy(string1, string2);

and assigns the contents of **string2** to **string1**. **string2** may be a character array variable or a string constant. For example, the statement

```
strcpy(city, "DELHI");
```

will assign the string "DELHI" to the string variable **city.** Similarly, the statement

```
strcpy(city1, city2);
```

will assign the contents of the string variable **city2** to the string variable **city1**. The size of the array **city1** should be large enough to receive the contents of **city2.**

strlen() Function

This function counts and returns the number of characters in a string. It takes the form

n = **strlen**(string);

Where **n** is an integer variable, which receives the value of the length of the **string.** The argument may be a string constant. The counting ends at the first null character.

Example 8.8 **s1, s2,** and **s3** are three string variables. Write a program to read two string constants into **s1** and **s2** and compare whether they are equal or not. If they are not, join them together. Then copy the contents of **s1** to the variable **s3**. At the end, the program should print the contents of all the three variables and their lengths.

The program is shown in Fig. 8.9. During the first run, the input strings are "New" and "York". These strings are compared by the statement

```
x = strcmp(s1, s2);
```

Since they are not equal, they are joined together and copied into **s3** using the statement

```
strcpy(s3, s1);
```

The program outputs all the three strings with their lengths.

During the second run, the two strings **s1** and **s2** are equal, and therefore, they are not joined together. In this case all the three strings contain the same string constant "London".

```
Program
   #include <string.h>
   main()
   { char s1[20], s2[20], s3[20];
     int x, l1, l2, l3;
     printf("\n\nEnter two string constants \n");
     printf("?");
     scanf("%s %s", s1, s2);
   /* comparing s1 and s2 */
     x = strcmp(s1, s2);
     if(x != 0)
     {    printf("\n\nStrings are not equal \n");
          strcat(s1, s2); /* joining s1 and s2 */
     }
     else
          printf("\n\nStrings are equal \n");
```

```
        /* copying s1 to s3
           strcpy(s3, s1);
        /* Finding length of strings */
           l1 = strlen(s1);
           l2 = strlen(s2);
           l3 = strlen(s3);
        /* output */
           printf("\ns1= %s\t length = %d characters\n", s1, l1);
           printf("s2 = %s\t length = %d characters\n", s2, l2);
           printf("s3 = %s\t length = %d characters\n", s3, l3);
        }
     Output
        Enter two string constants
        ? New York

        Strings are not equal
        s1 = NewYork  length = 7 characters
        s2 = York     length = 4 characters
        s3 = NewYork  length = 7 characters

        Enter two string constants
        ? London London

        Strings are equal

        s1 = London length = 6 characters
        s2 = London length = 6 characters
        s3 = London length = 6 characters
```

Fig. 8.9 *Illustration of string handling functions*

Other String Functions

The header file **<string.h>** contains many more string manipulation functions. They might be useful in certain situations.

strncpy

In addition to the function **strcpy** that copies one string to another, we have another function **strncpy** that copies only the left-most n characters of the source string to the target string variable. This is a three-parameter function and is invoked as follows:

```
strncpy(s1, s2, 5);
```

This statement copies the first 5 characters of the source string **s2** into the target string **s1.** Since the first 5 characters may not include the terminating null character, we have to place it explicitly in the 6th position of **s2** as shown below:

```
s1[6] ='\0';
```

Now, the string **s1** contains a proper string.

strncmp

A variation of the function **strcmp** is the function **strncmp**. This function has three parameters as illustrated in the function call below:

```
strncmp (s1, s2, n);
```

this compares the left-most n characters of **s1** to **s2** and returns.

(a) 0 if they are equal,
(b) negative number, if s1 sub-string is less than s2, and
(c) positive number, otherwise.

strncat

This is another concatenation function that takes three parameters as shown below:

```
strncat (s1, s2, n);
```

This call will concatenate the left-most n characters of **s2** to the end of **s1.** Example:

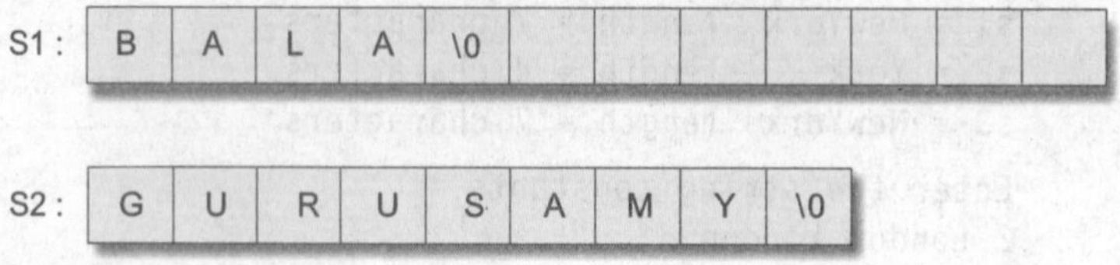

After **strncat** (s1, s2, 4); execution:

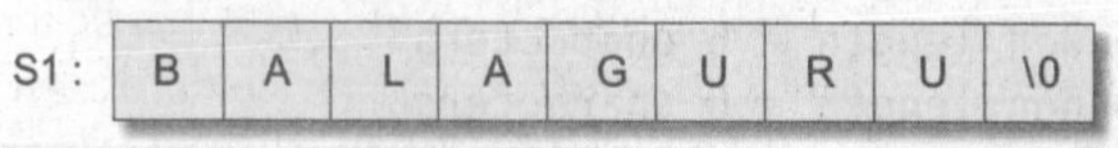

strstr

It is a two-parameter function that can be used to locate a sub-string in a string. This takes the forms:

```
strstr (s1, s2);
strstr (s1, "ABC");
```

The function **strstr** searches the string **s1** to see whether the string **s2** is contained in **s1**. If yes, the function returns the position of the first occurrence of the sub-string. Otherwise, it returns a NULL pointer. Example.

```
if (strstr (s1, s2) == NULL)
    printf("substring is not found");
else
    printf("s2 is a substring of s1");
```

We also have functions to determine the existence of a character in a string. The function call

```
strchr(s1, 'm');
```

will locate the first occurrence of the character 'm' and the call

```
strrchr(s1, 'm');
```

will locate the last occurrence of the character 'm' in the string **s1**.

Warnings

- When allocating space for a string during declaration, remember to count the terminating null character.
- When creating an array to hold a copy of a string variable of unknown size, we can compute the size required using the expression

  strlen (stringname) +1.
- When copying or concatenating one string to another, we must ensure that the target (destination) string has enough space to hold the incoming characters. Remember that no error message will be available even if this condition is not satisfied. The copying may overwrite the memory and the program may fail in an unpredictable way.
- When we use **strncpy** to copy a specific number of characters from a source string, we must ensure to append the null character to the target string, in case the number of characters is less than or equal to the source string.

8.9 TABLE OF STRINGS

We often use lists of character strings, such as a list of the names of students in a class, list of the names of employees in an organization, list of places, etc. A list of names can be treated as a table of strings and a two-dimensional character array can be used to store the entire list. For example, a character array **student[30][15]** may be used to store a list of 30 names, each of length not more than 15 characters. Shown below is a table of five cities:

C	h	a	n	d	i	g	a	r	h
M	a	d	r	a	s				
A	h	m	e	d	a	b	a	d	
H	y	d	e	r	a	b	a	d	
B	o	m	b	a	y				

This table can be conveniently stored in a character array city by using the following declaration:

```
char city[ ] [ ]
        {
           "Chandigarh",
           "Madras",
           "Ahmedabad",
           "Hyderabad",
           "Bombay"
        } ;
```

To access the name of the ith city in the list, we write

city[i-1]

and therefore **city[0]** denotes "Chandigarh", **city[1]** denotes "Madras" and so on. This shows that once an array is declared as two-dimensional, it can be used like a one-dimensional array in further manipulations. That is, the table can be treated as a column of strings.

Example 8.9 Write a program that would sort a list of names in alphabetical order.

A program to sort the list of strings in alphabetical order is given in Fig. 8.10. It employs the method of bubble sorting described in Case Study 1 in the previous chapter.

Program

```
#define ITEMS 5
#define MAXCHAR 20
main( )
{
  char string[ITEMS][MAXCHAR], dummy[MAXCHAR];
  int i = 0, j = 0;
  /* Reading the list */
  printf ("Enter names of %d items \n ",ITEMS);
  while (i < ITEMS)
    scanf ("%s", string[i++]);
  /* Sorting begins */
  for (i=1; i < ITEMS; i++) /* Outer loop begins */
  {
    for (j=1; j <= ITEMS-i ; j++) /*Inner loop begins*/
    {
      if (strcmp (string[j-1], string[j]) > 0)
      { /* Exchange of contents */
        strcpy (dummy, string[j-1]);
        strcpy (string[j-1], string[j]);
        strcpy (string[j], dummy );
      }
    } /* Inner loop ends */
  } /* Outer loop ends */
  /* Sorting completed */
  printf ("\nAlphabetical list \n\n");
  for (i=0; i < ITEMS ; i++)
    printf ("%s", string[i]);
}
```

Output

```
Enter names of 5 items
London Manchester Delhi Paris Moscow
Alphabetical list
Delhi
London
Manchester
Moscow
Paris
```

Fig. 8.10 *Sorting of strings in alphabetical order*

Note that a two-dimensional array is used to store the list of strings. Each string is read using a **scanf** function with **%s** format. Remember, if any string contains a white space, then the part of the string after the white space will be treated as another item in the list by the **scanf.** In such cases, we should read the entire line as a string using a suitable algorithm. For example, we can use **gets** function to read a line of text containing a series of words. We may also use **puts** function in place of **scanf** for output.

8.10 OTHER FEATURES OF STRINGS

Other aspects of strings we have not discussed in this chapter include:

- Manipulating strings using pointers
- Using string as function parameters
- Declaring and defining strings as members of structures.

These topics will be dealt with later when we discuss functions, structures and pointers.

Just Remember

- ✍ Character constants are enclosed in single quotes and string constants are enclosed in double quotes.
- ✍ Allocate sufficient space in a character array to hold the null character at the end.
- ✍ Avoid processing single characters as strings.
- ✍ Using the address operator **&** with a **string** variable in the **scanf** function call is an error.
- ✍ It is a compile time error to assign a string to a character variable.
- ✍ Using a string variable name on the left of the assignment operator is illegal.
- ✍ When accessing individual characters in a string variable, it is logical error to access outside the array bounds.
- ✍ Strings cannot be manipulated with operators. Use string functions.
- ✍ Do not use string functions on an array **char** type that is not terminated with the null character.
- ✍ Do not forget to append the null character to the target string when the number of characters copied is less than or equal to the source string.
- ✍ Be aware the return values when using the functions **strcmp** and **strncmp** for comparing strings.
- ✍ When using string functions for copying and concatenating strings, make sure that the target string has enough space to store the resulting string. Otherwise memory overwriting may occur.
- ✍ The header file <stdio.h> is required when using standard I/O functions.
- ✍ The header file <ctype.h> is required when using character handling functions.
- ✍ The header file <stdlib.h> is required when using general utility functions.
- ✍ The header file <string.h> is required when using string manipulation functions.

CASE STUDIES

1. Counting Words in a Text

One of the practical applications of string manipulations is counting the words in a text. We assume that a word is a sequence of any characters, except escape characters and blanks, and that two words are separated by one blank character. The algorithm for counting words is as follows:

1. Read a line of text.
2. Beginning from the first character in the line, look for a blank. If a blank is found, increment words by 1.
3. Continue steps 1 and 2 until the last line is completed.

The implementation of this algorithm is shown in Fig. 8.11. The first **while** loop will be executed once for each line of text. The end of text is indicated by pressing the 'Return' key an extra time after the entire text has been entered. The extra 'Return' key causes a newline character as input to the last line and as a result, the last line contains only the null character.

The program checks for this special line using the test

if (line[0] == '\0')

and if the first (and only the first) character in the line is a null character, then counting is terminated. Note the difference between a null character and a blank character.

Program

```
#include <stdio.h>
main()
{
   char line[81], ctr;
   int i,c,
       end = 0,
       characters = 0,
       words = 0,
       lines = 0;
   printf("KEY IN THE TEXT.\n");
   printf("GIVE ONE SPACE AFTER EACH WORD.\n");
   printf("WHEN COMPLETED, PRESS 'RETURN'.\n\n");
   while( end == 0)
   {
      /* Reading a line of text */
      c = 0;
      while((ctr=getchar()) != '\n')
          line[c++] = ctr;
      line[c] = '\0';
      /* counting the words in a line */
      if(line[0] == '\0')
          break ;
      else
      {
          words++;
```

```
            for(i=0; line[i] != '\0';i++)
                if(line[i] == ' ' || line[i] == '\t')
                    words++;
        }
        /* counting lines and characters */
        lines = lines +1;
        characters = characters + strlen(line);
    }
    printf ("\n");
    printf("Number of lines = %d\n", lines);
    printf("Number of words = %d\n", words);
    printf("Number of characters = %d\n", characters);
}
```

Output

```
KEY IN THE TEXT.
GIVE ONE SPACE AFTER EACH WORD.
WHEN COMPLETED, PRESS 'RETURN'.
Admiration is a very short-lived passion.
Admiration involves a glorious obliquity of vision.
Always we like those who admire us but we do not
like those whom we admire.
Fools admire, but men of sense approve.
Number of lines = 5
Number of words = 36
Number of characters = 205
```

Fig. 8.11 *Counting of characters, words and lines in a text*

The program also counts the number of lines read and the total number of characters in the text. Remember, the last line containing the null string is not counted.

After the first **while** loop is exited, the program prints the results of counting.

2. Processing of a Customer List

Telephone numbers of important customers are recorded as follows:

Full name	**Telephone number**
Joseph Louis Lagrange	869245
Jean Robert Argand	900823
Carl Freidrich Gauss	806788
-----	-----
-----	-----

It is desired to prepare a revised alphabetical list with surname (last name) first, followed by a comma and the initials of the first and middle names. For example,

Argand,J.R

We create a table of strings, each row representing the details of one person, such as first_name, middle_name, last_name, and telephone_number. The columns are interchanged as required and the list is sorted on the last_name. Figure 8.12 shows a program to achieve this.

Program

```
#define  CUSTOMERS   10

main( )
{
   char  first_name[20][10], second_name[20][10],
         surname[20][10], name[20][20],
         telephone[20][10], dummy[20];

    int   i,j;

     printf("Input names and telephone numbers \n");
     printf("?");
     for(i=0; i < CUSTOMERS ; i++)
     {
        scanf("%s %s %s %s", first_name[i],
             second_name[i], surname[i], telephone[i]);

        /* converting full name to surname with initials */

        strcpy(name[i], surname[i] );
        strcat(name[i], ",");
        dummy[0] = first_name[i][0];
        dummy[1] = '\0';
        strcat(name[i], dummy);
        strcat(name[i], ".");
        dummy[0] = second_name[i][0];
        dummy[1] = '\0';
        strcat(name[i], dummy);
     }
     /* Alphabetical ordering of surnames */

        for(i=1; i <= CUSTOMERS-1; i++)
           for(j=1; j <= CUSTOMERS-i; j++)
              if(strcmp (name[j-1], name[j]) > 0)
              {
              /* Swaping names */
                 strcpy(dummy, name[j-1]);
                 strcpy(name[j-1], name[j]);
                 strcpy(name[j], dummy);
```

```
                /* Swaping telephone numbers */
                    strcpy(dummy, telephone[j-1]);
                    strcpy(telephone[j-1],telephone[j]);
                    strcpy(telephone[j], dummy);
                }
            /* printing alphabetical list */
        printf("\nCUSTOMERS LIST IN ALPHABETICAL ORDER \n\n");
        for(i=0; i < CUSTOMERS ; i++)
            printf("    %-20s\t %-10s\n", name[i], telephone[i]);
    }
```

Output

```
    Input names and telephone numbers
    ?Gottfried Wilhelm Leibniz 711518
    Joseph Louis Lagrange 869245
    Jean Robert Argand 900823
    Carl Freidrich Gauss 806788
    Simon Denis Poisson 853240
    Friedrich Wilhelm Bessel 719731
    Charles Francois Sturm 222031
    George Gabriel Stokes 545454
    Mohandas Karamchand Gandhi 362718
    Josian Willard Gibbs 123145

  CUSTOMERS LIST IN ALPHABETICAL ORDER

          Argand,J.R    900823
          Bessel,F.W    719731
          Gandhi,M.K    362718
          Gauss,C.F     806788
          Gibbs,J.W     123145
          Lagrange,J.L 869245
          Leibniz,G.W   711518
          Poisson,S.D   853240
          Stokes,G.G    545454
          Sturm,C.F     222031
```

Fig. 8.12 *Program to alphabetize a customer list*

REVIEW QUESTIONS

8.1 State whether the following statements are *true* or *false*

(a) When initializing a string variable during its declaration, we must include the null character as part of the string constant, like "GOOD\0".

(b) The **gets** function automatically appends the null character at the end of the string read from the keyboard.

(c) When reading a string with **scanf**, it automatically inserts the terminating null character.
(d) String variables cannot be used with the assignment operator.
(e) We cannot perform arithmetic operations on character variables.
(f) We can assign a character constant or a character variable to an **int** type variable.
(g) The function **scanf** cannot be used in any way to read a line of text with the white-spaces.
(h) The ASCII character set consists of 128 distinct characters.
(i) In the ASCII collating sequence, the uppercase letters precede lowercase letters.
(j) In C, it is illegal to mix character data with numeric data in arithmetic operations.
(k) The function **getchar** skips white-space during input.
(l) In C, strings cannot be initialized at run time.
(m) The input function **gets** has one string parameter.
(n) The function call **strcpy(s2, s1);** copies string s2 into string s1.
(o) The function call **strcmp("abc", "ABC");** returns a positive number.

8.2 Fill in the blanks in the following statements.
(a) We can use the conversion specification ______ in **scanf** to read a line of text.
(b) We can initialize a string using the string manipulation function ______.
(c) The function **strncat** has ______ parameters.
(d) To use the function **atoi** in a program, we must include the header file ______.
(e) The function ______ does not require any conversion specification to read a string from the keyboard.
(f) The function ______ is used to determine the length of a string.
(g) The ______ string manipulation function determines if a character is contained in a string.
(h) The function ______ is used to sort the strings in alphabetical order.
(i) The function call **strcat (s2, s1);** appends ______ to ______.
(j) The **printf** may be replaced by ______ function for printing strings.

8.3 Describe the limitations of using **getchar** and **scanf** functions for reading strings.

8.4 Character strings in C are automatically terminated by the *null* character. Explain how this feature helps in string manipulations.

8.5 Strings can be assigned values as follows:

(a) During type declaration	`char string[ ] = {"......."};`
(b) Using **strcpy** function	`strcpy(string, ".......");`
(c) Reading using **scanf** function	`scanf("%s", string);`
(d) Reading using **gets** function	`gets(string);`

Compare them critically and describe situations where one is superior to the others.

8.6 Assuming the variable **string** contains the value "The sky is the limit.", determine what output of the following program segments will be.

(a) `printf("%s", string);`
(b) `printf("%25.10s", string);`
(c) `printf("%s", string[0]);`
(d)
```
for (i=0; string[i] != "."; i++)
    printf("%c", string[i]);
```
(e) `for (i=0; string[i] != '\0'; i++;)`

```
        printf("%d\n", string[i]);
    (f) for (i=0; i <= strlen[string]; ;)
        {
            string[i++] = i;
            printf("%s\n", string[i]);
        }
    (g) printf("%c\n", string[10] + 5);
    (h) printf("%c\n", string[10] + 5')
```

8.7 Which of the following statements will correctly store the concatenation of strings **s1** and **s2** in string **s3**?

```
    (a) s3 = strcat (s1, s2);
    (b) strcat (s1, s2, s3);
    (c) strcat (s3, s2, s1);
    (d) strcpy (s3, strcat (s1, s2));
    (e) strcmp (s3, strcat (s1, s2));
    (f) strcpy (strcat (s1, s2), s3);
```

8.8 What will be the output of the following statement?

```
printf ("%d", strcmp ("push", "pull"));
```

8.9 Assume that s1, s2 and s3 are declared as follows:

```
char s1[10] = "he", s2[20] = "she", s3[30], s4[30];
```

What will be the output of the following statements executed in sequence.

```
printf("%s", strcpy(s3, s1));
printf("%s", strcat(strcat(strcpy(s4, s1), "or"), s2));
printf("%d %d", strlen(s2)+strlen(s3), strlen(s4));
```

8.10 Find errors, if any, in the following code segments;

```
    (a) char str[10]
        strncpy(str, "GOD", 3);
        printf("%s", str);
    (b) char str[10];
        strcpy(str, "Balagurusamy");
    (c) if strstr("Balagurusamy", "guru") = = 0);
        printf("Substring is found");
    (d) char s1[5], s2[10],
        gets(s1, s2);
```

PROGRAMMING EXERCISES

8.1 Write a program, which reads your name from the keyboard and outputs a list of ASCII codes, which represent your name.

8.2 Write a program to do the following:

(a) To output the question "Who is the inventor of C ?"

(b) To accept an answer.

(c) To print out "Good" and then stop, if the answer is correct.

(d) To output the message 'try again', if the answer is wrong.

(e) To display the correct answer when the answer is wrong even at the third attempt and stop.

8.3 Write a program to extract a portion of a character string and print the extracted string. Assume that m characters are extracted, starting with the nth character.

8.4 Write a program which will read a text and count all occurrences of a particular word.

8.5 Write a program which will read a string and rewrite it in the alphabetical order. For example, the word STRING should be written as GINRST.

8.6 Write a program to replace a particular word by another word in a given string. For example, the word "PASCAL" should be replaced by "C" in the text "It is good to program in PASCAL language."

8.7 A Maruti car dealer maintains a record of sales of various vehicles in the following form:

Vehicle type	**Month of sales**	**Price**
MARUTI-800	02/01	210000
MARUTI-DX	07/01	265000
GYPSY	04/02	315750
MARUTI-VAN	08/02	240000

Write a program to read this data into a table of strings and output the details of a particular vehicle sold during a specified period. The program should request the user to input the vehicle type and the period (starting month, ending month).

8.8 Write a program that reads a string from the keyboard and determines whether the string is a *palindrome* or not. (A string is a palindrome if it can be read from left and right with the same meaning. For example, Madam and Anna are palindrome strings. Ignore capitalization).

8.9 Write program that reads the cost of an item in the form RRRR.PP (Where RRRR denotes Rupees and PP denotes Paise) and converts the value to a string of words that expresses the numeric value in words. For example, if we input 125.75, the output should be "ONE HUNDRED TWENTY FIVE AND PAISE SEVENTY FIVE".

8.10 Develop a program that will read and store the details of a list of students in the format

Roll No.	**Name**	**Marks obtained**
....	....	....
....	....	....
....	....	....

and produce the following output lits:

(a) Alphabetical list of names, roll numbers and marks obtained.

(b) List sorted on roll numbers.

(c) List sorted on marks (rank-wise list)

Chapter 9

User-Defined Functions

9.1 INTRODUCTION

We have mentioned earlier that one of the strengths of C language is that C functions are easy to define and use. We have used functions in every program that we have discussed so far. However, they have been primarily limited to the three functions, namely, **main, printf**, and **scanf**. In this chapter, we shall consider in detail how a function is designed, how two or more functions are put together and how they communicate with one another.

C functions can be classified into two categories, namely, *library* functions and *user-defined* functions. **main** is an example of user-defined functions. **printf** and **scanf** belong to the category of library functions. We have also used other library functions such as **sqrt, cos, strcat,** etc. The main distinction between these two categories is that library functions are not required to be written by us whereas a user-defined function has to be developed by the user at the time of writing a program. However, a user-defined function can later become a part of the C program library. In fact, this is one of the strengths of C language.

9.2 NEED FOR USER-DEFINED FUNCTIONS

As pointed out earlier, **main** is a specially recognized function in C. Every program must have a **main** function to indicate where the program has to begin its execution. While it is possible to code any program utilizing only **main** function, it leads to a number of problems. The program may become too large and complex and as a result the task of debugging, testing, and maintaining becomes difficult. If a program is divided into functional parts, then each part may be independently coded and later combined into a single unit. These subprograms called 'functions' are much easier to understand, debug, and test.

There are times when certain type of operations or calculations is repeated at many points throughout a program. For instance, we might use the factorial of a number at several points in the program. In such situations, we may repeat the program statements wherever they are needed. Another approach is to design a function that can be called and used whenever required. This saves both time and space.

This "division" approach clearly results in a number of advantages.

1. It facilitates top-down modular programming as shown in Fig. 9.1. In this programming style, the high level logic of the overall problem is solved first while the details of each lower-level function are addressed later.
2. The length of a source program can be reduced by using functions at appropriate places. This factor is particularly critical with microcomputers where memory space is limited.
3. It is easy to locate and isolate a faulty function for further investigations.
4. A function may be used by many other programs. This means that a C programmer can build on what others have already done, instead of starting all over again from scratch.

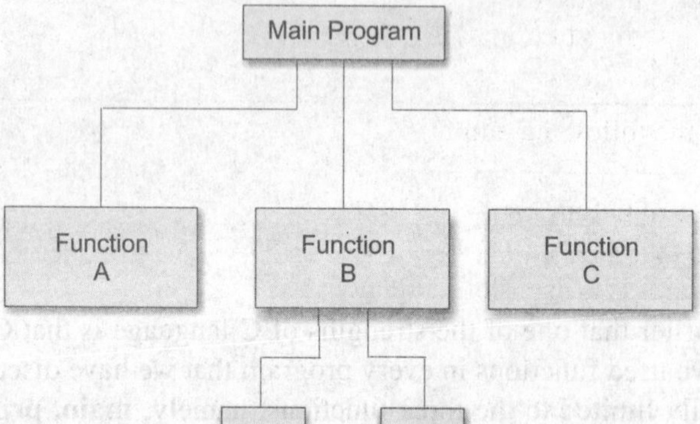

Fig. 9.1 *Top-down modular programming using functions*

9.3 A MULTI-FUNCTION PROGRAM

A function is a self-contained block of code that performs a particular task. Once a function has been designed and packed, it can be treated as a 'black box' that takes some data from the main program and returns a value. The inner details of operation are invisible to the rest of the program. All that the program knows about a function is: What goes in and what comes out. Every C program can be designed using a collection of these black boxes known as *functions*.

Consider a set of statements as shown below:

```
void  printline(void)
{
    int i;
    for (i=1; i<40; i++)
        printf("-");
    printf("\n");
}
```

The above set of statements defines a function called **printline,** which could print a line of 39-character length. This function can be used in a program as follows:

```
void printline(void);  /* declaration  */
 main( )
 {
      printline( );
      printf("This illustrates the use of C functions\n");
      printline();
 }
  void printline(void)
 {
   int i;
   for(i=1; i<40; i++)
   printf("-");
   printf("\n");
 }
```

This program will print the following output:

This illustrates the use of C functions

The above program contains two user-defined functions:

main() function

printline() function

As we know, the program execution always begins with the **main** function. During execution of the **main,** the first statement encountered is

```
printline( );
```

which indicates that the function **printline** is to be executed. At this point, the program control is transferred to the function **printline.** After executing the **printline** function, which outputs a line of 39 character length, the control is transferred back to the **main.** Now, the execution continues at the point where the function call was executed. After executing the **printf** statement, the control is again transferred to the **printline** function for printing the line once more.

The **main** function calls the user-defined **printline** function two times and the library function **printf** once. We may notice that the **printline** function itself calls the library function **printf** 39 times repeatedly.

Any function can call any other function. In fact, it can call itself. A 'called function' can also call another function. A function can be called more than once. In fact, this is one of the main features of using functions. Figure 9.2 illustrates the flow of control in a multi-function program.

Except the starting point, there are no other predetermined relationships, rules of precedence, or hierarchies among the functions that make up a complete program. The functions can be placed in any order. A called function can be placed either before or after the calling function. However, it is the usual practice to put all the called functions at the end. See the box "Modular Programming"

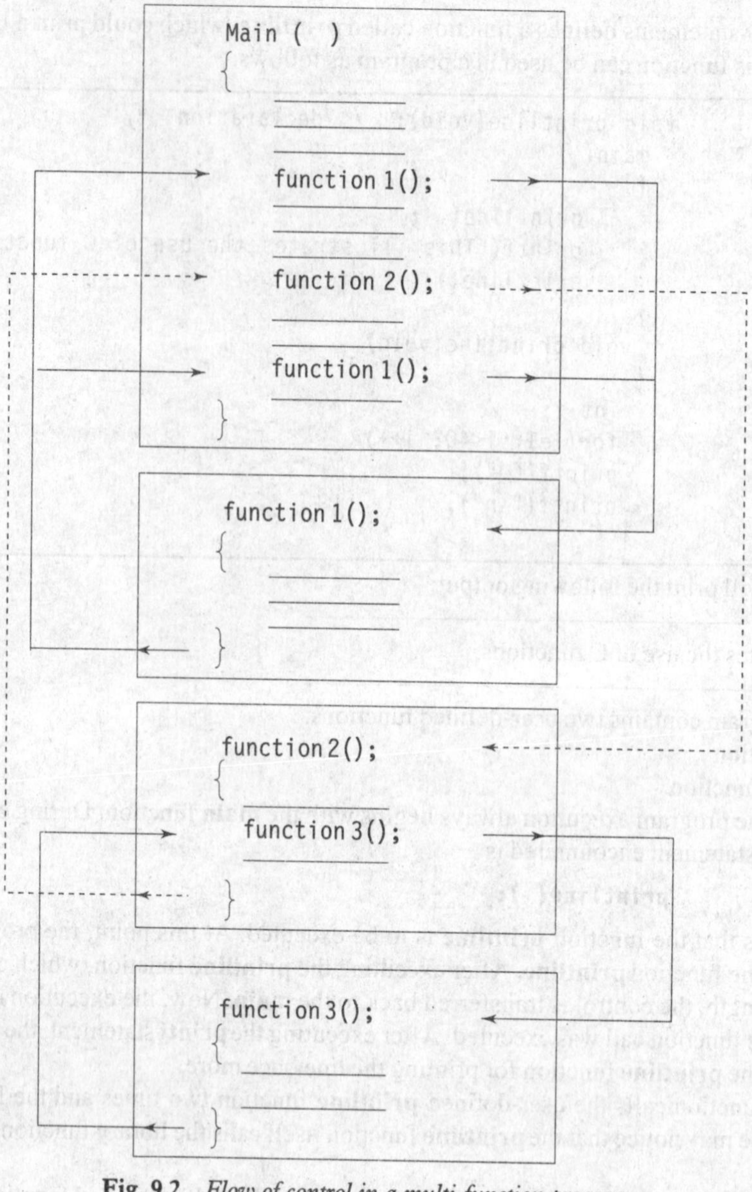

Fig. 9.2 *Flow of control in a multi-function program*

Modular Programming

Modular programming is a strategy applied to the design and development of software systems. It is defined as organizing a large program into small, independent program segments called ***modules*** that are separately named and individually callable *program units*. These modules are carefully integrated to become a software system that satisfies the system requirements. It is basically a "divide-and-conquer" approach to problem solving.

Modules are identified and designed such that they can be organized into a top-down hierarchical structure (similar to an organization chart). In C, each module refers to a function that is responsible for a single task.

Some characteristics of modular programming are:

1. Each module should do only one thing.
2. Communication between modules is allowed only by a calling module.
3. A module can be called by one and only one higher module.
4. No communication can take place directly between modules that do not have calling-called relationship.
5. All modules are designed as *single-entry, single-exit* systems using control structures.

9.4 ELEMENTS OF USER-DEFINED FUNCTIONS

We have discussed and used a variety of data types and variables in our programs so far. However, declaration and use of these variables were primarily done inside the **main** function. As we mentioned in Chapter 4, functions are classified as one of the derived data types in C. We can therefore define functions and use them like any other variables in C programs. It is therefore not a surprise to note that there exist some similarities between functions and variables in C.

- Both function names and variable names are considered identifiers and therefore they must adhere to the rules for identifiers.
- Like variables, functions have types (such as int) associated with them.
- Like variables, function names and their types must be declared and defined before they are used in a program.

In order to make use of a user-defined function, we need to establish three elements that are related to functions.

1. Function definition
2. Function call
3. Function declaration

The *function definition* is an independent program module that is specially written to implement the requirements of the function. In order to use this function we need to invoke it at a required place in the program. This is known as the *function call.* The program (or a function) that calls the function is referred to as the *calling program* or *calling function.* The calling program should declare any function (like declaration of a variable) that is to be used later in the program. This is known as the *function declaration* or *function prototype.*

9.5 DEFINITION OF FUNCTIONS

A *function definition,* also known as *function implementation* shall include the following elements.

1. Function name
2. Function type
3. List of parameters
4. Local variable declarations
5. Function statements
6. A return statement

All the six elements are grouped into two parts, namely,

- Function header (First three elements)
- Function body (Second three elements)

A general format of a function definition to implement these two parts is given below:

```
function_type  function_name(parameter list)
{
    local variable declaration;
    executable statement1;
    executable statement2;
    . . . . .
    . . . . .
    return statement;
}
```

The first line

function_type function_name(parameter list)

is known as the *function header* and the statements within the opening and closing braces constitute the *function body,* which is a compound statement.

Function Header

The function header consists of three parts: The function type (also known as *return* type, the function name and the *formal* parameter list. Note that a semicolon is not used at the end of the function header.

Name and Type

The *function type* specifies the type of value (*like float or double*) that the function is expected to return to the program calling the function. If the return type is not explicitly specified, C will assume that it is an integer type. If the function is not returning anything, then we need to specify the return type as **void**. Remember, **void** is one of the fundamental data types in C. It is a good programming practice to code explicitly the return type, even when it is an integer. (The value returned is the output produced by the function).

The *function name* is any valid C identifier and therefore must follow the same rules of formation as other variable names in C. The name should be appropriate to the task performed by the function. However, care must be exercised to avoid duplicating library routine names or operating system commands.

Formal Parameter List

The *parameter list* declares the variables that will receive the data sent by the calling program. They serve as input data to the function to carry out the specified task. Since they represent actual input values, they are often referred to as *formal* parameters. These parameters can also be used to send values to the calling programs. This aspect will be covered later when we discuss more about functions. The parameters are also known as *arguments*.

The parameter list contains declaration of variables separated by commas and surrounded by parentheses. Examples;

```
float quadratic (int a, int b, int c) {. . . . }
double power (double x, int n) {. . . ..}
float mul (float x, float y) {. . . . }
int sum (int a, int b) {. . . . }
```

Remember, there is no semicolon after the closing parenthesis. Note that the declaration of parameter variables cannot be combined. That is,

```
int sum (int a,b)
```

is illegal

A function need not always receive values from the calling program. In such cases, functions have no formal parameters. To indicate that the parameter list is empty, we use the keyword **void** between the parentheses as in

```
void printline (void)
{
    . . . .
}
```

This function neither receives any input values nor returns back any value. Many compilers accept an empty set of parentheses, without specifying anything as in

```
void printline ( )
```

But, it is a good programming style to use **void** to indicate a nill parameter list.

Function Body

The *function body* contains the declarations and statements necessary for performing the required task. The body enclosed in braces, contains three parts, in the order given below:

1. Local declarations that specify the variables needed by the function.
2. Function statements that perform the task of the function.
3. A **return** statement that returns the value evaluated by the function.

If a function does not return any value (like the **printline** function), we can omit the **return** statement. However, note that its return type should be specified as **void.** Again, it is nice to have a return statement even for **void** functions.

Some examples of typical function definitions are;

```
(a) float mul (float x, float y)
    {
        float result;            /* local variable */
        result = x * y;          /* computes the product */
        return (result);         /* returns the result */
    }
(b) void sum (int a, int b)
    {
        printf ("sum = %s", a + b); /* no local variables */
        return;                  /* optional */
    }
(c) void display (void)
    {                            /* no local variables */
        printf ("No type, no parameters");
                                 /* no return statement */
    }
```

Note:

1. When a function reaches its return statement, the control is transferred back to the calling program. In the absence of a return statement, the closing brace acts as a *void return*.
2. A *local variable* is a variable that is defined inside a function and used without having any role in the communication between functions.

9.6 RETURN VALUES AND THEIR TYPES

As pointed out earlier, a function may or may not send back any value to the calling function. If it does, it is done through the **return** statement. While it is possible to pass to the called function any number of values, the called function can only return *one value* per call, at the most.

The **return** statement can take one of the following forms

```
return;
or
return(expression);
```

The first, the 'plain' **return** does not return any value; it acts much as the closing brace of the function. When a **return** is encountered, the control is immediately passed back to the calling function. An example of the use of a simple **return** is as follows:

```
if(error)
    return;
```

The second form of **return** with an expression returns the value of the expression. For example, the function

```
int mul (int x, int y)
{
    int p;
```

```
        p = x*y;
        return(p);
    }
```

returns the value of **p** which is the product of the values of **x** and **y.** The last two statements can be combined into one statement as follows:

```
    return (x*y);
```

A function may have more than one **return** statements. This situation arises when the value returned is based on certain conditions. For example:

```
    if( x <= 0 )
        return(0);
    else
        return(1);
```

What type of data does a function return? All functions by default return **int** type data. But what happens if a function must return some other type? We can force a function to return a particular type of data by using a *type specifier* in the function header as discussed earlier.

When a value is returned, it is automatically cast to the function's type. In functions that do computations using **doubles**, yet return **ints**, the returned value will be truncated to an integer. For instance, the function

```
    int product (void)
    {
        return (2.5 * 3.0);
    }
```

will return the value 7, only the integer part of the result.

9.7 FUNCTION CALLS

A function can be called by simply using the function name followed by a list of *actual parameters* (or arguments), if any, enclosed in parentheses. Example:

```
    main( )
    {
        int y;
        y = mul(10,5);          /* Function call */
        printf("%d\n", y);
    }
```

When the compiler encounters a function call, the control is transferred to the function **mul()**. This function is then executed line by line as described and a value is returned when a **return** statement is encountered. This value is assigned to y. This is illustrated below:

```
main ()
{
   int y;
   y = mul(10,5);   /* call*/
   . . . . .
}
int mul(int x,int y)
{

   int p;          /*local variable*/

   p = x* y;       /* x = 10, y = 5*/
   return (p);
}
```

The function call sends two integer values 10 and 5 to the function.

int mul(int x, int y)

which are assigned to **x** and **y** respectively. The function computes the product **x** and **y**, assigns the result to the local variable **p**, and then returns the value 25 to the **main** where it is assigned to **y** again.

There are many different ways to call a function. Listed below are some of the ways the function **mul** can be invoked.

mul (10, 5)
mul (m, 5)
mul (10, n)
mul (m, n)
mul (m + 5, 10)
mul (10, mul(m,n))
mul (expression1, expression2)

Note that the sixth call uses its own call as its one of the parameters. When we use expressions, they should be evaluated to single values that can be passed as actual parameters.

A function which returns a value can be used in expressions like any other variable. Each of the following statements is valid:

```
printf("%d\n", mul(p,q));
y = mul(p,q) / (p+q);
if (mul(m,n)>total) printf("large");
```

However, a function cannot be used on the right side of an assignment statement. For instance,

```
mul(a,b) = 15;
```

is invalid.

A function that does not return any value may not be used in expressions; but can be called in to perform certain tasks specified in the function. The function **println( )** discussed in Section 9.3 belongs to this category. Such functions may be called in by simply stating their names as independent statements.

Example:

```
main( )
{
printline( );
}
```

Note the presence of a semicolon at the end.

Function Call

A function call is a postfix expression. The operator (. .) is at a very high level of precedence. (See Table 3.8) Therefore, when a function call is used as a part of an expression, it will be evaluated first, unless parentheses are used to change the order of precedence.

In a function call, the function name is the operand and the parentheses set (. .) which contains the *actual parameters* is the operator. The actual parameters must match the function's formal parameters in type, order and number. Multiple actual parameters must be separated by commas.

Note:

1. If the actual parameters are more than the formal parameters, the extra actual arguments will be discarded.
2. On the other hand, if the actuals are less than the formals, the unmatched formal arguments will be initialized to some garbage.
3. Any mismatch in data types may also result in some garbage values.

9.8 FUNCTION DECLARATION

Like variables, all functions in a C program must be declared, before they are invoked. A *function declaration* (also known as *function prototype*) consists of four parts.

- Function type (return type)
- Function name
- Parameter list
- Terminating semicolon

They are coded in the following format:

```
Function-type function-name (parameter list);
```

This is very similar to the function header line except the terminating semicolon. For example, **mul** function defined in the previous section will be declared as:

int mul (int m, int n); /* Function prototype */

Points to note:

1. The parameter list must be separated by commas.
2. The parameter names do not need to be the same in the prototype declaration and the function definition.
3. The types must match the types of parameters in the function definition, in number and order.
4. Use of parameter names in the declaration is optional.
5. If the function has no formal parameters, the list is written as (void).
6. The return type is optional, when the function returns **int** type data.
7. The retype must be **void** if no value is returned.
8. When the declared types do not match with the types in the function definition, compiler will produce an error.

Equally acceptable forms of declaration of **mul** function are:

```
int mul (int, int);
    mul (int a, int b);
    mul (int, int);
```

When a function does not take any parameters and does not return any value, its prototype is written as:

```
void display (void);
```

A prototype declaration may be placed in two places in a program.

1. Above all the functions (including **main**)
2. Inside a function definition.

When we place the declaration above all the functions (in the global declaration section), the prototype is referred to as a *global prototype*. Such declarations are available for all the functions in the program.

When we place it in a function definition (in the local declaration section), the prototype is called a *local prototype*. Such declarations are primarily used by the functions containing them.

The place of declaration of a function defines a region in a program in which the function may be used by other functions. This region is known as the *scope* of the function. (Scope is discussed later in this chapter.) It is a good programming style to declare prototypes in the global declaration section before **main**. It adds flexibility, provides an excellent quick reference to the functions used in the program, and enhances documentation.

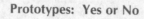

Prototypes: Yes or No

Prototype declarations are not essential. If a function has not been declared before it is used, C will assume that its details available at the time of linking. Since the prototype is not available, C will assume that the return type is an integer and that the types of parameters match the formal definitions. If these assumptions are wrong, the linker will fail and we will have to change the program. The moral is that we must always include prototype declarations, preferably in global declaration section.

Parameters Everywhere!

Parameters (also known as arguments) are used in three places;

1. In declaration (prototypes)
2. In function call
3. In function definition.

The parameters used in prototypes and function definitions are called *formal parameters* and those used in function calls are called *actual parameters*. Actual parameters used in a calling statement may be simple constants, variables or expressions.

The formal and actual parameters must match exactly in type, order and number. Their names, however, do not need to match.

9.9 CATEGORY OF FUNCTIONS

A function, depending on whether arguments are present or not and whether a value is returned or not, may belong to one of the following categories.

Category 1: Functions with no arguments and no return values.
Category 2: Functions with arguments and no return values.
Category 3: Functions with arguments and one return value.
Category 4: Functions with no arguments but return a value.
Category 5: Functions that return multiple values.

In the sections to follow, we shall discuss these categories with examples. Note that, from now on, we shall use the term arguments (rather than parameters) more frequently.

9.10 NO ARGUMENTS AND NO RETURN VALUES

When a function has no arguments, it does not receive any data from the calling function. Similarly, when it does not return a value, the calling function does not receive any data from the called function. In effect, there is no data transfer between the calling function and the called function. This is depicted in Fig. 9.3. The dotted lines indicate that there is only a transfer of control but not data.

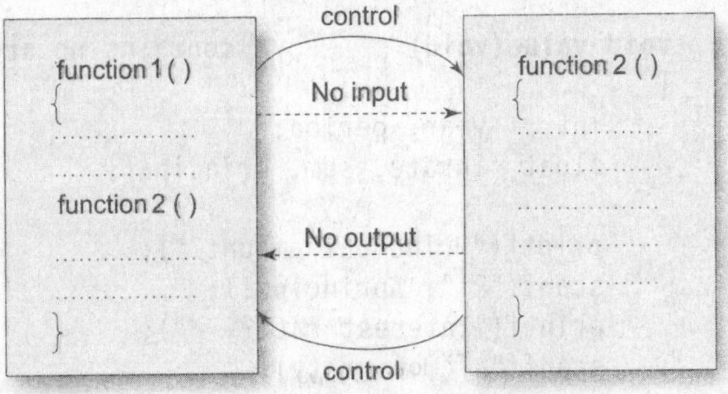

Fig. 9.3 *No data communication between functions*

As pointed out earlier, a function that does not return any value cannot be used in an expression. It can only be used as an independent statement.

Example 9.1 Write a program with multiple functions that do not communicate any data between them.

A program with three user-defined functions is given in Fig. 9.4. **main** is the calling function that calls **printline** and **value** functions. Since both the called functions contain no arguments, there are no argument declarations. The **printline** function, when encountered, prints a line with a length of 35 characters as prescribed in the function. The **value** function calculates the value of principal amount after a certain period of years and prints the results. The following equation is evaluated repeatedly:

value = principal(1+interest-rate)

```
Program

          /* Function declaration */
          void printline (void);
          void value (void);

          main()
          {
               printline();
               value();
               printline();
          }
          /*          Function1: printline( )          */

          void printline(void)      /* contains no arguments */
          {
               int i ;

               for(i=1; i <= 35; i++)
                    printf("%c",'-');
               printf("\n");
          }

          /*          Function2: value( )              */

          void value(void)          /* contains no arguments */
          {
               int    year, period;
               float  inrate, sum, principal;

               printf("Principal amount?");
               scanf("%f", &principal);
               printf("Interest rate?    ");
               scanf("%f", &inrate);
               printf("Period?           ");
```

```
        scanf("%d", &period);

        sum = principal;
        year = 1;
        while(year <= period)
        {
            sum = sum *(1+inrate);
            year = year +1;
        }
        printf("\n%8.2f %5.2f %5d %12.2f\n",
                principal,inrate,period,sum);
    }
```

Output

```
--------------------------------------
    Principal amount?   5000
    Interest rate?      0.12
    Period?             5

    5000.00  0.12       5       8811.71
--------------------------------------
```

Fig. 9.4 *Functions with no arguments and no return values*

It is important to note that the function **value** receives its data directly from the terminal. The input data include principal amount, interest rate and the period for which the final value is to be calculated. The **while** loop calculates the final value and the results are printed by the library function **printf.** When the closing brace of **value( )** is reached, the control is transferred back to the calling function **main.** Since everything is done by the value itself there is in fact nothing left to be sent back to the called function. Return types of both **printline** and **value** are declared as **void.**

Note that no **return** statement is employed. When there is nothing to be returned, the **return** statement is optional. The closing brace of the function signals the end of execution of the function, thus returning the control, back to the calling function.

9.11 ARGUMENTS BUT NO RETURN VALUES

In Fig. 9.4 the **main** function has no control over the way the functions receive input data. For example, the function **printline** will print the same line each time it is called. Same is the case with the function **value.** We could make the calling function to read data from the terminal and pass it on to the called function. This approach seems to be wiser because the calling function can check for the validity of data, if necessary, before it is handed over to the called function.

The nature of data communication between the calling function and the called function with arguments but no return value is shown in Fig. 9.5.

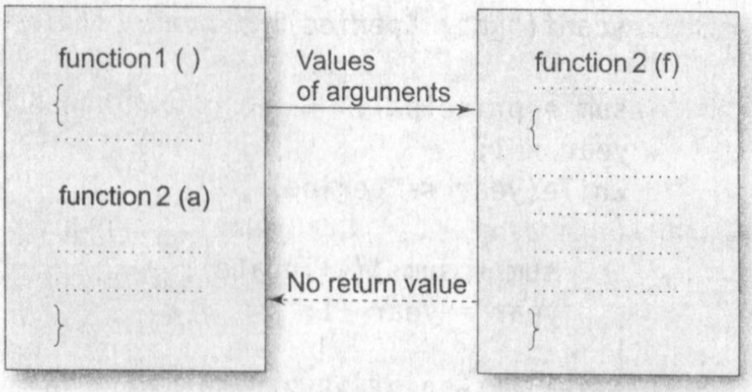

Fig. 9.5 *One-way data communication*

We shall modify the definitions of both the called functions to include arguments as follows:

void printline(char ch)

void value(float p, float r, int n)

The arguments **ch, p, r,** and **n** are called the *formal arguments.* The calling function can now send values to these arguments using function calls containing appropriate arguments. For example, the function call

value(500,0.12,5)

would send the values 500,0.12 and 5 to the function

void value(float p, float r, int n)

and assign 500 to **p**, 0.12 to **r** and 5 to **n**. The values 500, 0.12 and 5 are the *actual arguments, which* become the values of the *formal arguments* inside the called function.

The *actual* and *formal* arguments should match in number, type, and order. The values of actual arguments are assigned to the formal arguments on a *one to one* basis, starting with the first argument as shown in Fig. 9.6.

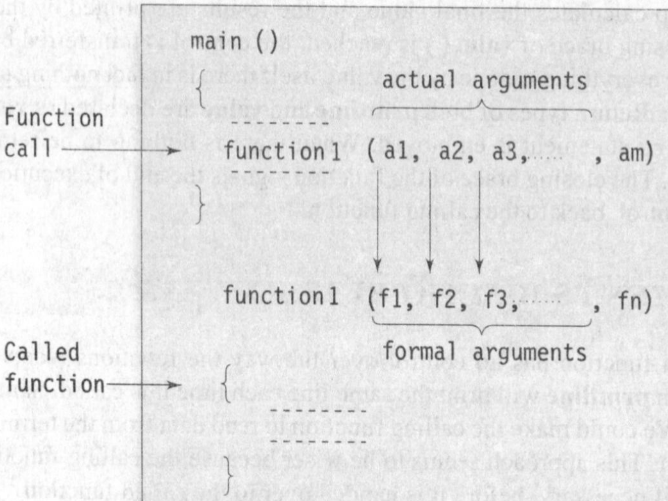

Fig. 9.6 *Arguments matching between the function call and the called function*

We should ensure that the function call has matching arguments. In case, the actual arguments are more than the formal arguments (m > n), the extra actual arguments are discarded. On the other hand, if the actual arguments are less than the formal arguments, the unmatched formal arguments are initialized to some garbage values. Any mismatch in data type may also result in passing of garbage values. Remember, no error message will be generated.

While the formal arguments must be valid variable names, the actual arguments may be variable names, expressions, or constants. The variables used in actual arguments must be assigned values before the function call is made.

Remember that, when a function call is made, only *a copy of the values of actual arguments is passed into the called function.* What occurs inside the function will have no effect on the variables used in the actual argument list.

Example 9.2 Modify the program of Example 9.1 to include the arguments in the function calls.

The modified program with function arguments is presented in Fig. 9.7. Most of the program is identical to the program in Fig. 9.4. The input prompt and **scanf** assignment statement have been moved from **value** function to **main.** The variables **principal, inrate,** and **period** are declared in **main** because they are used in main to receive data. The function call

```
value(principal, inrate, period);
```

passes information it contains to the function **value.**

The function header of **value** has three formal arguments **p,r,** and **n** which correspond to the actual arguments in the function call, namely, **principal, inrate,** and **period.** On execution of the function call, the values of the actual arguments are assigned to the corresponding formal arguments. In fact, the following assignments are accomplished across the function boundaries:

```
p = principal;
r = inrate;
n = period;
```

```
Program

    /* prototypes */
    void printline (char c);
    void value (float, float, int);

    main( )
    {
          float principal, inrate;
          int period;

          printf("Enter principal amount, interest");
          printf(" rate, and period \n");
          scanf("%f %f %d",&principal, &inrate, &period);
          printline('Z');
          value(principal,inrate,period);
```

```
        printline('C');
    }
    void printline(char ch)
    {
        int i ;
        for(i=1; i <= 52; i++)
            printf("%c",ch);
        printf("\n");
    }

    void value(float p, float r, int n)
    {
        int year ;
        float sum ;
        sum = p ;
        year = 1;
        while(year <= n)
        {
            sum = sum * (1+r);
            year = year +1;
        }
        printf("%f\t%f\t%d\t%f\n",p,r,n,sum);
    }
```

Output

```
    Enter principal amount, interest rate, and period
    5000 0.12   5
    ZZZZZZZZZZZZZZZZZZZZZZZZZZZZZZZZZZZZZZZZZZZZZZZZZZZZ
    5000.000000     0.120000        5     8811.708984
    CCCCCCCCCCCCCCCCCCCCCCCCCCCCCCCCCCCCCCCCCCCCCCCCCCCC
```

Fig. 9.7 *Functions with arguments but no return values*

The variables declared inside a function are known as *local variables* and therefore their values are local to the function and cannot be accessed by any other function. We shall discuss more about this later in the chapter.

The function **value** calculates the final amount for a given period and prints the results as before. Control is transferred back on reaching the closing brace of the function. Note that the function does not return any value.

The function **printline** is called twice. The first call passes the character 'Z', while the second passes the character 'C' to the function. These are assigned to the formal argument **ch** for printing lines (see the output).

Variable Number of Arguments

Some functions have a variable number of arguments and data types which cannot be known at compile time. The **printf** and **scanf** functions are typical examples. The ANSI standard proposes new symbol called the *ellipsis* to handle such functions. The *ellipsis* consists of three periods (...) and used as shown below:

double area(float d,...)

Both the function declaration and definition should use ellipsis to indicate that the arguments are arbitrary both in number and type.

9.12 ARGUMENTS WITH RETURN VALUES

The function **value** in Fig. 9.7 receives data from the calling function through arguments, but does not send back any value. Rather, it displays the results of calculations at the terminal. However, we may not always wish to have the result of a function displayed. We may use it in the calling function for further processing. Moreover, to assure a high degree of portability between programs, a function should generally be coded without involving any I/O operations. For example, different programs may require different output formats for display of results. These shortcomings can be overcome by handing over the result of a function to its calling function where the returned value can be used as required by the program.

A self-contained and independent function should behave like a 'black box' that receives a predefined form of input and outputs a desired value. Such functions will have two-way data communication as shown in Fig. 9.8

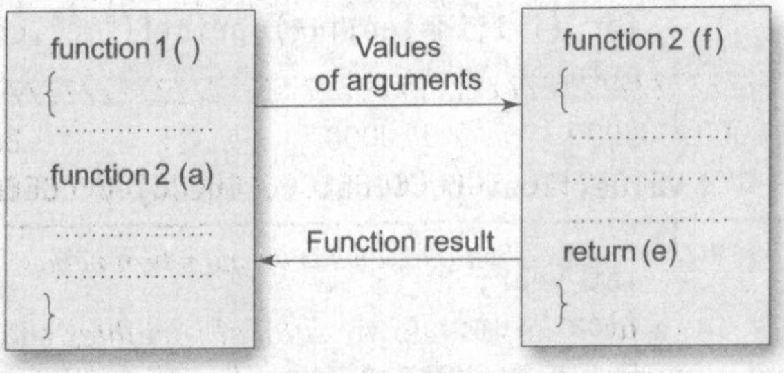

Fig. 9.8 *Two-way data communication between functions*

We shall modify the program in Fig. 9.7 to illustrate the use of two-way data communication between the calling and the called functions.

Example 9.3 In the program presented in Fig. 9.7 modify the function **value,** to return the final amount calculated to the **main**, which will display the required output at the terminal. Also extend the versatility of the function **printline** by having it to take the length of the line as an argument.

The modified program with the proposed changes is presented in Fig. 9.9. One major change is the movement of the **printf** statement from **value** to **main.**

```
Program

    void printline (char ch, int len);
    value (float, float, int);

      main( )
      {
        float principal, inrate, amount;
        int period;
        printf("Enter principal amount, interest");
        printf("rate, and period\n");
        scanf(%f %f %d", &principal, &inrate, &period);
        printline ('*'  , 52);
        amount = value (principal, inrate, period);
        printf("\n%f\t%f\t%d\t%f\n\n",principal,
           inrate,period,amount);
        printline('=',52);
      }
      void printline(char ch, int len)
      {
        int i;
        for (i=1;i<=len;i++) printf("%c",ch);
        printf("\n");
      }

      value(float p, float r, int n) /* default return type */
      {
        int year;
        float sum;
        sum = p; year = 1;
        while(year <=n)
        {
          sum = sum * (l+r);
          year = year +1;
        }
        return(sum);       /* returns int part of sum */
      }
```

```
Output

    Enter principal amount, interest rate, and period
    5000   0.12   5
    ************************************************

    5000.000000   0.1200000  5   8811.000000

    = = = = = = = = = = = = = = = = = = = = = = = =
```

Fig. 9.9 *Functions with arguments and return values*

The calculated value is passed on to **main** through statement:

```
return(sum);
```

Since, by default, the return type of **value** function is **int,** the 'integer' value of **sum** at this point is returned to **main** and assigned to the variable **amount** by the functional call

```
amount = value (principal, inrate, period);
```

The following events occur, in order, when the above function call is executed:

1. The function call transfers the control along with copies of the values of the actual arguments to the function **value** where the formal arguments **p, r,** and **n** are assigned the actual values of **principal, inrate** and **period** respectively.
2. The called function **value** is executed line by line in a normal fashion until the **return(sum);** statement is encountered. At this point, the integer value of **sum** is passed back to the function-call in the **main** and the following indirect assignment occurs:

```
value(principal, inrate, period) = sum;
```

3. The calling statement is executed normally and the returned value is thus assigned to **amount,** a **float** variable.
4. Since **amount** is a **float** variable, the returned integer part of sum is converted to floating-point value. See the output.

Another important change is the inclusion of second argument to **printline** function to receive the value of length of the line from the calling function. Thus, the function call

```
printline('*', 52);
```

will transfer the control to the function **printline** and assign the following values to the formal arguments **ch**, and **len;**

```
ch = '*' ;
len = 52;
```

Returning Float Values

We mentioned earlier that a C function returns a value of the type **int** as the default case when no other type is specified explicitly. For example, the function **value** of Example 9.3 does all calculations using **floats** but the return statement

```
return(sum);
```

returns only the integer part of **sum.** This is due to the absence of the *type-specifier* in the function header. In this case, we can accept the integer value of **sum** because the truncated decimal part is insignificant compared to the integer part. However, there will be times when we may find it necessary to receive the **float** or **double** type of data. For example, a function that calculates the mean or standard deviation of a set of values should return the function value in either **float** or **double.**

In all such cases, we must explicitly specify the *return type* in both the function definition and the prototype declaration.

If we have a mismatch between the type of data that the called function returns and the type of data that the calling function expects, we will have unpredictable results. We must, therefore, be very careful to make sure that both types are compatible.

Example 9.4 Write a function **power** that computes x raised to the power y for integers x and y and returns double-type value.

Fig. 9.10 shows a **power** function that returns a **double.** The prototype declaration

```
double power(int, int);
```

appears in **main**, before **power** is called.

```
Program
            main( )
            {
              int x,y;            /*input data */
              double power(int, int);/* prototype declaration*/
              printf("Enter x,y:");
              scanf("%d %d" , &x,&y);
              printf("%d to power %d is %f\n", x,y,power (x,y));
            }
            double power (int x, int y);
            {
              double p;
              p = 1.0 ;       /* x to power zero */

              if(y >=0)
                while(y--)    /* computes positive powers */
                  p *= x;
              else
                while (y++)   /* computes negative powers */
                  p /= x;
              return(p);      /* returns double type */

            }
Output
```

```
Enter x,y:16 2
16 to power 2 is 256.000000

Enter x,y:16 -2
16 to power -2 is 0.003906
```

Fig. 9.10 *Power fuctions: Illustration of return of float values*

Another way to guarantee that **power**'s type is declared before it is called in **main** is to define the **power** function before we define **main. Power**'s type is then known from its definition, so we no longer need its type declaration in **main.**

9.13 NO ARGUMENTS BUT RETURNS A VALUE

There could be occasions where we may need to design functions that may not take any arguments but returns a value to the calling function. A typical example is the **getchar** function declared in the header file **<stdio.h>.** We have used this function earlier in a number of places. The **getchar** function has no parameters but it returns an integer type data that represents a character.

We can design similar functions and use in our programs. Example:

```
int get_number(void);
main
{
        int m = get_number( );
        printf("%d",m);
}
int get_number(void)
{
        int number;
        scanf("%d", &number);
        return(number);
}
```

9.14 FUNCTIONS THAT RETURN MULTIPLE VALUES

Up to now, we have illustrated functions that return just one value using a return statement. That is because, a return statement can return only value. Suppose, however, that we want to get more information from a function. We can achieve this in C using the arguments not only to receive information but also to send back information to the calling function. The arguments that are used to "send out" information are called *output parameters.*

The mechanism of sending back information through arguments is achieved using what are known as the *address operator* (&) and *indirection operator* (*). Let us consider an example to illustrate this.

```
void mathoperation (int x, int y, int *s, int *d);
main( )
```

```
{
    int x = 20, y = 10, s, d;
    mathoperation(x,y, &s, &d);

    printf("s=%d\n d=%d\n", s,d);
}

void mathoperation (int a, int b, int *sum, int *diff)
{
    *sum  = a+b;
    *diff = a-b;
}
```

The actual arguments **x** and **y** are input arguments, **s** and **d** are output arguments. In the function call, while we pass the actual values of **x** and **y** to the function, we pass the addresses of locations where the values of **s** and **d** are stored in the memory. (That is why, the operator & is called the address operator.) When the function is called the following assignments occur:

value of x to a
value of y to b
address of s to sum
address of d to diff

Note that indirection operator * in the declaration of **sum** and **diff** in the header indicates these variables are to store addresses, not actual values of variables. Now, the variables **sum** and **diff** point to the memory locations of **s** and **d** respectively.

(The operator * is known as indirection operator because it gives an indirect reference to a variable through its address.)

In the body of the function, we have two statements:

```
* sum  = a+b;
* diff = a-b;
```

The first one adds the values **a** and **b** and the result is stored in the memory location pointed to by **sum.** Remember, this memory location is the same as the memory location of **s.** Therefore, the value stored in the location pointed to by **sum** is the value of **s.**

Similarly, the value of a–b is stored in the location pointed to by **diff,** which is the same as the location **d.** After the function call is implemented, the value of **s** is a+b and the value of **d** is a–b. Output will be:

s = 30
d = 10

The variables ***sum** and ***diff** are known as *pointers* and **sum** and **diff** as *pointer* variables. Since they are declared as **int**, they can point to locations of **int** type data.

The use of pointer variables as actual parameters for communicating data between functions is called "pass by pointers" or "call by address or reference". (Pointers and their applications are discussed in detail in Chapter 11).

Rules for Pass by Pointers

1. The types of the actual and formal arguments must be same.
2. The actual arguments (in the function call) must be the addresses of variables that are local to the calling function.
3. The formal arguments in the function header must be prefixed by the indirection operatior *.
4. In the prototype, the arguments must be prefixed by the symbol *.
5. To access the value of an actual argument in the called function, we must use the corresponding formal argument prefixed with the indirection operator *.

9.15 NESTING OF FUNCTIONS

C permits nesting of functions freely. **main** can call **function1,** which calls **function2,** which calls **function3,** .... and so on. There is in principle no limit as to how deeply functions can be nested.

Consider the following program:

```
float ratio (int x, int y, int z);
int difference (int x, int y);
main( )
{
    int a, b, c;
    scanf("%d %d %d", &a, &b, &c);
    printf("%f \n", ratio(a,b,c));
}

float ratio(int x, int y, int z)
{
    if(difference(y, z))
        return(x/(y-z));
    else
        return(0.0);
}
int difference(int p, int q)
{
    if(p != q)
         return (1);
    else
         return(0);
}
```

The above program calculates the ratio

$$\frac{a}{b - c}$$

and prints the result. We have the following three functions:

main( )
ratio( )
difference( )

main reads the values of a, b and c and calls the function **ratio** to calculate the value a/(b–c). This ratio cannot be evaluated if (b–c) = 0. Therefore, **ratio** calls another function **difference** to test whether the difference (b–c) is zero or not; **difference** returns 1, if b is not equal to c; otherwise returns zero to the function **ratio**. In turn, **ratio** calculates the value a/(b–c) if it receives 1 and returns the result in **float.** In case, **ratio** receives zero from **difference,** it sends back 0.0 to **main** indicating that (b–c) = 0.

Nesting of function calls is also possible. For example, a statement like

```
P = mul(mul(5,2),6);
```

is valid. This represents two sequential function calls. The inner function call is evaluated first and the returned value is again used as an actual argument in the outer function call. If **mul** returns the product of its arguments, then the value of **p** would be 60 (= 5×2×6).

Note that the nesting does not mean defining one function within another. Doing this is illegal.

9.16 RECURSION

When a called function in turn calls another function a process of 'chaining' occurs. *Recursion* is a special case of this process, where a function calls itself. A very simple example of recursion is presented below:

```
main( )
{
        printf("This is an example of recursion\n")
        main( );
}
```

When executed, this program will produce an output something like this:

This is an example of recursion
This is an example of recursion
This is an example of recursion
This is an ex

Execution is terminated abruptly; otherwise the execution will continue indefinitely.

Another useful example of recursion is the evaluation of factorials of a given number. The factorial of a number n is expressed as a series of repetitive multiplications as shown below:

factorial of n = n(n–1)(n–2)..........1.

For example,

factorial of 4 = 4×3×2×1 = 24

A function to evaluate factorial of n is as follows:

```
factorial(int n)
{
    int fact;
    if (n==1)
        return(1);
    else
        fact = n*factorial(n-1);
    return(fact);
}
```

Let us see how the recursion works. Assume n = 3. Since the value of n is not 1, the statement

fact = n * factorial(n–1);

will be executed with n = 3. That is,

fact = 3 * factorial(2);

will be evaluated. The expression on the right-hand side includes a call to **factorial** with n = 2. This call will return the following value:

2 * factorial(1)

Once again, **factorial** is called with n = 1. This time, the function returns 1. The sequence of operations can be summarized as follows:

fact = 3 * factorial(2)
= 3 * 2 * factorial(1)
= 3 * 2 * 1
= 6

Recursive functions can be effectively used to solve problems where solution is expressed in terms of successively applying the same solution to subsets of the problem. When we write recursive functions, we must have an **if** statement somewhere to force the function to return without the recursive call being executed. Otherwise, the function will never return.

9.17 PASSING ARRAYS TO FUNCTIONS

One-Dimensional Arrays

Like the values of simple variables, it is also possible to pass the values of an array to a function. To pass a one-dimensional an array to a called function, it is sufficient to list the name of the array, *without any subscripts,* and the size of the array as arguments. For example, the call

largest(a,n)

will pass the whole array **a** to the called function. The called function expecting this call must be appropriately defined. The **largest** function header might look like:

float largest(float array[ ], int size)

The function **largest** is defined to take two arguments, the array name and the size of the array to specify the number of elements in the array. The declaration of the formal argument array is made as follows:

float array[ ];

The pair of brackets informs the compiler that the argument **array** is an array of numbers. It is not necessary to specify the size of the **array** here.

Let us consider a problem of finding the largest value in an array of elements. The program is as follows:

```
main( )
{
    float largest(float a[ ], int n);
    float value[4] = {2.5,-4.75,1.2,3.67};
    printf("%f\n", largest(value,4));
}
float largest(float a[], int n)
{
    int i;
    float max;
    max = a[0];
    for(i = 1; i < n; i++)
        if(max < a[i])
        max = a[i];
    return(max);
}
```

When the function call **largest**(value,4) is made, the values of all elements of array **value** become the corresponding elements of array **a** in the called function. The **largest** function finds the largest value in the array and returns the result to the **main.**

In C, the name of the array represents the address of its first element. By passing the array name, we are, in fact, passing the address of the array to the called function. The array in the called function now refers to the same array stored in the memory. Therefore, any changes in the array in the called function will be reflected in the original array.

Passing addresses of parameters to the functions is referred to as *pass by address* (or pass by pointers). Note that we cannot pass a whole array by value as we did in the case of ordinary variables.

Example 9.5 Write a program to calculate the standard deviation of an array of values. The array elements are read from the terminal. Use functions to calculate standard deviation and mean.

Standard deviation of a set of n values is given by

$$S.D = \sqrt{\frac{1}{n}\sum_{i=1}^{n}(\bar{x} - x_i)^2}$$

Where $\bar{x}$ is the mean of the values.

Program

```
#include     <math.h>
#define SIZE     5
float std_dev(float a[], int n);
float mean (float a[], int n);

main( )
{
    float value[SIZE];
    int i;

    printf("Enter %d float values\n", SIZE);
    for (i=0 ;i < SIZE ; i++)
        scanf("%f", &value[i]);
    printf("Std.deviation is %f\n", std_dev(value,SIZE));
}
float std_dev(float a[], int n)
{
    int i;
    float x, sum = 0.0;
    x = mean (a,n);
    for(i=0; i < n; i++)
     sum += (x-a[i])*(x-a[i]);
    return(sqrt(sum/(float)n));
}
float mean(float a[],int n)
{
    int i ;
    float sum = 0.0;
    for(i=0 ; i < n ; i++)
        sum = sum + a[i];
    return(sum/(float)n);
}
```

Output

```
Enter 5 float values
35.0 67.0 79.5 14.20 55.75

Std.deviation is 23.231582
```

Fig. 9.11 *Passing of arrays to a function*

A multifunction program consisting of **main, std_dev,** and **mean** functions is shown in Fig. 9.11. **main** reads the elements of the array **value** from the terminal and calls the function **std_dev** to print the standard deviation of the array elements. **Std_dev,** in turn, calls another function **mean** to supply the average value of the array elements.

Both **std_dev** and **mean** are defined as **floats** and therefore they are declared as **floats** in the global section of the program.

Three Rules to Pass an Array to a Function

1. The function must be called by passing only the name of the array.
2. In the function definition, the formal parameter must be an array type; the size of the array does not need to be specified.
3. The function prototype must show that the argument is an array.

When dealing with array arguments, we should remember one major distinction. If a function changes the values of the elements of an array, then these changes will be made to the original array that passed to the function. When an entire array is passed as an argument, the contents of the array are not copied into the formal parameter array; instead, information about the addresses of array elements are passed on to the function. Therefore, any changes introduced to the array elements are truly reflected in the original array in the calling function. However, this does not apply when an individual element is passed on as argument. Example 9.6 highlights these concepts.

Example 9.6 Write a program that uses a function to sort an array of integers.

A program to sort an array of integers using the function **sort()** is given in Fig. 9.12. Its output clearly shows that a function can change the values in an array passed as an argument.

Program

```
void sort(int m, int x[ ]);
main()
{
    int i;
    int marks[5] = {40, 90, 73, 81, 35};

    printf("Marks before sorting\n");
    for(i = 0; i < 5; i++)
       printf("%d ", marks[i]);
    printf("\n\n");

    sort (5, marks);

    printf("Marks after sorting\n");
    for(i = 0; i < 5; i++)
       printf("%4d", marks[i]);
    printf("\n");
```

```
        }
        void sort(int m, int x[ ])
        {
            int i, j, t;

            for(i = 1; i <= m-1; i++)
               for(j = 1; j <= m-i; j++)
                  if(x[j-1] >= x[j])
                  {
                     t = x[j-1];
                     x[j-1] = x[j];
                     x[j] = t;
                  }
        }
Output
        Marks before sorting
        40 90 73 81 35

        Marks after sorting
        35  40  73  81  90
```

Fig. 9.12 *Sorting of array elements using a function*

Two-Dimensional Arrays

Like simple arrays, we can also pass multidimensional arrays to functions. The approach is similar to the one we did with one-dimensional arrays. The rules are simple.

1. The function must be called by passing only the array name.
2. In the function definition, we must indicate that the array has two dimensions by including two sets of brackets.
3. The size of the second dimension must be specified.
4. The prototype declaration should be similar to the function header.

The function given below calculates the average of the values in a two-dimensional matrix.

```
double average(int x[][N], int M, int N)
{
    int i, j;
    double sum = 0.0;
    for (i=0; i<M; i++)
         for(j=1; j<N; j++)
       sum += x[i][j];
    return(sum/(M*N));
}
```

This function can be used in a main function as illustrated below:

```
main( )
{
        int M=3, N=2;
        double average(int [ ] [N], int, int);
        double mean;
        int matrix [M][N]=
                {
                  {1,2},
                  {3,4},
                  {5,6}
                };

        mean = average(matrix, M, N);
        . . . . . .
        . . . . . .
}
```

9.18 PASSING STRINGS TO FUNCTIONS

Because the strings are treated as character arrays in C, the rules for passing strings to functions are very similar to those for passing arrays to functions.

Basic rules are:

1. The string to be passed must be declared as a formal argument of the function when it is defined. Example:

```
void display(char item_name[ ])
{
        ......
        ......
}
```

2. The function prototype must show that the argument is a string. For the above function definition, the prototype can be written as

```
void display(char str[ ]);
```

3. A call to the function must have a string array name without subscripts as its actual argument. Example:

```
display (names);
```

where **names** is a properly declared string array in the calling function.

We must note here that, like arrays, strings in C cannot be passed by value to functions.

Pass by Value versus Pass by Pointers

The technique used to pass data from one function to another is known as *parameter passing*. Parameter passing can be done in two ways.

- Pass by value (also known as call by value)
- Pass by Pointers (also known as call by pointers)

In *pass by value*, values of actual parameters are copied to the variables in the parameter list of the called function. The called function works on the copy and not on the original values of the actual parameters. This ensures that the original data in the calling function cannot be changed accidentally.

In *pass by pointers* (also known as pass by address), the memory addresses of the variables rather than the copies of values are sent to the called function. In this case, the called function directly works on the data in the calling function and the changed values are available in the calling function for its use.

Pass by pointers method is often used when manipulating arrays and strings. This method is also used when we require multiple values to be returned by the called function.

9.19 THE SCOPE, VISIBILITY AND LIFETIME OF VARIABLES

Variables in C differ in behaviour from those in most other languages. For example, in a BASIC program, a variable retains its value throughout the program. It is not always the case in C. It all depends on the 'storage' class a variable may assume.

In C not only do all variables have a data type, they also have a *storage class*. The following variable storage classes are most relevant to functions:

1. Automatic variables
2. External variables
3. Static variables
4. Register variables

We shall briefly discuss the *scope, visibility* and *longevity* of each of the above class of variables. The *scope* of variable determines over what region of the program a variable is actually available for use ('active'). *Longevity* refers to the period during which a variable retains a given value during execution of a program ('alive'). So longevity has a direct effect on the utility of a given variable. The *visibility* refers to the accessibility of a variable from the memory.

The variables may also be broadly categorized, depending on the place of their declaration, as *internal* (local) or *external* (global). Internal variables are those which are declared within a particular function, while external variables are declared outside of any function.

It is very important to understand the concept of storage classes and their utility in order to develop efficient multifunction programs.

Automatic Variables

Automatic variables are declared inside a function in which they are to be utilized. They are *created* when the function is called and *destroyed* automatically when the function is exited, hence the name automatic. Automatic variables are therefore private (or local) to the function in which they are declared. Because of this property, automatic variables are also referred to as *local* or *internal* variables.

A variable declared inside a function without storage class specification is, by default, an automatic variable. For instance, the storage class of the variable **number** in the example below is automatic.

```
main( )
{
        int number;
        -----
        -----
}
```

We may also use the keyword **auto** to declare automatic variables explicitly.

```
main( )
{
        auto int number;
        -----
        -----
}
```

One important feature of automatic variables is that their value cannot be changed accidentally by what happens in some other function in the program. This assures that we may declare and use the same variable name in different functions in the same program without causing any confusion to the compiler.

Example 9.7 Write a multifunction to illustrate how automatic variables work.

A program with two subprograms **function1** and **function2** is shown in Fig. 9.13. **m** is an automatic variable and it is declared at the beginning of each function. **m** is initialized to 10, 100, and 1000 in function1, function2, and **main** respectively.

When executed, **main** calls **function2** which in turn calls **function1**. When **main** is active, m = 1000; but when **function2** is called, the **main**'s **m** is temporarily put on the shelf and the new local **m** = 100 becomes active. Similarly, when **function1** is called, both the previous values of **m** are put on the shelf and the latest value of **m** (=10) becomes active. As soon as **function1** (m=10) is finished, **function2** (m=100) takes over again. As soon as it is done, **main** (m=1000) takes over. The output clearly shows that the value assigned to **m** in one function does not affect its value in the other functions; and the local value of **m** is destroyed when it leaves a function.

Program

```
void function1(void);
void function2(void);
main( )
{
```

```
        int m = 1000;
        function2();

        printf("%d\n",m); /* Third output */
    }
    void function1(void)
    {
        int m = 10;

        printf("%d\n",m); /* First output */
    }

    void function2(void)
    {
        int m = 100;

        function1();
        printf("%d\n",m); /* Second output */
    }


Output
    10
    100
    1000
```

Fig. 9.13 *Working of automatic variables*

There are two consequences of the scope and longevity of **auto** variables worth remembering. First, any variable local to **main** will normally *alive* throughout the whole program, although it is *active* only in **main**. Secondly, during recursion, the nested variables are unique **auto** variables, a situation similar to function-nested **auto** variables with identical names.

External Variables

Variables that are both *alive* and *active* throughout the entire program are known as *external* variables. They are also known as *global* variables. Unlike local variables, global variables can be accessed by any function in the program. External variables are declared outside a function. For example, the external declaration of integer **number** and float **length** might appear as:

```
int number;
float length = 7.5;
main( )
{
  -------
  -------
```

```
}
function1( )
{
    --------
    --------
}
function2( )
{
    --------
    --------
}
```

The variables **number** and **length** are available for use in all the three functions. In case a local variable and a global variable have the same name, the local variable will have precedence over the global one in the function where it is declared. Consider the following example:

```
int count;
main( )
{
    count = 10;
    -----
    -----
}
function( )
{
    int count = 0;
    ------
    ------
    count = count+1;
}
```

When the **function** references the variable **count,** it will be referencing only its local variable, not the global one. The value of **count** in **main** will not be affected.

Example 9.8 Write a multifunction program to illustrate the properties of global variables.

A program to illustrate the properties of global variables is presented in Fig. 9.14. Note that variable **x** is used in all functions but none except **fun2,** has a definition for **x.** Because **x** has been declared 'above' all the functions, it is available to each function without having to pass x as a function argument. Further, since the value of **x** is directly available, we need not use **return(x)** statements in **fun1** and **fun3.** However, since **fun2** has a definition of **x,** it returns its local value of **x** and therefore uses a **return** statement. In **fun2**, the global **x** is not visible. The local **x** hides its visibility here.

Program

```
int fun1(void);
int fun2(void);
int fun3(void);
```

```
int x ;        /* global */
main( )
{
     x = 10 ;   /* global x */
     printf("x = %d\n", x);
     printf("x = %d\n", fun1());
     printf("x = %d\n", fun2());
     printf("x = %d\n", fun3());
}
fun1(void)
{
     x = x + 10 ;
}
int fun2(void)
{
     int x ;            /* local */
     x = 1 ;
     return (x);
}
fun3(void)
{
     x = x + 10 ;     /* global x */
}
```

Output

```
x = 10
x = 20
x = 1
x = 30
```

Fig. 9.14 *Illustration of properties of global variables*

Once a variable has been declared as global, any function can use it and change its value. Then, subsequent functions can reference only that new value.

Global Variables as Parameters

Since all functions in a program source file can access global variables, they can be used for passing values between the functions. However, using global variables as parameters for passing values poses certain problems.

- The values of global variables which are sent to the called function may be changed inadvertently by the called function.
- Functions are supposed to be independent and isolated modules. This character is lost, if they use global variables.
- It is not immediately apparent to the reader which values are being sent to the called function.
- A function that uses global variables suffers from reusability.

One other aspect of a global variable is that it is available only from the point of declaration to the end of the program. Consider a program segment as shown below:

```
main( )
{
        y = 5;
        . . . .
        . . . .
}
int y;          /* global declaration */
func1( )
{
            y = y+1;
}
```

We have a problem here. As far as **main** is concerned, **y** is not defined. So, the compiler will issue an error message. Unlike local variables, global variables are initialized to zero by default. The statement

```
y = y+1;
```

in **fun1** will, therefore, assign 1 to y.

External Declaration

In the program segment above, the **main** cannot access the variable y as it has been declared after the **main** function. This problem can be solved by declaring the variable with the storage class **extern.**

For example:

```
main( )
{
        extern int y;    /* external declaration */
        . . . . .
        . . . . .
}
func1( )
{
        extern int y;    /* external declaration */
        . . . . .
        . . . . .
}
int y;                   /* definition */
```

Although the variable **y** has been defined after both the functions, the *external declaration* of **y** inside the functions informs the compiler that y is an integer type defined somewhere else in the program. Note that **extern** declaration does not allocate storage space for variables. In case of arrays, the definition should include their size as well.

Example:

```
main( )
{    int i;
     void print_out(void);
     extern float height [ ];
     . . . . .
     . . . . .
     print_out( );
}
void print_out(void)
{
     extern float height [ ];
     int i;
     . . . . .
     . . . . .
}
float height[SIZE];
```

An **extern** within a function provides the type information to just that one function. We can provide type information to all functions within a file by placing external declarations before any of them.

Example:

```
extern float height[ ];
main( )
{
     int i;
     void print_out(void);
     . . . . .
     . . . . .
     print_out( );
}
void print_out(void)
{
     int i;
     . . . . .
     . . . . .
}
float height[SIZE];
```

The distinction between definition and declaration also applies to functions. A function is defined when its parameters and function body are specified. This tells the compiler to allocate space for the function code and provides type information for the parameters. Since functions are external by default, we declare them (in the calling functions) without the qualifier **extern.** Therefore, the declaration

```
void print_out(void);
```

is equivalent to

```
extern void print_out(void);
```

Function declarations outside of any function behave the same way as variable declarations.

Static Variables

As the name suggests, the value of static variables persists until the end of the program. A variable can be declared *static* using the keyword **static** like

```
static int x;
static float y;
```

A static variable may be either an internal type or an external type depending on the place of declaration.

Internal static variables are those which are declared inside a function. The scope of internal static variables extend up to the end of the function in which they are defined. Therefore, internal **static** variables are similar to **auto** variables, except that they remain in existence (alive) throughout the remainder of the program. Therefore, internal **static** variables can be used to retain values between function calls. For example, it can be used to count the number of calls made to a function.

Example 9.9 Write a program to illustrate the properties of a static variable.

The program in Fig. 9.15 explains the behaviour of a static variable.

Program

```
void stat(void);
main ( )
{
   int i;
   for(i=1; i<=3; i++)
   stat( );
}
void stat(void)
{
   static int x = 0;

   x = x+1;
   printf("x = %d\n", x);
}
```

Output

```
x = 1
x = 2
x = 3
```

Fig. 9.15 *Illustration of static variable*

A static variable is initialized only once, when the program is compiled. It is never initialized again. During the first call to **stat, x** is incremented to 1. Because **x** is static, this value persists and therefore, the next call adds another 1 to **x** giving it a value of 2. The value of **x** becomes three when the third call is made.

Had we declared **x** as an **auto** variable, the output would have been:

x = 1
x = 1
x = 1

This is because each time **stat** is called, the auto variable x is initialized to zero. When the function terminates, its value of 1 is lost.

An external **static** variable is declared outside of all functions and is available to all the functions in that program. The difference between a **static** external variable and a simple external variable is that the **static** external variable is available only within the file where it is defined while the simple external variable can be accessed by other files.

It is also possible to control the scope of a function. For example, we would like a particular function accessible only to the functions in the file in which it is defined, and not to any function in other files. This can be accomplished by defining 'that' function with the storage class **static**.

Register Variables

We can tell the compiler that a variable should be kept in one of the machine's registers, instead of keeping in the memory (where normal variables are stored). Since a register access is much faster than a memory access, keeping the frequently accessed variables (e.g., loop control variables) in the register will lead to faster execution of programs. This is done as follows:

```
register int count;
```

Although, ANSI standard does not restrict its application to any particular data type, most compilers allow only **int** or **char** variables to be placed in the register.

Since only a few variables can be placed in the register, it is important to carefully select the variables for this purpose. However, C will automatically convert **register** variables into non-register variables once the limit is reached.

Table 9.1 summarizes the information on the visibility and lifetime of variables in functions and files.

Table 9.1 *Scope and Lifetime of Variables*

Storage Class	*Where declared*	*Visibility (Active)*	*Lifetime (Alive)*
None	Before all functions in a file (may be initialized)	Entire file plus other files where variable is declared with **extern**	Entire program (Global)

(Contd.)

Storage Class	*Where declared*	*Visibility (Active)*	*Lifetime (Alive)*
extern	Before all functions in a file (cannot be initialized)	Entire file plus other files where variable is declared **extern** and the file where originally declared as global.	Global
static	Before all functions in a file	Only in that file	Global
None or **auto**	Inside a function (or a block)	Only in that function or block	Until end of function or block
register	Inside a function or block	Only in that function or block	Until end of function or block
static	Inside a function	Only in that function	Global

Nested Blocks

A set of statements enclosed in a set of braces is known a *block* or a *compound* statement. Note that all functions including the **main** use compound *statement.* A block can have its own declarations and other statements. It is also possible to have a block of such statements inside the body of a function or another block, thus creating what is known as *nested blocks* as shown below:

```
main()
{                    <----------------+
    int a = 20;                       |
    int b = 10;                       |
    ....                              |
    {                <---+            |  Outer
                         |            |  block
        int a = 0;       |  Inner     |
        int c = a + b;   |  block     |
        ....             |            |
    }                <---+            |
    b = a;                            |
}                    <----------------+
```

When this program is executed, the value c will be 10, not 30. The statement b = a; assigns a value of 20 to **b** and not zero. Although the scope of **a** extends up to the end of **main** it is not "visible" inside the inner block where the variable **a** has been declared again. The inner **a** hides the visibility of the outer **a** in the inner block. However, when we leave the inner block, the inner **a** is no longer in scope and the outer **a** becomes visible again.

Remember, the variable **b** is not re-declared in the inner block and therefore it is visible in both the blocks. That is why when the statement

```
int c = a + b;
```

is evaluated, **a** assumes a values of 0 and **b** assumes a value of 10.

Although main's variables are visible inside the nested block, the reverse is not true.

Scope Rules

Scope

The region of a program in which a variable is available for use.

Visibility

The program's ability to access a variable from the memory.

Lifetime

The lifetime of a variable is the duration of time in which a variable exists in the memory during execution.

Rules of use

1. The scope of a global variable is the entire program file.
2. The scope of a local variable begins at point of declaration and ends at the end of the block or function in which it is declared.
3. The scope of a formal function argument is its own function.
4. The lifetime (or longevity) of an **auto** variable declared in **main** is the entire program execution time, although its scope is only the **main** function.
5. The life of an **auto** variable declared in a function ends when the function is exited.
6. A **static** local variable, although its scope is limited to its function, its lifetime extends till the end of program execution.
7. All variables have visibility in their scope, provided they are not declared again.
8. If a variable is redeclared within its scope again, it loses its visibility in the scope of the redeclared variable.

9.20 MULTIFILE PROGRAMS

So far we have been assuming that all the functions (including the **main**) are defined in one file. However, in real-life programming environment, we may use more than one source files which may be compiled separately and linked later to form an executable object code. This approach is very useful because any change in one file does not affect other files thus eliminating the need for recompilation of the entire program.

Multiple source files can share a variable provided it is declared as an external variable appropriately. Variables that are shared by two or more files are global variables and therefore we must declare them accordingly in one file and then explicitly define them with **extern** in other files. Figure 9.16 illustrates the use of **extern** declarations in a multifile program.

The function main in **file1** can reference the variable **m** that is declared as global in **file2**. Remember, **function1** cannot access the variable **m**. If, however, the **extern int m;** statement is placed before **main**, then both the functions could refer to **m**. This can also be achieved by using **extern int m;** statement inside each function in **file1**.

The **extern** specifier tells the compiler that the following variable types and names have already been declared elsewhere and no need to create storage space for them. It is the responsibility of the *linker* to resolve the reference problem. It is important to note that a multifile global variable should be declared *without* **extern** in one (and only one) of the files. The **extern** declaration is done in places where secondary references are made. If we declare a variable as global in two different files used by a single program, then the linker will have a conflict as to which variable to use and, therefore, issues a warning.

file1.c

```
main( )
{
    extern int m;
    int i;
    . . . . .
    . . . . .
}
function1( )
{
    int j;
    . . . . .
    . . . . .
}
```

file2.c

```
int m /* global variable */
function2( )
{
    int i;
    . . . . .
    . . . . .
}
function3( )
{
    int count;
    . . . . . . . .
    . . . . . . . .
}
```

Fig. 9.16 *Use of extern in a multifile program*

The multifile program shown in Fig. 9.16 can be modified as shown in Fig. 9.17.

file1.c

```
int m; /* global variable */

main( )
{    {
     int i;
     . . . . .
}
function1( )
{
     int j;
     . . . . .
}
```

file2.c

```
extern int m;

function2( )

          int i;
          . . . . .
}
function3( )
{
          int count;
          . . . . .
}
```

Fig. 9.17 *Another version of a multifile program*

When a function is defined in one file and accessed in another, the later file must include a function *declaration*. The declaration identifies the function as an external function whose definition appears elsewhere. We usually place such declarations at the beginning of the file, before all functions. Although all functions are assumed to be external, it would be a good practice to explicitly declare such functions with the storage class **extern.**

Just Remember

- It is a syntax error if the types in the declaration and function definition do not match.
- It is a syntax error if the number of actual parameters in the function call do not match the number in the declaration statement.
- It is a logic error if the parameters in the function call are placed in the wrong order.
- It is illegal to use the name of a formal argument as the name of a local variable.
- Using **void** as return type when the function is expected to return a value is an error.
- Trying to return a value when the function type is marked **void** is an error.
- Variables in the parameter list must be individually declared for their types. We cannot use multiple declarations (like we do with local or global variables).
- A **return** statement is required if the return type is anything other than **void.**
- If a function does not return any value, the return type must be declared **void.**
- If a function has no parameters, the parameter list must be declared **void.**
- Placing a semicolon at the end of header line is illegal.
- Forgetting the semicolon at the end of a prototype declaration is an error.
- Defining a function within the body of another function is not allowed.
- It is an error if the type of data returned does not match the return type of the function.
- It will most likely result in logic error if there is a mismatch in data types between the actual and formal arguments.
- Functions return integer value by default.
- A function without a return statement cannot return a value, when the parameters are passed by value.
- A function that returns a value can be used in expressions like any other C variable.
- When the value returned is assigned to a variable, the value will be converted to the type of the variable receiving it.
- Function cannot be the target of an assignment.
- A function with void return type cannot be used in the right-hand side of an assignment statement. It can be used only as a stand-alone statement.
- A function that returns a value cannot be used as a stand-alone statement.
- A **return** statement can occur anywhere within the body of a function.
- A function can have more than one return statement.
- A function definition may be placed either after or before the **main** function.

- Where more functions are used, they may be placed in any order.
- A global variable used in a function will retain its value for future use.
- A local variable defined inside a function is known only to that function. It is destroyed when the function is exited.
- A global variable is visible only from the point of its declaration to the end of the program.
- When a variable is redeclared within its scope either in a function or in a block, the original variable is not visible within the scope of the redeclared variable.
- A local variable declared **static** retains its value even after the function is exited.
- Static variables are initialized at compile time and therefore they are initialized only once.
- Use parameter passing by values as far as possible to avoid inadvertent changes to variables of calling function in the called function.
- Although not essential, include parameter names in the prototype declarations for documentation purposes.
- Avoid the use of names that hide names in outer scope.

CASE STUDY

Calculation of Area under a Curve

One of the applications of computers in numerical analysis is computing the area under a curve. One simple method of calculating the area under a curve is to divide the area into a number of trapezoids of same width and summing up the area of individual trapezoids. The area of a trapezoid is given by

$$\text{Area} = 0.5 * (h1 + h2) * b$$

where h1 and h2 are the heights of two sides and b is the width as shown in Fig. 9.18.

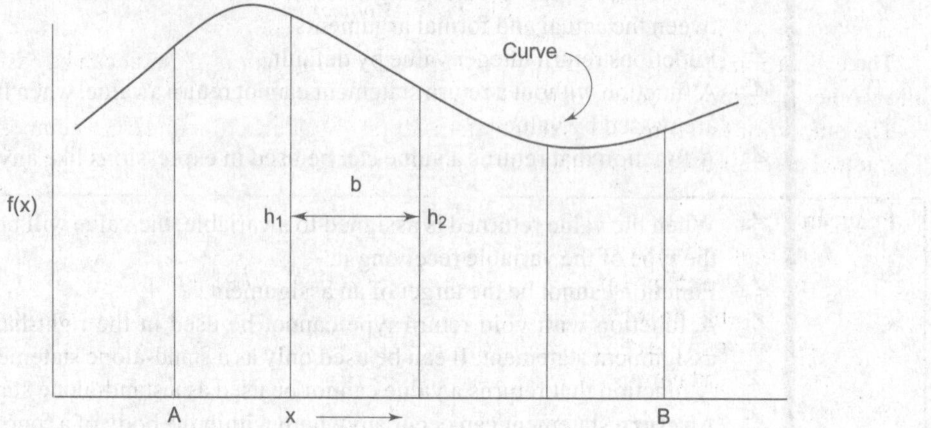

Fig. 9.18 *Area under a curve*

The program in Fig. 9.20 calculates the area for a curve of the function

$$f(x) = x^2 + 1$$

between any two given limits, say, A and B.

Input

Lower limit (A)
Upper limit (B)
Number of trapezoids

Output

Total area under the curve between the given limits.

Algorithm

1. Input the lower and upper limits and the number of trapezoids.
2. Calculate the width of trapezoids.
3. Initialize the total area.
4. Calculate the area of trapezoid and add to the total area.
5. Repeat step-4 until all the trapezoids are completed.
6. Print total area.

The algorithm is implemented in top-down modular form as in Fig. 9.19.

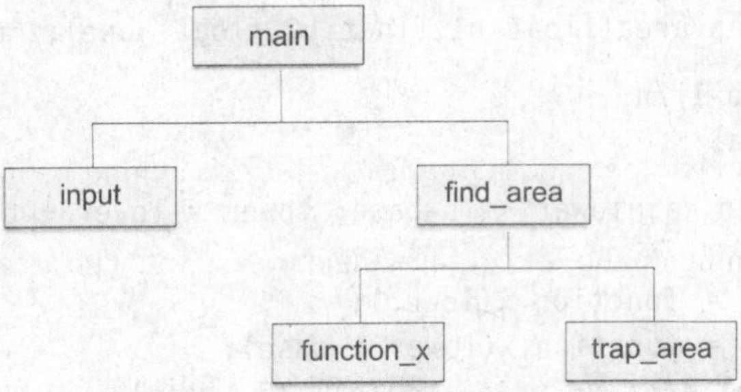

Fig. 9.19 *Modular chart*

The evaluation of f(x) has been done using a separate function so that it can be easily modified to allow other functions to be evaluated.

The output for two runs shows that better accuracy is achieved with larger number of trapezoids. The actual area for the limits 0 and 3 is 12 units (by analytical method).

Program

```
#include <stdio.h>
float start_point,              /* GLOBAL VARIABLES */
      end_point,
      total_area;
int   numtraps;
main( )
{
    void   input(void);
    float  find_area(float a,float b,int n); /* prototype */
```

```
    print("AREA UNDER A CURVE");
    input( );
    total_area = find_area(start_point, end_point, numtraps);
    printf("TOTAL AREA = %f", total_area);
}
void input(void)
{
    printf("\n Enter lower limit:");
    scanf("%f", &start_point);
    printf("Enter upper limit:");
    scanf("%f", &end_point);
    printf("Enter number of trapezoids:");
    scanf("%d", &numtraps);
}
float find_area(float a, float b, int n)
{
    float base, lower, h1, h2;  /* LOCAL VARIABLES */
    float function_x(float x);  /* prototype */
    float trap_area(float h1,float h2,float base);/*prototype*/

    base = (b-1)/n;
    lower = a;

     for(lower =a; lower <= b-base; lower = lower + base)
    {
        h1  = function_x(lower);
        h1  = function_x(lower + base);
        total_area += trap_area(h1, h2, base);
    }
        return(total_area);
float trap_area(float height_1,float height_2,float base)
{
  float area;      /* LOCAL VARIABLE */
  area = 0.5 * (height_1 + height_2) * base;
  return(area);
}
float function_x(float x)
{
    /* F(X) = X * X + 1 */

    return(x*x + 1);
}
```

Output

```
    AREA UNDER A CURVE
```

```
Enter lower limit: 0
Enter upper limit: 3
Enter number of trapezoids: 30
TOTAL AREA = 12.005000

AREA UNDER A CURVE
Enter lower limit: 0
Enter upper limit: 3
Enter number of trapezoids: 100
TOTAL AREA = 12.000438
```

Fig. 9.20 *Computing area under a curve*

REVIEW QUESTIONS

9.1 State whether the following statements are *true* or *false*.

(a) C functions can return only one value under their function name.
(b) A function in C should have at least one argument.
(c) A function can be defined and placed before the **main** function.
(d) A function can be defined within the **main** function.
(e) An user-defined function must be called at least once; otherwise a warning message will be issued.
(f) Any name can be used as a function name.
(g) Only a **void** type function can have **void** as its argument.
(h) When variable values are passed to functions, a copy of them are created in the memory.
(i) Program execution always begins in the main function irrespective of its location in the program.
(j) Global variables are visible in all blocks and functions in the program.
(k) A function can call itself.
(l) A function without a **return** statement is illegal.
(m) Global variables cannot be declared as **auto** variables.
(n) A function prototype must always be placed outside the calling function.
(o) The return type of a function is **int** by default.
(p) The variable names used in prototype should match those used in the function definition.
(q) In parameter passing by pointers, the formal parameters must be prefixed with the symbol * in their declarations.
(r) In parameter passing by pointers, the actual parameters in the function call may be variables or constants.
(s) In passing arrays to functions, the function call must have the name of the array to be passed without brackets.
(t) In passing strings to functions, the actual parameter must be name of the string post-fixed with size in brackets.

9.2 Fill in the blanks in the following statements.

(a) The parameters used in a function call are called ______.
(b) A variable declared inside a function is called ______.
(c) By default, ______ is the return type of a C function.
(d) In passing by pointers, the variables of the formal parameters must be prefixed with ______ in their declaration.
(e) In prototype declaration, specifying ____ is optional.
(f) ______ refers to the region where a variable is actually available for use.
(g) A function that calls itself is known as a ______ function.
(h) If a local variable has to retain its value between calls to the function, it must be declared as ______.
(i) A ______ aids the compiler to check the matching between the actual arguments and the formal ones.
(j) A variable declared inside a function by default assumes ______ storage class.

9.3 The **main** is a user-defined function. How does it differ from other user-defined functions?

9.4 Describe the two ways of passing parameters to functions. When do you prefer to use each of them?

9.5 What is prototyping? Why is it necessary?

9.6 Distinguish between the following:
(a) Actual and formal arguments
(b) Global and local variables
(c) Automatic and static variables
(d) Scope and visibility of variables
(e) & operator and * operator

9.7 Explain what is likely to happen when the following situations are encountered in a program.
(a) Actual arguments are less than the formal arguments in a function.
(b) Data type of one of the actual arguments does not match with the type of the corresponding formal argument.
(c) Data type of one of the arguments in a prototype does not match with the type of the corresponding formal parameter in the header line.
(d) The order of actual parameters in the function call is different from the order of formal parameters in a function where all the parameters are of the same type.
(e) The type of expression used in **return** statement does not match with the type of the function.

9.8 Which of the following prototype declarations are invalid? Why?
(a) `int (fun) void;`
(b) `double fun (void)`
(c) `float fun (x, y, n);`
(d) `void fun (void, void);`
(e) `int fun (int a, b);`
(f) `fun (int, float, char);`
(g) `void fun (int a, int &b);`

9.9 Which of the following header lines are invalid? Why?
(a) `float average (float x, float y, float z);`
(b) `double power (double a, int n - 1)`

(c) `int product (int m, 10)`
(d) `double minimum (double x; double y;)`
(e) `int mul (int x, y)`
(f) `exchange (int *a, int *b)`
(g) `void sum (int a, int b, int &c)`

9.10 Find errors, if any, in the following function definitions:

(a)
```
void abc (int a, int b)
{
        int c;
        . . . .
        return (c);
}
```
(b)
```
int abc (int a, int b)
{
        . . . .
        . . . .
}
```
(c)
```
int abc (int a, int b)
{
        double c = a + b;
        return (c);
}
```
(d)
```
void abc (void)
{
        . . . .
        . . . .
        return;
}
```
(e)
```
int abc(void)
{
        . . . .
        . . . .
        return;
}
```

9.11 Find errors in the following function calls:

(a) `void xyz ( );`
(b) `xyx ( void );`
(c) `xyx ( int x, int y);`
(d) `xyzz ( );`
(e) `xyz ( ) + xyz ( );`

9.12 A function to divide two floating point numbers is as follows:

```
divide (float x, float y)
{
    return (x / y);
}
```

What will be the value of the following function calls”

(a) divide (10, 2)

(b) divide (9, 2)

(c) divide (4.5, 1.5)

(d) divide (2.0, 3.0)

9.13 What will be the effect on the above function calls if we change the header line as follows:

(a) int divide (int x, int y)

(b) double divide (float x, float y)

9.14 Determine the output of the following program?

```
int prod( int m, int n);
main ( )
{
        int x = 10;
        int y = 20;
        int p, q;
        p = prod (x,y);
        q = prod (p, prod (x,z));
        printf ("%d %d\n", p,q);
}
int prod( int a, int b)
{
        return (a * b);
}
```

9.15 What will be the output of the following program?

```
void test (int *a);
main ( )
{
        int x = 50;
        test ( &x);
        printf("%d\n", x);
}
void test (int *a);
{
        *a = *a + 50;
}
```

9.16 The function **test** is coded as follows:

```
int test (int number)
{
        int m, n = 0;
        while (number)
        {
                m = number % 10;
                if (m % 2)
                    n = n + 1;
                number = number /10;
        }
        return (n);
}
```

What will be the values of **x** and **y** when the following statements are executed?

```
int x = test (135);
int y = test (246);
```

PROGRAMMING EXERCISES

9.1 Write a function **exchange** to interchange the values of two variables, say **x** and **y.** Illustrate the use of this function, in a calling function. Assume that **x** and **y** are defined as global variables.

9.2 Write a function **space(x)** that can be used to provide a space of x positions between two output numbers. Demonstrate its application.

9.3 Use recursive function calls to evaluate

$$f(x) = x - \frac{x^3}{3!} + \frac{x^5}{5!} - \frac{x^7}{7!} + \ldots$$

9.4 An n_order polynomial can be evaluated as follows:

$$P = (\ldots(((a_0x+a_1)x+a_2)x+a_3)x+..+a_n)$$

Write a function to evaluate the polynomial, using an array variable. Test it using a main program.

9.5 The Fibonacci numbers are defined recursively as follows:

$F_1 = 1$

$F_2 = 1$

$F_n = F_{n-1}+F_{n-2}$, $n > 2$

Write a function that will generate and print the first n Fibonacci numbers. Test the function for n = 5, 10, and 15.

9.6 Write a function that will round a floating-point number to an indicated decimal place. For example the number 17.457 would yield the value 17.46 when it is rounded off to two decimal places.

9.7 Write a function **prime** that returns 1 if its argument is a prime number and returns zero otherwise.

9.8 Write a function that will scan a character string passed as an argument and convert all lower-case characters into their uppercase equivalents.

9.9 Develop a top_down modular program to implement a calculator. The program should request the user to input two numbers and display one of the following as per the desire of the user:

(a) Sum of the numbers
(b) Difference of the numbers
(c) Product of the numbers
(d) Division of the numbers

Provide separate functions for performing various tasks such as reading, calculating and displaying. Calculating module should call second level modules to perform the individual mathematical operations. The main function should have only function calls.

9.10 Develop a modular interactive program using functions that reads the values of three sides of a triangle and displays either its area or its perimeter as per the request of the user. Given the three sides a, b and c.

$$\text{Perimeter} = a + b + c$$

$$\text{Area} = \sqrt{(s-a)(s-b)(s-c)}$$

$$\text{where } s = (a+b+c)/2$$

9.11 Write a function that can be called to find the largest element of an m by n matrix.

9.12 Write a function that can be called to compute the product of two matrices of size m by n and n by m. The main function provides the values for m and n and two matrices.

9.13 Design and code an interactive modular program that will use functions to a matrix of m by n size, compute column averages and row averages, and then print the entire matrix with averages shown in respective rows and columns.

9.14 Develop a top-down modular program that will perform the following tasks:
- (a) Read two integer arrays with unsorted elements.
- (b) Sort them in ascending order
- (c) Merge the sorted arrays
- (d) Print the sorted list

Use functions for carrying out each of the above tasks. The main function should have only function calls.

9.15 Develop your own functions for performing following operations on strings:
- (a) Copying one string to another
- (b) Comparing two strings
- (c) Adding a string to the end of another string

Write a driver program to test your functions.

Chapter

10

Structures and Unions

10.1 INTRODUCTION

We have seen that arrays can be used to represent a group of data items that belong to the same type, such as **int** or **float**. However, we cannot use an array if we want to represent a collection of data items of different types using a single name. Fortunately, C supports a constructed data type known as *structures,* a mechanism for packing data of different types. A structure is a convenient tool for handling a group of logically related data items. For example, it can be used to represent a set of attributes, such as student_name, roll_number and marks. The concept of a structure is analogous to that of a 'record' in many other languages. More examples of such structures are:

time	:	seconds, minutes, hours
date	:	day, month, year
book	:	author, title, price, year
city	:	name, country, population
address	:	name, door-number, street, city
inventory	:	item, stock, value
customer	:	name, telephone, city, category

Structures help to organize complex data in a more meaningful way. It is a powerful concept that we may often need to use in our program design. This chapter is devoted to the study of structures and their applications in program development. Another related concept known as *unions* is also discussed.

10.2 DEFINING A STRUCTURE

Unlike arrays, structures must be defined first for their format that may be used later to declare structure variables. Let us use an example to illustrate the process of structure definition and the creation of structure variables. Consider a book database consisting of book name, author, number of pages, and price. We can define a structure to hold this information as follows:

```
struct book_bank
{
        char   title[20];
        char   author[15];
        int    pages;
        float  price;
};
```

The keyword **struct** declares a structure to hold the details of four data fields, namely **title, author, pages**, and **price**. These fields are called *structure elements* or *members*. Each member may belong to a different type of data. **book_bank** is the name of the structure and is called the *structure tag*. The tag name may be used subsequently to declare variables that have the tag's structure.

Note that the above definition has not declared any variables. It simply describes a format called *template* to represent information as shown below:

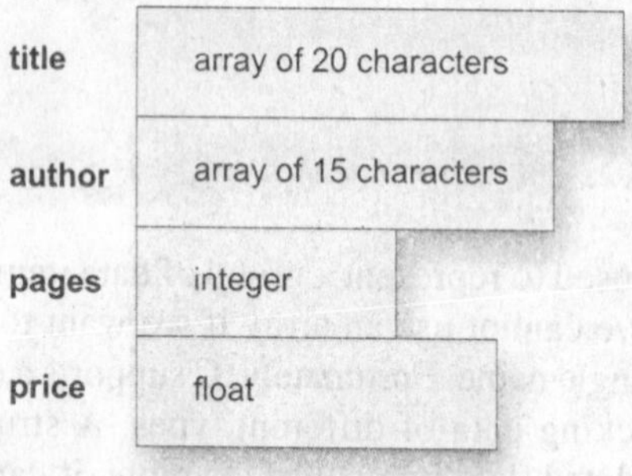

The general format of a structure definition is as follows:

```
struct   tag_name
{
        data_type       member1;
        data_type       member2;
        ----            ----
        ----            ----
};
```

In defining a structure you may note the following syntax:

1. The template is terminated with a semicolon.
2. While the entire definition is considered as a statement, each member is declared independently for its name and type in a separate statement inside the template.
3. The tag name such as **book_bank** can be used to declare structure variables of its type, later in the program.

Arrays Vs Structures

Both the arrays and structures are classified as structured data types as they provide a mechanism that enable us to access and manipulate data in a relatively easy manner. But they differ in a number of ways.

1. An array is a collection of related data elements of same type. Structure can have elements of different types.
2. An array is derived data type whereas a structure is a programmer-defined one.
3. Any array behaves like a built-in data type. All we have to do is to declare an array variable and use it. But in the case of a structure, first we have to design and declare a data structure before the variables of that type are declared and used.

10.3 DECLARING STRUCTURE VARIABLES

After defining a structure format we can declare variables of that type. A structure variable declaration is similar to the declaration of variables of any other data types. It includes the following elements.

1. The keyword **struct**
2. The structure tag name
3. List of variable names separated by commas
4. A terminating semicolon

For example, the statement

```
struct book_bank, book1, book2, book3;
```

declares **book1, book2**, and **book3** as variables of type **struct book_bank.**

Each one of these variables has four members as specified by the template. The complete declaration might look like this:

```
struct book_bank
{
   char  title[20];
   char  author[15];
   int   pages;
   float price;
};
struct book_bank book1, book2, book3;
```

Remember that the members of a structure themselves are not variables. They do not occupy any memory until they are associated with the structure variables such as **book1.** When the compiler comes across a declaration statement, it reserves memory space for the structure variables. It is also allowed to combine both the structure definition and variables declaration in one statement.

The declaration

```
struct book_bank
{
    char title[20];
    char author[15];
    int pages;
    flat price;
} book1, book2, book3;
```

is valid. The use of tag name is optional here. For example:

```
struct
{ ........
  ........
  ........
} book1, book2, book3;
```

declares **book1, book2,** and **book3** as structure variables representing three books, but does not include a tag name. However, this approach is not recommended for two reasons.

1. Without a tag name, we cannot use it for future declarations.
2. Normally, structure definitions appear at the beginning of the program file, before any variables or functions are defined. They may also appear before the **main**, along with macro definitions, such as **#define.** In such cases, the definition is *global* and can be used by other functions as well.

Type-Defined Structures

We can use the keyword **typedef** to define a structure as follows:

```
typedef struct
{ . . . . .
    type member1;
    type member2;
    . . . . .
    . . . . .
} type_name;
```

The type_name represents structure definition associated with it and therefore can be used to declare structure variables as shown below:

type_name variable1, variable2, ...;

Remember that (1) the name *type_name* is the type definition name, not a variable and (2) we cannot define a variable with *typedef* declaration.

10.4 ACCESSING STRUCTURE MEMBERS

We can access and assign values to the members of a structure in a number of ways. As mentioned earlier, the members themselves are not variables. They should be linked to the structure variables in order to make them meaningful members. For example, the word **title,** has no meaning whereas the phrase 'title of book3' has a meaning. The link between a member and a variable is established using the *member operator* '.' which is also known as 'dot operator' or 'period operator'. For example,

```
book1.price
```

is the variable representing the price of **book1** and can be treated like any other ordinary variable. Here is how we would assign values to the members of **book1**:

```
strcpy(book1.title, "BASIC");
strcpy(book1.author, "Balagurusamy");
book1.pages = 250;
book1.price = 120.50;
```

We can also use **scanf** to give the values through the keyboard.

```
scanf("%s\n", book1.title);
scanf("%d\n", &book1.pages);
```

are valid input statements.

Example 10.1 Define a structure type, **struct personal** that would contain person name, date of joining and salary. Using this structure, write a program to read this information for one person from the keyboard and print the same on the screen.

Structure definition along with the program is shown in Fig. 10.1. The **scanf** and **printf** functions illustrate how the member operator '.' is used to link the structure members to the structure variables. The variable name with a period and the member name is used like an ordinary variable.

```
Program
  struct  personal
  {
      char  name[20];
      int   day;
      char  month[10];
      int   year;
      float salary;
  };
  main()
  {
      struct personal person;
      printf("Input Values\n");
      scanf("%s %d %s %d %f",
                person.name,
               &person.day,
                person.month,
               &person.year,
               &person.salary);
```

```
        printf("%s %d %s %d %f\n",
                person.name,
                person.day,
                person.month,
                person.year,
                person.salary);
    }
```

Output

```
    Input Values
    M.L.Goel 10 January 1945 4500
    M.L.Goel 10 January 1945 4500.00
```

Fig. 10.1 *Defining and accessing structure members*

10.5 STRUCTURE INITIALIZATION

Like any other data type, a structure variable can be initialized at compile time.

```
main()
{
    struct
    {
        int weight;
        float height;
    }
    student = {60, 180.75};
    .....
    .....
}
```

This assigns the value 60 to **student. weight** and 180.75 to **student. height.** There is a one-to-one correspondence between the members and their initializing values.

A lot of variation is possible in initializing a structure. The following statements initialize two structure variables. Here, it is essential to use a tag name.

```
main()
{
    struct st_record
    {
      int weight;
      float height;
    };
    struct st_record student1 = { 60, 180.75 };
    struct st_record student2 = { 53, 170.60 };
    .....
    .....
}
```

Another method is to initialize a structure variable outside the function as shown below:

```
struct st_record
{
   int weight;
   float height;
} student1 = {60, 180.75};
main()
{
   struct st_record student2 = {53, 170.60};
   .....
   .....
}
```

C language does not permit the initialization of individual structure members within the template. The initialization must be done only in the declaration of the actual variables.

Note that the compile-time initialization of a structure variable must have the following elements:

1. The keyword **struct**
2. The structure tag name.
3. The name of the variable to be declared.
4. The assignment operator =
5. A set of values for the members of the structure variable, separated by commas and enclosed in braces.
6. A terminating semicolon.

Rules for Initializing Structures

There are a few rules to keep in mind while initializing structure variables at compile-time.

1. We cannot initialize individual members inside the structure template.
2. The order of values enclosed in braces must match the order of members in the structure definition.
3. It is permitted to have a partial initialization. We can initialize only the first few members and leave the remaining blank. The uninitialized members should be only at the end of the list.
4. The uninitialized members will be assigned default values as follows:
   - Zero for integer and floating point numbers.
   - '\0' for characters and strings.

10.6 COPYING AND COMPARING STRUCTURE VARIABLES

Two variables of the same structure type can be copied the same way as ordinary variables. If **person1** and **person2** belong to the same structure, then the following statements are valid:

```
person1 = person2;
person2 = person1;
```

However, the statements such as

```
person1 == person2
person1 != person2
```

are not permitted. C does not permit any logical operations on structure variables. In case, we need to compare them, we may do so by comparing members individually.

Example 10.2 Write a program to illustrate the comparison of structure variables.

The program shown in Fig. 10.2 illustrates how a structure variable can be copied into another of the same type. It also performs member-wise comparison to decide whether two structure variables are identical.

```
Program
   struct class
   {
       int  number;
       char name[20];
       float marks;
   };

   main()
   {
       int  x;
       struct class student1 = {111,"Rao",72.50};
       struct class student2 = {222,"Reddy", 67.00};
       struct class student3;

       student3 = student2;

       x = ((student3.number ==  student2.number) &&
            (student3.marks  ==  student2.marks)) ? 1 : 0;

       if(x == 1)
         {
           printf("\nstudent2 and student3 are same\n\n");
           printf("%d %s %f\n", student3.number,
                                student3.name,
                                student3.marks);
       }
       else
           printf("\nstudent2 and student3 are different\n\n");

   }
Output

   student2 and student3 are same

   222 Reddy 67.000000
```

Fig. 10.2 *Comparing and copying structure variables*

Word Boundaries and Slack Bytes

Computer stores structures using the concept of "word boundary". The size of a word boundary is machine dependent. In a computer with two bytes word boundary, the members of a structure are stored left_aligned on the word boundary as shown below. A character data takes one byte and an integer takes two bytes. One byte between them is left unoccupied. This unoccupied byte is known as the *slack byte.*

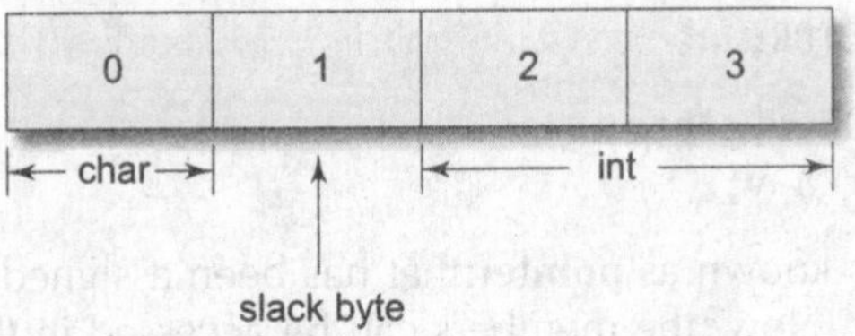

When we declare structure variables, each one of them may contain slack bytes and the values stored in such slack bytes are undefined. Due to this, even if the members of two variables are equal, their structures do not necessarily compare equal. C, therefore, does not permit comparison of structures. However, we can design our own function that could compare individual members to decide whether the structures are equal or not.

10.7 OPERATIONS ON INDIVIDUAL MEMBERS

As pointed out earlier, the individual members are identified using the member operator, the dot. A member with the dot operator along with its structure variable can be treated like any other variable name and therefore can be manipulated using expressions and operators. Consider the program in Fig. 10.2. We can perform the following operations:

```
if (student1.number == 111)
        student1.marks += 10.00;

float sum = student1.marks + student2.marks;
student2.marks * = 0.5;
```

We can also apply increment and decrement operators to numeric type members. For example, the following statements are valid:

```
student1.number ++;
++ student1.number;
```

The precedence of the member operator is higher than all arithmetic and relational operators and therefore no parentheses are required.

Three Ways to Access Members

We have used the dot operator to access the members of structure variables. In fact, there are two other ways. Consider the following structure:

```
typedef struct
{
        int x;
        int y;
} VECTOR;

VECTOR v, *ptr;
ptr = & v;
```

The identifier **ptr** is known as **pointer** that has been assigned the address of the structure variable v. Now, the members can be accessed in three ways:

- using dot notation : v.x
- using indirection notation : (*ptr).x
- using selection notation : ptr –> x

The second and third methods will be considered in Chapter 11.

10.8 ARRAYS OF STRUCTURES

We use structures to describe the format of a number of related variables. For example, in analyzing the marks obtained by a class of students, we may use a template to describe student name and marks obtained in various subjects and then declare all the students as structure variables. In such cases, we may declare an array of structures, each element of the array representing a structure variable. For example:

```
struct class student[100];
```

defines an array called **student**, that consists of 100 elements. Each element is defined to be of the type **struct class.** Consider the following declaration:

```
struct marks
{
   int subject1;
   int subject2;
   int subject3;
};
main()
{
   struct marks student[3] =
       {{45,68,81}, {75,53,69}, {57,36,71}};
```

This declares the **student** as an array of three elements **student[0], student[1],** and **student[2]** and initializes their members as follows:

```
student[0].subject1 = 45;
student[0].subject2 = 65;
  ....
  ....
student[2].subject3 = 71;
```

Note that the array is declared just as it would have been with any other array. Since **student** is an array, we use the usual array-accessing methods to access individual elements and then the member operator to access members. Remember, each element of **student** array is a structure variable with three members.

An array of structures is stored inside the memory in the same way as a multi-dimensional array. The array **student** actually looks as shown in Fig. 10.3.

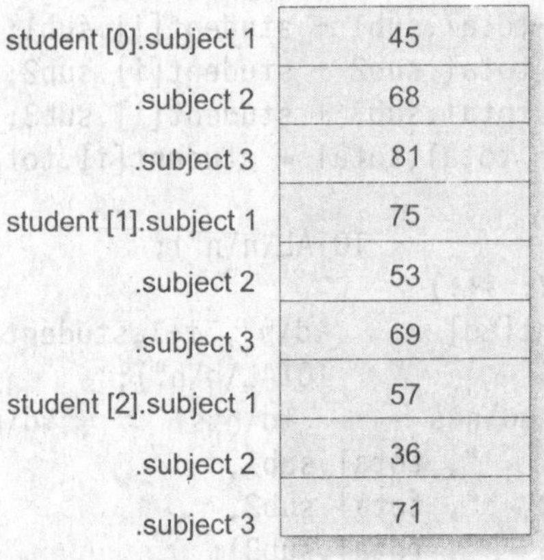

Fig. 10.3 *The array student inside memory*

Example 10.3 For the **student** array discussed above, write a program to calculate the subject-wise and student-wise totals and store them as a part of the structure.

The program is shown in Fig. 10.4. We have declared a four-member structure, the fourth one for keeping the student-totals. We have also declared an **array** total to keep the subject-totals and the grand-total. The grand-total is given by **total.total.** Note that a member name can be any valid C name and can be the same as an existing structure variable name. The linked name **total.total** represents the **total** member of the structure variable **total.**

Program

```
struct marks
{
    int  sub1;
    int  sub2;
    int  sub3;
    int  total;
};
```

```
main()
{
    int  i;
    struct marks student[3] =  {{45,67,81,0},
                                {75,53,69,0},
                                {57,36,71,0}};
    struct marks total;
    for(i = 0; i <= 2; i++)
    {
        student[i].total = student[i].sub1 +
                           student[i].sub2 +
                           student[i].sub3;
        total.sub1 = total.sub1 + student[i].sub1;
        total.sub2 = total.sub2 + student[i].sub2;
        total.sub3 = total.sub3 + student[i].sub3;
        total.total = total.total + student[i].total;
    }
    printf(" STUDENT          TOTAL\n\n");
    for(i = 0; i <= 2; i++)
       printf("Student[%d]       %d\n", i+1,student[i].total);
    printf("\n SUBJECT          TOTAL\n\n");
    printf("%s        %d\n%s        %d\n%s        %d\n",
          "Subject 1    ", total.sub1,
          "Subject 2    ", total.sub2,
          "Subject 3    ", total.sub3);

    printf("\nGrand Total = %d\n", total.total);
}
```

Output

```
STUDENT          TOTAL
Student[1]        193
Student[2]        197
Student[3]        164

SUBJECT          TOTAL
Subject 1         177
Subject 2         156
Subject 3         221

Grand Total  = 554
```

Fig. 10.4 *Arrays of structures: Illustration of subscripted structure variables*

10.9 ARRAYS WITHIN STRUCTURES

C permits the use of arrays as structure members. We have already used arrays of characters inside a structure. Similarly, we can use single- or multi-dimensional arrays of type **int** or **float.** For example, the following structure declaration is valid:

```
struct marks
{
 int number;
 float subject[3];
} student[2];
```

Here, the member **subject** contains three elements, **subject[0], subject[1]** and **subject[2].** These elements can be accessed using appropriate subscripts. For example, the name

```
student[1].subject[2];
```

would refer to the marks obtained in the third subject by the second student.

Example 10.4 Rewrite the program of Example 10.3 using an array member to represent the three subjects.

The modified program is shown in Fig. 10.5. You may notice that the use of array name for subjects has simplified in code.

```
Program
  main()
  {
      struct  marks
      {
         int  sub[3];
         int  total;
      };
      struct marks student[3] =
      {45,67,81,0,75,53,69,0,57,36,71,0};
      struct marks total;
      int  i,j;

      for(i = 0; i <= 2; i++)
      {
        for(j = 0; j <= 2; j++)
        {
           student[i].total += student[i].sub[j];
           total.sub[j] += student[i].sub[j];
        }
        total.total += student[i].total;
      }
      printf("STUDENT          TOTAL\n\n");
```

```
    for(i = 0; i <= 2; i++)
        printf("Student[%d]        %d\n", i+1, student[i].total);

    printf("\nSUBJECT            TOTAL\n\n");
    for(j = 0; j <= 2; j++)
        printf("Subject-%d          %d\n", j+1, total.sub[j]);

    printf("\nGrand Total   =   %d\n", total.total);

}
```

Output

```
STUDENT         TOTAL
Student[1]       193
Student[2]       197
Student[3]       164
SUBJECT         TOTAL
Subject-1        177
Subject-2        156
Subject-3        221

Grand Total  =   554
```

Fig. 10.5 *Use of subscripted members arrays in structures*

10.10 STRUCTURES WITHIN STRUCTURES

Structures within a structure means nesting of structures. Nesting of structures is permitted in C. Let us consider the following structure defined to store information about the salary of employees.

```
struct salary
{
    char name;
    char department;
    int  basic_pay;
    int  dearness_allowance;
    int  house_rent_allowance;
    int  city_allowance;
}
employee;
```

This structure defines name, department, basic pay and three kinds of allowances. We can group all the items related to allowance together and declare them under a substructure as shown below:

```
struct salary
{
   char name;
   char department;
   struct
   {
      int dearness;
      int house_rent;
      int city;
   }
   allowance;
}
employee;
```

The salary structure contains a member named **allowance** which itself is a structure with three members. The members contained in the inner structure namely **dearness, house_rent**, and **city** can be referred to as:

employee.allowance.dearness
employee.allowance.house_rent
employee.allowance.city

An inner-most member in a nested structure can be accessed by chaining all the concerned structure variables (from outer-most to inner-most) with the member using dot operator. The following are invalid:

employee.allowance (actual member is missing)
employee.house_rent (inner structure variable is missing)

An inner structure can have more than one variable. The following form of declaration is legal:

```
struct salary
{
   .....
   struct
   {
     int dearness;
     .....
   }
   allowance,
   arrears;
}
employee[100];
```

The inner structure has two variables, **allowance** and **arrears**. This implies that both of them have the same structure template. Note the comma after the name **allowance.** A base member can be accessed as follows:

employee[1].allowance.dearness
employee[1].arrears.dearness

We can also use tag names to define inner structures. Example:

```
struct pay
  {
    int dearness;
    int house_rent;
    int city;
  };
  struct salary
  {
    char name;
    char department;
    struct pay allowance;
    struct pay arrears;
  };
  struct salary employee[100];
```

pay template is defined outside the **salary** template and is used to define the structure of **allowance** and **arrears** inside the **salary** structure.

It is also permissible to nest more than one type of structures.

```
struct personal_record
{
  struct name_part name;
  struct addr_part address;
  struct date date_of_birth;
  .....
  .....
};
struct personal_record person1;
```

The first member of this structure is **name**, which is of the type **struct name_part.** Similarly, other members have their structure types.

10.11 STRUCTURES AND FUNCTIONS

We know that the main philosophy of C language is the use of functions. And therefore, it is natural that C supports the passing of structure values as arguments to functions. There are three methods by which the values of a structure can be transferred from one function to another.

1. The first method is to pass each member of the structure as an actual argument of the function call. The actual arguments are then treated independently like ordinary variables. This is the most elementary method and becomes unmanageable and inefficient when the structure size is large.
2. The second method involves passing of a copy of the entire structure to the called function. Since the function is working on a copy of the structure, any changes to structure members within the function are not reflected in the original structure (in the calling function). It is,

therefore, necessary for the function to return the entire structure back to the calling function. All compilers may not support this method of passing the entire structure as a parameter.

3. The third approach employs a concept called *pointers* to pass the structure as an argument. In this case, the address location of the structure is passed to the called function. The function can access indirectly the entire structure and work on it. This is similar to the way arrays are passed to function. This method is more efficient as compared to the second one.

In this section, we discuss in detail the second method, while the third approach using pointers is discussed in the next chapter, where pointers are dealt in detail.

The general format of sending a copy of a structure to the called function is:

function_name (structure_variable_name);

The called function takes the following form:

```
data_type function_name(struct_type st_name)
{
    ......
    ......
    return(expression);
}
```

The following points are important to note:

1. The called function must be declared for its type, appropriate to the data type it is expected to return. For example, if it is returning a copy of the entire structure, then it must be declared as **struct** with an appropriate tag name.
2. The structure variable used as the actual argument and the corresponding formal argument in the called function must be of the same **struct** type.
3. The **return** statement is necessary only when the function is returning some data back to the calling function. The *expression* may be any simple variable or structure variable or an expression using simple variables.
4. When a function returns a structure, it must be assigned to a structure of identical type in the calling function.
5. The called functions must be declared in the calling function appropriately.

Example 10.5 Write a simple program to illustrate the method of sending an entire structure as a parameter to a function.

A program to update an item is shown in Fig. 10.6. The function **update** receives a copy of the structure variable **item** as one of its parameters. Note that both the function **update** and the formal parameter **product** are declared as type **struct stores.** It is done so because the function uses the parameter **product** to receive the structure variable **item** and also to return the updated values of **item.**

The function **mul** is of type **float** because it returns the product of **price** and **quantity.** However, the parameter **stock,** which receives the structure variable **item** is declared as type **struct stores.**

The entire structure returned by **update** can be copied into a structure of identical type. The statement

```
item = update(item,p_increment,q_increment);
```

replaces the old values of **item** by the new ones.

Program

```
/*      Passing a copy of the entire structure          */
 struct stores
 {
     char  name[20];
     float price;
     int   quantity;
 };
 struct stores update (struct stores product, float p, int q);
 float mul (struct stores stock);
 main()
 {
     float     p_increment, value;
     int       q_increment;

     struct stores item = {"XYZ", 25.75, 12};

     printf("\nInput increment values:");
     printf("   price increment and quantity increment\n");
     scanf("%f %d", &p_increment, &q_increment);

 /* - - - - - - - - - - - - - - - - - - - - - - - - - - - */
     item  = update(item, p_increment, q_increment);
 /* - - - - - - - - - - - - - - - - - - - - - - - - - - - */
     printf("Updated values of item\n\n");
     printf("Name      : %s\n",item.name);
     printf("Price     : %f\n",item.price);
     printf("Quantity  : %d\n",item.quantity);

 /* - - - - - - - - - - - - - - - - - - - - - - - - - - - */
     value  = mul(item);
 /* - - - - - - - - - - - - - - - - - - - - - - - - - - - */
     printf("\nValue of the item  =  %f\n" value);
 }
 struct stores update(struct stores product, float p, int q)
 {
     product.price += p;
     product.quantity += q;
     return(product);
 }
```

```
    float mul(struct stores stock)
    {
        return(stock.price * stock.quantity);
    }

Output
Input increment values:    price increment and quantity increment
10 12
Updated values of item
Name        : XYZ
Price       : 35.750000
Quantity    : 24
Value of the item   =   858.000000
```

Fig. 10.6 *Using structure as a function parameter*

You may notice that the template of **stores** is defined before **main().** This has made the data type **struct stores** as *global* and has enabled the functions **update** and **mul** to make use of this definition.

10.12 UNIONS

Unions are a concept borrowed from structures and therefore follow the same syntax as structures. However, there is major distinction between them in terms of storage. In structures, each member has its own storage location, whereas all the members of a union use the same location. This implies that, although a union may contain many members of different types, it can handle only one member at a time. Like structures, a union can be declared using the keyword union as follows:

```
union item
{
    int m;
    float x;
    char c;
} code;
```

This declares a variable **code** of type **union item.** The union contains three members, each with a different data type. However, we can use only one of them at a time. This is due to the fact that only one location is allocated for a union variable, irrespective of its size.

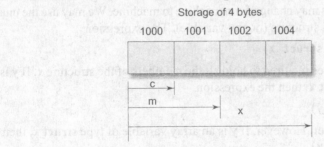

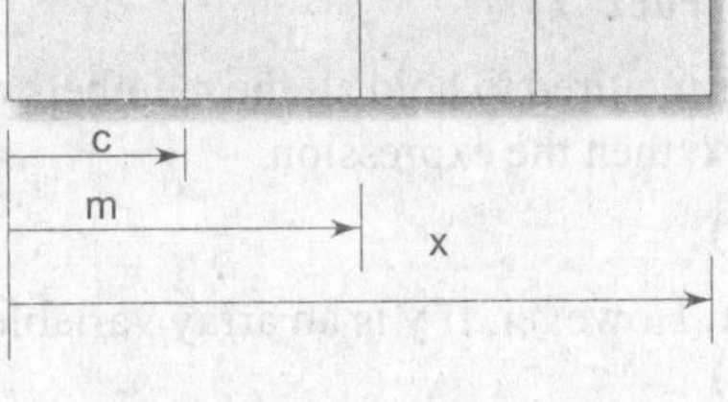

Fig. 10.7 *Sharing of a storage locating by union members*

The compiler allocates a piece of storage that is large enough to hold the largest variable type in the union. In the declaration above, the member x requires 4 bytes which is the largest among the members. Figure 10.7 shows how all the three variables share the same address. This assumes that a float variable requires 4 bytes of storage.

To access a union member, we can use the same syntax that we use for structure members. That is,

```
code.m
code.x
code.c
```

are all valid member variables. During accessing, we should make sure that we are accessing the member whose value is currently stored. For example, the statements such as

```
code.m = 379;
code.x = 7859.36;
printf("%d", code.m);
```

would produce erroneous output (which is machine dependent).

In effect, a union creates a storage location that can be used by any one of its members at a time. When a different member is assigned a new value, the new value supersedes the previous member's value.

Unions may be used in all places where a structure is allowed. The notation for accessing a union member which is nested inside a structure remains the same as for the nested structures.

Unions may be initialized when the variable is declared. But, unlike structures, it can be initialized only with a value of the same type as the first union member. For example, with the preceding, the declaration

```
union item abc = {100};
```

is valid but the declaration

```
union item abc = {10.75};
```

is invalid. This is because the type of the first member is **int.** Other members can be initialized by either assigning values or reading from the keyboard.

10.13 SIZE OF STRUCTURES

We normally use structures, unions, and arrays to create variables of large sizes. The actual size of these variables in terms of bytes may change from machine to machine. We may use the unary operator **sizeof** to tell us the size of a structure (or any variable). The expression

```
sizeof(struct x)
```

will evaluate the number of bytes required to hold all the members of the structure **x.** If **y** is a simple structure variable of type **struct x**, then the expression

```
sizeof(y)
```

would also give the same answer. However, if **y** is an array variable of type **struct x,** then

```
sizeof(y)
```

would give the total number of bytes the array **y** requires.

This kind of information would be useful to determine the number of records in a database. For example, the expression

```
sizeof(y)/sizeof(x)
```

would give the number of elements in the array **y**.

10.14 BIT FIELDS

So far, we have been using integer fields of size 16 bits to store data. There are occasions where data items require much less than 16 bits space. In such cases, we waste memory space. Fortunately, C permits us to use small bit fields to hold data items and thereby to pack several data items in a word of memory. Bit fields allow direct manipulation of string of a string of preselected bits as if it represented an integral quantity.

A bit field is a set of adjacent bits whose size can be from 1 to 16 bits in length. A word can therefore be divided into a number of bit fields. The name and size of bit fields are defined using a structure. The general form of bit field definition is;

```
struct tag-name
{
      data-type name1: bit-length;
      data-type name2: bit-length;
      . . . . . .
      . . . . . .
      data-type nameN: bit-length;
}
```

The *data-type* is either **int** or **unsigned int** or **signed int** and the *bit-length* is the number of bits used for the specified name. Remember that a **signed** bit field should have at least 2 bits (one bit for sign). Note that the field name is followed by a colon. The *bit-length* is decided by the range of value to be stored. The largest value that can be stored is 2^{n-1}, where n is bit-length.

The internal representation of bit fields is machine dependent. That is, it depends on the size of **int** and the ordering of bits. Some machines store bits from left to right and others from right to left. The sketch below illustrates the layout of bit fields, assuming a 16-bit word that is ordered from right to left.

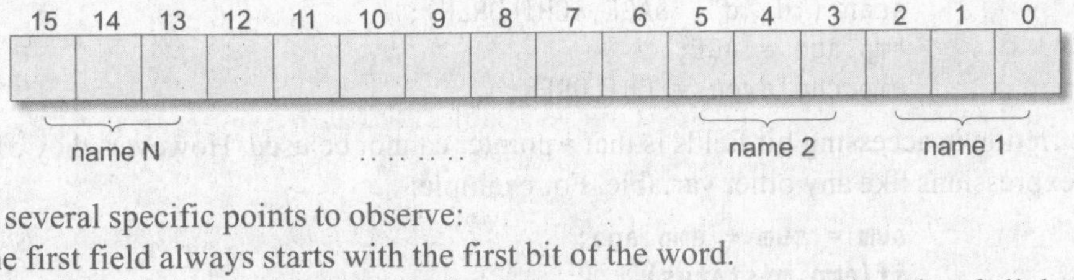

There are several specific points to observe:

1. The first field always starts with the first bit of the word.
2. A bit field cannot overlap integer boundaries. That is, the sum of lengths of all the fields in a structure should not be more than the size of a word. In case, it is more, the overlapping field is automatically forced to the beginning of the next word.

3. There can be unnamed fields declared with size. Example:

   Unsigned : *bit-length*

   Such fields provide padding within the word.
4. There can be unused bits in a word.
5. We cannot take the address of a bit field variable. This means we cannot use **scanf** to read values into bit fields. We can neither use pointer to access the bit fields.
6. Bit fields cannot be arrayed.
7. Bit fields should be assigned values that are within the range of their size. If we try to assign larger values, behaviour would be unpredicted.

Suppose, we want to store and use personal information of employees in compressed form, this can be done as follows:

```
struct personal
{
unsigned sex         :   1
unsigned age         :   7
unsigned m_status    :   1
unsigned children    :   3
unsigned             :   4
} emp;
```

This defines a variable name **emp** with four bit fields. The range of values each field could have is follows:

Bit field	*Bit length*	*Range of value*
sex	1	0 or 1
age	7	0 or 127 $(2^7 - 1)$
m_status	1	0 or 1
children	3	0 to 7 (2^3-1)

Once bit fields are defined, they can be referenced just as any other structure-type data item would be referenced. The following assignment statements are valid.

```
emp.sex = 1;
emp.age = 50;
```

Remember, we cannot use **scanf** to read values into a bit field. We may have to read into a temporary variable and then assign its value to the bit field. For example:

```
scanf(%d %d", &AGE,&CHILDREN);
emp.age = AGE;
emp.children = CHILDREN;
```

One restriction in accessing bit fields is that a pointer cannot be used. However, they can be used in normal expressions like any other variable. For example:

```
sum = sum + emp.age;
if(emp.m_status). . . . .;
printf("%d\n", emp.age);
```

are valid statements.

It is possible to combine normal structure elements with bit field elements. For example:

```
struct personal
{
        char          name[20];   /* normal variable */
        struct addr address;      /* structure variable */
        unsigned      sex : 1;
        unsigned      age : 7;
        . . . . .
        . . . . .
}
emp[100];
```

This declares **emp** as a 100 element array of type **struct personal.** This combines normal variable name and structure type variable **address** with bit fields.

Bit fields are packed into words as they appear in the definition. Consider the following definition.

```
struct pack
{
        unsigned a:2;
        int count;
        unsigned b : 3;
};
```

Here, the bit field **a** will be in one word, the variable **count** will be in the second word and the bit field **b** will be in the third word. The fields **a** and **b** would not get packed into the same word.

Just Remember

- Remember to place a semicolon at the end of definition of structures and unions.
- We can declare a structure variable at the time of definition of a structure by placing it after the closing brace but before the semicolon.
- Do not place the structure tag name after the closing brace in the definition. That will be treated as a structure variable. The tag name must be placed before the opening brace but after the keyword **struct.**
- When we use **typedef** definition, the *type_name* comes after the closing brace but before the semicolon.
- We cannot declare a variable at the time of creating a **typedef** definition. We must use the *type_name* to declare a variable in an independent statement.
- It is an error to use a structure variable as a member of its own **struct** type structure.
- Assigning a structure of one type to a structure of another type is an error.
- Declaring a variable using the tag name only (without the keyword struct) is an error.
- It is an error to compare two structure variables.
- It is illegal to refer to a structure member using only the member name.
- When structures are nested, a member must be qualified with all levels of structures nesting it.

- ✍ When accessing a member with a pointer and dot notation, parentheses are required around the pointer, like (*ptr).number.
- ✍ The selection operator (->) is a single token. Any space between the symbols – and > is an error.
- ✍ When using **scanf** for reading values for members, we must use address operator & with non-string members.
- ✍ Forgetting to include the array subscript when referring to individual structures of an array of structures is an error.
- ✍ A union can store only one of its members at a time. We must exercise care in accessing the correct member. Accessing a wrong data is a logic error.
- ✍ It is an error to initialize a union with data that does not match the type of the first member.
- ✍ Always provide a structure tag name when creating a structure. It is convenient to use tag name to declare new structure variables later in the program.
- ✍ Use short and meaningful structure tag names.
- ✍ Avoid using same names for members of different structures (although it is not illegal).
- ✍ Passing structures to functions by pointers is more efficient than passing by value. (Passing by pointers are discussed in Chapter 11.)
- ✍ We cannot take the address of a bit field. Therefore, we cannot use **scanf** to read values in bit fields. We can neither use pointer to access the bit fields.
- ✍ Bit fields cannot be arrayed.

CASE STUDY

Book Shop Inventory

A book shop uses a personal computer to maintain the inventory of books that are being sold at the shop. The list includes details such as author, title, price, publisher, stock position, etc. Whenever a customer wants a book, the shopkeeper inputs the title and author of the book and the system replies whether it is in the list or not. If it is not, an appropriate message is displayed. If book is in the list, then the system displays the book details and asks for number of copies. If the requested copies are available, the total cost of the books is displayed; otherwise the message "Required copies not in stock" is displayed.

A program to accomplish this is shown in Fig. 10.8. The program uses a template to define the structure of the book. Note that the date of publication, a member of **record** structure, is also defined as a structure.

When the title and author of a book are specified, the program searches for the book in the list using the function

look_up(table, s1, s2, m)

The parameter **table** which receives the structure variable **book** is declared as type **struct record.** The parameters **s1** and **s2** receive the string values of **title** and **author** while **m** receives the total number of books in the list. Total number of books is given by the expression

sizeof(book)/sizeof(struct record)

The search ends when the book is found in the list and the function returns the serial number of the book. The function returns –1 when the book is not found. Remember that the serial number of the first book in the list is zero. The program terminates when we respond "NO" to the question

Do you want any other book?

Note that we use the function

get(string)

to get title, author, etc. from the terminal. This enables us to input strings with spaces such as "C Language". We cannot use **scanf** to read this string since it contains two words.

Since we are reading the quantity as a string using the **get(string)** function, we have to convert it to an integer before using it in any expressions. This is done using the **atoi()** function.

Programs

```
#include   <stdio.h>
#include   <string.h>
struct  record
{
   char    author[20];
   char    title[30];
   float   price;
   struct
   {
      char   month[10];
      int    year;
   }
   date;
   char   publisher[10];
   int    quantity;
};
  int look_up(struct record table[],char s1[],char s2[],int m);
  void get (char string [ ] );
  main()
  {
       char title[30], author[20];
       int  index, no_of_records;
       char response[10], quantity[10];
       struct record book[] =  {
        {"Ritche","C Language",45.00,"May",1977,"PHI",10},
        {"Kochan","Programming in C",75.50,"July",1983,"Hayden",5},
        {"Balagurusamy","BASIC",30.00,"January",1984,"TMH",0},
        {"Balagurusamy","COBOL",60.00,"December",1988,"Macmillan",25}
                                     };

  no_of_records = sizeof(book)/ sizeof(struct record);
```

```
    do
    {
      printf("Enter title and author name as per the list\n");
      printf("\nTitle:    ");
      get(title);
      printf("Author:   ");
      get(author);
      index = look_up(book, title, author, no_of_records);
      if(index != -1)     /*  Book found  */
      {
          printf("\n%s %s %.2f %s %d %s\n\n",
                    book[index].author,
                    book[index].title,
                    book[index].price,
                    book[index].date.month,
                    book[index].date.year,
                    book[index].publisher);

          printf("Enter number of copies:");
          get(quantity);
          if(atoi(quantity) < book[index].quantity)

             printf("Cost of %d copies = %.2f\n",atoi(quantity),
                   book[index].price * atoi(quantity));
          else
             printf("\nRequired copies not in stock\n\n");
      }
      else
             printf("\nBook not in list\n\n");

      printf("\nDo you want any other book? (YES / NO):");
      get(response);
    }
    while(response[0] == 'Y' || response[0] == 'y');
    printf("\n\nThank you.  Good bye!\n");
}
void get(char string [] )
{
    char  c;
    int  i = 0;
    do
    {
      c = getchar();
      string[i++] = c;
    }
    while(c != '\n');
```

```
    string[i-1] = '\0';
  }

int look_up(struct record table[],char s1[],char s2[],int m)
{
    int  i;
    for(i = 0; i < m;  i++)
        if(strcmp(s1, table[i].title) == 0  &&
           strcmp(s2, table[i].author) == 0)
           return(i);              /* book found         */
    return(-1);                    /* book not found     */
}
```

Output

```
  Enter title and author name as per the list
  Title:     BASIC
  Author:    Balagurusamy
  Balagurusamy BASIC 30.00 January 1984 TMH

  Enter number of copies:5
  Required copies not in stock

  Do you want any other book? (YES / NO):y
  Enter title and author name as per the list
  Title:     COBOL
  Author:    Balagurusamy
  Balagurusamy COBOL 60.00 December 1988 Macmillan

  Enter number of copies:7
  Cost of 7 copies = 420.00

  Do you want any other book? (YES / NO):y
  Enter title and author name as per the list
  Title:     C Programming
  Author:    Ritche

  Book not in list


  Do you want any other book? (YES / NO):n


  Thank you.  Good bye!
```

Fig. 10.8 *Program of bookshop inventory*

REVIEW QUESTIONS

10.1 State whether the following statements are *true* or *false*.

(a) A **struct** type in C is a built-in data type.

(b) The tag name of a structure is optional.

(c) Structures may contain members of only one data type.

(d) A structure variable is used to declare a data type containing multiple fields.

(e) It is legal to copy a content of a structure variable to another structure variable of the same type.

(f) Structures are always passed to functions by printers.

(g) Pointers can be used to access the members of structure variables.

(h) We can perform mathematical operations on structure variables that contain only numeric type members.

(i) The keyword **typedef** is used to define a new data type.

(j) In accessing a member of a structure using a pointer p, the following two are equivalent: (*p).member_name and p-> member_name

(k) A union may be initialized in the same way a structure is initialized.

(l) A union can have another union as one of the members.

(m) A structure cannot have a union as one of its members.

(n) An array cannot be used as a member of a structure.

(o) A member in a structure can itself be a structure.

10.2 Fill in the blanks in the following statements:

(a) The ______________ can be used to create a synonym for a previously defined data type.

(b) A______________ is a collection of data items under one name in which the items share the same storage.

(c) The name of a structure is referred to as ______________.

(d) The selection operator -> requires the use of a ______________ to access the members of a structure.

(e) The variables declared in a structure definition are called its ______________.

10.3 A structure tag name **abc** is used to declare and initialize the structure variables of type **struct abc** in the following statements. Which of them are incorrect? Why? Assume that the structure **abc** has three members, **int, float** and **char** in that order.

(a) `struct a,b,c;`

(b) `struct abc a,b,c`

(c) `abc x,y,z;`

(d) `struct abc a[ ];`

(e) `struct abc a = { };`

(f) `struct abc = b, { 1+2, 3.0, "xyz"}`

(g) `struct abc c = {4,5,6};`

(h) `struct abc a = 4, 5.0, "xyz";`

10.4 Given the declaration

```
struct abc a,b,c;
```

which of the following statements are legal?

(a) `scanf ("%d, &a);`

(b) `printf ("%d", b);`

(c) `a = b;`

(d) `a = b + c;`

(e) `if (a>b)`

`. . . . .`

10.5 Given the declaration

```
struct item_bank
{
        int number;
        double cost;
};
```

which of the following are correct statements for declaring one dimensional array of structures of type **struct item_bank?**

(a) `int item_bank items[10];`

(b) `struct items[10] item_bank;`

(c) `struct item_bank items (10);`

(d) `struct item_bank items [10];`

(e) `struct items item_bank [10];`

10.6 Given the following declaration

```
typedef struct abc
{
        char x;
        int y;
        float z[10];
} ABC;
```

State which of the following declarations are invalid? Why?

(a) `struct abc v1;`

(b) `struct abc v2[10];`

(c) `struct ABC v3;`

(d) `ABC a,b,c;`

(e) `ABC a[10];`

10.7 How does a structure differ from an array?

10.8 Explain the meaning and purpose of the following:

(a) Template

(b) **struct** keyword

(c) **typedef** keyword

(d) **sizeof** operator

(e) Tag name

10.9 Explain what is wrong in the following structure declaration:

```
struct
{
        int number;
        float price;
}
main( )
{
        . . . . .
        . . . . .
}
```

10.10 When do we use the following?

(a) Unions
(b) Bit fields
(c) The **sizeof** operator

10.11 What is meant by the following terms?

(a) Nested structures
(b) Array of structures

Give a typical example of use of each of them.

10.12 Given the structure definitions and declarations

```
struct abc
{
        int a;
        float b;
};
struct xyz
{
        int x;
        float y;
};
abc a1, a2;
xyz x1, x2;
```

find errors, if any, in the following statements:

(a) `a1 = x1;`
(b) `abc.a1 = 10.75;`
(c) `int m = a + x;`
(d) `int n = x1.x + 10;`
(e) `a1 = a2;`
(f) `if (a.a1 > x.x1) . . .`
(g) `if (a1.a < x1.x) . . .`
(h) `if (x1 != x2) . . .`

PROGRAMMING EXERCISES

10.1 Define a structure data type called **time_struct** containing three members integer **hour,** integer **minute** and integer **second**. Develop a program that would assign values to the individual members and display the time in the following form:

16:40:51

10.2 Modify the above program such that a function is used to input values to the members and another function to display the time.

10.3 Design a function **update** that would accept the data structure designed in Exercise 10.1 and increments time by one second and returns the new time. (If the increment results in 60 seconds, then the second member is set to zero and the minute member is incremented by one. Then, if the result is 60 minutes, the minute member is set to zero and the hour member is incremented by one. Finally when the hour becomes 24, it is set to zero.)

10.4 Define a structure data type named **date** containing three integer members **day, month** and **year.** Develop an interactive modular program to perform the following tasks;

- To read data into structure members by a function
- To validate the date entered by another function
- To print the date in the format

  April 29, 2002

by a third function.

The input data should be three integers like 29, 4, and 2002 corresponding to day, month and year. Examples of invalid data:

31, 4, 2002 – April has only 30 days

29, 2, 2002 – 2002 is not a leap year

10.5 Design a function **update** that accepts the **date** structure designed in Exercise 10.4 to increment the date by one day and return the new date. The following rules are applicable:

- If the date is the last day in a month, month should be incremented
- If it is the last day in December, the year should be incremented
- There are 29 days in February of a leap year

10.6 Modify the input function used in Exercise 10.4 such that it reads a value that represents the date in the form of a long integer, like 19450815 for the date 15-8-1945 (August 15, 1945) and assigns suitable values to the members **day, month** and **year.**

Use suitable algorithm to convert the long integer 19450815 into year, month and day.

10.7 Add a function called **nextdate** to the program designed in Exercise 10.4 to perform the following task;

- Accepts two arguments, one of the structure **data** containing the present date and the second an integer that represents the number of days to be added to the present date.
- Adds the days to the present date and returns the structure containing the next date correctly.

Note that the next date may be in the next month or even the next year.

10.8 Use the **date** structure defined in Exercise 10.4 to store two dates. Develop a function that will take these two dates as input and compares them.
- It returns 1, if the **date1** is earlier than **date2**
- It returns 0, if **date1** is later date

10.9 Define a structure to represent a vector (a series of integer values) and write a modular program to perform the following tasks:
- To create a vector
- To modify the value of a given element
- To multiply by a scalar value
- To display the vector in the form (10, 20, 30, ...)

10.10 Add a function to the program of Exercise 10.9 that accepts two vectors as input parameters and return the addition of two vectors.

10.11 Create two structures named **metric** and **British** which store the values of distances. The **metric** structure stores the values in metres and centimetres and the British structure stores the values in feet and inches. Write a program that reads values for the structure variables and adds values contained in one variable of **metric** to the contents of another variable of **British.** The program should display the result in the format of feet and inches or metres and centimetres as required.

10.12 Define a structure named **census** with the following three members:
- A character array city [ ] to store names
- A long integer to store population of the city
- A float member to store the literacy level

Write a program to do the following:
- To read details for 5 cities randomly using an array variable
- To sort the list alphabetically
- To sort the list based on literacy level
- To sort the list based on population
- To display sorted lists

10.13 Define a structure that can describe an hotel. It should have members that include the name, address, grade, average room charge, and number of rooms.
Write functions to perform the following operations:
- To print out hotels of a given grade in order of charges
- To print out hotels with room charges less than a given value

10.14 Define a structure called **cricket** that will describe the following information:

player name
team name
batting average

Using **cricket,** declare an array **player** with 50 elements and write a program to read the information about all the 50 players and print a team-wise list containing names of players with their batting average.

10.15 Design a structure **student_record** to contain name, date of birth and total marks obtained. Use the **date** structure designed in Exercise 10.4 to represent the date of birth.
Develop a program to read data for 10 students in a class and list them rank-wise.

Chapter

11

Pointers

11.1 INTRODUCTION

A pointer is a derived data type in C. It is built from one of the fundamental data types available in C. Pointers contain memory addresses as their values. Since these memory addresses are the locations in the computer memory where program instructions and data are stored, pointers can be used to access and manipulate data stored in the memory.

Pointers are undoubtedly one of the most distinct and exciting features of C language. It has added power and flexibility to the language. Although they appear little confusing and difficult to understand for a beginner, they are a powerful tool and handy to use once they are mastered.

Pointers are used frequently in C, as they offer a number of benefits to the programmers. They include:

1. Pointers are more efficient in handling arrays and data tables.
2. Pointers can be used to return multiple values from a function via function arguments.
3. Pointers permit references to functions and thereby facilitating passing of functions as arguments to other functions.
4. The use of pointer arrays to character strings results in saving of data storage space in memory.
5. Pointers allow C to support dynamic memory management.
6. Pointers provide an efficient tool for manipulating dynamic data structures such as structures, linked lists, queues, stacks and trees.
7. Pointers reduce length and complexity of programs.
8. They increase the execution speed and thus reduce the program execution time.

Of course, the real power of C lies in the proper use of pointers. In this chapter, we will examine the pointers in detail and illustrate how to use them in program development. Chapter 13 examines the use of pointers for creating and managing linked lists.

11.2 UNDERSTANDING POINTERS

The computer's memory is a sequential collection of 'storage cells' as shown in Fig. 11.1. Each cell, commonly known as a *byte,* has a number called *address* associated with it. Typically, the addresses are numbered consecutively, starting from zero. The last address depends on the memory size. A computer system having 64 K memory will have its last address as 65,535.

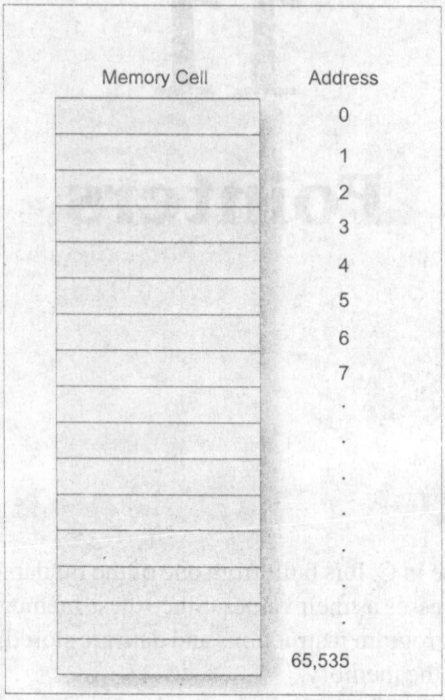

Fig. 11.1 *Memory organisation*

Whenever we declare a variable, the system allocates, somewhere in the memory, an appropriate location to hold the value of the variable. Since, every byte has a unique address number, this location will have its own address number. Consider the following statement:

```
int quantity = 179;
```

This statement instructs the system to find a location for the integer variable **quantity** and puts the value 179 in that location. Let us assume that the system has chosen the address location 5000 for **quantity.** We may represent this as shown in Fig. 11.2. (Note that the address of a variable is the address of the first bye occupied by that variable.)

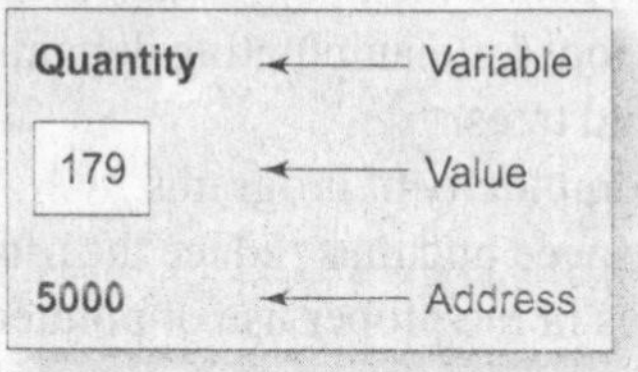

Fig. 11.2 *Representation of a variable*

During execution of the program, the system always associates the name **quantity** with the address 5000. (This is something similar to having a house number as well as a house name.) We may have access to the value 179 by using either the name **quantity** or the address 5000. Since memory addresses are simply numbers, they can be assigned to some variables, which can be stored in memory, like any other variable. Such variables that hold memory addresses are called *pointer variables*. A pointer variable is, therefore, nothing but a variable that contains an address, which is a location of another variable in memory.

Remember, since a pointer is a variable, its value is also stored in the memory in another location. Suppose, we assign the address of **quantity** to a variable **p**. The link between the variables **p** and **quantity** can be visualized as shown in Fig.11.3. The address of **p** is 5048.

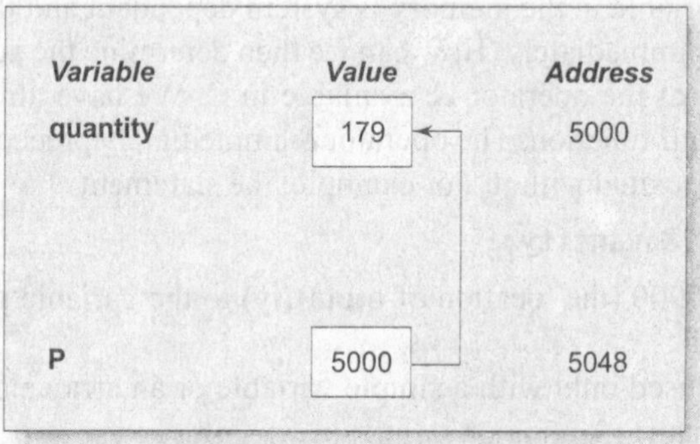

Fig. 11.3 *Pointer variable*

Since the value of the variable **p** is the address of the variable **quantity,** we may access the value of **quantity** by using the value of **p** and therefore, we say that the variable **p** 'points' to the variable **quantity.** Thus, **p** gets the name 'pointer'. (We are not really concerned about the actual values of pointer variables. They may be different every-time we run the program. What we are concerned about is the relationship between the variables **p** and **quantity**.)

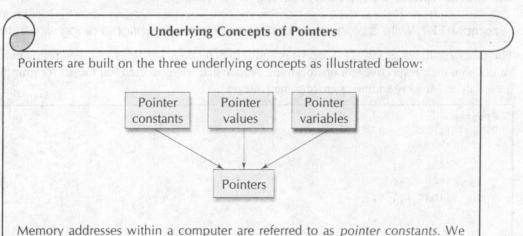

Underlying Concepts of Pointers

Pointers are built on the three underlying concepts as illustrated below:

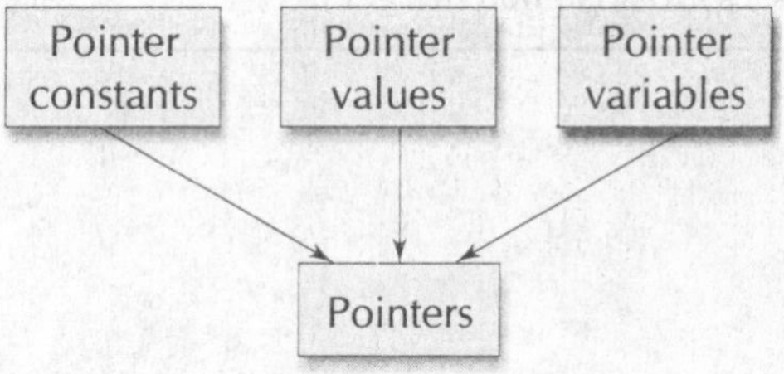

Memory addresses within a computer are referred to as *pointer constants.* We cannot change them; we can only use them to store data values. They are like house numbers.

We cannot save the value of a memory address directly. We can only obtain the value through the variable stored there using the address operator (&). The value thus obtained is known as *pointer value*. The pointer value (i.e. the address of a variable) may change from one run of the program to another.

Once we have a pointer value, it can be stored into another variable. The variable that contains a pointer value is called a *pointer variable*.

11.3 ACCESSING THE ADDRESS OF A VARIABLE

The actual location of a variable in the memory is system dependent and therefore, the address of a variable is not known to us immediately. How can we then determine the address of a variable? This can be done with the help of the operator **&** available in C. We have already seen the use of this *address operator* in the scanf function. The operator **&** immediately preceding a variable returns the address of the variable associated with it. For example, the statement

```
p = &quantity;
```

would assign the address 5000 (the location of **quantity)** to the variable **p**. The **&** operator can be remembered as 'address of'.

The **&** operator can be used only with a simple variable or an array element. The following are illegal use of address operator:

1. **&125** (pointing at constants).
2. int x[10];
   &x (pointing at array names).
3. **&(x+y)** (pointing at expressions).

If **x** is an array, then expressions such as

&x[0] and &x[i+3]

are valid and represent the addresses of 0th and (i+3)th elements of x.

Example 11.1 Write a program to print the address of a variable along with its value.

The program shown in Fig. 11.4, declares and initializes four variables and then prints out these values with their respective storage locations. Notice that we have used %u format for printing address values. Memory addresses are unsigned integers.

```
Program
  main()
  {
     char   a;
     int    x;
     float  p, q;

     a  = 'A';
     x  = 125;
```

```
    p  = 10.25, q = 18.76;
    printf("%c is stored at addr %u.\n", a, &a);
    printf("%d is stored at addr %u.\n", x, &x);
    printf("%f is stored at addr %u.\n", p, &p);
    printf("%f is stored at addr %u.\n", q, &q);

}
```

Output

```
A is stored at addr 4436.
125 is stored at addr 4434.
10.250000 is stored at addr 4442.
18.760000 is stored at addr 4438.
```

Fig. 11.4 *Accessing the address of a variable*

11.4 DECLARING POINTER VARIABLES

In C, every variable must be declared for its type. Since pointer variables contain addresses that belong to a separate data type, they must be declared as pointers before we use them. The declaration of a pointer variable takes the following form:

data_type ***pt_name;**

This tells the compiler three things about the variable **pt_name.**

1. The asterisk (*) tells that the variable **pt_name** is a pointer variable.
2. **pt_name** needs a memory location.
3. **pt_name** points to a variable of type *data_type.*

For example,

```
int *p;                    /* integer pointer */
```

declares the variable **p** as a pointer variable that points to an integer data type. Remember that the type **int** refers to the data type of the variable being pointed to by **p** and not the type of the value of the pointer. Similarly, the statement

```
float *x;                  / * float pointer */
```

declares **x** as a pointer to a floating-point variable.

The declarations cause the compiler to allocate memory locations for the pointer variables **p** and **x.** Since the memory locations have not been assigned any values, these locations may contain some unknown values in them and therefore they point to unknown locations as shown:

int *p;

Pointer Declaration Style

Pointer variables are declared similar to normal variables except for the addition of the unary * operator. This symbol can appear anywhere between the type name and the printer variable name. Programmers use the following styles:

```
int*    p;      /* style 1 */
int     *p;     /* style 2 */
int  *  p;      /* style 3 */
```

However the style2 is becoming increasingly popular due to the following reasons:

1. This style is convenient to have multiple declarations in the same statement. Example:

```
int *p, x, *q;
```

2. This style matches with the format used for accessing the target values. Example:

```
int x, *p, y;
x = 10;
p = & x;
y = *p;        /* accessing x through p */
*p = 20;       /* assigning 20 to x */
```

We use in this book the style 2, namely,

```
int *p;
```

11.5 INITIALIZATION OF POINTER VARIABLES

The process of assigning the address of a variable to a pointer variable is known as *initialization*. As pointed out earlier, all uninitialized pointers will have some unknown values that will be interpreted as memory addresses. They may not be valid addresses or they may point to some values that are wrong. Since the compilers do not detect these errors, the programs with uninitialized pointers will produce erroneous results. It is therefore important to initialize pointer variables carefully before they are used in the program.

Once a pointer variable has been declared we can use the assignment operator to initialize the variable. Example:

```
int quantity;
int *p;               /* declaration    */
p = &quantity;        /* initialization */
```

We can also combine the initialization with the declaration. That is,

```
int *p = &quantity;
```

is allowed. The only requirement here is that the variable **quantity** must be declared before the initialization takes place. Remember, this is an initialization of **p** and not ***p**.

We must ensure that the pointer variables always point to the corresponding type of data. For example,

```
float a, b;
int x, *p;
p = &a;            /* wrong */
b = *p;
```

will result in erroneous output because we are trying to assign the address of a **float** variable to an integer pointer. When we declare a pointer to be of **int** type, the system assumes that any address that the pointer will hold will point to an integer variable. Since the compiler will not detect such errors, care should be taken to avoid wrong pointer assignments.

It is also possible to combine the declaration of data variable, the declaration of pointer variable and the initialization of the pointer variable in one step. For example,

```
int x, *p = &x;        /* three in one */
```

is perfectly valid. It declares **x** as an integer variable and **p** as a pointer variable and then initializes **p** to the address of **x.** And also remember that the target variable **x** is declared first. The statement

```
int *p = &x, x;
```

is not valid.

We could also define a pointer variable with an initial value of NULL or 0 (zero). That is, the following statements are valued:

```
int *p = NULL;
int *p = 0;
```

With the exception of NULL and 0, no other constant value can be assigned to a pointer variable. For example, the following is wrong:

```
int *p = 5360;          / *absolute address */
```

Pointer Flexibility

Pointers are flexible. We can make the same pointer to point to different data variables in different statements. Example;

```
int x, y, z, *p;
. . . . .
p = &x;
. . . . .
p = &y;
. . . . .
p = &z;
. . . . .
```

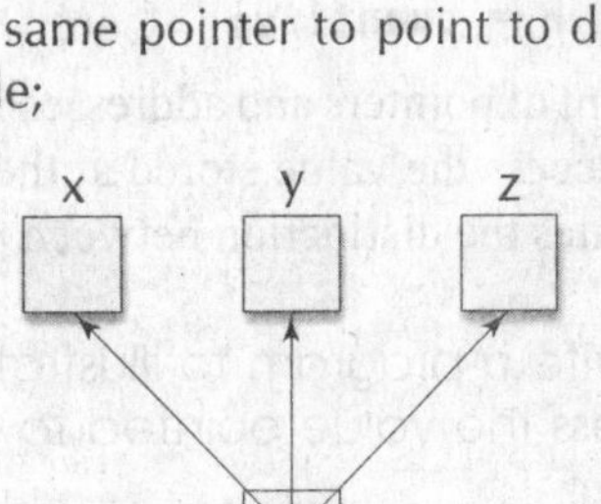

We can also use different pointers to point to the same data variable. Example.

```
int x;
int *p1 = &x;
int *p2 = &x;
int *p3 = &x;
.....
.....
```

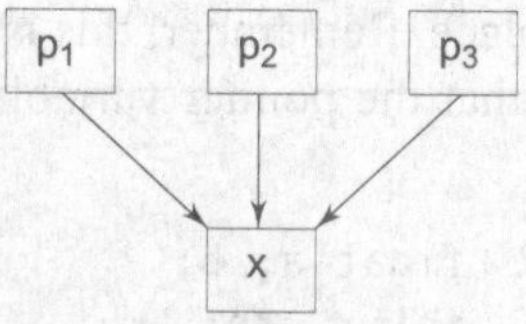

11.6 ACCESSING A VARIABLE THROUGH ITS POINTER

Once a pointer has been assigned the address of a variable, the question remains as to how to access the value of the variable using the pointer. This is done by using another unary operator * (asterisk), usually known as the *indirection operator*. Another name for the indirection operator is the *dereferencing operator*. Consider the following statements:

```
int quantity, *p, n;
quantity = 179;
p = &quantity;
n = *p;
```

The first line declares **quantity** and **n** as integer variables and **p** as a pointer variable pointing to an integer. The second line assigns the value 179 to **quantity** and the third line assigns the address of **quantity** to the pointer variable **p**. The fourth line contains the indirection operator *. When the operator * is placed before a pointer variable in an expression (on the right-hand side of the equal sign), the pointer returns the value of the variable of which the pointer value is the address. In this case, ***p** returns the value of the variable **quantity**, because **p** is the address of **quantity.** The * can be remembered as 'value at address'. Thus the value of **n** would be 179. The two statements

```
p = &quantity;
n = *p;
```

are equivalent to

```
n = *&quantity;
```

which in turn is equivalent to

```
n = quantity;
```

In C, the assignment of pointers and addresses is always done symbolically, by means of symbolic names. You cannot access the value stored at the address 5368 by writing *5368. It will not work. Example 11.2 illustrates the distinction between pointer value and the value it points to.

Example 11.2 Write a program to illustrate the use of indirection operator '*' to access the value pointed to by a printer.

The program and output are shown in Fig.11.5. The program clearly shows how we can access the value of a variable using a pointer. You may notice that the value of the pointer **ptr** is 4104 and the value it points to is 10. Further, you may also note the following equivalences:

```
x = *(&x) = *ptr = y
&x = &*ptr
```

Program

```
main()
{
    int   x, y;
    int   *ptr;
    x = 10;
    ptr = &x;
    y = *ptr;
    printf("Value of x is %d\n\n",x);
    printf("%d is stored at addr %u\n", x, &x);
    printf("%d is stored at addr %u\n", *&x, &x);
    printf("%d is stored at addr %u\n", *ptr, ptr);
    printf("%d is stored at addr %u\n", ptr, &ptr);
    printf("%d is stored at addr %u\n", y, &y);
    *ptr = 25;
    printf("\nNow x = %d\n",x);

}
```

Output

```
Value of x is 10
10      is stored at addr 4104
10      is stored at addr 4104
10      is stored at addr 4104
4104    is stored at addr 4106
10      is stored at addr 4108
Now x = 25
```

Fig. 11.5 *Accessing a variable through its pointer*

The actions performed by the program are illustrated in Fig. 11.6. The statement **ptr = &x** assigns the address of **x** to **ptr** and **y = *ptr** assigns the value pointed to by the pointer **ptr** to **y**.

Note the use of the assignment statement

```
*ptr = 25;
```

This statement puts the value of 25 at the memory location whose address is the value of **ptr**. We know that the value of **ptr** is the address of **x** and therefore the old value of **x** is replaced by 25. This, in effect, is equivalent to assigning 25 to **x**. This shows how we can change the value of a variable *indirectly* using a pointer and the *indirection operator*.

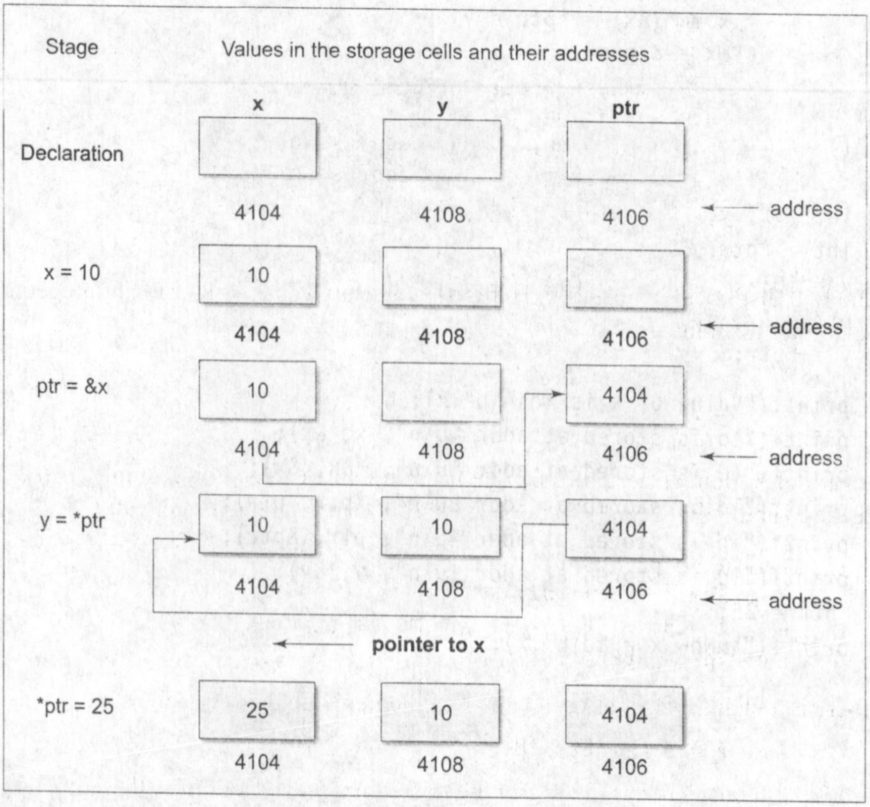

Fig. 11.6 *Illustration of pointer assignments*

11.7 CHAIN OF POINTERS

It is possible to make a pointer to point to another pointer, thus creating a chain of pointers as shown.

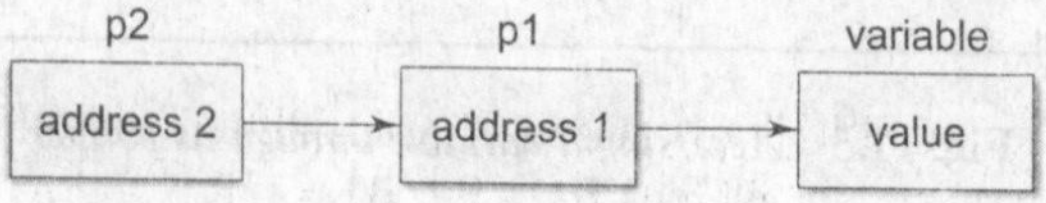

Here, the pointer variable **p2** contains the address of the pointer variable **p1**, which points to the location that contains the desired value. This is known as *multiple indirections.*

A variable that is a pointer to a pointer must be declared using additional indirection operator symbols in front of the name. Example:

```
int **p2;
```

This declaration tells the compiler that **p2** is a pointer to a pointer of **int** type. Remember, the pointer **p2** is not a pointer to an integer, but rather a pointer to an integer pointer.

We can access the target value indirectly pointed to by pointer to a pointer by applying the indirection operator twice. Consider the following code:

```
main ( )
{
        int x, *p1,   **p2;
        x = 100;
        p1 = &x;        /* address of x */
        p2 = &p1        /* address of p1*/
        printf ("%d", **p2);
}
```

This code will display the value 100. Here, **p1** is declared as a pointer to an integer and **p2** as a pointer to a pointer to an integer.

11.8 POINTER EXPRESSIONS

Like other variables, pointer variables can be used in expressions. For example, if **p1** and **p2** are properly declared and initialized pointers, then the following statements are valid.

```
y = *p1 * *p2;          same as (*p1) * (*p2)
sum = sum + *p1;
z = 5* - *p2/ *p1;      same as (5 * (- (*p2)))/(*p1)
*p2 = *p2 + 10;
```

Note that there is a blank space between / and * in the item3 above. The following is wrong.

```
z = 5* - *p2 /*p1;
```

The symbol /* is considered as the beginning of a comment and therefore the statement fails.

C allows us to add integers to or subtract integers from pointers, as well as to subtract one pointer from another. p1 + 4, p2–2 and p1 – p2 are all allowed. If p1 and p2 are both pointers to the same array, then **p2 – p1** gives the number of elements between **p1** and **p2**.

We may also use short-hand operators with the pointers.

```
p1++;
–p2;
sum += *p2;
```

In addition to arithmetic operations discussed above, pointers can also be compared using the relational operators. The expressions such as **p1 > p2, p1 = = p2**, and **p1 != p2** are allowed. However, any comparison of pointers that refer to separate and unrelated variables makes no sense. Comparisons can be used meaningfully in handling arrays and strings.

We may not use pointers in division or multiplication. For example, expressions such as

p1 / p2 or p1 * p2 or p1 / 3

are not allowed. Similarly, two pointers cannot be added. That is, p1 + p2 is illegal.

Example 11.3 Write a program to illustrate the use of pointers in arithmetic operations.

The program in Fig.11.7 shows how the pointer variables can be directly used in expressions. It also illustrates the order of evaluation of expressions. For example, the expression

4* – *p2 / *p1 + 10

is evaluated as follows:

((4 * (–(*p2))) / (*p1)) + 10

When *p1 = 12 and *p2 = 4, this expression evaluates to 9. Remember, since all the variables are of type int, the entire evaluation is carried out using the integer arithmetic.

Program

```
main()
{
    int  a, b, *p1, *p2, x, y, z;
    a  = 12;
    b  =  4;
    p1 = &a;
    p2 = &b;
    x  =  *p1 * *p2 - 6;
    y  =  4*  - *p2 / *p1 + 10;
    printf("Address of a = %u\n", p1);
    printf("Address of b = %u\n", p2);
    printf("\n");
    printf("a = %d, b = %d\n", a, b);
    printf("x = %d, y = %d\n", x, y);
    *p2  = *p2 + 3;
    *p1  = *p2 - 5;
    z    = *p1 * *p2 - 6;
    printf("\na = %d, b = %d,", a, b);
    printf(" z = %d\n", z);
}
```

Output

```
Address of a = 4020
Address` of b = 4016
a = 12, b = 4
x = 42, y = 9
a = 2, b = 7, z = 8
```

Fig. 11.7 *Evaluation of pointer expressions*

11.9 POINTER INCREMENTS AND SCALE FACTOR

We have seen that the pointers can be incremented like

```
p1 = p2 + 2;
p1 = p1 + 1;
```

and so on. Remember, however, an expression like

```
p1++;
```

will cause the pointer **p1** to point to the next value of its type. For example, if **p1** is an integer pointer with an initial value, say 2800, then after the operation **p1 = p1 + 1**, the value of **p1** will be 2802, and not 2801. That is, when we increment a pointer, its value is increased by the 'length' of the data type that it points to. This length called the *scale factor.*

For an IBM PC, the length of various data types are as follows:

characters	1 byte
integers	2 bytes
floats	4 bytes
long integers	4 bytes
doubles	8 bytes

The number of bytes used to store various data types depends on the system and can be found by making use of the **sizeof** operator. For example, if **x** is a variable, then **sizeof(x)** returns the number of bytes needed for the variable. (Systems like Pentium use 4 bytes for storing integers and 2 bytes for short integers.)

Rules of Pointer Operations

The following rules apply when performing operations on pointer variables.

1. A pointer variable can be assigned the address of another variable.
2. A pointer variable can be assigned the values of another pointer variable.
3. A pointer variable can be initialized with NULL or zero value.
4. A pointer variable can be pre-fixed or post-fixed with increment or decrement operators.
5. An integer value may be added or subtracted from a pointer variable.
6. When two pointers point to the same array, one pointer variable can be subtracted from another.
7. When two pointers point to the objects of the same data types, they can be compared using relational operators.
8. A pointer variable cannot be multiplied by a constant.
9. Two pointer variables cannot be added.
10. A value cannot be assigned to an arbitrary address (i.e &x = 10; is illegal).

11.10 POINTERS AND ARRAYS

When an array is declared, the compiler allocates a base address and sufficient amount of storage to contain all the elements of the array in contiguous memory locations. The base address is the location of the first element (index 0) of the array. The compiler also defines the array name as a constant pointer to the first element. Suppose we declare an array **x** as follows:

```
int x[5] = {1, 2, 3, 4, 5};
```

Suppose the base address of x is 1000 and assuming that each integer requires two bytes, the five elements will be stored as follows:

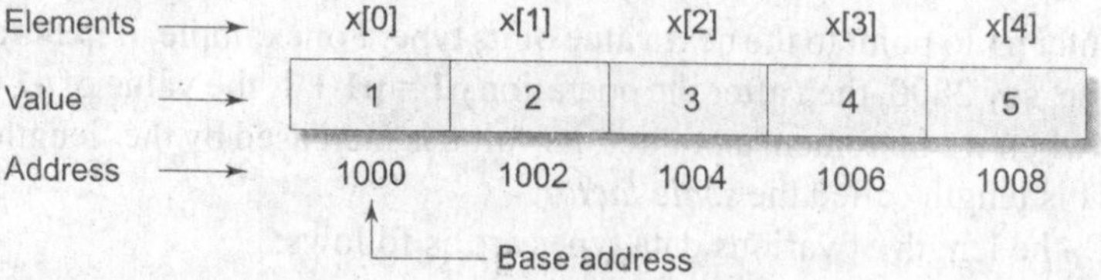

The name **x** is defined as a constant pointer pointing to the first element, **x[0]** and therefore the value of **x** is 1000, the location where **x[0]** is stored. That is,

```
x = &x[0] = 1000
```

If we declare **p** as an integer pointer, then we can make the pointer **p** to point to the array **x** by the following assignment:

```
p = x;
```

This is equivalent to

```
p = &x[0];
```

Now, we can access every value of **x** using p++ to move from one element to another. The relationship between **p** and **x** is shown as:

p = &x[0] (= 1000)
p+1 = &x[1] (= 1002)
p+2 = &x[2] (= 1004)
p+3 = &x[3] (= 1006)
p+4 = &x[4] (= 1008)

You may notice that the address of an element is calculated using its index and the scale factor of the data type. For instance,

address of **x[3]** = base address + (3 x scale factor of **int**)
= 1000 + (3 x 2) = 1006

When handling arrays, instead of using array indexing, we can use pointers to access array elements. Note that ***(p+3)** gives the value of **x[3]**. The pointer accessing method is much faster than array indexing.

The example 11.4 illustrates the use of pointer accessing method.

Example 11.4 Write a program using pointers to compute the sum of all elements stored in an array.

The program shown in Fig. 11.8 illustrates how a pointer can be used to traverse an array element. Since incrementing an array pointer causes it to point to the next element, we need only to add one to **p** each time we go through the loop.

Program

```
main()
{
     int *p, sum, i;
     int x[5] = {5,9,6,3,7};
     i  = 0;
     p  = x;        /* initializing with base address of x */
     printf("Element   Value    Address\n\n");
     while(i < 5)
     {
         printf(" x[%d] %d %u\n", i, *p, p);
         sum = sum + *p;     /* accessing array element   */
         i++, p++;          /* incrementing pointer     */
     }
     printf("\n  Sum      =  %d\n", sum);
     printf("\n  &x[0]    =  %u\n", &x[0]);
     printf("\n  p        =  %u\n", p);
}
```

Output

```
Element      Value       Address
x[0]            5          166
x[1]            9          168
x[2]            6          170
x[3]            3          172
x[4]            7          174
Sum       =  55
&x[0]     =  166
p         =  176
```

Fig. 11.8 *Accessing one-dimensional array elements using the pointer*

It is possible to avoid the loop control variable **i** as shown:

```
.....
p = x;
while(p <= &x[4])
{
sum += *p;
p++;
}
.....
```

Here, we compare the pointer **p** with the address of the last element to determine when the array has been traversed.

Pointers can be used to manipulate two-dimensional arrays as well. We know that in a one-dimensional array **x,** the expression

```
*(x+i) or *(p+i)
```

represents the element **x[i]**. Similarly, an element in a two-dimensional array can be represented by the pointer expression as follows:

```
*(*(a+i)+j) or *(*(p+i)+j)
```

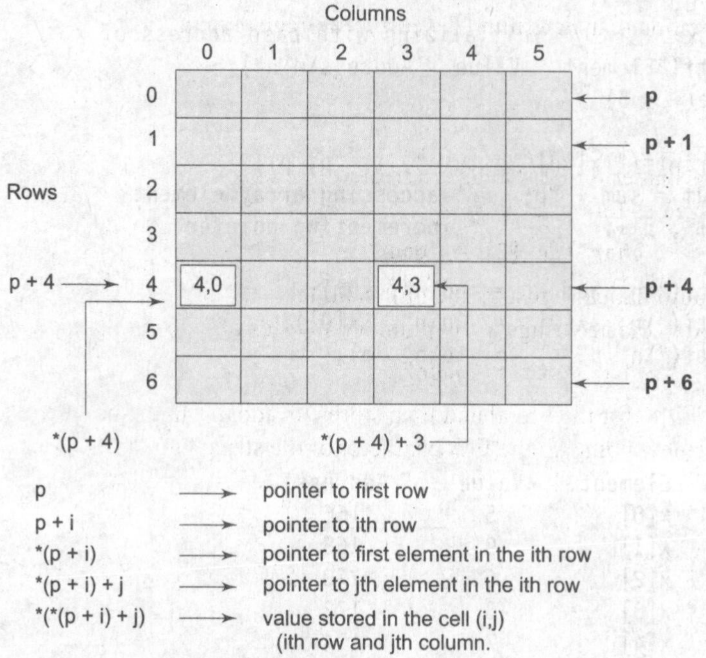

Fig. 11.9 *Pointers to two-dimensional arrays*

Figure 11.9 illustrates how this expression represents the element **a[i][j].** The base address of the array **a** is &a[0][0] and starting at this address, the compiler allocates contiguous space for all the elements, *row-wise*. That is, the first element of the second row is placed immediately after the last element of the first row, and so on. Suppose we declare an array **a** as follows:

```
int a[3][4] = { {15,27,11,35},
                {22,19,31,17},
                {31,23,14,36}
              };
```

The elements of **a** will be stored as:

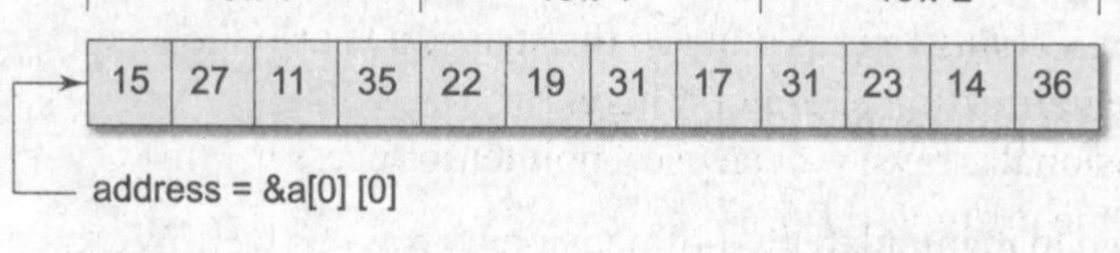

If we declare **p** as an **int** pointer with the initial address of &a[0][0], then

a[i][j] is equivalent to *(p+4 × i+j)

You may notice that, if we increment **i** by 1, the **p** is incremented by 4, the size of each row. Then the element **a[2][3]** is given by ***(p+2 × 4+3) = *(p+11).**

This is the reason why, when a two-dimensional array is declared, we must specify the size of each row so that the compiler can determine the correct storage mapping.

11.11 POINTERS AND CHARACTER STRINGS

We have seen in Chapter 8 that strings are treated like character arrays and therefore they are declared and initialized as follows:

```
char str [5] = "good";
```

The compiler automatically inserts the null character '\0' at the end of the string. C supports an alternative method to create strings using pointer variables of type **char.** Example:

```
char *str = "good";
```

This creates a string for the literal and then stores its address in the pointer variable **str.**

The pointer **str** now points to the first character of the string "good" as:

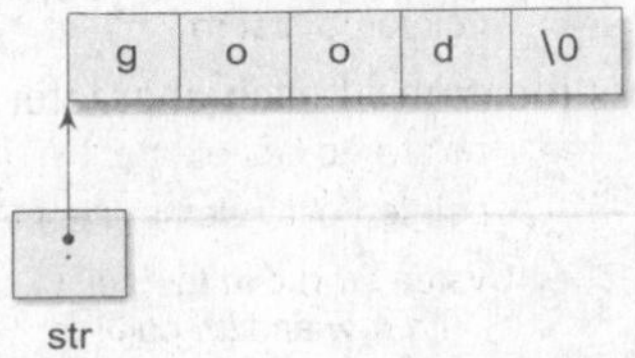

We can also use the run-time assignment for giving values to a string pointer. Example

```
char * string1;
string1 = "good";
```

Note that the assignment

```
string1 = "good";
```

is not a string copy, because the variable **string1** is a pointer, not a string.

(As pointed out in Chapter 8, C does not support copying one string to another through the assignment operation.)

We can print the content of the string **string1** using either **printf** or **puts** functions as follows:

```
printf("%s", string1);
puts (string1);
```

Remember, although **string1** is a pointer to the string, it is also the name of the string. Therefore, we do not need to use indirection operator * here.

Like in one-dimensional arrays, we can use a pointer to access the individual characters in a string. This is illustrated by the example 11.5.

Example 11.5 Write a program using pointers to determine the length of a character string.

A program to count the length of a string is shown in Fig.11.10. The statement

```
char *cptr = name;
```

declares **cptr** as a pointer to a character and assigns the address of the first character of **name** as the initial value. Since a string is always terminated by the null character, the statement

```
while(*cptr != '\0')
```

is true until the end of the string is reached.

When the **while** loop is terminated, the pointer **cptr** holds the address of the null character. Therefore, the statement

```
length = cptr - name;
```

gives the length of the string **name.**

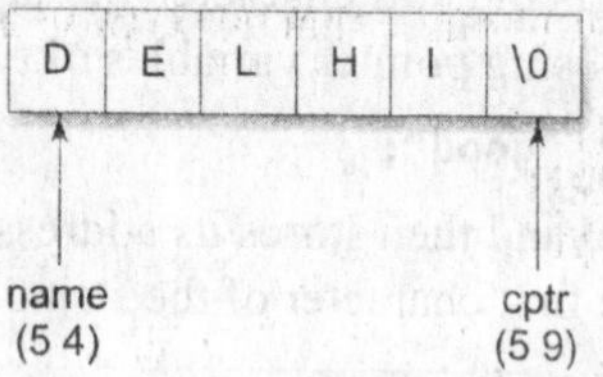

The output also shows the address location of each character. Note that each character occupies one memory cell (byte).

Program

```
main()
{
    char  *name;
    int  length;
    char  *cptr = name;
    name  = "DELHI";
    printf ("%s\n", name);
    while(*cptr != '\0')
    {
        printf("%c is stored at address %u\n", *cptr, cptr);
        cptr++;
    }
    length = cptr - name;
    printf("\nLength of the string = %d\n", length);
}
```

Output

```
DELHI
D is stored at address 54
```

```
E is stored at address 55
L is stored at address 56
H is stored at address 57
I is stored at address 58

Length of the string = 5
```

Fig. 11.10 *String handling by pointers*

In C, a constant character string always represents a pointer to that string. And therefore the following statements are valid:

```
char *name;
name = "Delhi";
```

These statements will declare **name** as a pointer to character and assign to **name** the constant character string “Delhi”. You might remember that this type of assignment does not apply to character arrays. The statements like

```
char name[20];
name = "Delhi";
```

do not work.

11.12 ARRAY OF POINTERS

One important use of pointers is in handling of a table of strings. Consider the following array of strings:

```
char name [3][25];
```

This says that the **name** is a table containing three names, each with a maximum length of 25 characters (including null character). The total storage requirements for the **name** table are 75 bytes.

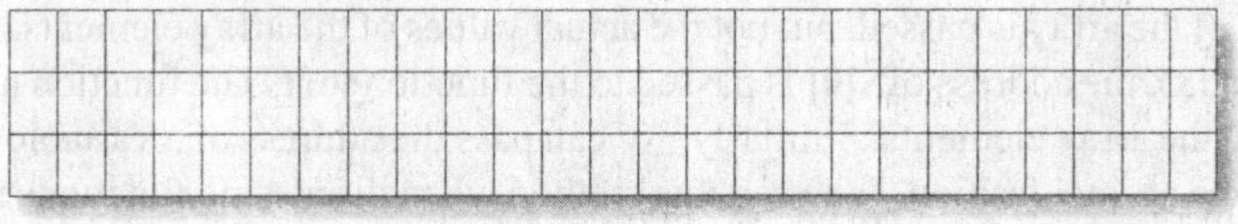

We know that rarely the individual strings will be of equal lengths. Therefore, instead of making each row a fixed number of characters, we can make it a pointer to a string of varying length. For example,

```
char *name[3] = {
                    "New Zealand",
                    "Australia",
                    "India"
                };
```

declares **name** to be an *array of three pointers* to characters, each pointer pointing to a particular name as:

name [0] ⟶ New Zealand
name [1] ⟶ Australia
name [2] ⟶ India

This declaration allocates only 28 bytes, sufficient to hold all the characters as shown

N	e	w		Z	e	a	l	a	n	d	\0
A	u	s	t	r	a	l	i	a	\0		
I	n	d	i	a	\0						

The following statement would print out all the three names:

```
for(i = 0; i <= 2; i++)
   printf("%s\n", name[i]);
```

To access the jth character in the ith name, we may write as

***(name[i]+j)**

The character arrays with the rows of varying length are called 'ragged arrays' and are better handled by pointers.

Remember the difference between the notations ***p[3]** and **(*p)[3]**. Since * has a lower precedence than [ ], *p[3] declares p as an array of 3 pointers while (*p)[3] declares **p** as a pointer to an array of three elements.

11.13 POINTERS AS FUNCTION ARGUMENTS

We have noted earlier that when an array is passed to a function as an argument, only the address of the first element of the array is passed, but not the actual values of the array elements. If **x** is an array, when we call **sort(x),** the address of **x[0]** is passed to the function **sort**. The function uses this address for manipulating the array elements. Similarly, we can pass the address of a variable as an argument to a function in the normal fashion. We used this method when discussing functions that return multiple values (see Chapter 9).

When we pass addresses to a function, the parameters receiving the addresses should be pointers. The process of calling a function using pointers to pass the addresses of variables is known as *'call by reference'*. (You know, the process of passing the actual value of variables is known as "call by value".) The function which is called by 'reference' can change the value of the variable used in the call.

Consider the following code:

```
main()
{
        int x;
```

```
        x = 20;
        change(&x);          /* call by reference or address */
        printf("%d\n",x);
    }
    change(int *p)
    {
        *p = *p + 10;
    }
```

When the function **change( )** is called, the address of the variable **x**, not its value, is passed into the function **change().** Inside **change( ),** the variable **p** is declared as a pointer and therefore **p** is the address of the variable **x.** The statement,

***p = *p + 10;**

means 'add 10 to the value stored at the address **p'**. Since **p** represents the address of **x,** the value of **x** is changed from 20 to 30. Therefore, the output of the program will be 30, not 20.

Thus, call by reference provides a mechanism by which the function can change the stored values in the calling function. Note that this mechanism is also known as "*call by address*" or "*pass by pointers*"

Example 11.6 Write a function using pointers to exchange the values stored in two locations in the memory.

The program in Fig. 11.11 shows how the contents of two locations can be exchanged using their address locations. The function **exchange()** receives the addresses of the variables **x** and **y** and exchanges their contents.

```
Program
  void exchange (int *, int *);     /* prototype */
  main()
  {
      int x, y;
      x = 100;
      y = 200;
      printf("Before exchange  : x = %d    y = %d\n\n", x, y);
      exchange(&x,&y);/* call */
      printf("After exchange   : x = %d    y = %d\n\n", x, y);
  }
  exchange (int *a, int *b)
  {
      int t;
      t = *a;    /* Assign the value at address a to t */
      *a = *b;   /* put b into a */
      *b = t;    /* put t into b */
  }
```

Output

```
Before exchange  : x = 100   y = 200
After exchange   : x = 200   y = 100
```

Fig. 11.11 *Passing of pointers as function parameters*

You may note the following points:

1. The function parameters are declared as pointers.
2. The dereferenced pointers are used in the function body.
3. When the function is called, the addresses are passed as actual arguments.

The use of pointers to access array elements is very common in C. We have used a pointer to traverse array elements in Example 11.4. We can also use this technique in designing user-defined functions discussed in Chapter 9. Let us consider the problem sorting an array of integers discussed in Example 9.6.

The function **sort** may be written using pointers (instead of array indexing) as shown:

```
void sort (int m, int *x)
{     int i j, temp;
      for (i=1; i<= m-1; i++)
          for (j=1; j<= m-1; j++)
          if(*(x+j-1) >= *(x+j))
          {
               temp = *(x+j-1);
               *(x+j-1) = *(x+j);
               *(x+j) = temp;
          }
}
```

Note that we have used the pointer x (instead of array x[ ]) to receive the address of array passed and therefore the pointer x can be used to access the array elements (as pointed out in Section 11.10). This function can be used to sort an array of integers as follows:

```
. . . . .
int score[4] = {45, 90, 71, 83};
. . . . .
sort(4, score);    /* Function call */
. . . . .
```

The calling function must use the following prototype declaration.

```
void sort (int, int *);
```

This tells the compiler that the formal argument that receives the array is a pointer, not array variable.

Pointer parameters are commonly employed in string functions. Consider the function copy which copies one string to another.

```
copy(char *s1, char *s2)
{
  while( (*s1++ = *s2++) != '\0')
  ;
}
```

This copies the contents of **s2** into the string **s1.** Parameters **s1** and **s2** are the pointers to character strings, whose initial values are passed from the calling function. For example, the calling statement

```
copy(name1, name2);
```

will assign the address of the first element of **name1** to **s1** and the address of the first element of **name2** to **s2.**

Note that the value of ***s2++** is the character that **s2** pointed to before **s2** was incremented. Due to the postfix ++, **s2** is incremented only after the current value has been fetched. Similarly, **s1** is incremented only after the assignment has been completed.

Each character, after it has been copied, is compared with '\0' and therefore copying is terminated as soon as the '\0' is copied.

11.14 FUNCTIONS RETURNING POINTERS

We have seen so far that a function can return a single value by its name or return multiple values through pointer parameters. Since pointers are a data type in C, we can also force a function to return a pointer to the calling function. Consider the following code:

```
int *larger (int *, int *);        /* prototype */
main ( )
{
          int a = 10;
          int b = 20;
          int *p;
          p = larger(&a, &b); /Function call */
          printf ("%d", *p);
}
int *larger (int *x, int *y)
{
          if (*x>*y)
                    return (x);      /*address of a */
          else
                    return (y);      /* address of b */
     }
```

The function **larger** receives the addresses of the variables **a** and **b**, decides which one is larger using the pointers **x** and **y** and then returns the address of its location. The returned value is then assigned to the pointer variable **p** in the calling function. In this case, the address of **b** is returned and assigned to **p** and therefore the output will be the value of **b**, namely, 20.

Note that the address returned must be the address of a variable in the calling function. It is an error to return a pointer to a local variable in the called function.

11.15 POINTERS TO FUNCTIONS

A function, like a variable, has a type and an address location in the memory. It is therefore, possible to declare a pointer to a function, which can then be used as an argument in another function. A pointer to a function is declared as follows:

```
type (*fptr) ();
```

This tells the compiler that **fptr** is a pointer to a function, which returns *type* value. The parentheses around ***fptr** are necessary. Remember that a statement like

```
type *gptr();
```

would declare **gptr** as a function returning a pointer to *type.*

We can make a function pointer to point to a specific function by simply assigning the name of the function to the pointer. For example, the statements

```
double mul(int, int);
double (*p1)();
p1 = mul;
```

declare **p1** as a pointer to a function and **mul** as a function and then make **p1** to point to the function **mul**. To call the function **mul,** we may now use the pointer **p1** with the list of parameters. That is,

(*p1)(x,y)/* Function call */

is equivalent to

mul(x,y)

Note the parentheses around ***p1.**

Example 11.7 Write a program that uses a function pointer as a function argument.

A program to print the function values over a given range of values is shown in Fig. 11.12. The printing is done by the function **table** by evaluating the function passed to it by the **main.**

With **table,** we declare the parameter **f** as a pointer to a function as follows:

```
double (*f)();
```

The value returned by the function is of type **double.** When **table** is called in the statement

```
table (y, 0.0, 2, 0.5);
```

we pass a pointer to the function **y** as the first parameter of **table**. Note that **y** is not followed by a parameter list.

During the execution of **table,** the statement

```
value = (*f)(a);
```

calls the function **y** which is pointed to by **f,** passing it the parameter **a.** Thus the function **y** is evaluated over the range 0.0 to 2.0 at the intervals of 0.5.

Similarly, the call

```
table (cos, 0.0, PI, 0.5);
```

passes a pointer to **cos** as its first parameter and therefore, the function **table** evaluates the value of **cos** over the range 0.0 to PI at the intervals of 0.5.

Program

```
#include  <math.h>
#define  PI  3.1415926
double y(double);
double cos(double);
double table (double(*f)(), double, double, double);

main()
{   printf("Table of y(x) = 2*x*x-x+1\n\n");
    table(y, 0.0, 2.0, 0.5);
    printf("\nTable of cos(x)\n\n");
    table(cos, 0.0, PI, 0.5);
}
double table(double(*f)(),double min, double max, double step)
{   double a, value;
    for(a = min; a <= max; a += step)
    {
        value = (*f)(a);
        printf("%5.2f  %10.4f\n", a, value);
    }
}
double y(double x)
{
   return(2*x*x-x+1);
}
```

Output

```
        Table of y(x) = 2*x*x-x+1
          0.00        1.0000
          0.50        1.0000
          1.00        2.0000
          1.50        4.0000
          2.00        7.0000
        Table of cos(x)
          0.00        1.0000
          0.50        0.8776
          1.00        0.5403
          1.50        0.0707
          2.00       -0.4161
          2.50       -0.8011
          3.00       -0.9900
```

Fig. 11.12 *Use of pointers to functions*

Compatibility and Casting

A variable declared as a pointer is not just a *pointer type* variable. It is also a pointer to a *specific* fundamental data type, such as a character. A pointer therefore always has a type associated with it. We cannot assign a pointer of one type to a pointer of another type, although both of them have memory addresses as their values. This is known as *incompatibility* of pointers.

All the pointer variables store memory addresses, which are compatible, but what is not compatible is the underlying data type to which they point to. We cannot use the assignment operator with the pointers of different types. We can however make explicit assignment between incompatible pointer types by using **cast** operator, as we do with the fundamental types. Example:

```
int x;
char *p;
p = (char *) & x;
```

In such cases, we must ensure that all operations that use the pointer **p** must apply casting properly.

We have an exception. The exception is the void pointer (void *). The void pointer is a ***generic pointer*** that can represent any pointer type. All pointer types can be assigned to a void pointer and a void pointer can be assigned to any pointer without casting. A void pointer is created as follows:

```
void *vp;
```

Remember that since a void pointer has no object type, it cannot be de-referenced.

11.16 POINTERS AND STRUCTURES

We know that the name of an array stands for the address of its zeroth element. The same thing is true of the names of arrays of structure variables. Suppose **product** is an array variable of **struct** type. The name **product** represents the address of its zeroth element. Consider the following declaration:

```
struct inventory
{
  char   name[30];
  int    number;
  float  price;
} product[2], *ptr;
```

This statement declares **product** as an array of two elements, each of the type **struct inventory** and **ptr** as a pointer to data objects of the type **struct inventory.** The assignment

```
ptr = product;
```

would assign the address of the zeroth element of **product** to **ptr**. That is, the pointer **ptr** will now point to **product[0]**. Its members can be accessed using the following notation.

```
ptr -> name
ptr -> number
ptr -> price
```

The symbol –> is called the *arrow operator* (also known as *member selection operator*) and is made up of a minus sign and a greater than sign. Note that **ptr–>** is simply another way of writing **product[0]**.

When the pointer **ptr** is incremented by one, it is made to point to the next record, i.e., product[1]. The following **for** statement will print the values of members of all the elements of **product** array.

```
for(ptr = product; ptr < product+2; ptr++)
        printf ("%s %d %f\n", ptr->name, ptr->number, ptr->price);
```

We could also use the notation

```
(*ptr).number
```

to access the member **number.** The parentheses around ***ptr** are necessary because the member operator '.' has a higher precedence than the operator *.

Example 11.8 Write a program to illustrate the use of structure pointers.

A program to illustrate the use of a structure pointer to manipulate the elements of an array of structures is shown in Fig. 11.13. The program highlights all the features discussed above. Note that the pointer **ptr** (of type **struct invent)** is also used as the loop control index in **for** loops.

```
Program
  struct invent
  {
     char  *name[20];
     int   number;
     float price;
  };
  main()
  {
    struct invent product[3], *ptr;
    printf("INPUT\n\n");
    for(ptr = product; ptr < product+3; ptr++)
      scanf("%s %d %f", ptr->name, &ptr->number, &ptr->price);
    printf("\nOUTPUT\n\n");
     ptr = product;
     while(ptr < product + 3)
     {
         printf("%-20s %5d %10.2f\n",
                   ptr->name,
                   ptr->number,
```

```
                    ptr->price);
            ptr++;
        }
    }

Output

    INPUT
    Washing_machine    5    7500
    Electric_iron     12     350
    Two_in_one         7    1250

    OUTPUT
    Washing machine    5   7500.00
    Electric_iron     12    350.00
    Two_in_one         7   1250.00
```

Fig. 11.13 *Pointer to structure variables*

While using structure pointers, we should take care of the precedence of operators.

The operators '–>' and '.', and () and [] enjoy the highest priority among the operators. They bind very tightly with their operands. For example, given the definition

```
struct
{
    int count;
    float *p;    /* pointer inside the struct */
} ptr;           /* struct type pointer */
```

then the statement

```
++ptr->count;
```

increments **count,** not **ptr.** However,

```
(++ptr)->count;
```

increments **ptr** first, and then links **count.** The statement

```
ptr++ -> count;
```

is legal and increments **ptr** after accessing **count.**

The following statements also behave in the similar fashion.

***ptr–>p**	Fetches whatever **p** points to.
***ptr–>p++**	Increments **p** after accessing whatever it points to.
(*ptr–>p)++	Increments whatever **p** points to.
***ptr++–>p**	Increments **ptr** after accessing whatever it points to.

In the previous chapter, we discussed about passing of a structure as an argument to a function. We also saw an example where a function receives a copy of an entire structure and returns it after working on it. As we mentioned earlier, this method is inefficient in terms of both, the execution speed and memory. We can overcome this drawback by passing a pointer to the structure and then using this pointer to work on the structure members. Consider the following function:

```
print_invent(struct invent *item)
{
        printf("Name: %s\n", item->name);
        printf("Price: %f\n", item->price);
}
```

This function can be called by

```
print_invent(&product);
```

The formal argument **item** receives the address of the structure **product** and therefore it must be declared as a pointer of type **struct invent**, which represents the structure of **product.**

Just Remember

- Only an address of a variable can be stored in a pointer variable.
- Do not store the address of a variable of one type into a pointer variable of another type.
- The value of a variable cannot be assigned to a pointer variable.
- A pointer variable contains garbage until it is initialized. Therefore we must not use a pointer variable before it is assigned, the address of a variable.
- Remember that the definition for a pointer variable allocates memory only for the pointer variable, not for the variable to which it is pointing.
- If we want a called function to change the value of a variable in the calling function, we must pass the address of that variable to the called function.
- When we pass a parameter by address, the corresponding formal parameter must be a pointer variable.
- It is an error to assign a numeric constant to a pointer variable.
- It is an error to assign the address of a variable to a variable of any basic data types.
- It is an error to assign a pointer of one type to a pointer of another type without a cast (with an exception of void pointer).
- A proper understanding of a precedence and associativity rules is very important in pointer applications. For example, expressions like *p++, *p[ ], (*p)[ ], (p).member should be carefully used.
- When an array is passed as an argument to a function, a pointer is actually passed. In the header function, we must declare such arrays with proper size, except the first, which is optional.
- A very common error is to use (or not to use) the address operator (&) and the indirection operator (*) in certain places. Be careful. The compiler may not warn such mistakes.

CASE STUDIES

1. Processing of Examination Marks

Marks obtained by a batch of students in the Annual Examination are tabulated as follows:

Student name	Marks obtained
S. Laxmi	45 67 38 55
V.S. Rao	77 89 56 69
-	- - - -

It is required to compute the total marks obtained by each student and print the rank list based on the total marks.

The program in Fig. 11.14 stores the student names in the array **name** and the marks in the array **marks.** After computing the total marks obtained by all the students, the program prepares and prints the rank list. The declaration

```
int marks[STUDENTS][SUBJECTS+1];
```

defines **marks** as a pointer to the array's first row. We use **rowptr** as the pointer to the row of **marks.** The **rowptr** is initialized as follows:

```
int (*rowptr)[SUBJECTS+1] = array;
```

Note that **array** is the formal argument whose values are replaced by the values of the actual argument **marks.** The parentheses around ***rowptr** makes the **rowptr** as a pointer to an array of **SUBJECTS+1** integers. Remember, the statement

```
int *rowptr[SUBJECTS+1];
```

would declare **rowptr** as an array of **SUBJECTS+1** elements.

When we increment the **rowptr** (by **rowptr+1**), the incrementing is done in units of the size of each row of **array,** making **rowptr** point to the next row. Since **rowptr** points to a particular row, **(*rowptr)[x]** points to the xth element in the row.

Program

```
#define  STUDENTS  5
#define  SUBJECTS  4
#include <string.h>

main()
{
   char name[STUDENTS][20];
   int  marks[STUDENTS][SUBJECTS+1];

   printf("Input students names & their marks in four subjects\n");
   get_list(name, marks, STUDENTS, SUBJECTS);
   get_sum(marks, STUDENTS, SUBJECTS+1);
   printf("\n");
   print_list(name,marks,STUDENTS,SUBJECTS+1);
   get_rank_list(name, marks, STUDENTS, SUBJECTS+1);
```

```
 printf("\nRanked List\n\n");
 print_list(name,marks,STUDENTS,SUBJECTS+1);
}
   /*   Input student name and marks         */
get_list(char *string[ ],
         int array [ ] [SUBJECTS +1], int m, int n)
{
    int   i, j, (*rowptr)[SUBJECTS+1] = array;
    for(i = 0; i < m; i++)
    {
       scanf("%s", string[i]);
       for(j = 0; j < SUBJECTS; j++)
          scanf("%d", &(*(rowptr + i))[j]);
    }
}
/*    Compute total marks obtained by each student   */
get_sum(int array [ ] [SUBJECTS +1], int m, int n)
{
    int   i, j, (*rowptr)[SUBJECTS+1] = array;
    for(i = 0; i < m; i++)
    {
       (*(rowptr + i))[n-1] = 0;
       for(j =0; j < n-1; j++)
          (*(rowptr + i))[n-1] += (*(rowptr + i))[j];
    }
}


/*    Prepare rank list based on total marks        */

get_rank_list(char *string [ ],
              int array [ ] [SUBJECTS + 1]
              int m,
              int n)
 {
   int i, j, k, (*rowptr)[SUBJECTS+1] = array;
   char *temp;

   for(i = 1; i <= m-1; i++)
      for(j = 1; j <= m-i; j++)
         if( (*(rowptr + j-1))[n-1] < (*(rowptr + j))[n-1])
         {
           swap_string(string[j-1], string[j]);

           for(k = 0; k < n; k++)
           swap_int(&(*(rowptr + j-1))[k],&(*(rowptr+j))[k]);
```

```
        }
}
/*      Print out the ranked list                  */
print_list(char *string[ ],
           int array [] [SUBJECTS + 1],
           int m,
           int n)
{
    int  i, j, (*rowptr)[SUBJECTS+1] = array;
    for(i = 0; i < m; i++)
    {
       printf("%-20s", string[i]);
       for(j = 0; j < n; j++)
          printf("%5d", (*(rowptr + i))[j]);
          printf("\n");
    }
}
/*      Exchange of integer values                  */
swap_int(int *p, int *q)
{
    int  temp;
    temp = *p;
    *p   = *q;
    *q   = temp;
}

/*      Exchange of strings          */
swap_string(char s1[ ], char s2[ ])
{
    char  swaparea[256];
    int   i;
    for(i = 0; i < 256; i++)
       swaparea[i] = '\0';
    i = 0;
    while(s1[i] != '\0' && i < 256)
    {
       swaparea[i] = s1[i];
       i++;
    }
    i = 0;
    while(s2[i] != '\0' && i < 256)
    {
       s1[i] = s2[i];
       s1[++i] = '\0';
    }
    i = 0;
```

```
    while(swaparea[i] != '\0')
    {
        s2[i] = swaparea[i];
        s2[++i] = '\0';
    }
}
```

Output

```
Input students names & their marks in four subjects
S.Laxmi 45 67 38 55
V.S.Rao 77 89 56 69
A.Gupta 66 78 98 45
S.Mani 86 72 0 25
R.Daniel 44 55 66 77

S.Laxmi                45   67   38   55  205
V.S.Rao                77   89   56   69  291
A.Gupta                66   78   98   45  287
S.Mani                 86   72    0   25  183
R.Daniel               44   55   66   77  242

Ranked List
V.S.Rao                77   89   56   69  291
A.Gupta                66   78   98   45  287
R.Daniel               44   55   66   77  242
S.Laxmi                45   67   38   55  205
S.Mani                 86   72    0   25  183
```

Fig. 11.14 *Preparation of the rank list of a class of students*

2. Inventory Updating

The price and quantity of items stocked in a store changes every day. They may either increase or decrease. The program in Fig. 11.15 reads the incremental values of price and quantity and computes the total value of the items in stock.

The program illustrates the use of structure pointers as function parameters. **&item,** the address of the structure **item,** is passed to the functions **update()** and **mul().** The formal arguments **product** and **stock,** which receive the value of **&item,** are declared as pointers of type **struct stores.**

Program

```
struct stores
{
    char  name[20];
    float price;
    int   quantity;
};
```

```
main()
{
    void update(struct stores *, float, int);
    float          p_increment, value;
    int            q_increment;

    struct stores item = {"XYZ", 25.75, 12};
    struct stores *ptr = &item;

    printf("\nInput increment values:");
    printf(" price increment and quantity increment\n");
    scanf("%f %d", &p_increment, &q_increment);

/* - - - - - - - - - - - - - - - - - - - - - - - - - - */
    update(&item, p_increment, q_increment);
/* - - - - - - - - - - - - - - - - - - - - - - - - - - */
    printf("Updated values of item\n\n");
    printf("Name       : %s\n",ptr->name);
    printf("Price      : %f\n",ptr->price);
    printf("Quantity   : %d\n",ptr->quantity);

/* - - - - - - - - - - - - - - - - - - - - - - - - - - */
    value  = mul(&item);
/* - - - - - - - - - - - - - - - - - - - - - - - - - - */
    printf("\nValue of the item   =   %f\n", value);
}


void update(struct stores *product, float p, int q)
{
    product->price += p;
    product->quantity += q;
}
float mul(struct stores *stock)
{
    return(stock->price * stock->quantity);
}
```

Output

```
Input increment values: price increment and quantity increment
10 12
Updated values of item

Name        : XYZ
Price       : 35.750000
Quantity    : 24

Value of the item   =   858.000000
```

Fig. 11.15 *Use of structure pointers as function parameters*

REVIEW QUESTIONS

11.1 State whether the following statements are *true* or *false*.

(a) Pointer constants are the addresses of memory locations.

(b) Pointer variables are declared using the address operator.

(c) The underlying type of a pointer variable is void.

(d) Pointers to pointers is a term used to describe pointers whose contents are the address of another pointer.

(e) It is possible to cast a pointer to float as a pointer to integer.

(f) An integer can be added to a pointer.

(g) A pointer can never be subtracted from another pointer.

(h) When an array is passed as an argument to a function, a pointer is passed.

(i) Pointers cannot be used as formal parameters in headers to function definitions.

(j) Value of a local variable in a function can be changed by another function.

11.2 Fill in the blanks in the following statements:

(a) A pointer variable contains as its value the ______ of another variable.

(b) The ______ operator is used with a pointer to de-reference the address contained in the pointer.

(c) The ______ operator returns the value of the variable to which its operand points.

(d) The only integer that can be assigned to a pointer variable is ______.

(e) The pointer that is declared as ______ cannot be de-referenced.

11.3 What is a pointer?

11.4 How is a pointer initialized?

11.5 Explain the effects of the following statements:

(a) `int a, *b = &a;`

(b) `int p, *p;`

(c) `char *s;`

(d) `a = (float *) &x);`

(e) `double(*f)();`

11.6 If **m** and **n** have been declared as integers and **p1** and **p2** as pointers to integers, then state errors, if any, in the following statements.

(a) `p1 = &m;`

(b) `p2 = n;`

(c) `*p1 = &n;`

(d) `p2 = &*&m;`

(e) `m = p2-p1;`

(f) `p1 = &p2;`

(g) `m = *p1 + *p2++;`

11.7 Distinguish between (*m)[5] and *m[5].

11.8 Find the error, if any, in each of the following statements:

(a) `int x = 10;`

(b) `int *y = 10;`

(c) `int a, *b = &a;`

(d)
```
int m;
int **x = &m;
```

11.9 Given the following declarations:

```
int x = 10, y = 10;
int *p1 = &x, *p2 = &y;
```

What is the value of each of the following expressions?

(a) (*p1) ++

(b) -- (*p2)

(c) *p1 + (*p2) --

(d) ++ (*p2) – *p1

11.10 Describe typical applications of pointers in developing programs.

PROGRAMMING EXERCISES

11.1 Write a program using pointers to read in an array of integers and print its elements in reverse order.

11.2 We know that the roots of a quadratic equation of the form

$$ax^2 + bx + c = 0$$

are given by the following equations:

$$x_1 = \frac{-b + \text{square - root } (b^2 - 4ac)}{2a}$$

$$x_2 = \frac{-b - \text{square - root } (b^2 - 4ac)}{2a}$$

Write a function to calculate the roots. The function must use two pointer parameters, one to receive the coefficients a, b, and c, and the other to send the roots to the calling function.

11.3 Write a function that receives a sorted array of integers and an integer value, and inserts the value in its correct place.

11.4 Write a function using pointers to add two matrices and to return the resultant matrix to the calling function.

11.5 Using pointers, write a function that receives a character string and a character as argument and deletes all occurrences of this character in the string. The function should return the corrected string with no holes.

11.6 Write a function **day_name** that receives a number n and returns a pointer to a character string containing the name of the corresponding day. The day names should be kept in a **static** table of character strings local to the function.

11.7 Write a program to read in an array of names and to sort them in alphabetical order. Use **sort** function that receives pointers to the functions **strcmp** and **swap.sort** in turn should call these functions via the pointers.

11.8 Given an array of sorted list of integer numbers, write a function to search for a particular item, using the method of *binary search.* And also show how this function may be used in a program. Use pointers and pointer arithmetic.
(Hint: In binary search, the target value is compared with the array's middle element. Since the table is sorted, if the required value is smaller, we know that all values greater than the middle element can be ignored. That is, in one attempt, we eliminate one half the list. This search can be applied recursively till the target value is found.)

11.9 Write a function (using a pointer parameter) that reverses the elements of a given array.

11.10 Write a function (using pointer parameters) that compares two integer arrays to see whether they are identical. The function returns 1 if they are identical, 0 otherwise.

Chapter 12

File Management in C

12.1 INTRODUCTION

Until now we have been using the functions such as **scanf** and **printf** to read and write data. These are console oriented I/O functions, which always use the terminal (keyboard and screen) as the target place. This works fine as long as the data is small. However, many real-life problems involve large volumes of data and in such situations, the console oriented I/O operations pose two major problems.

1. It becomes cumbersome and time consuming to handle large volumes of data through terminals.
2. The entire data is lost when either the program is terminated or the computer is turned off.

It is therefore necessary to have a more flexible approach where data can be stored on the disks and read whenever necessary, without destroying the data. This method employs the concept of *files* to store data. A file is a place on the disk where a group of related data is stored. Like most other languages, C supports a number of functions that have the ability to perform basic file operations, which include:

- naming a file,
- opening a file,
- reading data from a file,
- writing data to a file, and
- closing a file.

There are two distinct ways to perform file operations in C. The first one is known as the *low-level I/O* and uses UNIX system calls. The second method is referred to as the *high-level I/O* operation and uses functions in C's standard I/O library. We shall discuss in this chapter, the important file handling functions that are available in the C library. They are listed in Table 12.1.

Table 12.1 *High Level I/O Functions*

Function name	*Operation*
fopen()	* Creates a new file for use. * Opens an existing file for use.
fclose()	* Closes a file which has been opened for use.
getc()	* Reads a character from a file.
putc()	* Writes a character to a file.
fprintf()	* Writes a set of data values to a file.
fscanf()	* Reads a set of data values from a file.
getw()	* Reads an integer from a file.
putw()	* Writes an integer to a file.
fseek()	* Sets the position to a desired point in the file.
ftell()	* Gives the current position in the file (in terms of bytes from the start).
rewind()	* Sets the position to the beginning of the file.

There are many other functions. Not all of them are supported by all compilers. You should check your C library before using a particular I/O function.

12.2 DEFINING AND OPENING A FILE

If we want to store data in a file in the secondary memory, we must specify certain things about the file, to the operating system. They include:

1. Filename.
2. Data structure.
3. Purpose.

Filename is a string of characters that make up a valid filename for the operating system. It may contain two parts, a primary name and an optional period with the extension. Examples:

Input.data
store
PROG.C
Student.c
Text.out

Data structure of a file is defined as **FILE** in the library of standard I/O function definitions. Therefore, all files should be declared as type FILE before they are used. **FILE** is a defined data type.

When we open a file, we must specify what we want to do with the file. For example, we may write data to the file or read the already existing data.

Following is the general format for declaring and opening a file:

```
FILE *fp;
fp = fopen("filename", "mode");
```

The first statement declares the variable **fp** as a "pointer to the data type **FILE**". As stated earlier, **FILE** is a structure that is defined in the I/O library. The second statement opens the file named filename and assigns an identifier to the **FILE** type pointer **fp**. This pointer which contains all the information about the file is subsequently used as a communication link between the system and the program.

The second statement also specifies the purpose of opening this file. The mode does this job. Mode can be one of the following:

r open the file for reading only.
w open the file for writing only.
a open the file for appending (or adding) data to it.

Note that both the filename and mode are specified as strings. They should be enclosed in double quotation marks.

When trying to open a file, one of the following things may happen:

1. When the mode is 'writing', a file with the specified name is created if the file does not exist. The contents are deleted, if the file already exists.
2. When the purpose is 'appending', the file is opened with the current contents safe. A file with the specified name is created if the file does not exist.
3. If the purpose is 'reading', and if it exists, then the file is opened with the current contents safe otherwise an error occurs.

Consider the following statements:

```
FILE *p1, *p2;
p1 = fopen("data", "r");
p2 = fopen("results", "w");
```

The file **data** is opened for reading and **results** is opened for writing. In case, the **results** file already exists, its contents are deleted and the file is opened as a new file. If **data** file does not exist, an error will occur.

Many recent compilers include additional modes of operation. They include:

r+ The existing file is opened to the beginning for both reading and writing.
w+ Same as **w** except both for reading and writing.
a+ Same as **a** except both for reading and writing.

We can open and use a number of files at a time. This number however depends on the system we use.

12.3 CLOSING A FILE

A file must be closed as soon as all operations on it have been completed. This ensures that all outstanding information associated with the file is flushed out from the buffers and all links to the file are broken. It also prevents any accidental misuse of the file. In case, there is a limit to the number of files that can be kept open simultaneously, closing of unwanted files might help open the required files. Another instance where we have to close a file is when we want to reopen the same file in a different mode. The I/O library supports a function to do this for us. It takes the following form:

```
fclose(file_pointer);
```

This would close the file associated with the **FILE** pointer **file_pointer.** Look at the following segment of a program.

```
.....
.....
FILE *p1, *p2;
p1 = fopen("INPUT", "w");
p2 = fopen("OUTPUT", "r");
.....
.....
fclose(p1);
fclose(p2);
.....
```

This program opens two files and closes them after all operations on them are completed. Once a file is closed, its file pointer can be reused for another file.

As a matter of fact all files are closed automatically whenever a program terminates. However, closing a file as soon as you are done with it is a good programming habit.

12.4 INPUT/OUTPUT OPERATIONS ON FILES

Once a file is opened, reading out of or writing to it is accomplished using the standard I/O routines that are listed in Table 12.1.

The getc and putc Functions

The simplest file I/O functions are **getc** and **putc.** These are analogous to **getchar** and **putchar** functions and handle one character at a time. Assume that a file is opened with mode **w** and file pointer **fp1**. Then, the statement

```
putc(c, fp1);
```

writes the character contained in the character variable **c** to the file associated with **FILE** pointer **fp1**. Similarly, **getc** is used to read a character from a file that has been opened in read mode. For example, the statement

```
c = getc(fp2);
```

would read a character from the file whose file pointer is fp2.

The file pointer moves by one character position for every operation of **getc** or **putc**. The **getc** will return an end-of-file marker EOF, when end of the file has been reached. Therefore, the reading should be terminated when EOF is encountered.

Example 12.1 Write a program to read data from the keyboard, write it to a file called **INPUT,** again read the same data from the **INPUT** file, and display it on the screen.

A program and the related input and output data are shown in Fig.12.1. We enter the input data via the keyboard and the program writes it, character by character, to the file **INPUT**. The end of the data is indicated by entering an **EOF** character, which is *control-Z* in the reference system. (This may be control-D in other systems.) The file INPUT is closed at this signal.

Program

```
#include  <stdio.h>

main()
{
    FILE *f1;
    char c;
    printf("Data Input\n\n");
    /* Open the file INPUT */
    f1 = fopen("INPUT", "w");

    /* Get a character from keyboard    */
    while((c=getchar()) != EOF)

        /* Write a character to INPUT  */
        putc(c,f1);

    /* Close the file INPUT    */

    fclose(f1);
    printf("\nData Output\n\n");

    /* Reopen the file INPUT    */
    f1 = fopen("INPUT","r");

   /* Read a character from INPUT*/
    while((c=getc(f1)) != EOF)

        /* Display a character on screen */
        printf("%c",c);

    /* Close the file INPUT         */
    fclose(f1);
}
```

Output

```
Data Input
This is a program to test the file handling
features on this system^Z

Data Output
This is a program to test the file handling
features on this system
```

Fig. 12.1 *Character oriented read/write operations on a file*

The file INPUT is again reopened for reading. The program then reads its content character by character, and displays it on the screen. Reading is terminated when **getc** encounters the end-of-file mark EOF.

Testing for the end-of-file condition is important. Any attempt to read past the end of file might either cause the program to terminate with an error or result in an infinite loop situation.

The getw and putw Functions

The **getw** and **putw** are integer-oriented functions. They are similar to the **getc** and **putc** functions and are used to read and write integer values. These functions would be useful when we deal with only integer data. The general forms of **getw** and **putw** are:

```
putw(integer, fp);
getw(fp);
```

Example 12.2 illustrates the use of **putw** and **getw** functions.

Example 12.2 A file named **DATA** contains a series of integer numbers. Code a program to read these numbers and then write all 'odd' numbers to a file to be called **ODD** and all 'even' numbers to a file to be called **EVEN.**

The program is shown in Fig. 12.2. It uses three files simultaneously and therefore we need to define three-file pointers **f1, f2** and **f3.**

First, the file DATA containing integer values is created. The integer values are read from the terminal and are written to the file **DATA** with the help of the statement

putw(number, f1);

Notice that when we type –1, the reading is terminated and the file is closed. The next step is to open all the three files, **DATA** for reading, **ODD** and **EVEN** for writing. The contents of **DATA** file are read, integer by integer, by the function **getw(f1)** and written to **ODD** or **EVEN** file after an appropriate test. Note that the statement

(number = getw(f1)) != EOF

reads a value, assigns the same to **number**, and then tests for the end-of-file mark.

Finally, the program displays the contents of ODD and EVEN files. It is important to note that the files **ODD** and **EVEN** opened for writing are closed before they are reopened for reading.

```
Program
   #include  <stdio.h>
   main()
   {
      FILE  *f1, *f2, *f3;
      int   number, i;

      printf("Contents of DATA file\n\n");
```

```
    f1 = fopen("DATA", "w");          /* Create DATA file     */
    for(i = 1; i <= 30; i++)
    {
      scanf("%d", &number);
      if(number == -1) break;
      putw(number,f1);
    }
    fclose(f1);

    f1 = fopen("DATA", "r");
    f2 = fopen("ODD", "w");
    f3 = fopen("EVEN", "w");

    /* Read from DATA file */
    while((number = getw(f1)) != EOF)
    {
       if(number %2 == 0)
         putw(number, f3);    /*  Write to EVEN file   */
       else
         putw(number, f2);    /*  Write to ODD file    */
    }
    fclose(f1);
    fclose(f2);
    fclose(f3);

    f2 = fopen("ODD","r");
    f3 = fopen("EVEN", "r");

    printf("\n\nContents of ODD file\n\n");
    while((number = getw(f2)) != EOF)
      printf("%4d", number);

    printf("\n\nContents of EVEN file\n\n");
    while((number = getw(f3)) != EOF)
      printf("%4d", number);

    fclose(f2);
    fclose(f3);

}
```

Output

```
Contents of DATA file
111 222 333 444 555 666 777 888 999 000 121 232 343 454 565 -1
```

```
Contents of ODD file
111 333 555 777 999 121 343 565

Contents of EVEN file
222 444 666 888   0 232 454
```

Fig. 12.2 *Operations on integer data*

The fprintf and fscanf Functions

So far, we have seen functions, which can handle only one character or integer at a time. Most compilers support two other functions, namely **fprintf** and **fscanf**, that can handle a group of mixed data simultaneously.

The functions **fprintf** and **fscanf** perform I/O operations that are identical to the familar **printf** and **scanf** functions, except of course that they work on files. The first argument of these functions is a file pointer which specifies the file to be used. The general form of **fprintf** is

```
fprintf(fp, "control string", list);
```

where *fp* is a file pointer associated with a file that has been opened for writing. The *control string* contains output specifications for the items in the list. The *list* may include variables, constants and strings. Example:

```
fprintf(f1, "%s %d %f", name, age, 7.5);
```

Here, **name** is an array variable of type char and **age** is an **int** variable.

The general format of **fscanf** is

```
fprintf(fp, "control string", list);
```

This statement would cause the reading of the items in the list from the file specified by fp, according to the specifications contained in the *control string*. Example:

```
fscanf(f2, "%s %d", item, &quantity);
```

Like **scanf, fscanf** also returns the number of items that are successfully read. When the end of file is reached, it returns the value **EOF.**

Example 12.3 Write a program to open a file named INVENTORY and store in it the following data:

Item name	Number	Price	Quantity
AAA-1	111	17.50	115
BBB-2	125	36.00	75
C-3	247	31.75	104

Extend the program to read this data from the file INVENTORY and display the inventory table with the value of each item.

The program is given in Fig.12.3. The filename INVENTORY is supplied through the keyboard. Data is read using the function **fscanf** from the file **stdin,** which refers to the terminal and it is then written to the file that is being pointed to by the file pointer **fp.** Remember that the file pointer **fp** points to the file INVENTORY.

After closing the file INVENTORY, it is again reopened for reading. The data from the file, along with the item values are written to the file **stdout,** which refers to the screen. While reading from a file, care should be taken to use the same format specifications with which the contents have been written to the file.…é

Program

```
#include  <stdio.h>

main()
{
     FILE  *fp;
     int     number, quantity, i;
     float  price, value;
     char    item[10], filename[10];

     printf("Input file name\n");
     scanf("%s", filename);
     fp = fopen(filename, "w");
     printf("Input inventory data\n\n");
     printf("Item name  Number   Price  Quantity\n");
     for(i = 1; i <= 3; i++)
     {
         fscanf(stdin, "%s %d %f %d",
                       item, &number, &price, &quantity);
         fprintf(fp, "%s %d %.2f %d",
                       item, number, price, quantity);
     }
     fclose(fp);
     fprintf(stdout, "\n\n");

     fp = fopen(filename, "r");

     printf("Item name  Number   Price   Quantity      Value\n");
     for(i = 1; i <= 3; i++)
     {
         fscanf(fp, "%s %d %f d",item,&number,&price,&quantity);
         value = price * quantity;
         fprintf(stdout, "%-8s %7d %8.2f %8d %11.2f\n",
                         item, number, price, quantity, value);
     }
     fclose(fp);
}
```

Output

```
Input file name
```

```
INVENTORY
Input inventory data

Item name  Number   Price   Quantity
AAA-1   111  17.50  115
BBB-2   125  36.00  75
C-3     247  31.75  104

Item name  Number   Price   Quantity     Value
AAA-1          111   17.50       115    2012.50
BBB-2          125   36.00        75    2700.00
C-3            247   31.75       104    3302.00
```

Fig. 12.3 *Operations on mixed data types*

12.5 ERROR HANDLING DURING I/O OPERATIONS

It is possible that an error may occur during I/O operations on a file. Typical error situations include:

1. Trying to read beyond the end-of-file mark.
2. Device overflow.
3. Trying to use a file that has not been opened.
4. Trying to perform an operation on a file, when the file is opened for another type of operation.
5. Opening a file with an invalid filename.
6. Attempting to write to a write-protected file.

If we fail to check such read and write errors, a program may behave abnormally when an error occurs. An unchecked error may result in a premature termination of the program or incorrect output. Fortunately, we have two status-inquiry library functions; **feof** and **ferror** that can help us detect I/O errors in the files.

The **feof** function can be used to test for an end of file condition. It takes a **FILE** pointer as its only argument and returns a nonzero integer value if all of the data from the specified file has been read, and returns zero otherwise. If **fp** is a pointer to file that has just been opened for reading, then the statement

```
if(feof(fp))
   printf("End of data.\n");
```

would display the message "End of data." on reaching the end of file condition.

The **ferror** function reports the status of the file indicated. It also takes a **FILE** pointer as its argument and returns a nonzero integer if an error has been detected up to that point, during processing. It returns zero otherwise. The statement

```
if(ferror(fp) != 0)
   printf("An error has occurred.\n");
```

would print the error message, if the reading is not successful.

We know that whenever a file is opened using **fopen** function, a file pointer is returned. If the file cannot be opened for some reason, then the function returns a NULL pointer. This facility can be used to test whether a file has been opened or not. Example:

```
if(fp == NULL)
    printf("File could not be opened.\n");
```

Example 12.4 Write a program to illustrate error handling in file operations.

The program shown in Fig. 12.4 illustrates the use of the **NULL** pointer test and **feof** function. When we input filename as TETS, the function call

```
fopen("TETS", "r");
```

returns a **NULL** pointer because the file TETS does not exist and therefore the message "Cannot open the file" is printed out.

Similarly, the call **feof(fp2)** returns a non-zero integer when the entire data has been read, and hence the program prints the message "Ran out of data" and terminates further reading.

Program

```
#include  <stdio.h>

main()
{
    char  *filename;
    FILE  *fp1, *fp2;
    int    i, number;

    fp1 = fopen("TEST", "w");
    for(i = 10; i <= 100; i += 10)
       putw(i, fp1);

    fclose(fp1);

    printf("\nInput filename\n");

open_file:
    scanf("%s", filename);

    if((fp2 = fopen(filename,"r")) == NULL)
    {
       printf("Cannot open the file.\n");
       printf("Type filename again.\n\n");
       goto open_file;
    }
    else

    for(i = 1; i <= 20; i++)
```

```
        {  number = getw(fp2);
           if(feof(fp2))
           {
               printf("\nRan out of data.\n");
               break;
           }
           else
               printf("%d\n", number);
        }

        fclose(fp2);
    }
```

Output

```
Input filename
TETS
Cannot open the file.
Type filename again.

TEST
10
20
30
40
50
60
70
80
90
100

Ran out of data.
```

Fig. 12.4 *Illustration of error handling in file operations*

12.6 RANDOM ACCESS TO FILES

So far we have discussed file functions that are useful for reading and writing data sequentially. There are occasions, however, when we are interested in accessing only a particular part of a file and not in reading the other parts. This can be achieved with the help of the functions **fseek, ftell,** and **rewind** available in the I/O library.

ftell takes a file pointer and return a number of type **long,** that corresponds to the current position. This function is useful in saving the current position of a file, which can be used later in the program. It takes the following form:

```
n = ftell(fp);
```

n would give the relative offset (in bytes) of the current position. This means that n bytes have already been read (or written).

rewind takes a file pointer and resets the position to the start of the file. For example, the statement

```
rewind(fp);
n = ftell(fp);
```

would assign 0 to n because the file position has been set to the start of the file by **rewind.** Remember, the first byte in the file is numbered as 0, second as 1, and so on. This function helps us in reading a file more than once, without having to close and open the file. Remember that whenever a file is opened for reading or writing, a **rewind** is done implicitly.

fseek function is used to move the file position to a desired location within the file. It takes the following form:

```
fseek(file_ptr, offset, position);
```

file_ptr is a pointer to the file concerned, *offset* is a number or variable of type long, and *position* is an integer number. The *offset* specifies the number of positions (bytes) to be moved from the location specified by *position.* The *position* can take one of the following three values:

Value	*Meaning*
0	Beginning of file
1	Current position
2	End of file

The offset may be positive, meaning move forwards, or negative, meaning move backwards. Examples in Table 12.2 illustrate the operations of the **fseek** function:

Table 12.2 *Operations of fseek Function*

Statement	*Meaning*
fseek(fp,0L,0);	Go to the beginning. (Similar to rewind)
fseek(fp,0L,1);	Stay at the current position. (Rarely used)
fseek(fp,0L,2);	Go to the end of the file, past the last character of the file.
fseek(fp,m,0);	Move to (m+1)th byte in the file.
fseek(fp,m,1);	Go forward by m bytes.
fseek(fp,-m,1);	Go backward by m bytes from the current position.
fseek(fp,-m,2);	Go backward by m bytes from the end. (Positions the file to the mth character from the end.)

When the operation is successful, **fseek** returns a zero. If we attempt to move the file pointer beyond the file boundaries, an error occurs and **fseek** returns –1 (minus one). It is good practice to check whether an error has occurred or not, before proceeding further.

Example 12.5 Write a program that uses the functions **ftell** and **fseek.**

A program employing **ftell** and **fseek** functions is shown in Fig. 12.5. We have created a file **RANDOM** with the following contents:

```
Position ----> 0   1   2   ... 25
Character
stored ---->   A   B   C   ... Z
```

We are reading the file twice. First, we are reading the content of every fifth position and printing its value along with its position on the screen. The second time, we are reading the contents of the file from the end and printing the same on the screen.

During the first reading, the file pointer crosses the end-of-file mark when the parameter **n** of **fsee(fp,n,0)** becomes 30. Therefore, after printing the content of position 30, the loop is terminated.

For reading the file from the end, we use the statement

```
fseek(fp,-1L,2);
```

to position the file pointer to the last character. Since every read causes the position to move forward by one position, we have to move it back by two positions to read the next character. This is achieved by the function

```
fseek(fp, -2L, 1);
```

in the while statement. This statement also tests whether the file pointer has crossed the file boundary or not. The loop is terminated as soon as it crosses it.

Program

```
#include <stdio.h>
main()
{
    FILE  *fp;
    long  n;
    char c;
    fp = fopen("RANDOM", "w");
    while((c = getchar()) != EOF)
        putc(c,fp);

    printf("No. of characters entered = %ld\n", ftell(fp));
    fclose(fp);
    fp = fopen("RANDOM","r");
    n = 0L;

    while(feof(fp) == 0)
    {
        fseek(fp, n, 0);  /*  Position to (n+1)th character */
        printf("Position of %c is %ld\n", getc(fp),ftell(fp));
        n = n+5L;
    }
    putchar('\n');
```

```
   fseek(fp,-1L,2);   /*  Position to the last character */
     do
     {
          putchar(getc(fp));
     }
     while(!fseek(fp,-2L,1));
     fclose(fp);
   }
```

Output

```
   ABCDEFGHIJKLMNOPQRSTUVWXYZ^Z
   No. of characters entered = 26
   Position of A is 0
   Position of F is 5
   Position of K is 10
   Position of P is 15
   Position of U is 20
   Position of Z is 25
   Position of    is 30

   ZYXWVUTSRQPONMLKJIHGFEDCBA
```

Fig. 12.5 *Illustration of **fseek** and **ftell** functions*

Example 12.6 Write a program to append additional items to the file INVENTORY created in Example 12.3 and print the total contents of the file.

The program is shown in Fig. 12.6. It uses a structure definition to describe each item and a function **append**() to add an item to the file.

On execution, the program requests for the filename to which data is to be appended. After appending the items, the position of the last character in the file is assigned to **n** and then the file is closed.

The file is reopened for reading and its contents are displayed. Note that reading and displaying are done under the control of a **while** loop. The loop tests the current file position against n and is terminated when they become equal.

Program

```
   #include  <stdio.h>

   struct invent_record
   {
        char   name[10];
        int    number;
        float  price;
        int    quantity;
   };
```

```
main()
{
    struct invent_record item;
    char  filename[10];
    int   response;
    FILE  *fp;
    long  n;
    void append (struct invent_record *x, file *y);
    printf("Type filename:");
    scanf("%s", filename);

    fp = fopen(filename, "a+");
    do
    {
       append(&item, fp);
       printf("\nItem %s appended.\n",item.name);
       printf("\nDo you want to add another item\
           (1 for YES /0 for NO)?");
       scanf("%d", &response);
    }  while (response == 1);

    n = ftell(fp);         /* Position of last character */
    fclose(fp);

    fp = fopen(filename, "r");

    while(ftell(fp) < n)
    {
       fscanf(fp,"%s %d %f %d",
       item.name, &item.number, &item.price, &item.quantity);
       fprintf(stdout,"%-8s %7d %8.2f %8d\n",
       item.name, item.number, item.price, item.quantity);
    }
    fclose(fp);
}
void append(struct invent_record *product, File *ptr)
{
    printf("Item name:");
    scanf("%s", product->name);
    printf("Item number:");
    scanf("%d", &product->number);
    printf("Item price:");
    scanf("%f", &product->price);
    printf("Quantity:");
    scanf("%d", &product->quantity);
    fprintf(ptr, "%s %d %.2f %d",
```

```
                product->name,
                product->number,
                product->price,
                product->quantity);
}
```

Output

```
Type filename:INVENTORY
Item name:XXX
Item number:444
Item price:40.50
Quantity:34

Item XXX appended.

Do you want to add another item(1 for YES /0 for NO)?1

Item name:YYY
Item number:555
Item price:50.50
Quantity:45

Item YYY appended.

Do you want to add another item(1 for YES /0 for NO)?0
AAA-1           111     17.50      115
BBB-2           125     36.00       75
C-3             247     31.75      104
XXX             444     40.50       34
YYY             555     50.50       45
```

Fig. 12.6 *Adding items to an existing file*

12.7 COMMAND LINE ARGUMENTS

What is a command line argument? It is a parameter supplied to a program when the program is invoked. This parameter may represent a filename the program should process. For example, if we want to execute a program to copy the contents of a file named **X_FILE** to another one named Y_FILE, then we may use a command line like

C > PROGRAM X_FILE Y_FILE

where **PROGRAM** is the filename where the executable code of the program is stored. This eliminates the need for the program to request the user to enter the filenames during execution. How do these parameters get into the program?

We know that every C program should have one **main** function and that it marks the beginning of the program. But what we have not mentioned so far is that it can also take arguments like other functions. In fact **main** can take two arguments called **argc** and **argv** and the information contained in the command line is passed on to the program through these arguments, when **main** is called up by the system.

The variable **argc** is an argument counter that counts the number of arguments on the command line. The **argv** is an argument vector and represents an array of character pointers that point to the command line arguments. The size of this array will be equal to the value of **argc**. For instance, for the command line given above, **argc** is three and **argv** is an array of three pointers to strings as shown below:

argv[0] –> PROGRAM
argv[1] –> X_FILE
argv[2] –> Y_FILE

In order to access the command line arguments, we must declare the main function and its parameters as follows:

```
main(int arge, char *argv[])
{
    .....
    .....
}
```

The first parameter in the command line is always the program name and therefore **argv[0]** always represents the program name.

Example 12.7 Write a program that will receive a filename and a line of text as command line arguments and write the text to the file.

Figure 12.7 shows the use of command line arguments. The command line is

F12_7 TEXT AAAAAA BBBBBB CCCCCC DDDDDD EEEEEE FFFFFF GGGGGG

Each word in the command line is an argument to the **main** and therefore the total number of arguments is 9.

The argument vector **argv[1]** points to the string TEXT and therefore the statement

```
fp = fopen(argv[1], "w");
```

opens a file with the name TEXT. The **for** loop that follows immediately writes the remaining 7 arguments to the file TEXT.

Program

```
#include  <stdio.h>

main(int arge, char *argv[])
{
    FILE   *fp;
    int  i;
    char word[15];
```

```
    fp = fopen(argv[1], "w"); /* open file with name argv[1] */
    printf("\nNo. of arguments in Command line = %d\n\n",argc);
    for(i = 2; i < argc; i++)
       fprintf(fp,"%s ", argv[i]); /* write to file argv[1]  */
    fclose(fp);

/*  Writing content of the file to screen                    */

    printf("Contents of %s file\n\n", argv[1]);
    fp = fopen(argv[1], "r");
    for(i = 2; i < argc; i++)
    {
       fscanf(fp,"%s", word);
       printf("%s ", word);
    }

    fclose(fp);
    printf("\n\n");

/* Writing the arguments from memory */

    for(i = 0; i < argc; i++)
       printf("%*s \n", i*5,argv[i]);
}
```

Output

```
C>F12_7 TEXT AAAAAA BBBBBB CCCCCC DDDDDD EEEEEE FFFFFF GGGGG

No. of arguments in Command line = 9

Contents of TEXT file

AAAAAA BBBBBB CCCCCC DDDDDD EEEEEE FFFFFF GGGGGG

C:\C\F12_7.EXE
 TEXT
    AAAAAA
          BBBBBB
               CCCCCC
                    DDDDDD
                         EEEEEE
                              FFFFFF
                                   GGGGGG
```

Fig. 12.7 *Use of command line arguments*

Just Remember

- Do not try to use a file before opening it.
- Remember, when an existing file is open using 'w' mode, the contents of file are deleted.
- When a file is used for both reading and writing, we must open it in 'w+' mode.
- EOF is integer type with a value –1. Therefore, we must use an integer variable to test EOF.
- It is an error to omit the file pointer when using a file function.
- It is an error to open a file for reading when it does not exist.
- It is an error to try to read from a file that is in write mode and vice versa.
- It is an error to attempt to place the file marker before the first byte of a file.
- It is an error to access a file with its name rather than its file pointer.
- It is a good practice to close all files before terminating a program.

REVIEW QUESTIONS

12.1 State whether the following statements are *true* or *false*.
  (a) A file must be opened before it can be used.
  (b) All files must be explicitly closed.
  (c) Files are always referred to by name in C programs.
  (d) Using **fseek** to position a file beyond the end of the file is an error.
  (e) Function **fseek** may be used to seek from the beginning of the file only.

12.2 Fill in the blanks in the following statements.
  (a) The mode _______ is used for opening a file for updating.
  (b) The function ___ may be used to position a file at the beginning.
  (c) The function _____gives the current position in the file.
  (d) The function _____ is used to write data to randomly accessed file.

12.3 Describe the use and limitations of the functions **getc** and **putc.**

12.4 What is the significance of EOF?

12.5 When a program is terminated, all the files used by it are automatically closed. Why is it then necessary to close a file during execution of the program?

12.6 Distinguish between the following functions:
  (a) getc and getchar
  (b) printf and fprintf
  (c) feof and ferror

12.7 How does an append mode differ from a write mode?

12.8 What are the common uses of **rewind** and **ftell** functions?

12.9 Explain the general format of **fseek** function?

12.10 What is the difference between the statements **rewind(fp);** and **fseek(fp,0L,0);?**

PROGRAMMING EXERCISES

12.1 Write a program to copy the contents of one file into another.

12.2 Two files DATA1 and DATA2 contain sorted lists of integers. Write a program to produce a third file DATA which holds a single sorted, merged list of these two lists. Use command line arguments to specify the file names.

12.3 Write a program that compares two files and returns 0 if they are equal and 1 is they are not.

12.4 Write a program that appends one file at the end of another.

12.5 Write a program that reads a file containing integers and appends at its end the sum of all the integers.

Chapter

13

Dynamic Memory Allocation and Linked Lists

13.1 INTRODUCTION

Most often we face situations in programming where the data is dynamic in nature. That is, the number of data items keep changing during execution of the program. For example, consider a program for processing the list of customers of a corporation. The list grows when names are added and shrinks when names are deleted. When list grows we need to allocate more memory space to the list to accommodate additional data items. Such situations can be handled more easily and effectively by using what is known as *dynamic data structures* in conjunction with *dynamic memory management* techniques.

Dynamic data structures provide flexibility in adding, deleting or rearranging data items at run time. Dynamic memory management techniques permit us to allocate additional memory space or to release unwanted space at run time, thus, optimizing the use of storage space. This chapter discusses the concept of *linked lists*, one of the basic types of dynamic data structures. Before we take up linked lists, we shall briefly introduce the dynamic storage management functions that are available in C. These functions would be extensively used in processing linked lists.

13.2 DYNAMIC MEMORY ALLOCATION

C language requires the number of elements in an array to be specified at compile time. But we may not be able to do so always. Our initial judgment of size, if it is wrong, may cause failure of the program or wastage of memory space.

Many languages permit a programmer to specify an array's size at run time. Such languages have the ability to calculate and assign, during execution, the memory space required by the variables in a program. The process of allocating memory at run time is known as *dynamic memory allocation*. Although C does not inherently have this facility, there are four library routines known as "memory management functions" that can be used for allocating and freeing memory during program execution. They are listed in Table 13.1. These functions help us build complex application programs that use the available memory intelligently.

Table 13.1 *Memory Allocation Functions*

Function	*Task*
malloc	Allocates request size of bytes and returns a pointer to the first byte of the allocated space
calloc	Allocates space for an array of elements, initializes them to zero and then returns a pointer to the memory.
free	Frees previously allocated space
realloc	Modifies the size of previously allocated space

Memory Allocation Process

Before we discuss these functions, let us look at the memory allocation process associated with a C program. Figure 13.1 shows the conceptual view of storage of a C program in memory.

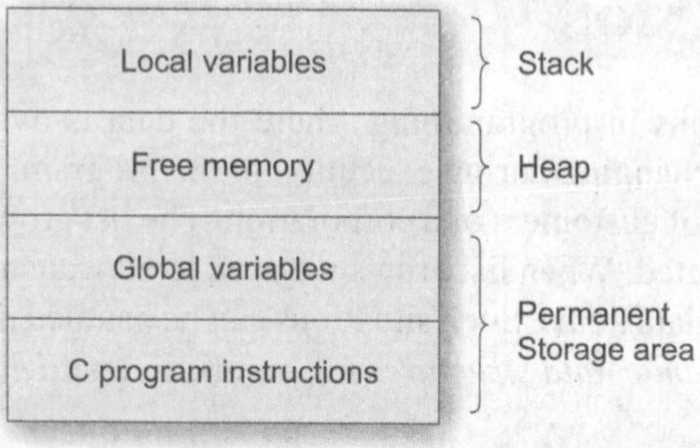

Fig. 13.1 *Storage of a C program*

The program instructions and global and static variables are stored in a region known as *permanent storage area* and the local variables are stored in another area called *stack*. The memory space that is located between these two regions is available for dynamic allocation during execution of the program. This free memory region is called the *heap*. The size of the heap keeps changing when program is executed due to creation and death of variables that are local to functions and blocks. Therefore, it is possible to encounter memory "overflow" during dynamic allocation process. In such situations, the memory allocation functions mentioned above return a NULL pointer (when they fail to locate enough memory requested).

13.3 ALLOCATING A BLOCK OF MEMORY: MALLOC

A block of memory may be allocated using the function **malloc**. The **malloc** function reserves a block of memory of specified size and returns a pointer of type **void**. This means that we can assign it to any type of pointer. It takes the following form:

```
ptr = (cast-type *) malloc(byte-size);
```

ptr is a pointer of type *cast-type*. The **malloc** returns a pointer (of *cast type*) to an area of memory with size *byte-size*.

Example:

```
x = (int *) malloc (100 *sizeof(int));
```

On successful execution of this statement, a memory space equivalent to "100 times the size of an **int**" bytes is reserved and the address of the first byte of the memory allocated is assigned to the pointer **x** of type of **int**.

Similarly, the statement

```
cptr = (char*) malloc(10);
```

allocates 10 bytes of space for the pointer **cptr** of type **char**. This is illustrated as:

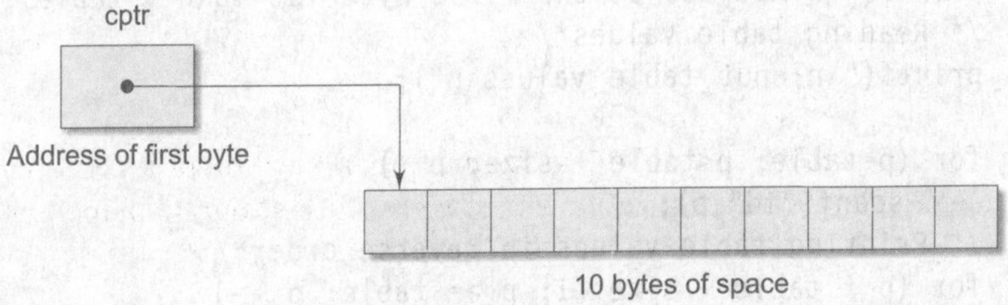

Note that the storage space allocated dynamically has no name and therefore its contents can be accessed only through a pointer.

We may also use **malloc** to allocate space for complex data types such as structures. Example:

```
st_var = (struct store *)malloc(sizeof(struct store));
```

where **st_var** is a pointer of type **struct store**

Remember, the **malloc** allocates a block of contiguous bytes. The allocation can fail if the space in the heap is not sufficient to satisfy the request. If it fails, it returns a NULL. We should therefore check whether the allocation is successful before using the memory pointer. This is illustrated in the program in Fig.13.2.

Example 13.1 Write a program that uses a table of integers whose size will be specified interactively at run time.

The program is given in Fig.13.2. It tests for availability of memory space of required size. If it is available, then the required space is allocated and the address of the first byte of the space allocated is displayed. The program also illustrates the use of pointer variable for storing and accessing the table values.

Program

```
#include <stdio.h>
#include <stdlib.h>
#define NULL 0
```

```
main()
{
        int *p, *table;
        int size;
        printf("\nWhat is the size of table?");
        scanf("%d",size);
        printf("\n")
         /*------------Memory allocation --------------*/
        if((table = (int*)malloc(size *sizeof(int))) == NULL)
         {
           printf("No space available \n");
           exit(1);
         }
        printf("\n Address of the first byte is  %u\n", table);
        /* Reading table values*/
        printf("\nInput table values\n");

        for (p=table; p<table + size; p++)
           scanf("%d",p);
        /* Printing table values in reverse order*/
        for (p = table + size -1; p >= table; p --)
          printf("%d is stored at address %u \n",*p,p);

}
```

Output

```
What is the size of the table? 5
Address of the first byte is 2262
Input table values
11 12 13 14 15
15 is stored at address 2270
14 is stored at address 2268
13 is stored at address 2266
12 is stored at address 2264
11 is stored at address 2262
```

Fig. 13.2 *Memory allocation with **malloc***

13.4 ALLOCATING MULTIPLE BLOCKS OF MEMORY: CALLOC

calloc is another memory allocation function that is normally used for requesting memory space at run time for storing derived data types such as arrays and structures. While **malloc** allocates a single block of storage space, **calloc** allocates multiple blocks of storage, each of the same size, and then sets all bytes to zero. The general form of **calloc** is:

```
ptr = (cast-type *) calloc (n, elem-size);
```

The above statement allocates contiguous space for *n* blocks, each of size *elem-size* bytes. All bytes are initialized to zero and a pointer to the first byte of the allocated region is returned. If there is not enough space, a NULL pointer is returned.

The following segment of a program allocates space for a structure variable:

```
. . . .
. . . .
struct student
{
    char name[25];
    float age;
    long int id_num;
};
typedef struct student record;
record *st_ptr;
int class_size = 30;
st_ptr=(record *)calloc(class_size, sizeof(record));
. . . .
. . . .
```

record is of type **struct student** having three members: **name, age** and **id_num**. The **calloc** allocates memory to hold data for 30 such records. We must be sure that the requested memory has been allocated successfully before using the **st_ptr**. This may be done as follows:

```
if(st_ptr == NULL)
{
    printf("Available memory not sufficient");
    exit(1);
}
```

13.5 RELEASING THE USED SPACE: FREE

Compile-time storage of a variable is allocated and released by the system in accordance with its storage class. With the dynamic run-time allocation, it is our responsibility to release the space when it is not required. The release of storage space becomes important when the storage is limited.

When we no longer need the data we stored in a block of memory, and we do not intend to use that block for storing any other information, we may release that block of memory for future use, using the **free** function:

```
free (ptr);
```

ptr is a pointer to a memory block which has already been created by **malloc** or **calloc**. Use of an invalid pointer in the call may create problems and cause system crash. We should remember two things here:

1. It is not the pointer that is being released but rather what it points to.
2. To release an array of memory that was allocated by **calloc** we need only to release the pointer once. It is an error to attempt to release elements individually.

The use of **free** function has been illustrated in Example 13.2.

13.6 ALTERING THE SIZE OF A BLOCK: REALLOC

It is likely that we discover later, the previously allocated memory is not sufficient and we need additional space for more elements. It is also possible that the memory allocated is much larger than necessary and we want to reduce it. In both the cases, we can change the memory size already allocated with the help of the function **realloc**. This process is called the *reallocation* of memory. For example, if the original allocation is done by the statement

```
ptr = malloc(size);
```

then reallocation of space may be done by the statement

```
ptr = realloc(ptr, newsize);
```

This function allocates a new memory space of size *newsize* to the pointer variable **ptr** and returns a pointer to the first byte of the new memory block. The *newsize* may be larger or smaller than the *size*. Remember, the new memory block may or may not begin at the same place as the old one. In case, it is not able to find additional space in the same region, it will create the same in an entirely new region and move the contents of the old block into the new block. The function guarantees that the old data will remain intact.

If the function is unsuccessful in locating additional space, it returns a NULL pointer and the original block is freed (lost). This implies that it is necessary to test the success of operation before proceeding further. This is illustrated in the program of Example 13.2.

Example 13.2 Write a program to store a character string in a block of memory space created by **malloc** and then modify the same to store a larger string.

The program is shown in Fig. 13.3. The output illustrates that the original buffer size obtained is modified to contain a larger string. Note that the original contents of the buffer remains same even after modification of the original size.

Program

```
#include <stdio.h>
#include<stdlib.h>
#define NULL 0
main()
{
        char *buffer;
        /* Allocating memory */
        if((buffer = (char *)malloc(10)) == NULL)
        {
```

```
        printf("malloc failed.\n");
        exit(1);
      }
      printf("Buffer of size %d created \n",_msize(buffer));
      strcpy(buffer, "HYDERABAD");
      printf("\nBuffer contains: %s \n ", buffer);
      /* Reallocation */
      if((buffer = (char *)realloc(buffer, 15)) == NULL)
      {
        printf("Reallocation failed. \n");
        exit(1);
      }
      printf("\nBuffer size modified. \n");
      printf("\nBuffer still contains: %s \n",buffer);
      strcpy(buffer, "SECUNDERABAD");
      printf("\nBuffer now contains: %s \n",buffer);
  /* Freeing memory */
  free(buffer);
  }
```

Output

```
  Buffer of size 10 created
  Buffer contains: HYDERABAD
  Buffer size modified
  Buffer still contains: HYDERABAD
  Buffer now contains: SECUNDERABAD
```

Fig. 13.3 *Reallocation and release of memory space*

13.7 CONCEPTS OF LINKED LISTS

We know that a list refers to a set of items organized sequentially. An array is an example of list. In an array, the sequential organization is provided implicitly by its index. We use the index for accessing and manipulation of array elements. One major problem with the arrays is that the size of an array must be specified precisely at the beginning. As pointed out earlier, this may be a difficult task in many real-life applications.

A completely different way to represent a list is to make each item in the list part of a structure that also contains a "link" to the structure containing the next item, as shown in Fig. 13.4. This type of list is called a *linked list* because it is a list whose order is given by links from one item to the next.

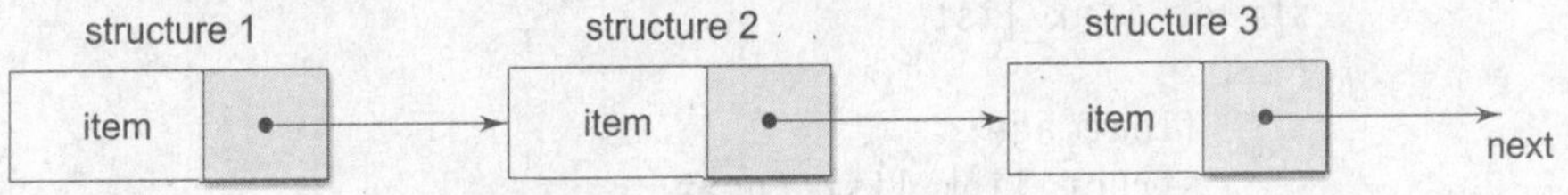

Fig. 13.4 *A linked list*

Each structure of the list is called a *node* and consists of two fields, one containing the item, and the other containing the address of the next item (a pointer to the next item) in the list. A linked list is therefore a collection of structures ordered not by their physical placement in memory (like an array) but by logical links that are stored as part of the data in the structure itself. The link is in the form of a pointer to another structure of the same type. Such a structure is represented as follows:

```
struct node
{
   int item;
   struct node *next;
};
```

The first member is an integer item and the second a pointer to the next node in the list as shown below. Remember, the **item** is an integer here only for simplicity, and could be any complex data type.

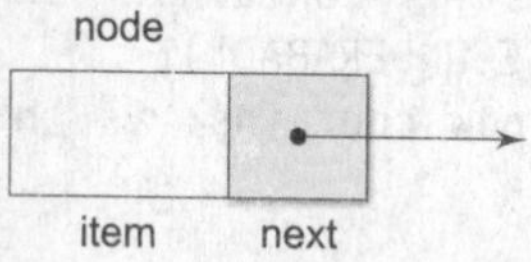

Such structures which contain a member field that points to the same structure type are called *self-refrential* structure.

A node may be represented in general form as follows:

```
struct tag-name
{
   type member1;
   type member2;
   . . . .
   . . . .
   struct tag-name *next;
};
```

The structure may contain more than one item with different data types. However, one of the items must be a pointer of the type **tag-name**.

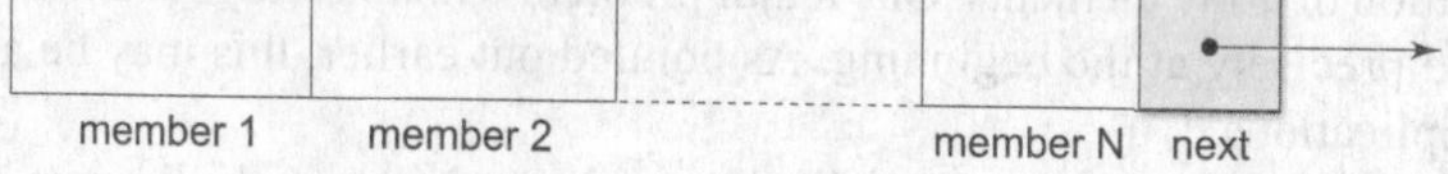

Let use consider a simple example to illustrate the concept of linking. Suppose we define a structure as follows:

```
struct link_list
{
     float age:
     struct link_list *next;
};
```

For simplicity, let as assume that the list contains two nodes **node1** and **node2**. They are of type **struct link_list** and are defined as follows:

```
struct link_list node1, node2;
```

This statement creates space for two nodes each containing two empty fields as shown:

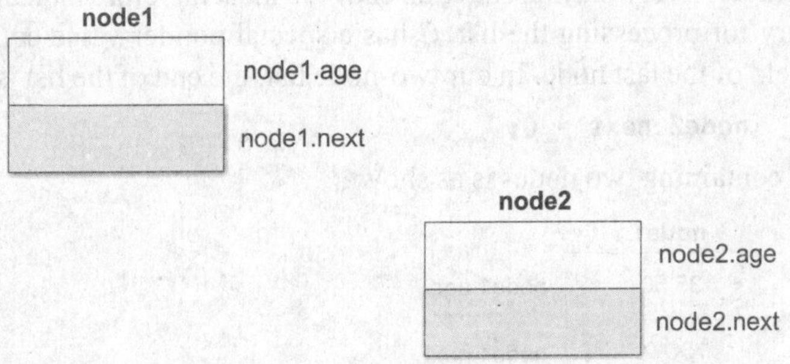

The **next** pointer of **node1** can be made to point to **node2** by the statement

```
node1.next = &node2;
```

This statement stores the address of **node2** into the field **node1.next** and thus establishes a "link" between **node1** and **node2** as shown:

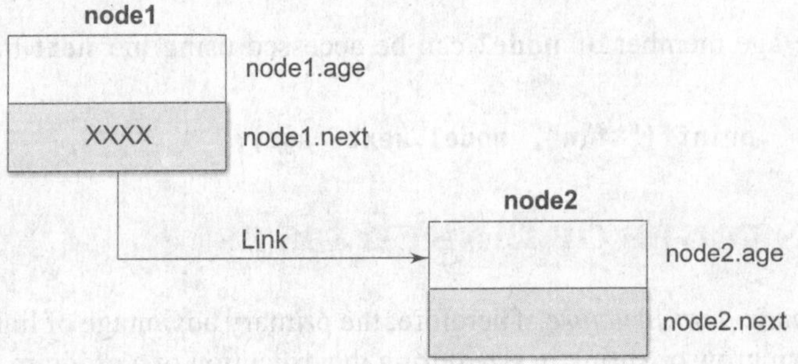

"xxxx" is the address of **node2** where the value of the variable **node2.age** will be stored. Now let us assign values to the field age.

```
node1.age = 35.50;
node2.age = 49.00;
```

The result is as follows:

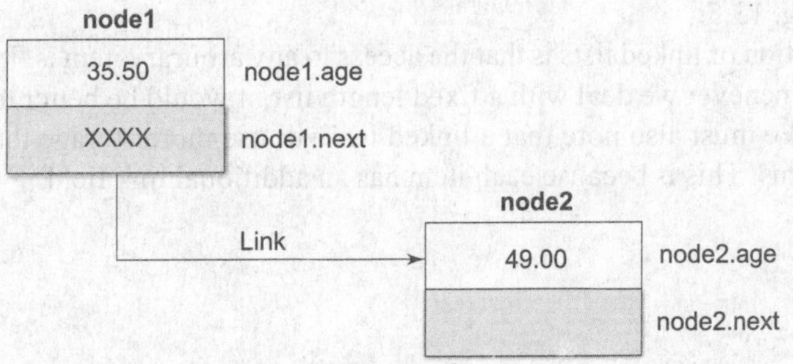

We may continue this process to create a liked list of any number of values.
For example:

```
node2.next = &node3;
```

would add another link provided **node3** has been declared as a variable of type **struct link list.**

No list goes on forever. Every list must have an end. We must therefore indicate the end of a linked list. This is necessary for processing the list. C has a special pointer value called **null** that can be stored in the **next** field of the last node. In our two-node list, the end of the list is marked as follows:

```
node2.next = 0;
```

The final linked list containing two nodes is as shown:

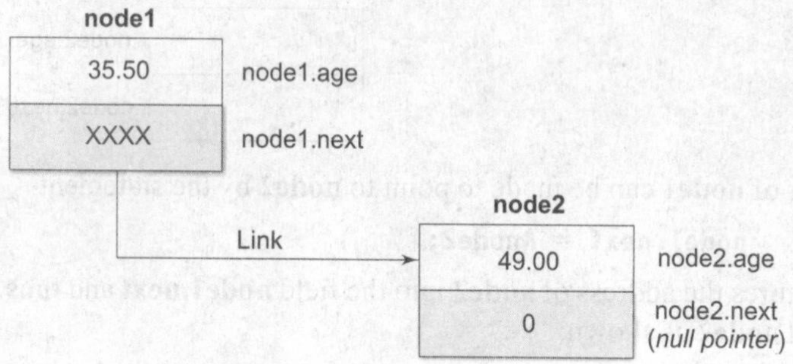

The value of the age member of **node2** can be accessed using the **next** member of **node1** as follows:

```
printf("%f\n", node1.next->age);
```

13.8 ADVANTAGES OF LINKED LISTS

A linked list is *dynamic data structure*. Therefore, the primary advantage of linked lists over arrays is that linked lists can grow or shrink in size during the execution of a program. A linked list can be made just as long as required.

Another advantage is that a linked list does not waste memory space. It uses the memory that is just needed for the list at any point of time. This is because it is not necessary to specify the number of nodes to be used in the list.

The third, and the more important advantage is that the linked lists provide flexibility is allowing the items to be rearranged efficiently. It is easier to insert or delete items by rearranging the links. This is shown in Fig. 13.5.

The major limitation of linked lists is that the access to any arbitrary item is little cumbersome and time consuming. Whenever we deal with a fixed length list, it would be better to use an array rather than a linked list. We must also note that a linked list will use more storage than an array with the same number of items. This is because each item has an additional link field.

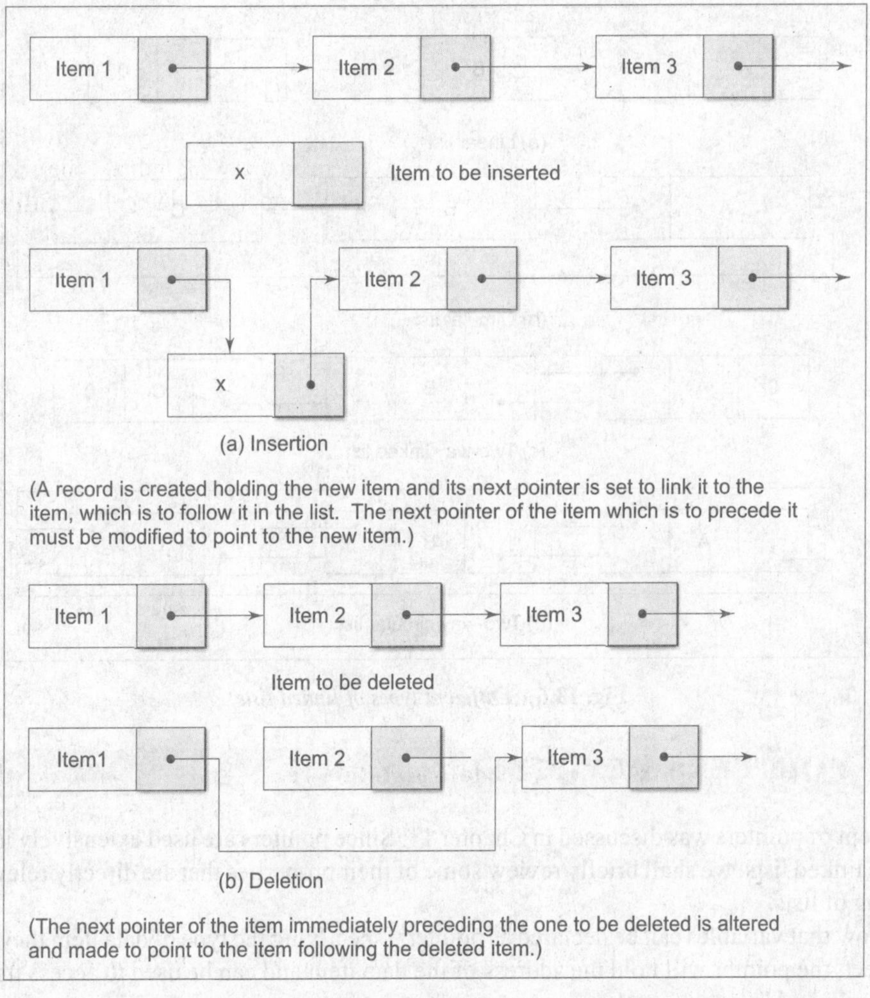
Item 1
Item 2
Item 3
x
Item to be inserted
Item 1
Item 2
Item 3
x
(a) Insertion
(A record is created holding the new item and its next pointer is set to link it to the item, which is to follow it in the list. The next pointer of the item which is to precede it must be modified to point to the new item.)
Item 1
Item 2
Item 3
Item to be deleted
Item1
Item 2
Item 3
(b) Deletion
(The next pointer of the item immediately preceding the one to be deleted is altered and made to point to the item following the deleted item.)

Fig. 13.5 *Insertion into and deletion from a linked list*

13.9 TYPES OF LINKED LISTS

There are different types of lined lists. The one we discussed so far is known as *linear singly* linked list. The other linked lists are:

- Circular linked lists
- Two-way or doubly linked lists
- Circular doubly linked lists

The circular linked lists have no beginning and no end. The last item points back to the first item. The doubly linked list uses double set of pointers, one pointing to the next item and other pointing to the preceding item. This allows us to traverse the list in either direction. Circular doubly linked lists employs both the forward pointer and backward pointer in circular form. Figure 13.6 illustrates various kinds of linked lists.

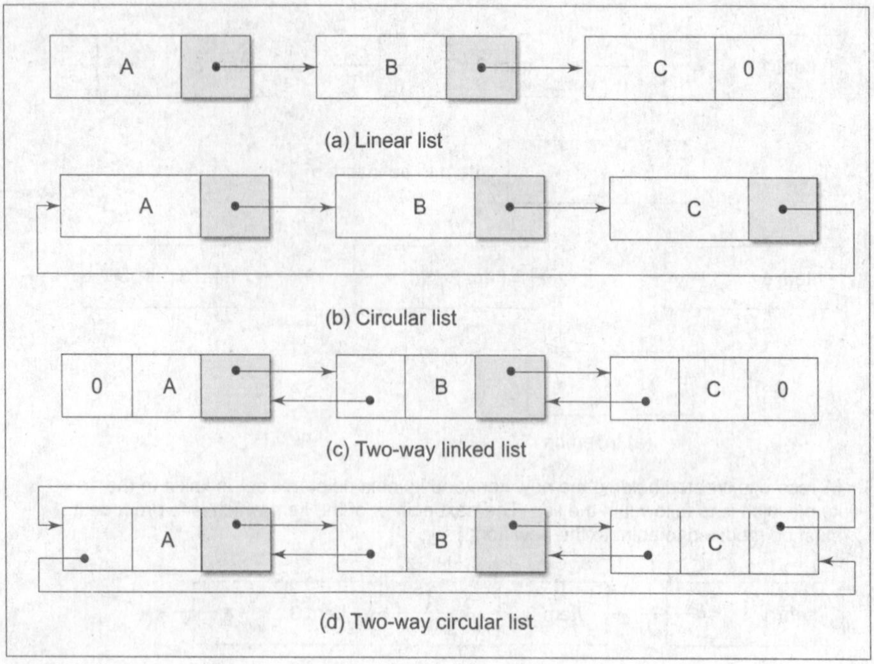

Fig. 13.6 *Different types of linked lists*

13.10 POINTERS REVISITED

The concept of pointers was discussed in Chapter 11. Since pointers are used extensively in processing of the linked lists, we shall briefly review some of their properties that are directly relevant to the processing of lists.

We know that variables can be declared as pointers, specifying the type of data item they can point to. In effect, the pointer will hold the address of the data item and can be used to access its value. In processing linked lists, we mostly use pointers of type structures.

It is most important to remember the distinction between the pointer variable **ptr**, which contain the address of a variable, and the referenced variable ***ptr**, which denotes the value of variable to which **ptr**'s value points. The following examples illustrate this distinction. In these illustrations, we assume that the pointers **p** and **q** and the variables **x** and **y** are declared to be of same type.

(a) Initialization

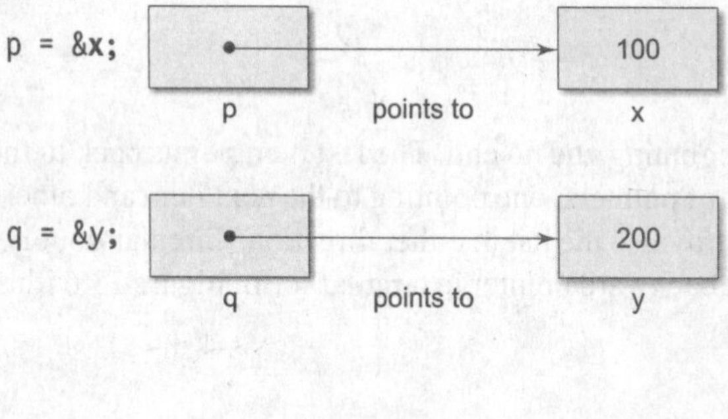

The pointer **p** contains the address of **x** and **q** contains the address of y.

***p =100 and *q = 200 and p<>q**

(b) Assignment p = q

The assignment **p = q** assigns the address of the variable **y** to the pointer variable **p** and therefore **p** now points to the variable y.

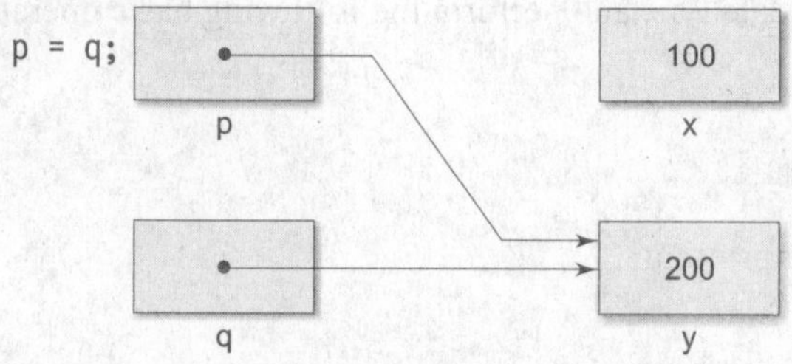

Both the pointer variables point to the same variable.

***p = *q = 200 but x <> y**

(c) Assignment *p = *q

This assignment statement puts the value of the variable pointed to by **q** in the location of the variable pointed to by **p**.

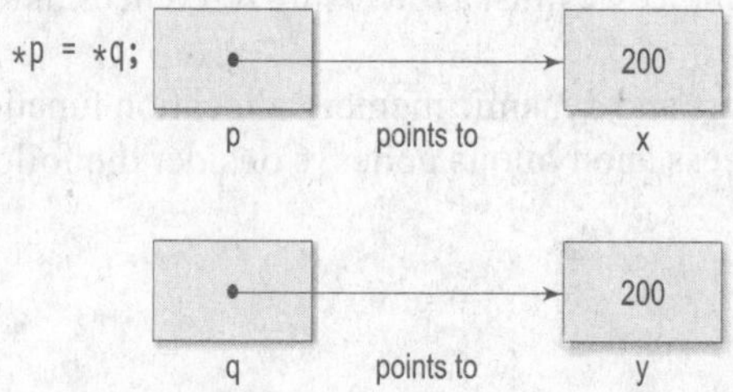

The pointer **p** still points to the same variable **x** but the old value of **x** is replaced by 200 (which is pointed to by **q**).

x = y = 200 but p <> q

(d) NULL pointers

A special constant known as NULL pointer (0) is available in C to initialize pointers that point to nothing. That is the statements

p = 0; (or p = NULL;)   p → [0]

q = 0; (q = NULL;)   q → [0]

make the pointers **p** and **q** point to nothing. They can be later used to point any values.

We know that a pointer must be initialized by assigning a memory address before using it. There are two ways of assigning memory address to a pointer.

1. Assigning an existing variable address (static assignment)

```
ptr = &count;
```

2. Using a memory allocation function (dynamic assignment)

```
ptr = (int*) malloc(sizeof(int));
```

13.11 CREATING A LINKED LIST

We can treat a linked list as an abstract data type and perform the following basic operations:

1. Creating a list
2. Traversing the list
3. Counting the items in the list
4. Printing the list (or sub list)
5. Looking up an item for editing or printing
6. Inserting an item
7. Deleting an item
8. Concatenating two lists

In Section 13.7 we created a two-element linked list using the structure variable names **node1** and **node2**. We also used the address operator **&** and member operators **.** and –> for creating and accessing individual items. The very idea of using a linked list is to avoid any reference to specific number of items in the list so that we can insert or delete items as and when necessary. This can be achieved by using "anonymous" locations to store nodes. Such locations are accessed not by name, but by means of pointers, which refer to them. (For example, we must avoid using references like **node1.age** and **node1.next –> age**.)

Anonymous locations are created using pointers and dynamic memory allocation functions such as **malloc**. We use a pointer **head** to create and access anonymous nodes. Consider the following:

```
struct linked_list
{
     int number;
     struct linked_list *next;
};
typedef struct linked_list node;
node *head;
head = (node *) malloc(sizeof(node));
```

The **struct** declaration merely describes the format of the nodes and does not allocate storage. Storage space for a node is created only when the function **malloc** is called in the statement

```
head = (node *) malloc(sizeof(node));
```

This statement obtains a piece of memory that is sufficient to store a node and assigns its address to the pointer variable **head**. This pointer indicates the beginning of the linked list.

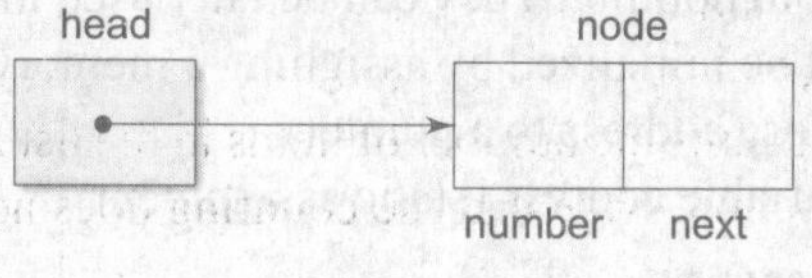

The following statements store values in the member fields:

```
head -> number = 10;
head -> next = NULL;
```

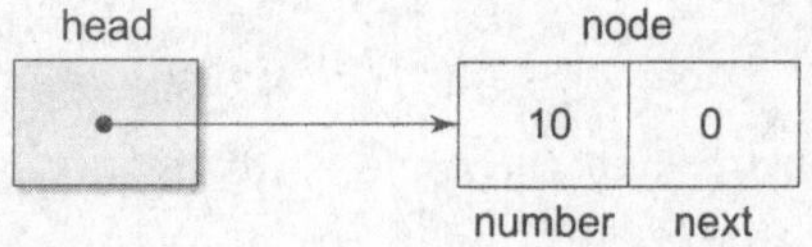

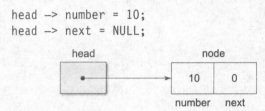

The second node can be added as follows:

```
head -> next = (node *)malloc(sizeof(node));
head -> next ->number = 20;
head->next->next = NULL;
```

Although this process can be continued to create any number of nodes, it becomes cumbersome and clumsy if nodes are more than two. The above process may be easily implemented using both recursion and iteration techniques. The pointer can be moved from the current node to the next node by a self-replacement statement such as

```
head = head -> next;
```

The Example 13.3 shows creation of a complete linked list and printing of its contents using recursion.

Example 13.3 Write a program to create a linear linked list interactively and print out the list and the total number of items in the list.

The program shown in Fig. 13.7 first allocates a block of memory dynamically for the first node using the statement

```
head = (node *)malloc(sizeof(node));
```

which returns a pointer to a structure of type **node** that has been type defined earlier. The linked list is then created by the function **create**. The function requests for the number to be placed in the current node that has been created. If the value assigned to the current node is –999, then null is assigned to the pointer variable **next** and the list ends. Otherwise, memory space is allocated to the next node using again the **malloc** function and the next value is placed into it. Not that the function **create** calls itself recursively and the process will continue until we enter the number –999.

The items stored in the linked list are printed using the function **print** which accept a pointer to the current node as an argument. It is a recursive function and stops when it receives a NULL pointer. Printing algorithm is as follows;

1. Start with the first node.
2. While there are valid nodes left to print
   (a) print the current item and
   (b) advance to next node

Similarly, the function **count** counts the number of items in the list recursively and return the total number of items to the **main** function. Note that the counting does not include the item –999 (contained in the dummy node).

Program

```
#include  <stdio.h>
#include  <stdlib.h>
#define   NULL 0

struct linked_list
{
        int number;
        struct linked_list *next;
};
typedef struct linked_list node;  /* node type defined */

main()
{
        node *head;
        void create(node *p);
        int count(node *p);
        void print(node *p);
        head = (node *)malloc(sizeof(node));
        create(head);
        printf("\n");
        printf(head);
        printf("\n");
        printf("\nNumber of items = %d \n", count(head));
}
void create(node *list)
{
        printf("Input a number\n");
        printf("(type -999 at end): ");
        scanf("%d", &list -> number); /* create current node */

        if(list->number == -999)
        {
          list->next = NULL;
        }
        else /*create next node */
        {
          list->next = (node *)malloc(sizeof(node));
          create(list->next);   */ Recursion occurs */
        }
        return;
}
void print(node *list)
{
          if(list->next != NULL)
```

```
    {
      printf("%d-->",list ->number);   /* print current item */

       if(list->next->next == NULL)
         printf("%d", list->next->number);

      print(list->next);    /* move to next item */
    }
    return;
  }

  int count(node *list)
  {
    if(list->next == NULL)
          return (0);
    else
          return(1+ count(list->next));
  }
```

Output

```
Input a number
(type -999 to end); 60
Input a number
(type -999 to end); 20
Input a number
(type -999 to end); 10
Input a number
(type -999 to end); 40
Input a number
(type -999 to end); 30
Input a number
(type -999 to end); 50
Input a number
(type -999 to end); -999

60 -->20 -->10 -->40 -->30 -->50 --> -999

Number of items = 6
```

Fig. 13.7 *Creating a linear linked list*

13.12 INSERTING AN ITEM

One of the advantages of linked lists is the comparative case with which new nodes can be inserted. It requires merely resetting of two pointers (rather than having to move around a list of data as would be the case with arrays).

Inserting a new item, say X, into the list has three situations:

1. Insertion at the front of the list.
2. Insertion in the middle of the list.
3. Insertion at the end of the list.

The process of insertion precedes a search for the place of insertion. The search involves in locating a node after which the new item is to be inserted.

A general algorithm for insertion is as follows:

Begin
  if the list is empty or
  the new node comes before the head node *then*,
  insert the new node as the head node,
  else
  if the new node comes after the last node, *then*,
  insert the new node as the end node,
  else
  insert the new node in the body of the list.
End

Algorithm for placing the new item at the beginning of a linked list:

1. Obtain space for new node.
2. Assign data to the item field of new node.
3. Set the *next* field of the new node to point to the start of the list.
4. Change the head pointer to point to the new node.

Algorithm for inserting the new node X between two existing nodes, say, N1 and N2;

1. Set space for new node X.
2. Assign value to the item field of X.
3. Set the *next* field of X to point to node N2.
4. Set the *next* field of N1 to point to X.

Algorithm for inserting an item at the end of the list is similar to the one for inserting in the middle, except the *next* field of the new node is set to NULL (or set to point to a dummy or sentinel node, if it exists).

Example 13.4 Write a function to insert a given item *before* a specified node known as key node.

The function **insert** shown in Fig. 13.8 requests for the item to be inserted as well as the "key node". If the insertion happens to be at the beginning, then memory space is created for the new node, the value of new item is assigned to it and the pointer **head** is assigned to the next member. The pointer **new** which indicates the beginning of the new node is assigned to **head.** Note the following statements:

```
new->number = x;
new->next = head;
head = new;
```

```
node *insert(node *head)
{
        node *find(node *p, int a);
        node *new;     /* pointer to new node */
        node *n1;   /* pointer to node preceding key node */
        int key;
        int x;      /* new item (number) to be inserted */

        printf("Value of new item?");
        scanf("%d", &x);
        printf("Value of key item ? (type -999 if last) ");
        scanf("%d", &key);

        if(head->number == key)   /* new node is first */
        {
          new = (node *)malloc(size of(node));
          new->number = x;
          new->next = head;
          head = new;
        }
        else    /* find key node and insert new node */
        {    /* before the key node */
          n1 = find(head, key);    /* find key node */

          if(n1 == NULL)
            printf("\n key is not found \n");
          else    /* insert new node */
          {
             new = (node *)malloc(sizeof(node));
             new->number = x;
             new->next = n1->next;
             n1->next = new;
          }
        }
        return(head);
}
node *find(node *lists, int key)
{
          if(list->next->number == key) /* key found */
            return(list);
        else

          if(list->next->next == NULL)  /* end */
            return(NULL);
        else
          find(list->next, key);
}
```

Fig. 13.8 *A function for inserting an item into a linked list*

However, if the new item is to be inserted after an existing node, then we use the function **find** recursively to locate the 'key node'. The new item is inserted before the key node using the algorithm discussed above. This is illustrated as:

Before insertion

```
new = (node *)malloc(sizeof(node));
new->number = x;
```

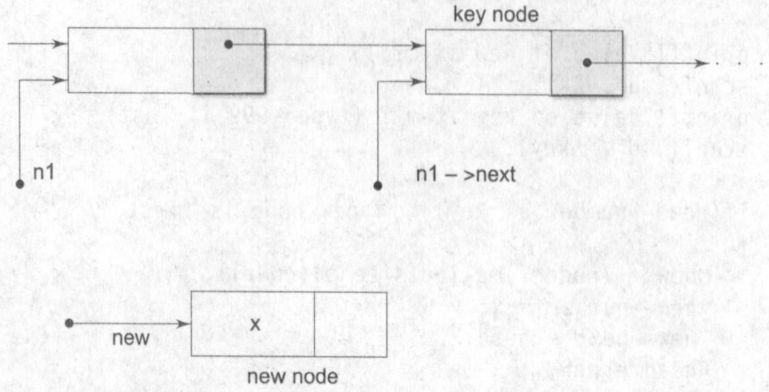

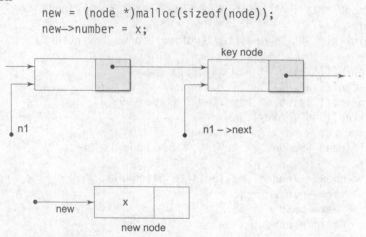

After insertion

```
new->next = n1->next;
n1->next = new;
```

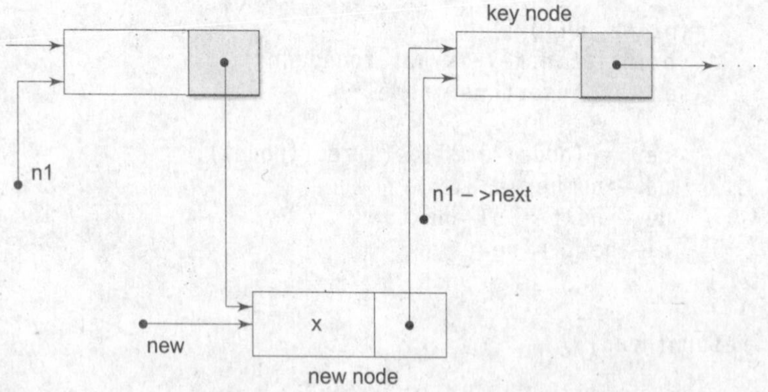

13.13 DELETING AN ITEM

Deleting a node from the list is even easier than insertion, as only one pointer value needs to be changed. Here again we have three situations.

1. Deleting the first item
2. Deleting the last item
3. Deleting between two nodes in the middle of the list

In the first case, the head pointer is altered to point to the second item in the list. In the other two cases, the pointer of the item immediately preceding the one to be deleted is altered to point to the item following the deleted item. The general algorithm for deletion is as follows:

Begin
if the list is empty, *then*,
node cannot be deleted
else
if node to be deleted is the first node, *then*,
make the head to point to the second node,
else
delete the node from the body of the list.
End

The memory space of deleted node may be released for re-use. As in the case of insertion, the process of deletion also involves search for the item to be deleted.

Example 13.5 Write a function to delete a specified node.

A function to delete a specified node is given in Fig. 13.9. The function first checks whether the specified item belongs to the first node. If yes, then the pointer to the second node is temporarily assigned the pointer variable **p**, the memory space occupied by the first node is freed and the location of the second node is assigned to **head**. Thus, the previous second node becomes the first node of the new list.

If the item to be deleted is not the first one, then we use the **find** function to locate the position of 'key node' containing the item to be deleted. The pointers are interchanged with the help of a temporary pointer variable making the pointer in the preceding node to point to the node following the key node. The memory space of key node that has been deleted if freed. The figure below shows the relative position of the key node.

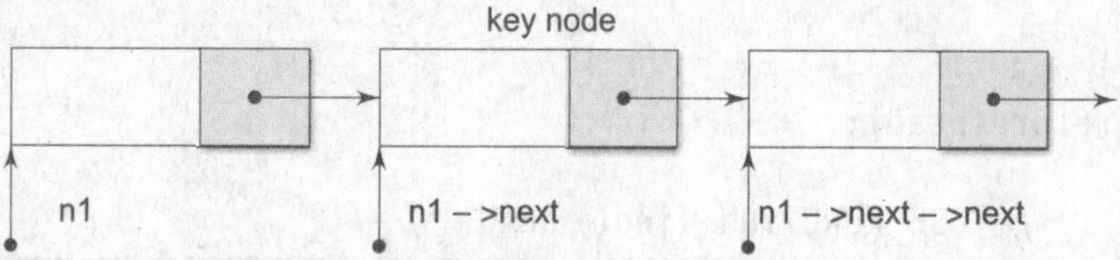

The execution of the following code deletes the key node.

```
p = n1->next->next;
free (n1->next);
n1->next = p;
```

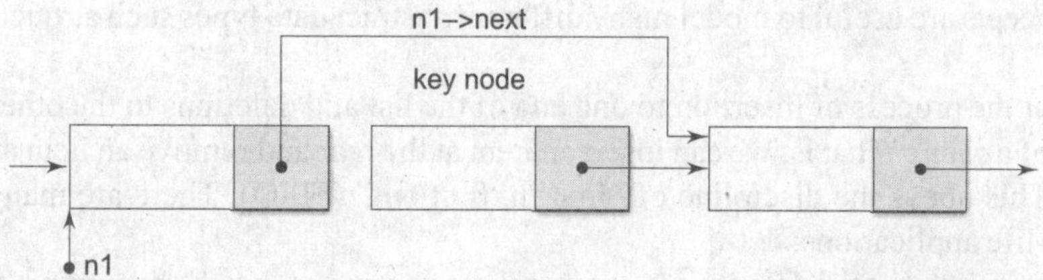

```
node *delete(node *head)
{
        node *find(node *p, int a);
        int  key;   /* item to be deleted */
        node *n1;   /* pointer to node preceding key node */
        node *p;    /* temporary pointer */
        printf("\n What is the item (number) to be deleted?");
        scanf("%d", &key);
        if(head->number == key)/* first node to be deleted) */
        {
          p = head->next;     /* pointer to 2nd node  in list */
          free(head);         /* release space of key node */
          head = p;           /* make head to point to 1st node */
        }
        else
        {
          n1 = find(head, key);
          if(n1 == NULL)
              printf("\n key not found \n");
          else                          /* delete key node */
          {
            p = n1->next->next;     /*  pointer to the node
                                        following the keynode */

            free(n1->next);         /* free key node */
            n1->next = p;           /* establish link */
          }
        }
        return(head);
}

          /* USE FUNCTION find() HERE */
```

Fig. 13.9 *A function for deleting an item from linked list*

13.14 APPLICATION OF LINKED LISTS

Linked list concepts are useful to model many different abstract data types such as queues, stacks and trees.

If we restrict the process of insertion to one end of the list and deletions to the other end, then we have a model of a *queue*. That is, we can insert an item at the rear and remove an item at the front (see Fig. 13.10a). This obeys the discipline of "first in, first out" (FIFO). There are many examples of queues in real-life applications.

If we restrict insertions and deletions to occur only at one end of .lst, the beginning, then we model another data structure known as *stack*. Stacks are also referred to as *push-down* lists. An example of a stack is the "in" tray of a busy executive. The files pile up in the tray, and whenever the executive has time to clear the files, he takes it off from the top. That is, files are added at the top and removed from the top (see Fig. 13.10b). Stacks are sometimes referred to as "last in, first out" (LIFO) structure.

Lists, queues and stacks are all inherently one-dimensional. A *tree* represents a two-dimensional linked list. Trees are frequently encountered in everyday life. One example is the organizational chart of a large company. Another example is the chart of sports tournaments.

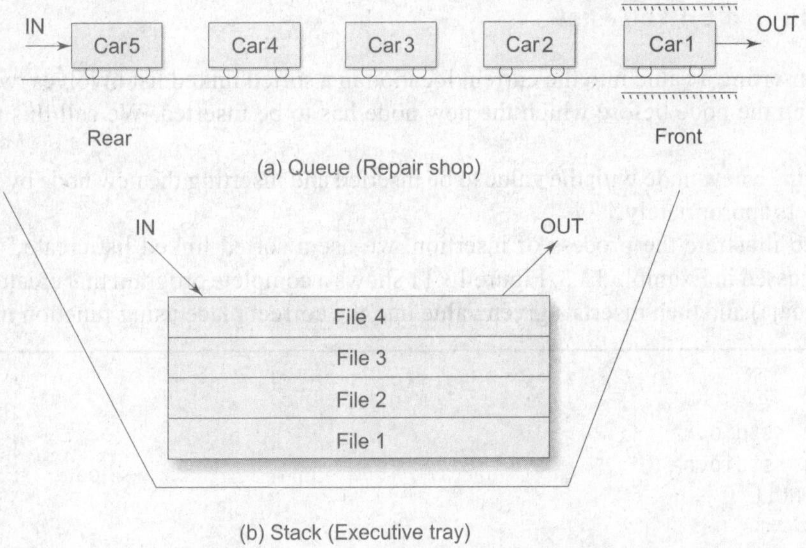

Fig. 13.10 *Application of linked lists*

Just Remember

- Use the **sizeof** operator to determine the size of a linked list.
- When using memory allocation functions **malloc** and **calloc,** test for a NULL pointer return value. Print appropriate message if the memory allocation fails.
- Never call memory allocation functions with a zero size.
- Release the dynamically allocated memory when it is no longer required to avoid any possible "memory leak".
- Using **free** function to release the memory not allocated dynamically with **malloc** or **calloc** is an error.
- Use of a invalid pointer with **free** may cause problems and, sometimes, system crash.
- Using a pointer after its memory has been released is an error.
- It is an error to assign the return value from **malloc** or **calloc** to anything other than a pointer.
- It is a logic error to set a pointer to NULL before the node has been released. The node is irretrievably lost.

- It is an error to declare a self-referential structure without a structure tag.
- It is an error to release individually the elements of an array created with **calloc**.
- It is a logic error to fail to set the link filed in the last node to null.

CASE STUDIES

1. Insertion in a Sorted List

The task of inserting a value into the current location in a sorted linked list involves two operations:

1. Finding the node before which the new node has to be inserted. We call this node as 'Key node'.
2. Creating a new node with the value to be inserted and inserting the new node by manipulating pointers appropriately.

In order to illustrate the process of insertion, we use a sorted linked list created by the create function discussed in Example 13.3. Figure 13.11 shows a complete program that creates a list (using sorted input data) and then inserts a given value into the correct place using function insert.

```
Program

#include <stdio.h>
#include <stdio.h>
#define NULL 0

struct linked_list
{
        int number;
        struct linked-list *next;
};
typedef struct linked_lit node;

main()
{
        int n;
        node *head;
        void create(node *p);
        node *insert(node *p, int n);
        void print(node *p);
        head = (node *)malloc(sizeof(node));
        create(head);
        printf("\n");
        printf("Original list: ");
        print(head);
        printf("\n\n");
        printf("Input number to be inserted: ");
        scanf("%d", &n);
```

```
        head = inert(head,n);
        printf("\n");
        printf("New list:  ");
        print(head);
}
void create(node *list)
{
        printf("Input a number \n");
        printf("(type -999 at end): ");
        scanf("%d", &list->number);

        if(list->number == -999)
        {
          list->next = NULL;
        }
        else /* create next node */
        {
          list->next = (node *)malloc(sizeof(node));
          create(list->next);
        }
        return:
}

void print(node *list)
{
        if(list->next != NULL)
        {
          printf("%d -->", list->number);

        if(list ->next->next = = NULL)
          printf("%d", list->next->number);

        print(list->next);
        }
        return:
}

node *insert(node *head, int x)
{
        node *p1, *p2, *p;
        p1 = NULL;
        p2 = head;  /* p2 points to first node */

        for( ; p2->number < x; p2 = p2->next)
        {
```

```
            p1 = p2;

            if(p2->next->next == NULL)
              {
                 p2 = p2->next;    /* insertion at end */
                 break;
              }
          }

        /*key node found and insert new node */

            p = (node )malloc(sizeof(node));   / space for new node */

            p->number = x; /* place value in the new node */

            p->next = p2; /*link new node to key node */

            if (p1 == NULL)
              head = p; /* new node becomes the first node */
            else
              p1->next = p; /* new node inserted in middle */

            return (head);
}
```

Output

```
  Input a number
  (type -999 at end ); 10

  Input a number
  (type -999 at end ); 20

  Input a number
  (type -999 at end ); 30

  Input a number
  (type -999 at end ); 40

  Input a number
  (type -999 at end ); -999

  Original list:  10 -->20-->30-->40-->-999

  Input number to be inserted: 25
  New list: 10-->20-->25-->30-->40-->-999
```

Fig. 13.11 *Inserting a number in a sorted linked list*

The function takes two arguments, one the value to be inserted and the other a pointer to the linked list. The function uses two pointers, **p1** and **p2** to search the list. Both the pointers are moved down the list with **p1** trailing **p2** by one node while the value **p2** points to is compared with the value to be inserted. The 'key node' is found when the number **p2** points to is greater (or equal) to the number to be inserted.

Once the key node is found, a new node containing the number is created and inserted between the nodes pointed to by **p1** and **p2**. The figures below illustrate the entire process.

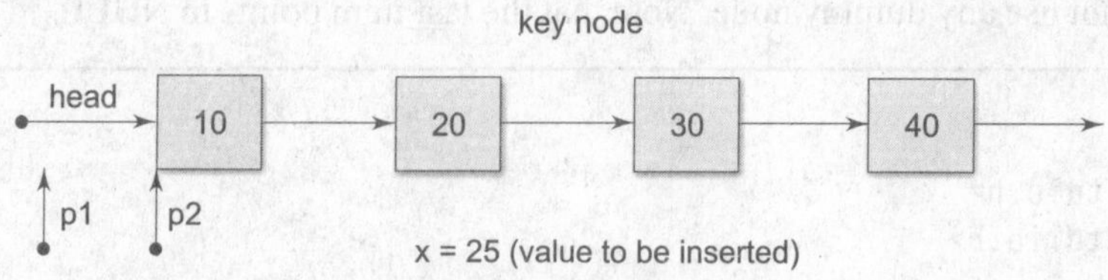

At the start of the search

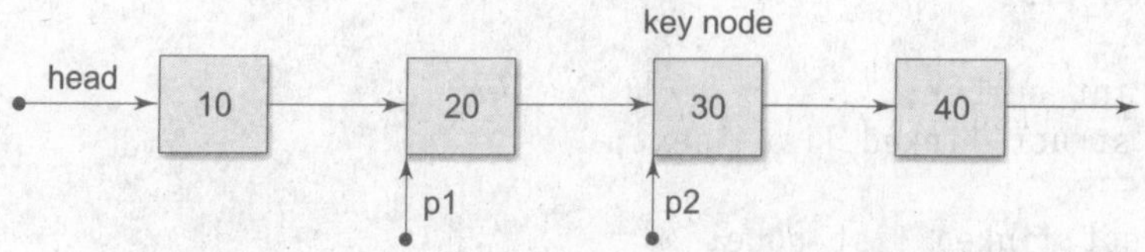

When key node is found

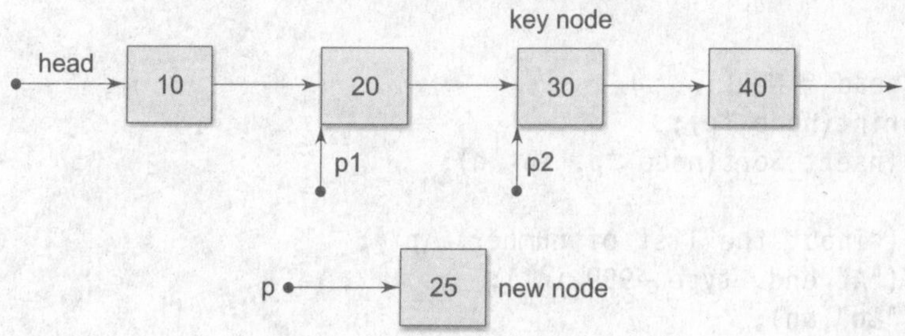

When new node is created

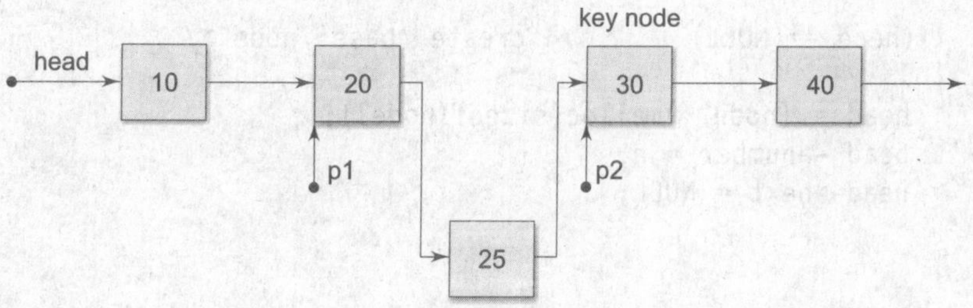

When new node is inserted

2. Building a Sorted List

The program in Fig. 13.11 can be used to create a sorted list. This is possible by creating 'one item' list using the create function and then inserting the remaining items one after another using insert function.

A new program that would build a sorted list from a given list of numbers is shown in Fig. 13.12. The **main** function creates a 'base node' using the first number in the list and then calls the function **insert_sort** repeatedly to build the entire sorted list. It uses the same sorting algorithm discussed above but does not use any dummy node. Note that the last item points to NULL.

Program

```
#include <stdio.h>
#include <stdlib.h>
#define NULL 0

struct linked_list
{
            int number;
            struct linked_list *next;
};
typedef struct linked_list node;

main ()
{
            int n;
            node *head = NULL;
            void print(node *p);
            node *insert_Sort(node *p, int n);

            printf("Input the list of numbers.\n");
            printf("At end, type -999.\n");
            scanf("%d",&n);

            while(n != -999)
            {
               if(head == NULL)        /* create 'base' node */
               {
                  head = (node *)malloc(sizeof(node));
                  head ->number = n;
                  head->next = NULL;

               }

               else          /* insert next item */
               {
```

```
            head = insert_sort(head,n);
          }
            scanf("%d", &n);
        }
        printf("\n");
        print(head);
        print("\n");
}
node *insert_sort(node *list, int x)
{
        node *p1, *p2, *p;
        p1 = NULL;
        p2 = list; /* p2 points to first node */

        for( ; p2->number < x ; p2 = p2->next)
        {
          p1 = p2;

          if(p2->next == NULL)
          {
            p2 = p2->next;          /* p2 set to NULL */
            break;              /* insert new node at end */
          }
        }

    /* key node found */
    p = (node *)malloc(sizeof(node)); /* space for new node */
    p->number = x;        /* place value in the new node */
    p->next = p2;         /* link new node to key node */
    if (p1 == NULL)
            list = p;       /* new node becomes the first node */
    else
            p1->next = p;  /* new node inserted after 1st node */


    return (list);
}
void print(node *list)
{
        if (list == NULL)
          printf("NULL");
        else
        {
          printf("%d-->",list->number);
          print(list->next);
```

```
        }
        return;
}
```

Output

```
Input the list of number.
At end, type -999.
80 70 50 40 60 -999
40-->50-->60-->70-->80 -->NULL
Input the list of number.
At end, type -999.
40 70 50 60 80 -999
40-->50-->60-->70-->80-->NULL
```

Fig. 13.12 *Creation of sorted list from a given list of numbers*

REVIEW QUESTIONS

13.1 State whether the following statements are *true* or *false*

(a) Dynamically allocated memory can only be accessed using pointers.

(b) **calloc** is used to change the memory allocation previously allocated with **malloc**.

(c) Only one call to free is necessary to release an entire array allocated with **calloc**.

(d) Memory should be freed when it is no longer required.

(e) To ensure that it is released, allocated memory should be freed before the program ends.

(f) The link field in a linked list always points to successor.

(g) The first step in a adding a node to a linked list is to allocate memory for the next node.

13.2 Fill in the blanks in the following statements

(a) Function ____________ is used to dynamically allocate memory to arrays.

(b) A____________ is an ordered collection of data in which each element contains the location of the next element.

(c) Data structures which contain a member field that points to the same structure type are called ____________ structures.

(d) A____________ identifies the last logical node in a linked list.

(e) Stacks are referred to as ____________

13.3 What is a linked list? How is it represented?

13.4 What is dynamic memory allocation? How does it help in building complex programs?

13.5 What is the principal difference between the functions **malloc** and **calloc**

13.6 Find errors, if any, in the following memory management statements:

a. `*ptr = (int *)malloc(m, sizeof(int));`

b. `table = (float *)calloc(100);`

c. `node = free(ptr);`

13.7 Why a linked list is called a dynamic data structure? What are the advantages of using linked lists over arrays?

13.8 Describe different types of linked lists.

13.9 Identify errors, if any, in the following structure definition statements:

```
struct
{
    char name[30]
    struct *next;
};
typedef struct node;
```

13.10 The following code is defined in a header file *list.h*

```
typedef struct
{
     char name[15];
     int age;
     float weight;
}DATA;

struct linked_list
{
     DATA person;
     Struct linked_list *next;
};
typedef struct linked_list NODE;
typedef NODE *NDPTR;
```

Explain how could we use this header file for writing programs.

PROGRAMMING EXERCISES

13.1 In Example 13.3, we have used print() in recursive mode. Rewrite this function using iterative technique in for loop.

13.2 Write a menu driven program to create a linked list of a class of students and perform the following operations:

a. Write out the contents of the list.
b. Edit the details of a specified student.
c. Count the number of students above a specified age and weight.

Make use of the header file defined in Exercise 13.7.

13.3 Write recursive and non-recursive functions for reversing the elements in a linear list. Compare the relative efficiencies of them.

13.4 Write an interactive program to create linear linked lists of customer names and their telephone numbers. The program should be menu driven and include features for adding a new customer and deleting an existing customer.

13.5 Modify the above program so that the list is always maintained in the alphabetical order of customer names.

13.6 Develop a program to combine two sorted lists to produce a third sorted lists which contains one occurrence of each of the elements in the original lists.

13.7 Write a program to create a circular linked list so that the input order of data item is maintained. Add function to carry out the following operations on circular linked list.

   a. Count the number of nodes
   b. Write out contents
   c. Locate and write the contents of a given node

13.8 Write a program to construct an ordered doubly linked list and write out the contents of a specified node.

13.9 Write a function that would traverse a linear singly linked list in reverse and write out the contents in reverse order.

13.10 Given two ordered singly linked lists, write a function that will merge them into a third ordered list.

Chapter

14

The Preprocessor

14.1 INTRODUCTION

C is a unique language in many respects. We have already seen features such as structures and pointers. Yet another unique feature of the C language is the *preprocessor*. The C preprocessor provides several tools that are unavailable in other high-level languages. The programmer can use these tools to make his program easy to read, easy to modify, portable, and more efficient.

The preprocessor, as its name implies, is a program that processes the source code before it passes through the compiler. It operates under the control of what is known as *preprocessor command lines or directives*. Preprocessor directives are placed in the source program before the main line. Before the source code passes through the compiler, it is examined by the preprocessor for any preprocessor directives. If there are any, appropriate actions (as per the directives) are taken and then the source program is handed over to the compiler.

Preprocessor directives follow special syntax rules that are different from the normal C syntax. They all begin with the symbol # in column one and do not require a semicolon at the end. We have already used the directives **#define** and **#include** to a limited extent. A set of commonly used preprocessor directives and their functions is given in Table 14.1.

Table 14.1 *Preprocessor Directives*

Directive	*Function*
#define	Defines a macro substitution
#undef	Undefines a macro
#include	Specifies the files to be included
#ifdef	Test for a macro definition
#endif	Specifies the end of #if.
#ifndef	Tests whether a macro is not defined.
#if	Test a compile-time condition
#else	Specifies alternatives when #if test fails.

These directives can be divided into three categories:

1. Macro substitution directives.
2. File inclusion directives.
3. Compiler control directives.

14.2 MACRO SUBSTITUTION

Macro substitution is a process where an identifier in a program is replaced by a predefined string composed of one or more tokens. The preprocessor accomplishes this task under the direction of **#define** statement. This statement, usually known as a *macro definition* (or simply a macro) takes the following general form:

#define *identifier string*

If this statement is included in the program at the beginning, then the preprocessor replaces every occurrence of the **identifier** in the source code by the string. The keyword **#define** is written just as shown (starting from the first column) followed by the *identifier* and a *string*, with at least one blank space between them. Note that the definition is not terminated by a semicolon. The *string* may be any text, while the *identifier* must be a valid C name.

There are different forms of macro substitution. The most common forms are:

1. Simple macro substitution.
2. Argumented macro substitution.
3. Nested macro substitution.

Simple Macro Substitution

Simple string replacement is commonly used to define constants. Examples of definition of constants are:

```
#define    COUNT       100
#define    FALSE       0
#define    SUBJECTS    6
#define    PI          3.1415926
#define    CAPITAL     "DELHI"
```

Notice that we have written all macros (identifiers) in capitals. It is a convention to write all macros in capitals to identify them as symbolic constants. A definition, such as

```
#define M 5
```

will replace all occurrences of M with 5, starting from the line of definition to the end of the program. However, a macro inside a string does not get replaced. Consider the following two lines:

```
total = M * value;
printf("M = %d\n", M);
```

These two lines would be changed during preprocessing as follows:

```
total = 5 * value;
printf("M = %d\n", 5);
```

Notice that the string **"M=%d\n"** is left unchanged.

A macro definition can include more than a simple constant value. It can include expressions as well. Following are valid definitions:

```
#define    AREA      5 * 12.46
#define    SIZE      sizeof(int) * 4
#define    TWO-PI    2.0 * 3.1415926
```

Whenever we use expressions for replacement, care should be taken to prevent an unexpected order of evaluation. Consider the evaluation of the equation

```
ratio = D/A;
```

where D and A are macros defined as follows:

```
#define  D  45 – 22
#define  A  78 + 32
```

The result of the preprocessor's substitution for D and A is:

```
ratio = 45-22/78+32;
```

This is certainly different from the expected expression

(45 – 22)/(78+32)

Correct results can be obtained by using parentheses around the strings as:

```
#define  D  (45 – 22)
#define  A  (78 + 32)
```

It is a wise practice to use parentheses for expressions used in macro definitions.

As mentioned earlier, the preprocessor performs a literal text substitution whenever the defined name occurs. This explains why we cannot use a semicolon to terminate the #define statement. This also suggests that we can use a macro to define almost anything. For example, we can use the definitions

```
#define    TEST     (45 – 22)
#define    AND
#define    PRINT    printf("Very Good. \n");
```

to build a statement as follows:

TEST AND PRINT

The preprocessor would translate this line to

```
if(x>y) printf("Very Good.\n");
```

Some tokens of C syntax are confusing or are error-prone. For example, a common programming mistake is to use the token = in place of the token == in logical expressions. Similar is the case with the token &&.

Following are a few definitions that might be useful in building error free and more readable programs:

```
#define    EQUALS    ==
#define    AND       &&
```

```
#define    OR            ||
#define    NOT_EQUAL     !=
#define    START         main() {
#define    END           }
#define    MOD           %
#define    BLANK_LINE    printf("\n");
#define    INCREMENT     ++
```

An example of the use of syntactic replacement is:

```
START
... .....
... .....
if(total EQUALS 240 AND average EQUALS 60)
INCREMENT count;
... .....
... ....
END
```

Macros with Arguments

The preprocessor permits us to define more complex and more useful form of replacements. It takes the form:

```
#define    identifier(f1, f2, . . . . . . fn)    string
```

Notice that there is no space between the macro *identifier* and the left parentheses. The identifiers f1, f2, ...,fn are the formal macro arguments that are analogous to the formal arguments in a function definition.

There is a basic difference between the simple replacement discussed above and the replacement of macros with arguments. Subsequent occurrence of a macro with arguments is known as a *macro call* (similar to a function call). When a macro is called, the preprocessor substitutes the string, replacing the formal parameters with the actual parameters. Hence, the string behaves like a template.

A simple example of a macro with arguments is

```
#define    CUBE(x)    (x*x*x)
```

If the following statement appears later in the program

```
volume = CUBE(side);
```

Then the preprocessor would expand this statement to:

```
volume = (side * side * side );
```

Consider the following statement:

```
volume = CUBE(a+b);
```

This would expand to:

```
volume = (a+b * a+b * a+b);
```

which would obviously not produce the correct results. This is because the preprocessor performs a blind test substitution of the argument a+b in place of x. This shortcoming can be corrected by using parentheses for each occurrence of a formal argument in the *string*.
Example:

```
#define    CUBE(x)    ( (x) * (x) *(x) )
```

This would result in correct expansion of **CUBE(a+b)** as:

```
volume = ( (a+b) * (a+b) * (a+b));
```

Remember to use parentheses for each occurrence of a formal argument, as well as the whole *string*.

Some commonly used definitions are:

```
#define    MAX(a,b)       (((a) > (b)) ? (a) : (b))
#define    MIN(a,b)       (((a) < (b)) ? (a) : (b))
#define    ABS(x)         (((x) > 0) ? (x) : (–(x)))
#define    STREQ(s1,s2)   (strcmp((s1,) (s2)) == 0)
#define    STRGT(s1,s2)   (strcmp((s1,) (s2)) > 0)
```

The argument supplied to a macro can be any series of characters. For example, the definition

```
#define PRINT(variable, format)   printf("variable = %format \n", variable)
```

can be called-in by

```
PRINT(price x quantity, f);
```

The preprocessor will expand this as

```
printf( "price x quantity = %f\n", price x quantity);
```

Note that the actual parameters are substituted for formal parameters in a macro call, although they are within a string. This definition can be used for printing integers and character strings as well.

Nesting of Macros

We can also use one macro in the definition of another macro. That is, macro definitions may be nested. For instance, consider the following macro definitions.

```
#define    M          5
#define    N          M+1
#define    SQUARE(x)  ( (x) * (x) )
#define    CUBE(x)    (SQUARE (x) * (x))
#define    SIXTH(x)   (CUBE(x) * CUBE(x))
```

The preprocessor expands each **#define** macro, until no more macros appear in the text. For example, the last definition is first expanded into

```
((SQUARE(x) * (x)) * (SQUARE(x) * (x)))
```

Since **SQUARE (x)** is still a macro, it is further expanded into

```
( ( ((x)*(x)) * (x) ) * ( ((x) * (x)) * (x)) )
```

which is finally evaluated as x^6.

Macros can also be used as parameters of other macros. For example, given the definitions of M and N, we can define the following macro to give the maximum of these two:

```
#define MAX(M,N)  (( (M) > (N) ) ? (M) : (N))
```

Macro calls can be nested in much the same fashion as function calls. Example:

```
#define        HALF(x)        ( (x)/2.0)
#define        Y              HALF(HALF(x))
```

Similarly, given the definition of MAX(a,b) we can use the following nested call to give the maximum of the three values x,y, and z:

```
MAX (x, MAX(y,z))
```

Undefining a Macro

A defined macro can be undefined, using the statement

#undef *identifier*

This is useful when we want to restrict the definition only to a particular part of the program.

14.3 FILE INCLUSION

An external file containing functions or macro definitions can be included as a part of a program so that we need not rewrite those functions or macro definitions. This is achieved by the preprocessor directive.

#include "filename"

where *filename* is the name of the file containing the required definitions or functions. At this point, the preprocessor inserts the entire contents of *filename* into the source code of the program. When the *filename* is included within the double quotation marks, the search for the file is made first in the current directory and then in the standard directories.

Alternatively this directive can take the form

#include <filename>

without double quotation marks. In this case, the file is searched only in the standard directories.

Nesting of included files is allowed. That is, an included file can include other files. However, a file cannot include itself.

If an included file is not found, an error is reported and compilation is terminated.

Let use assume that we have created the following three files:

SYNTAX.C	contains syntax definitions.
STAT.C	contains statistical functions.
TEST.C	contains test functions.

We can make use of a definition or function contained in any of these files by including them in the program as:

```
#include    <stdio.h>
#include    "SYNTAX.C"
#include    "STAT.C"
#include    "TEST.C"
#define     M      100
main ()
{
      -------------
      -------------
      -------------
}
```

14.4 COMPILER CONTROL DIRECTIVES

While developing large programs, you may face one or more of the following situations:

1. You have included a file containing some macro definitions. It is not known whether a particular macro (say, TEST) has been defined in that header file. However, you want to be certain that Test is defined (or not defined).
2. Suppose a customer has two different types of computers and you are required to write a program that will run on both the systems. You want to use the same program, although certain lines of code must be different for each system.
3. You are developing a program (say, for sales analysis) for selling in the open market. Some customers may insist on having certain additional features. However, you would like to have a single program that would satisfy both types of customers.
4. Suppose you are in the process of testing your program, which is rather a large one. You would like to have print calls inserted in certain places to display intermediate results and messages in order to trace the flow of execution and errors, if any. Such statements are called 'debugging' statements. You want these statements to be a part of the program and to become 'active' only when you decide so.

One solution to these problems is to develop different programs to suit the needs of different situations. Another method is to develop a single, comprehensive program that includes all optional codes and then directs the compiler to skip over certain parts of source code when they are not required. Fortunately, the C preprocessor offers a feature known as *conditional compilation*, which can be used to 'switch' on or off a particular line or group of lines in a program.

Situation 1

This situation refers to the conditional definition of a macro. We want to ensure that the macro TEST is always defined, irrespective of whether it has been defined in the header file or not. This can be achieved as follows:

```
#include    "DEFINE.H"
#ifndef     TEST
#define     TEST 1
#endif
... ...
```

DEFINE.H is the header file that is supposed to contain the definition of **TEST** macro. The directive.

```
#ifndef TEST
```

searches for the definition of **TEST** in the header file and *if not defined*, then all the lines between the **#ifndef** and the corresponding **#endif** directive are left 'active' in the program. That is, the preprocessor directive

```
# define TEST     is processed.
```

In case, the TEST has been defined in the header file, the **#ifndef** condition becomes false, therefore the directive **#define TEST** is ignored. Remember, you cannot simply write

```
# define TEST 1
```

because if **TEST** is already defined, an error will occur.

Similar is the case when we want the macro **TEST** never to be defined. Looking at the following code:

```
... ... ...
#ifdef   TEST
#undef   TEST
#endif
... ...
... ...
```

This ensures that even if **TEST** is defined in the header file, its definition is removed. Here again we cannot simply say

```
#undef   TEST
```

because, if TEST is not defined, the directive is erroneous.

Situation 2

The main concern here is to make the program portable. This can be achieved as follows:

```
......
......
main()
{
    ......
    ... ...
#ifdef IBM_PC
{
    ... ...
    ... ...          code for IBM_PC
    ... ...
}
#else
{
```

```
        … …
        … …                 code for HP machine
        … …
    }
    #endif
        … ..
        … ..
    }
```

If we want the program to run on IBM PC, we include the directive

#define IBM_PC

in the program; otherwise we don't. Note that the compiler control directives are inside the function. Care must be taken to put the # character at column one.

The compiler complies the code for IBM PC if **IBM-PC** is defined, or the code for the HP machine if it is not.

Situation 3

This is similar to the above situation and therefore the control directives take the following form:

```
#ifdef    ABC
    group-A lines
#else
    group-B lines
#endif
```

Group-A lines are included if the customer **ABC** is defined. Otherwise, group-B lines are included.

Situation 4

Debugging and testing are done to detect errors in the program. While the Compiler can detect syntactic and semantic errors, it cannot detect a faulty algorithm where the program executes, but produces wrong results.

The process of error detection and isolation begins with the testing of the program with a known set of test data. The program is divided down and printf statements are placed in different parts to see intermediate results. Such statements are called debugging statements and are not required once the errors are isolated and corrected. We can either delete all of them or, alternately, make them inactive using control directives as:

```
... ...
... ...
#ifdef TEST
{
        printf("Array elements\n");
        for (i = 0; i< m; i++)
            printf("x[%d] = %d\n", i, x[i]);
```

```
}
#endif
… ..
… ..
#ifdef TEST
        printf(….);
#endif
… …
```

The statements between the directives **#ifdef** and **#endif** are included only if the macro **TEST** is defined. Once everything is OK., delete or undefine the **TEST**. This makes the **#ifdef TEST** conditions false and therefore all the debugging statements are left out.

The C preprocessor also supports a more general form of test condition - **#if** directive. This takes the following form:

```
#if constant expression
{
        statement-1;
        statement-2;
        … …
        … …
}
#endif
```

The *constant-expression* may be any logical expression such as

TEST <= 3
(LEVEL == 1 || LEVEL == 2)
MACHINE == 'A'

If the result of the constant-expression is nonzero (true), then all the statements between the **#if** and **#endif** are included for processing; otherwise they are skipped. The names **TEST, LEVEL**, etc. may be defined as macros.

14.5 ANSI ADDITIONS

ANSI committee has added some more preprocessor directives to the existing list given in Table 14.1. They are:

#elif	Provides alternative test facility
#pragma	Specifies certain instructions
#error	Stops compilation when an error occurs

The ANSI standard also includes two new preprocessor operations:

#	Stringizing operator
##	Token-pasting operator

elif Directive

The #elif enables us to establish an "if..else..if.." sequence for testing multiple conditions. The general form of use of **#elif** is:

```
#if   expression 1
      statement sequence 1
    #elif expression 2
          statement sequence 2
          .....
          .....
          #elif expression N
                statement sequence N
#endif
```

For example:

```
#if MACHINE == HCL
    #define FILE "hcl.h"
        #elif    MACHINE == WIPRO
              #define FILE "wipro.h"
              #elif     MACHINE == DCM
                        #define FILE "dcm.h"
#endif
#include FILE
```

#pragma Directive

The **#pragma** is an implementation oriented directive that allows us to specify various instructions to be given to the compiler. It takes the following form

#pragma ***name***

where *name* is the name of the **pragma** we want. For example, under Microsoft C,

```
#pragma loop_opt(on)
```

causes loop optimization to be performed. It is ignored, if the compiler does not recognize it.

#error Directive

The **#error** directive is used to produce diagnostic messages during debugging. The general form is

#error ***error message***

When the **#error** directive is encountered, it displays the error message and terminates processing. Example.

```
#if !defined(FILE_G)
#error NO GRAPHICS FACILITY
#endif
```

Note that we have used a special processor operator **defined** along with **#if**. **defined** is a new addition and takes a *name* surrounded by parentheses. If a compiler does not support this, we can replace it as follows:

```
#if !defined     by     #ifndef
#if defined      by     #ifdef
```

Stringizing Operator

ANSI C provides an operator # called *stringizing operator* to be used in the definition of macro functions. This operator allows a formal argument within a macro definition to be converted to a string. Consider the example below:

```
#define sum(xy) printf(#xy " = %f\n", xy)
main()
{
    ... ...
    ... ...
    sum(a+b);
    ... ...
}
```

The preprocessor will convert the line

```
sum(a+b);
```

into

```
printf("a+b" "=%f\n", a+b);
```

which is equivalent to

```
printf("a+b =%f\n", a+b);
```

Note that the ANSI standard also stipulates that adjacent strings will be concatenated.

Token Pasting Operator

The token pasting operator ## defined by ANSI standard enables us to combine two tokens within a macro definition to form a single token. For example:

```
#define combine(s1,s2) s1 ## s2
main()
{
        ... ..
        ... ..
        printf("%f", combine(total, sales));
        ... ..
        ... ..
}
```

The preprocessor transforms the statement

```
printf("%f", combine(total, sales));
```

into the statement

```
printf("%f", totalsales);
```

Consider another macro definition:

```
#define print(i) printf("a" #i "=%f", a##i)
```

This macro will convert the statement

```
print(5);
```

into the statement

```
printf("a5 = %f", a5)
```

REVIEW QUESTIONS

14.1 Explain the role of the C preprocessor.

14.2 What is a macro and how is it different from a C variable name?

14.3 What precautions one should take when using macros with argument?

14.4 What are the advantages of using macro definitions in a program?

14.5 When does a programmer use **#include** directive?

14.6 The value of a macro name cannot be changed during the running of a program. Comment?

14.7 What is conditional compilation? How does it help a programmer?

14.8 Distinguish between **#ifdef** and **#if** directives.

14.9 Comment on the following code fragment:

```
#if 0
{
        line-1;
        line-2;
        ... ...
        ... ...
        line-n;
}
#endif
```

14.10 Identify errors, if any, in the following macro definitions:

(a) #define until(x) while(!x)

(b) #define ABS(x) (x > 0) ? (x) : (–x)

(c) #ifdef(FLAG)
    #undef FLAG
#endif

(d) #if n == 1 update(item)
#else print-out(item)
#endif

14.11 State whether the following statements are true or false.

(a) The keyword **#define** must be written starting from the first column.

(b) Like other statements, a processor directive must end with a semicolon.

(c) All preprocessor directives begin with #.

(d) We cannot use a macro in the definition of another macro.

14.12 Fill in the blanks in the following statements.

(a) The ______________ directive discords a macro.

(b) The operator ______________ is used to concatenate two arguments.

(c) The operator ______________ converts its operand

(d) The ______________ directive causes an implementation-oriented action.

PROGRAMMING EXERCISES

14.1 Define a macro PRINT_VALUE that can be used to print two values of arbitrary type.

14.2 Write a nested macro that gives the minimum of three values.

14.3 Define a macro with one parameter to compute the volume of a sphere. Write a program using this macro to compute the volume for spheres of radius 5, 10 and 15 metres.

14.4 Define a macro that receives an array and the number of elements in the array as arguments. Write a program using this macro to print out the elements of an array.

14.5 Using the macro defined in the exercise 14.4, write a program to compute the sum of all elements in an array.

Chapter 15

Developing a C Program: Some Guidelines

15.1 INTRODUCTION

We have discussed so far various features of C language and are ready to write and execute programs of modest complexity. However, before attempting to develop complex programs, it is worthwhile to consider some programming techniques that would help design efficient and error-free programs.

The program development process includes three important stages, namely, program design, program coding and program testing. All the three stages contribute to the production of high-quality programs. In this chapter we shall discuss some of the techniques used for program design, coding and testing.

15.2 PROGRAM DESIGN

Program design is the foundation for a good program and is therefore an important part of the program development cycle. Before coding a program, the program should be well conceived and all aspects of the program design should be considered in detail.

Program design is basically concerned with the development of a strategy to be used in writing the program, in order to achieve the solution of a problem. This includes mapping out a solution procedure and the form the program would take. The program design involves the following four stages:

1. Problem analysis.
2. Outlining the program structure.
3. Algorithm development.
4. Selection of control structures.

Problem Analysis

Before we think of a solution procedure to the problem, we must fully understand the nature of the problem and what we want the program to do. Without the comprehension and definition of the problem at hand, program design might turn into a hit-or-miss approach. We must carefully decide the following at this stage;

What kind of data will go in,

What kind of outputs are needed, and

What are the constraints and conditions under which the program has to operate?

Outlining the Program Structure

Once we have decided what we want and what we have, then the next step is to decide how to do it. C as a structured language lends itself to a *top-down* approach. Top-down means decomposing of the solution procedure into tasks that form a hierarchical structure as shown in Fig. 15.1. The essence of the top-down design is to cut the whole problem into a number of independent constituent tasks, and then to cut the tasks into smaller subtasks, and so on, until they are small enough to be grasped mentally and to code easily. These tasks and subtasks can form the basis of functions in the program.

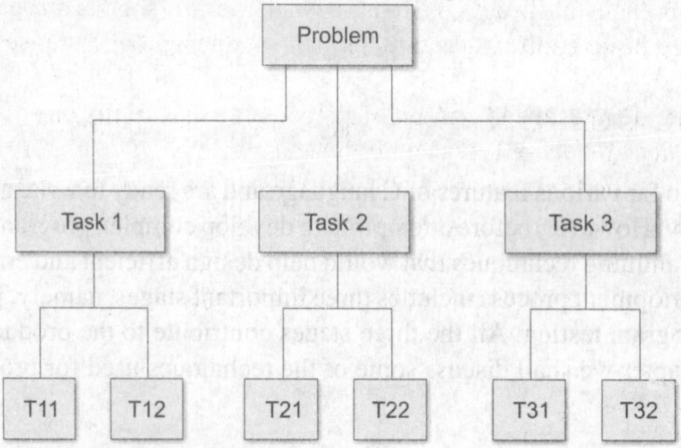

Fig. 15.1 *Hierarchical structure*

An important feature of this approach is that at each level, the details of the design of lower levels are hidden. The higher-level functions are designed first, assuming certain broad tasks of the immediately lower level functions. The actual details of the lower level functions are not considered until that level is reached. Thus the design of functions proceeds from top to bottom, introducing progressively more and more refinements.

This approach will produce a readable and modular code that can be easily understood and maintained. It also helps us classify the overall functioning of the program in terms of lower-level functions.

Algorithm Development

After we have decided a solution procedure and an overall outline of the program, the next step is to work out a detailed definite, step-by-step procedure, known as *algorithm* for each function. The most common method of describing an algorithm is through the use of *flowcharts*. The other method is to write what is known as *pseudocode*. The flow chart presents the algorithm pictorially, while the pseudocode describe the solution steps in a logical order. Either method involves concepts of logic and creativity.

Since algorithm is the key factor for developing an efficient program, we should devote enough attention to this step. A problem might have many different approaches to its solution. For example, there are many sorting techniques available to sort a list. Similarly, there are many methods of finding the area under a curve. We must consider all possible approaches and select the one, which is simple to follow, takes less execution time, and produces results with the required accuracy.

Control Structures

A complex solution procedure may involve a large number of control statements to direct the flow of execution. In such situations, indiscriminate use of control statements such as **goto** may lead to unreadable and uncomprehensible programs. It has been demonstrated that any algorithm can be structured, using the three basic control structure, namely, sequence structure, selection structure, and looping structure.

Sequence structure denotes the execution of statements sequentially one after another. Selection structure involves a decision, based on a condition and may have two or more branches, which usually join again at a later point. **if . . . .else** and **switch** statements in C can be used to implement a selection structure. Looping structure is used when a set of instructions is evaluated repeatedly. This structure can be implemented using **do**, **while**, or **for** statements.

A well-designed program would provide the following benefits:

1. Coding is easy and error-free.
2. Testing is simple.
3. Maintenance is easy.
4. Good documentation is possible.
5. Cost estimates can be made more accurately.
6. Progress of coding may be controlled more precisely.

15.3 PROGRAM CODING

The algorithm developed in the previous section must be translated into a set of instructions that a computer can understand. The major emphasis in coding should be simplicity and clarity. A program written by one may have to be ready by others later. Therefore, it should be readable and simple to understand. Complex logic and tricky coding should be avoided. The elements of coding style include:

- internal documentation.
- construction of statements.
- generality of the program.
- input/output formats.

Internal Documentation

Documentation refers to the details that describe a program. Some details may be built-in as an integral part of the program. These are known as *internal documentation*.

Two important aspects of internal documentation are, selection of meaningful variable names and the use of comments. Selection of meaningful names is crucial for understanding the program. For example,

```
area = breadth * length
```

is more meaningful than

```
a = b * l;
```

Names that are likely to be confused must be avoided. The use of meaningful function names also aids in understanding and maintenance of programs.

Descriptive comments should be embedded within the body of source code to describe processing steps.

The following guidelines might help the use of comments judiciously:

1. Describe blocks of statements, rather than commenting on every line.
2. Use blank lines or indentation, so that comments are easily readable.
3. Use appropriate comments; an incorrect comment is worse than no comment at all.

Statement Construction

Although the flow of logic is decided during design, the construction of individual statements is done at the coding stage. Each statement should be simple and direct. While multiple statements per line are allowed, try to use only one statement per line with necessary indentation. Consider the following code:

```
if(quantify>0){code = 0; quantity = rate;}
else { code = 1; sales = 0:)
```

Although it is perfectly valid, it could be reorganized as follows:

```
if(quantify>0)
{
    code = 0;
    quantify = rate;
}
else
{
    code = 1;
    sales = 0:
}
```

The general guidelines for construction of statements are:

1. Use one statement per line.
2. Use proper indentation when selection and looping structures are implemented.

3. Avoid heavy nesting of loops, preferably not more than three levels.
4. Use simple conditional tests; if necessary break complicated conditions into simple conditions.
5. Use parentheses to clarify logical and arithmetic expressions.
6. Use spaces, wherever possible, to improve readability.

Input/Output Formats

Input/output formats should be simple and acceptable to users. A number of guidelines should be considered during coding.

1. Keep formats simple.
2. Use end –of-file indicators, rather than the user requiring to specify the number of items.
3. Label all interactive input requests.
4. Label all output reports.
5. Use output messages when the output contains some peculiar results.

Generality of Programs

Care should be taken to minimize the dependence of a program on a particular set of data, or on a particular value of a parameter. Example:

```
for(sum = 0, i=1; i <= 10; i++)
    sum = sum + i;
```

This loop adds numbers 1,2, ...10. This can be made more general as follows;

```
sum =0;
for(i =m; i <=n; i = i+ step);
    sum = sum + i;
```

The initial value **m**, the final value **n**, and the increment size **step** can be specified interactively during program execution. When **m**=2, **n**=100, and **step** =2, the loop adds all even numbers up to, and including 100.

15.4 COMMON PROGRAMMING ERRORS

By now you must be aware that C has certain features that are easily amenable to bugs. Added to this, it does not check and report all kinds of run-time errors. It is therefore advisable to keep track of such errors and to see that these known errors are not present in the program. This section examines some of the more common mistakes that a less experienced C programmer could make.

Missing Semicolons

Every C statement must end with a semicolon. A missing semicolon may cause considerable confusion to the compiler and result in 'misleading' error messages. Consider the following statements:

```
a = x+y
b = m/n;
```

The compiler will treat the second line as a part of the first one and treat b as a variable name. You may therefore get an "undefined name" error message in the second line. Note that both the message and location are incorrect. In such situations where there are no errors in a reported line, we should check the preceding line for a missing semicolon.

There may be an instance when a missing semicolon might cause the compiler to go 'crazy' and to produce a series of error messages. If they are found to be dubious errors, check for a missing semicolon in the beginning of the error list.

Misuse of Semicolon

Another common mistake is to put a semicolon in a wrong place. Consider the following code:

```
for(i = 1; i<=10; i++);
        sum = sum + i;
```

This code is supposed to sum all the integers from 1 to 10. But what actually happens is that only the 'exit' value of i is added to the sum. Other examples of such mistake are:

```
1. while (x < Max);
   {
   
   }
2. if(T>= 200);
   grade = 'A';
```

A simple semicolon represents a null statement and therefore it is syntactically valid. The compiler does not produce any error message. Remember, these kinds of errors are worse than syntax errors.

Use of = Instead of = =

It is quite possible to forget the use of double equal sings when we perform a relational test. Example:

```
if(code = 1)
    count ++;
```

It is a syntactically valid statement. The variable code is assigned 1 and then, because code = 1 is true, the count is incremented. In fact, the above statement does not perform any relational test on code. Irrespective of the previous value of code, count ++: is always executed.

Similar mistakes can occur in other control statements, such as **for** and **while**. Such a mistake in the loop control statements might cause infinite loops.

Missing Braces

It is common to forget a closing brace when coding a deeply nested loop. It will be usually detected by the compiler because the number of opening braces should match with the closing ones. However, if we put a matching brace in a wrong place, the compiler won't notice the mistake and the program will produce unexpected results.

Another serious problem with the braces is, not using them when multiple statements are to be grouped together. For instance, consider the following statements:

```
for(i=1; i <= 10; i++)
        sum1 = sum 1 +i;
        sum2 = sum2 + i*i;
printf("%d %d\n", sum1,sum2);
```

This code is intended to compute **sum1, sum2** for i varying from 1 to 10, in steps of 1 and then to print their values. But, actually the **for** loop treats only the first statement, namely,

```
sum = sum1 + i;
```

as its body and therefore the statement

```
sum2 = sum2 + i*i;
```

is evaluated only once when the loop is exited. The correct way to code this segment is to place braces as follows:

```
for(i=1; i<=10; i++)
{
        sum1 = sum1 + i;
        sum2 = sum2 +i*i;
}
printf("%d %d\n", sum1 sum2);
```

In case, only one brace is supplied, the behaviour of the compiler becomes unpredictable.

Missing Quotes

Every string must be enclosed in double quotes, while a single character constant in single quotes. If we miss them out, the string (or the character) will be interpreted as a variable name. Examples:

```
if(response ==YES)    /* YES is a string */
Grade = A;            /* A is a character constant */
```

Here YES and A are treated as variables and therefore, a message "undefined names" may occur.

Misusing Quotes

It is likely that we use single quotes whenever we handle single characters. Care should be exercised to see that the associated variables are declared properly. For example, the statement

```
city = 'M';
```

would be invalid if **city** has been declared as a **char** variable with dimension (i.e., pointer to **char**).

Improper Comment Characters

Every comment should start with a /* and end with a */. Anything between them is ignored by the compiler. If we miss out the closing */, then the compiler searches for a closing */ further down in the program, treating all the lines as comments. In case, it fails to find a closing */, we may get an error message. Consider the following lines:

```
.....
/* comment line 1
statement1;
statement2;
/* comment line 2 */
statement 3;
.....
```

Since the closing */ is missing in the comment line 1, all the statements that follow, until the closing comment */ in comment line 2 are ignored.

We should remember that C does not support nested comments. Assume that we want to comment out the following segment:

```
.....
x = a-b;
Y = c-d;
/* compute ratio */
ratio = x/y;
.....
.....
```

we may be tempted to add comment characters as follows:

```
/* x = a–b;
   y = c–d;
   /* Compute ratio */
   ratio = x/y; */
```

This is incorrect. The first opening comment matches with the first closing comment and therefore the lines between these two are ignored. The statement

```
ratio = x/y;
```

is not commented out. The correct way to comment out this segment is shown as:

```
/* x = a–b;
   y = c–d; */
   /* compute ratio */
   /* ratio = x/y; */
```

Undeclared Variables

C requires every variable to be declared for its type, before it is used. During the development of a large program, it is quite possible to use a variable to hold intermediate results and to forget to declare it.

Forgetting the Precedence of Operators

Expressions are evaluated according to the precedence of operators. It is common among beginners to forget this. Consider the statement

```
if (value = product ( ) >= 100)
        tax = 0.05 * value;
```

The call **product ( )** returns the product of two numbers, which is compared to 100. If it is equal to or greater than 100, the relational test is true, and a 1 is assigned to **value**; otherwise a 0 is assigned. In either case, the only values **value** can take on are 1 or 0. This certainly is not what the programmer wanted.

The statement was actually expected to assign the value returned by **product( )** to **value** and then compare **value** with 100. If **value** was equal to or greater than 100, tax should have been computed, using the statement

```
tax = 0.05 * value;
```

The error is due to the higher precedence of the relational operator compared to the assignment operator. We can force the assignment to occur first by using parentheses as follows:

```
if(value = product()) >=100)
tax = 0.05 * value;
```

Similarly, the logical operators **&&** and || have lower precedence than arithmetic and relational operators and among these two, **&&** has higher precedence than ||. Try, if there is any difference between the following statements:

1. if(p > 50|| c > 50 && m > 60 && T > 180)
   x = 1;
2. if((p > 50|| c > 50) && m > 60 && T > 180)
   x = 1;
3. if((p > 50|| c > 50 && m > 60) && T > 180)
   x = 1;

Ignoring the Order of Evaluation of Increment/Decrement Operators

We often use increment or decrement operators in loops. Example

```
... ...
i = 0;
while ((c = getchar()) != '\n';
{
        string[i++] = c;
}
string[i-1] = '\n';
```

The statement **string[i++]** = c; is equivalent to :

```
string[i] = c;
i = i+1;
```

This is not the same as the statement **string[++i]** = c; which is equivalent to

```
i =i+1;
string[i] = c;
```

Forgetting to Declare Function Parameters

Remember to declare all function parameters in the function header.

Mismatching of Actual and Formal Parameter Types in Function Calls

When a function with parameters is called, we should ensure that the type of values passed, match with the type expected by the called function. Otherwise, erroneous results may occur. If necessary, we may use the *type* cast operator to change the type locally. Example:

```
y = cos((double)x);
```

Nondeclaration of Functions

Every function that is called should be declared in the calling function for the types of value it returns. Consider the following program:

```
main()
{
      float a =12.75;
      float b = 7.36;
      printf("%f\n", division(a,b));
}
double division(float x, float y)
{
      return(x/y);
}
```

The function returns a **double** type value but this fact is not known to the calling function and therefore it expects to receive an **int** type value. The program produces either meaningless results or error message such as "redefinition".

The function **division** is like any other variable for the **main** and therefore it should be declared as **double** in the main.

Now, let us assume that the function division is coded as follows:

```
division(float x, float y)
{
   return(x/y);
}
```

Although the values x and y are floats and the result of x/y is also float, the function returns only integer value because no type specifier is given in the function definition. This is wrong too. The function header should include the type specifier to force the function to return a particular type of value.

Missing & Operator in scanf Parameters

All non-pointer variables in a scanf call should be preceded by an **&** operator. If the variable code is declared as an integer, then the statement

```
scanf("%d", code);
```

is wrong. The correct one is scanf("%d", &code);

Remember, the compiler will not detect this error and you may get a crazy output.

Crossing the Bounds of an Array

All C indices start from zero. A common mistake is to start the index from 1. For example, the segment

```
int x[10], sum i;
Sum = 0;
for (i = 1; i < = 10; i++)
        sum = sum + x[i];
```

would not find the correct sum of the elements of array x. The for loop expressions should be corrected as follows:

```
for(i=0;i<10;i++)
```

Forgetting a Space for Null character in a String

All character arrays are terminated with a null character and therefore their size should be declared to hold one character more than the actual string size.

Using Uninitialized Pointers

An uninitialized pointer points to garbage. The following program is wrong.

```
main()
{
        int a, *ptr;
        a = 25;
        *ptr = a+5;
}
```

The pointer **ptr** has not been initialized.

Missing Indirection and Address Operators

Another common error is to forget to use the operators * and **&** in certain places. Consider the following program:

```
main()
{
        int m, *p1;
```

```
        m = 5;
        p1 = m;
        printf("%d\n", *p1);
    }
```

This will print some unknown value because the pointer assignment

```
p1 =m;
```

is wrong. It should be:

```
p1 = &m;
```

Consider the following expression:

```
y = p1 + 10;
```

Perhaps, **y** was expected to be assigned the value at location **p1** plus 10. But it does not happen. **y** will contain some unknown address value. The above expression should be rewritten as

```
y = *p1 + 10;
```

Missing Parentheses in Pointer Expressions

The following two statements are not the same:

```
x = *p1 + 1;
x = *(p1 + 1);
```

The first statement would assign the value at location **p1** plus 1 to **x** while the second would assign the value at location **p1 + 1**.

Omitting Parentheses around Arguments in Macro Definitions

This would cause incorrect evaluation of expression when the macro definition is substituted.

Example: **# define** f(x) x * x + 1

The call **y = f(a+b);**

will be evaluated as **y = a+b * a+b+1;** which is wrong.

Some other mistakes that we commonly make are:

- Wrong indexing of loops.
- Wrong termination of loops.
- Unending loops.
- Use of incorrect relational test.
- Failure to consider all possible conditions of a variable.
- Trying to divide by zero.
- Mismatching of data specifications and variables in **scanf** and **printf** statements.
- Forgetting truncation and rounding off errors.

15.5 PROGRAM TESTING AND DEBUGGING

Testing and debugging refer to the tasks of detecting and removing errors in a program, so that the program produces the desired results on all occasions. Every programmer should be aware of the fact that rarely does a program run perfectly the first time. No matter how thoroughly the design is carried out, and no matter how much care is taken in coding, one can never say that the program would be 100 per cent error-free. It is therefore necessary to make efforts to detect, isolate and correct any errors that are likely to be present in the program.

Types of Errors

We have discussed a number of common errors. There might be many other errors, some obvious and others not so obvious. All these errors can be classified under four types, namely, syntax errors, run-time errors, logical errors, and latent errors.

Syntax errors: Any violation of rules of the language results in syntax errors. The compiler can detect and isolate such errors. When syntax errors are present, the compilation fails and is terminated after listing the errors and the line numbers in the source program, where the errors have occurred. Remember, in some cases, the line number may not exactly indicate the place of the error. In other cases, one syntax error may result in a long list of errors. Correction of one or two errors at the beginning of the program may eliminate the entire list.

Run-time errors: Errors such as a mismatch of data types or referencing an out-of-range array element go undetected by the compiler. A program with these mistakes will run, but produce erroneous results and therefore the name run-time errors. Isolating a run-time error is usually a difficult task.

Logical errors: As the name implies, these errors are related to the logic of the program execution. Such actions as taking a wrong path, failure to consider a particular condition, and incorrect order of evaluation of statements belong to this category. Logical errors do not show up as compiler-generated error messages. Rather, they cause incorrect results. These errors are primarily due to a poor understanding of the problem, incorrect translation of the algorithm into the program and a lack of clarity of hierarchy of operators. Consider the following statement:

```
if(x ==y)
    printf("They are equal\n");
```

when **x** and **y** are float types values, they rarely become equal, due to truncation errors. The printf call may not be executed at all. A test like **while(x != y)** might create an infinite loop.

Latent errors: It is a 'hidden' error that shows up only when a particular set of data is used. For example, consider the following statement:

```
ratio = (x+y)/(p-q);
```

An error occurs only when p and q are equal. An error of this kind can be detected only by using all possible combinations of test data.

Program Testing

Testing is the process of reviewing and executing a program with the intent of detecting errors, which may belong to any of the four kinds discussed above. We know that while the compiler can detect syntactic and semantic errors, it cannot detect run-time and logical errors that show up during the execution of the program. Testing, therefore, should include necessary steps to detect all possible errors in the program. It is, however, important to remember that it is impractical to find all errors. Testing process may include the following two stages:

1. Human testing.
2. Computer-based testing.

Human testing is an effective error-detection process and is done before the computer-based testing begins. Human testing methods include code inspection by the programmer, code inspection by a test group, and a review by a peer group. The test is carried out statement by statement and is analyzed with respect to a checklist of common programming errors. In addition to finding the errors, the programming style and choice of algorithm are also reviewed.

Computer-based testing involves two stages, namely compiler testing and run-time testing. Compiler testing is the simplest of the two and detects yet undiscovered syntax errors. The program executes when the compiler detects no more errors. Should it mean that the program is correct? Will it produce the expected results? The answer is negative. The program may still contain run-time and logic errors.

Run-time errors may produce run-time error messages such as "null pointer assignment" and "stack overflow". When the program is free from all such errors, it produces output which might or might not be correct. Now comes the crucial test, the test for the *expected output*. The goal is to ensure that the program produces expected results under all conditions of input data.

Test for correct output is done using *test data* with known results for the purpose of comparison. The most important consideration here is the design or invention of effective test data. A useful criteria for test data is that all the various conditions and paths that the processing may take during execution must be tested.

Program testing can be done either at module (function) level or at program level. Module level test, often known as *unit test*, is conducted on each of the modules to uncover errors within the boundary of the module. Unit testing becomes simple when a module is designed to perform only one function.

Once all modules are unit tested, they should be *integrated together* to perform the desired function(s). There are likely to be interfacing problems, such as data mismatch between the modules. An *integration test* is performed to discover errors associated with interfacing.

Program Debugging

Debugging is the process of isolating and correcting the errors. One simple method of debugging is to place print statements throughout the program to display the values of variables. It displays the dynamics of a program and allows us to examine and compare the information at various points. Once the location of an error is identified and the error corrected, the debugging statements may be removed. We can use the conditional compilation statements discussed in Chapter 14 to switch on or off the debugging statements.

Another approach is to use the process of deduction. The location of an error is arrived at using the process of elimination and refinement. This is done using a list of possible causes of the error.

The third error-locating method is to backtrack the incorrect results through the logic of the program until the mistake is located. That is, beginning at the place where the symptom has been uncovered, the program is traced backward until the error is located.

15.6 PROGRAM EFFICIENCY

Two critical resources of a computer system are execution time and memory. The efficiency of a program is measured in terms of these two resources. Efficiency can be improved with good design and coding practices.

Execution Time

The execution time is directly tied to the efficiency of the algorithm selected. However, certain coding techniques can considerably improve the execution efficiency. The following are some of the techniques, which could be applied while coding the program.

1. Select the fastest algorithm possible.
2. Simplify arithmetic and logical expressions.
3. Use fast arithmetic operations, whenever possible.
4. Carefully evaluate loops to avoid any unnecessary calculations within the loops.
5. If possible, avoid the use of multi-dimensional arrays.
6. Use pointers for handling arrays and strings.

However, remember the following, while attempting to improve efficiency.

1. Analyse the algorithm and various parts of the program before attempting any efficiency changes.
2. Make it work before making it faster.
3. Keep it right while trying to make it faster.
4. Do not sacrifice clarity for efficiency.

Memory Requirement

Memory restrictions in the microcomputer environment is a real concern to the programmer. It is therefore desirable to take all necessary steps to compress memory requirements.

1. Keep the program simple. This is the key to memory efficiency.
2. Use an algorithm that is simple and requires less steps.
3. Declare arrays and strings with correct sizes.
4. When possible, limit the use of multi-dimensional arrays.
5. Try to evaluate and incorporate memory compression features available with the language.

REVIEW QUESTIONS

15.1 Discuss the various aspects of program design.

15.2 How does program design relate to program efficiency?

15.3 Readability is more important than efficiency, Comment.

15.4 Distinguish between the following:

a. Syntactic errors and semantic errors.

b. Run-time errors and logical errors.

c. Run-time errors and latent errors.

d. Debugging and testing.
e. Compiler testing and run-time testing.

15.5 A program has been compiled and linked successfully. When you run this program you face one or more of the following situations.
a. Program is executed but no output.
b. It produces incorrect answers.
c. It does not stop running.

15.6 List five common programming mistakes. Write a small program containing these errors and try to locate them with the help of computer.

15.7 In a program, two values are compared for convergence, using the statement

```
if( (x-y) < 0.00001) ....
```

Does the statement contain any error? If yes, explain the error.

15.8 A program contains the following if statements:

```
... ..
... ..
if(x>1&&y == 0)p = p/x;
if(x == 5|| p > 2) p = p+2;
... ..
... ..
```

Draw a flow chart to illustrate various logic paths for this segment of the program and list test data cases that could be used to test the execution of every path shown.

15.9 Given below is a function to compute the yth power of an integer x.

```
power(int x, int y)
{
    int p;
    p = y;
    while(y > 0)
          x *= y --;
    return(x);
}
```

This function contains some bugs. Write a test procedure to locate the errors with the help of a computer.

15.10 A program reads three values from the terminal, representing the lengths of three sides of a box namely length, width and height and prints a message stating whether the box is a cube, rectangle, or semi-rectangle. Prepare sets of data that you feel would adequately test this program.

Appendix I

Bit-Level Programming

1. INTRODUCTION

One of the unique features of C language as compared to other high-level languages is that it allows direct manipulation of individual bits within a word. Bit-level manipulations are used in setting a particular bit or group of bits to 1 or 0. They are also used to perform certain numerical computations faster. As pointed out in Chapter 3, C supports the following operators:

1. Bitwise logical operators.
2. Bitwise shift operators.
3. One's complement operator.

All these operators work only on integer type operands.

2. BITWISE LOGICAL OPERATORS

There are three logical bitwise operators. They are:

- *Bitwise* AND (&)
- *Bitwise* OR (|)
- *Bitwise exclusive* OR (^)

These are binary operators and require two integer-type operands. These operators work on their operands bit by bit starting from the least significant (i.e. the rightmost) bit, setting each bit in the result as shown in Table 1.

Table 1 *Result of Logical Bitwise Operations*

op1	*op2*	*op1 & op2*	*op1 | op2*	*op1 ^ op2*
1	1	1	1	0
1	0	0	1	1
0	1	0	1	1
0	0	0	0	0

Bitwise AND

The bitwise AND operator is represented by a single ampersand (&) and is surrounded on both sides by integer expressions. The result of ANDing operation is 1 if both the bits have a value of 1; otherwise it is 0. Let us consider two variables **x** and **y** whose values are 13 and 25. The binary representation of these two variables are

```
x - - -> 0000 0000 0000 1101
y - - -> 0000 0000 0001 1001
```

If we execute statement

```
z = x & y ;
```

then the result would be:

```
z - - -> 0000 0000 0000 1001
```

Although the resulting bit pattern represents the decimal number 9, there is no apparent connection between the decimal values of these three variables.

Bitwise ANDing is often used to test whether a particular bit is 1 or 0. For example, the following program tests whether the fourth bit of the variable **flag** is 1 or 0.

```
#define TEST 8 /* represents 00........01000 */
main()
{
          int flag;
          ....
          ....
          if((flag & TEST) != 0) /* test 4th bit */
          {
             printf(" Fourth bit is set \n");
          }
          ....
          ....
```

Note that the bitwise logical operators have lower precedence than the relational operators and therefore additional parentheses are necessary as shown above.

The following program tests whether a given number is odd or even.

```
main()
{
        int test = 1;
        int number;

        printf("Input a number \n");
        scanf("%d", &number);

        while (number != -1)
        {
            if(number & test)
                print("Number is odd\n\n");
            else
                printf("Number is even\n\n");
                printf("Input a number \n");
                scanf("%d", &number);
        }
}
```

Output

```
Input a number
20
Number is even

Input a number
9
Number is odd

Input a number
-1
```

Bitwise OR

The bitwise OR is represented by the symbol | (vertical bar) and is surrounded by two integer operands. The result of OR operation is 1 if *at least* one of the bits has a value of 1; otherwise it is zero. Consider the variables **x** and **y** discussed above.

```
x - - ->       0000 0000 0000 1101
y - - ->       0000 0000 0001 1001
              _____________________
x|y - - ->     0000 0000 0001 1101
              _____________________
```

The bitwise inclusion OR operation is often used to set a particular bit to 1 in a flag. Example:

```
#define SET 8
main()
{
     int flag;
     ....
     ....
     flag = flag | SET;
     if (( flag & SET) != 0)
     {
        printf("flag is set \n");
     }
     ....
     ....
}
```

The statement

```
flag = flag | SET;
```

causes the fourth bit of flag to set 1 if it is 0 and does not change it if it is already 1.

Bitwise Exclusive OR

The bitwise *exclusive* OR is represented by the symbol ^. The result of exclusive OR is 1 if *only one* of the bits is 1; otherwise it is 0. Consider again the same variable **x** and **y** discussed above.

```
x - - ->       0000 0000 0000 1101
y - - ->       0000 0000 0001 1001
               ___________________
x^y - - ->     0000 0000 0001 0100
               ___________________
```

3. BITWISE SHIFT OPERATORS

The shift operators are used to move bit patterns either to the left or to the right. The shift operators are represented by the symbols << and >> and are used in the following form:

```
Left shift:   op << n
Right shift:  op >> n
```

op is the integer expression that is to be shifted and *n* is the number of bit positions to be shifted.

The left-shift operation causes all the bits in the operand *op* to be shifted to the left by *n* positions. The leftmost *n* bits in the original bit pattern will be lost and the rightmost *n* bit positions that are vacated will be filled with 0s.

Similarly, the right-shift operation causes all the bits in the operand *op* to be shifted to the right by *n* positions. The rightmost *n* bits will be lost. The leftmost *n* bit positions that are vacated will be filled with zero, if the *op* is an *unsigned integer*. If the variable to be shifted is **signed**, then the operation is machine dependent.

Both the operands *op* and *n* can be constants or variables. There are two restrictions on the value of *n*. It may not be negative and it may not exceed the number of bits used to represent the left operand *op*.

Let us suppose **x** is an unsigned integer whose bit pattern is

```
0100 1001 1100 1011
```

then,

```
                      vacated
                      positions
x << 13 =0100 1110 0101 1000
x >> 3 =  0000 1001 00111001
          vacated
          positions
```

Shift operators are often used for multiplication and division by powers of two.

Consider the following statement:

```
x = y << 1;
```

This statement shifts one bit to the left in **y** and then the result is assigned to **x**. The decimal value of **x** will be the value of **y** multiplied by 2. Similarly, the statement

```
x = y >> 1;
```

shifts **y** one bit to the right and assigns the result to **x**. In this case, the value of **x** will be the value of **y** divided by 2.

The shift operators, when combined with the logical bitwise operators, are useful for extracting data from an integer field that holds multiple pieces of information. This process is known as *masking*. Masking is discussed in Section 5.

4. BITWISE COMPLEMENT OPERATORS

The complement operator ~ (also called the one's complement operator) is an unary operator and inverts all the bits represented by its operand. That is, 0s become 1s and 1s become zero. Example:

```
 x  =  1001 0110 1100 1011
~x  =  0110 1001 0011 0100
```

This operator is often combined with the bitwise AND operator to turn off a particular bit. For example, the statement

```
x = 8;          /* 0000 0000 0000 1000 */
flag = flag & ~x;
```

would turn off the fourth bit in the variable **flag**.

5. MASKING

Masking refers to the process of extracting desired bits from (or transforming desired bits in) a variable by using logical bitwise operation. The operand (a constant or variable) that is used to perform masking is called the *mask*. Examples:

```
y = x & mask;
y = x | mask;
```

Masking is used in many different ways.

- To decide bit pattern of an integer variable.
- To copy a portion of a given bit pattern to a new variable, while the remainder of the new variable is filled with 0s (using bitwise AND).
- To copy a portion of a given bit pattern to a new variable, while the remainder of the new variable is filled with 1s (using bitwise OR).
- To copy a portion of a given bit pattern to a new variable, while the remainder of the original bit pattern is inverted within the new variable (using bitwise *exclusive* OR).

The following function uses a mask to display the bit pattern of a variable.

```
void bit_pattern(int u)
{
    int i, x, word;
    unsigned mask;
    mask = 1;
    word = 8 * sizeof(int);
    mask = mask << (word - 1);
            /* shift 1 to the leftmost position */
    for(i = 1; i<= word; i++)
    {
      x = (u & mask) ? 1 : 0; /* identify the bit */
      printf("%d", x); /* print bit value */
      mask >>= 1; /* shift mask by 11 position to right */
```

Appendix II

ASCII Values of Characters

ASCII Value	Character	ASCII Value	Character	ASCII Value	Character	ASCII Value	Character
000	NUL	032	blank	064	@	096	←
001	SOH	033	!	065	A	097	a
002	STX	034	“	066	B	098	b
003	ETX	035	#	067	C	099	c
004	EOT	036	$	068	D	100	d
005	ENQ	037	%	069	E	101	e
006	ACK	038	&	070	F	102	f
007	BEL	039	‘	071	G	103	g
008	BS	040	(	072	H	104	h
009	HT	041	)	073	I	105	i
010	LF	042	*	074	J	106	j
011	VT	043	+	075	K	107	k
012	FF	044	,	076	L	108	l
013	CR	045	–	077	M	109	m
014	SO	046	.	078	N	110	n
015	SI	047	/	079	O	111	o
016	DLE	048	0	080	P	112	p
017	DC1	049	1	081	Q	113	q
018	DC2	050	2	082	R	114	r
019	DC3	051	3	083	S	115	s
020	DC4	052	4	084	T	116	t
021	NAK	053	5	085	U	117	u
022	SYN	054	6	086	V	118	v
023	ETB	055	7	087	W	119	w
024	CAN	056	8	088	X	120	x
025	EM	057	9	089	Y	121	y
026	SUB	058	:	090	Z	122	z
027	ESC	059	;	091	[	123	{
028	FS	060	<	092	\	124	|
029	GS	061	=	093	]	125	}
030	RS	062	>	094	↑	126	~
031	US	063	?	095	-	127	DEL

Note: The first 32 characters and the last character are control characters; they cannot be printed.

Appendix III

ANSI C Library Functions

The C language is accompanied by a number of library functions that perform various tasks. The ANSI committee has standardized header files which contain these functions. What follows is a slit of commonly used functions and the header files where they are defined. For a more complete list, the reader should refer to the manual of the version of C that is being used.

The header files that are included in this Appendix are:

<ctype.h>	Character testing and conversion functions
<math.h>	Mathematical functions
<stdio.h>	Standard I/O library functions
<stdlib.h>	Utility functions such as string conversion routines, memory allocation routines, random number generator, etc.
<string.h>	String manipulation functions
<time.h>	Time manipulation functions

Note: The following function parameters are used:

c - character type argument
d - double precision argument
f - file argument
i - integer argument
l - long integer argument
p - pointer argument
s - string argument
u - unsigned integer argument

An asterisk (*) denotes a pointer

Function	*Data type returned*	*Task*
<ctype.h>		
isalnum(c)	int	Determine if argument is alphanumeric. Return nonzero value if true; 0 otherwise.
isalpha(c)	int	Determine if argument is alphabetic. Return nonzero value if true; 0 otherwise.
isascii(c)	int	Determine if argument is an ASCII character. Return nonzero value if true; 0 otherwise.
iscntrl(c)	int	Determine if argument is an ASCII control character. Return nonzero value if true; 0 otherwise.
isdigit(c)	int	Determine if argument is a decimal digit. Return nonzero value if true; 0 otherwise.
isgraph(c)	int	Determine if argument is a graphic printing ASCII character. Return nonzero value if true; 0 otherwise.
islower(c)	int	Determine if argument is lowercase. Return nonzero value if true; 0 otherwise.
isodigit(c)	int	Determine if argument is an octal digit. Return nonzero value if true; 0 otherwise.
isprint(c)	int	Determine if argument is a printing ASCII character. Return nonzero value if true; 0 otherwise.
ispunct(c)	int	Determine if argument is a punctuation character. Return non-zero value if true; 0 otherwise.
isspace(c)	int	Determine if argument is a whitespace character. Return non-zero value if true; 0 otherwise.
isupper(c)	int	Determine if argument is uppercase. Return nonzero value if true; 0 otherwise.
isxdigit(c)	int	determine if argument is a hexadecimal digit. Return nonzero value if true; 0 otherwise.
toascii(c)	int	Convert value of argument to ASCII.
tolower(c)	int	Convert letter to lowercase.
toupper(c)	int	Convert letter to uppercase.
<math.h>		
acos(d)	double	Return the arc cosine of d.
asin(d)	double	Return the arc sine of d.
atan(d)	double	Return the arc tangent of d.
atan2(d1,d2)	double	Return the arc tangent of d1/d2.
ceil(d)	double	Return a value rounded up to the next higher integer.
cos(d)	double	Return the cosine of d.
cosh(d)	double	Return the hyperbolic cosine of d.
exp(d)	double	Raise e to the power d.
fabs(d)	double	Return the absolute value of d.
floor(d)	double	Return a value rounded down to the next lower integer.

Function	*Data type returned*	*Task*
fmod(d1, d2)	double	Return the remainder of d1/d2 (with same sign as d1).
labs(l)	long int	Return the absolute value of 1.
log(d)	double	Return the natural logarithm of d.
log10(d)	double	Return the logarithm (base 10) of d.
pow(d1,d2)	double	Return d1 raised to the d2 power.
sin(d)	double	Return the sine of d.
sinh(d)	double	Return the hyperbolic sine of d.
sqrt(d)	double	Return the square root of d.
tan(d)	double	Return the tangent of d.
tanh(d)	double	Return the hyperbolic tangent of d.
<stdio.h>		
fclose(f)	int	Close file f. Return 0 if file is successfully closed.
feof(f)	int	Determine if an end-of-file condition has been reached. If so, return a nonzero value; otherwise, return 0.
fgetc(f)	int	Enter a single character form file f.
fgets(s, i, f)	char*	Enter string s, containing i characters, from file f.
fopen(s1,s2)	file*	Open a file named s1 of type s2. Return a pointer to the file.
fprint(f,...)	int	Send data items to file f.
fputc(c,f)	int	Send a single character to file f.
fputs(s,f)	int	Send string s to file f.
fread(s,i1,i2,f)	int	Enter i2 data items, each of size i1 bytes, from file f to string s.
fscanf(f,...)	int	Enter data items from file f
fseek(f,1,i)	int	Move the pointer for file f a distance 1 bytes from location i.
ftell(f)	long int	Return the current pointer position within file f.
fwrite(s,i1,i2,f)	int	Send i2 data items, each of size i1 bytes from string s to file f.
getc(f)	int	Enter a single character from file f.
getchar(void)	int	Enter a single character from the standard input device.
gets(s)	char*	Enter string s from the standard input device.
printf(...)	int	Send data items to the standard output device.
putc(c,f)	int	Send a single character to file f.
putchar(c)	int	Send a single character to the standard output device.
puts(s)	int	Send string s to the standard output device.
rewind(f)	void	Move the pointer to the beginning of file f.
scanf(...)	int	Enter data items from the standard input device.
<stdlib.h>		
abs(i)	int	Return the absolute value of i.
atof(s)	double	Convert string s to a double-precision quantity.
atoi(s)	int	Convert string s to an integer.
atol(s)	long	Convert string s to a long integer.

Function	*Data type returned*	*Task*
calloc(u1,u2)	void*	Allocate memory for an array having u1 elements, each of length u2 bytes. Return a pointer to the beginning of the allocated space.
exit(u)	void	Close all files and buffers, and terminate the program. (Value of u is assigned by the function, to indicate termination status).
free(p)	void	Free a block of allocated memory whose beginning is indicated by p.
malloc(u)	void*	Allocate u bytes of memory. Return a pointer to the beginning of the allocated space.
rand(void)	int	Return a random positive integer.
realloc(p, u)	void*	Allocate u bytes of new memory to the pointer variable p. Return a pointer to the beginning of the new memory space.
srand(u)	void	Initialize the random number generator.
system(s)	int	Pass command string s to the operating system. Return 0 if the command is successfully executed; otherwise, return a nonzero value typically –1.
<string.h>		
strcmp(s1, s2)	int	Compare two strings lexicographically. Return a negative value if s1<s2; 0 if s1 and s2 are identical; and a positive value if s1>s2.
strcmpi(s1, s2)	int	Compare two strings lexicographically, without regard to case. Return a negative value if s1<s2; 0 if s1 and s2 are identical; and a value of s1 > s2.
strcpy(s1, s2)	char*	Copy string s2 to string s1.
strlen(s)	int	Return the number of characters in string s.
strset(s, c)	char*	Set all characters within s to c(excluding the terminating null character \0).
<time.h>		
difftime(11,12)	double	Return the time difference 11 ~ 12, where 11 and 12 represent elapsed time beyond a designated base time (see the time function).
time(p)	long int	Return the number of seconds elapsed beyond a designated base time.

Appendix IV

A Phone Book

After reading the book, one would like to apply the gained knowledge to some practical work. This case study, *Phone Book* is a simple application that incorporates most of the features of C that you have learnt in the book. I will discuss each of the features of this application between the code, although most of the code has comments and you by now would have become quite an expert in writing code in C.

The *Phone Book* application provides features like storing a room/phone number into a database, sorting, finding the room number/phone number etc.

I will refer to any particular line of code during explanation using the line number against each line. Well then let's begin,

```
1  /************************************************************************
2  Program: Phone Book (phoneb.c)
3  Programmer: Jude D'souza
4  TESTED/COMPILED - Windows 2000 Pro/Borland Turbo C++ 3.0
5  ************************************************************************/
6  #include <stdio.h>
7  #include <conio.h>
8  #include <stdlib.h>
9  #include <graphics.h>
10 #include <ctype.h>
11 #include <string.h>
12 #define MAXDB 500 /* Maximum number of Entries in the phone book */
13
14
15 /* List of Globe variables */
16 int i; /*globe index*/
17 long int phone[MAXDB+1];
18 int room[MAXDB+1];
19 /* phone_tmp & room_tmp array's are temp storage used for delete recovery */
20 long int phone_tmp[MAXDB+1];
21 int room_tmp[MAXDB+1];
22 void AddEntry(int, long int);
23 int add_count=0; /* master counter for entries added */
24 int current_e_add; /* counter for current entries added within a giventime.*/
25 int DeleteEntry(int, long int);
26 int FindPhone(long int);
27 int FindRoom(int);
```

```
int phone_found,room_found;
int del_entry; /* counts del entry at a given time */
int tot_del_entry=0; /* master del counter */
int ListAll(void);
int SortAllEntries(char);
int GetTotalEntries(void);
int chkstrdig (char str[], int range);
char menu(void);
void LoadDB(void); /* load database from file function */
void exitmenu(void);
void drawscreen(void);
void refreshscreen(void);

char dbload[80]; /* loaded database */

void main(void)
{
char iroom[80],iphone[80],add_quit;
char option,sortopt,exit_opt; /* menu,sort and exit option*/
int  phone_check,room_check,delete_check,sort_check,list_check;
int iroom_search,iroom_del;
int int_iroom,total_entries;
int error_iphone,error_iroom; /* used to check inputs error's  */
long int longint_iphone;
long int iphone_search;
long int iphone_del;

/* Init while no valid database file is loaded program will work in RAM! */
strcpy(dbload, "No database file loaded (RAM MODE!).");

/* MAIN MENU */
do
 {
  do
   { option = menu();
     if (option == '1') /* AddEntry Option */
     {  current_e_add=0; /*init current entries added to zero.*/
  for (i=add_count; i < MAXDB; i++)
  {    clrscr();
       refreshscreen();
       drawscreen();
       gotoxy(1,4);
       printf(">> Add Entry <<");
       gotoxy(1,25);
       cprintf("Please Add Your Entry, leave blank to quit to Main Menu");
       gotoxy(1,6);
```

```
    printf("Enter Room  Number[%3d]: ",i+1);
    gets(iroom);

    if (iroom[0] == '\0' ) /* user hits enter - quits */
    {  gotoxy(1,25);
       cprintf("You chose to quit: Entry %d was not added to the
database.",i+1);
       getch();
       break;
    }
    printf("Enter Phone Number[%3d]: ",i+1);
    gets(iphone);

    if (iphone[0] == '\0') /* user hits enter - quits */
    {  gotoxy(1,25);
       cprintf("You chose to quit: Entry %d was not added to the
 database.",i+1);
       getch();
       break;
    }
    /* check the string for valid inputs */
    error_iroom = chkstrdig(iroom,4);
    error_iphone = chkstrdig(iphone,8);
    /* loop's while room input error (out of range/character) */
    while(error_iroom != 0)
    { if (error_iroom == -1)
      {  clrscr();
         refreshscreen();
         drawscreen();
         gotoxy(1,4);
         printf(">> Add Entry <<");
         gotoxy(1,25);
         cprintf("Error: Room  Number - out of Range, Your entry was greater
 than 4 digits. ");
         gotoxy(1,6);
         printf("Renter Room  Number[%3d]: ",i+1);
         gets(iroom);
      }
      if (error_iroom == -2)
      {  clrscr();
         refreshscreen();
         drawscreen();
         gotoxy(1,4);
         printf("*** Add Entry ***");
         gotoxy(1,25);
         cprintf("Error: Room  Number - Character(s) detected, character(s)
```

```
are not allowed.");
            gotoxy(1,6);
            printf("Renter Room  Number[%3d]: ",i+1);
            gets(iroom);
        }/* checks string room input if valid */
        error_iroom = chkstrdig(iroom,4);
      }/*loop's while phone input error (out of range/character) */
      while(error_iphone !=0)
      { if (error_iphone == -1)
        {  clrscr();
            refreshscreen();
            drawscreen();
            gotoxy(1,4);
            printf(">> Add Entry <<");
            gotoxy(1,25);
            cprintf("Error: Phone Number - out of Range, Your entry was greater
than 8 digits. ");
            gotoxy(1,6);
            printf("Room  Number[%3d] Entry: %s",i+1,iroom);
            gotoxy(1,7);
            printf("Renter Phone Number[%3d]: ",i+1);
            gets(iphone);
        }
        if (error_iphone == -2)
        {  clrscr();
            refreshscreen();
            drawscreen();
            gotoxy(1,4);
            printf(">> Add Entry <<");
            gotoxy(1,25);
            cprintf("Error: Phone Number - Character(s) detected, character(s)
are not allowed.");
            gotoxy(1,6);
            printf("Room  Number[%3d] Entry: %s",i+1,iroom);
            gotoxy(1,7);
            printf("Renter Phone Number[%3d]: ",i+1);
            gets(iphone);
        }/* checks phone input valid */
        error_iphone = chkstrdig(iphone,8);
      }
      /* no room or phone input error - addentry */
      if (error_iroom == 0 && error_iphone == 0)
      {  int_iroom = atoi(iroom); /* converts string to int */
         longint_iphone = atol(iphone); /* converts string to long int */
         current_e_add++;
         AddEntry(int_iroom,longint_iphone);
```

```
    }
  }
  if (add_count == MAXDB) /* database full */
  {  gotoxy(1,25);
     cprintf("\aDatabase is full!: %d entries were added, ",add_count);
     cprintf("that is the Maximum No. I can hold.");
     getch();
  }
     }
     else
     if (option == '2') /* DeleteEntry option */
     {  del_entry = 0; /* Initialize del_entry counter zero */
      clrscr();
      refreshscreen();
      drawscreen();
      gotoxy(1,4);
      printf(">> Delete Entry <<");
      gotoxy(1,6);
      printf("Enter room  number to delete: ");
      scanf("%d",&iroom_del);
      flushall(); /* clears buffer */

      printf("Enter phone number to delete: ");
      scanf("%ld",&iphone_del);
      flushall();

      delete_check = DeleteEntry(iroom_del,iphone_del);

      if (delete_check == 0)/*successfully found or deleted entries display*/
      {  gotoxy(1,25);
         cprintf("Successful: There are currently %d entries in the database,
 ",add_count);
         cprintf("deleted %d.",del_entry);
         getch();
      }
      if (delete_check == -1) /* error: does not delete if db not found */
      {  gotoxy(1,25);
         cprintf("Error: The Room No./Phone No. Your looking for was Not Found.
 ");
         getch();
      }

   }
   else
   if (option == '3') /* FindPhone Option */
   {  phone_found = 0; /*initialize phone no. found to zero */
```

```
    clrscr();
    refreshscreen();
    drawscreen();
    gotoxy(1,4);
    printf(">> Find Room Number <<");

    gotoxy(1,6);
    printf("Enter the phone number to search for: ");
    scanf("%ld",&iphone_search);
    flushall(); /* clears buffer */

    phone_check = FindPhone(iphone_search);

    if (phone_check == 0) /* return = 0 Phone found */
    {  gotoxy(1,25);
        cprintf("Successful: There are currently %d entries in the database,
",add_count);
        /* phone_found(globe), counts phone no. found(within FindPhone
        function */
        printf("found %d.",phone_found);
        getch();
    }
    if (phone_check == -1) /* return = -1 Phone not found */
    {  gotoxy(1,25);
        cprintf("Error: The Phone No. Your looking for was Not Found.");
        getch();
    }
    }
    else
    if (option == '4') /* FindRoom Option */
    {  room_found = 0;  /* initialize room no. found to zero */
        clrscr();
        refreshscreen();
        drawscreen();
        gotoxy(1,4);
        printf(">> Find Phone Number <<");

        gotoxy(1,6);
        printf("Enter the room number to search for: ");
        scanf("%d",&iroom_search);
        flushall();

        room_check = FindRoom(iroom_search);

        if (room_check == 0) /* return = 0 Room found */
        {  gotoxy(1,25);
```

```
                cprintf("Successful: There are currently %d entries in the data
                base,
", add_count);
            /* room_found is globe it counts room no. found in FindRoom
            function */
            cprintf("found %d.",room_found);
            getch();
        }
        if (room_check == -1) /* return = -1 Room was not found */
        {  gotoxy(1,25);
           cprintf("Error: The Room No. Your looking for was Not Found.");
           getch();
        }

      }
      else
      if (option == '5') /* ListAll option */
      {  clrscr();
         refreshscreen();
         drawscreen();
         gotoxy(1,4);
         printf(">> ListAll <<\n\n");

         list_check = ListAll();

         if (list_check == 0) /* return 0 if entries are in database */
         {  gotoxy(1,25);
            cprintf("List Sucuessful");
            getch();
         }
         if (list_check == -1) /* return -1 - emptylist */
         {
            gotoxy(1,25);
            cprintf("Empty List");
            getch();
     }
      }
      else
      if (option == '6') /* Getotalentries option */
      {  total_entries = GeTotalEntries();
  gotoxy(1,25);
  cprintf("There are currently %d entries stored in the
 Database.",total_entries);
     getch();
    }
    else
```

```
    if (option == '7') /* Sort Option */
    {  clrscr();
     refreshscreen();
     drawscreen();
     gotoxy(1,4);
     printf(">> Sort All Entries <<");
     gotoxy(1,6);
     printf("Press 'A' to sort database in [A]scending order");
     gotoxy(1,7);
     printf("Press 'D' to sort database in [D]escending order.");
     gotoxy(1,9);
     printf("Note: Database is sorted by phone no. entries.");
     sortopt = getch();
     flushall();

     sort_check = SortAllEntries(sortopt);
     getch();
     if (sort_check == 0) /* return = 0 - entries, in db & was sorted */
     {  gotoxy(1,25);
        cprintf("Database was successfully Sorted.
");
        getch();
     }
     if (sort_check == -1) /* return = -1 - if db is empty */
     {  gotoxy(1,25);
        cprintf("Database was not sorted - Database is empty!");
        getch();
     }
    }
    else
    if (option == '8') /* Load Database from file option */
    { clrscr();
     refreshscreen();
     drawscreen();
     gotoxy(1,4);
     printf(">> Load Database <<");
     LoadDB();
    }
    else
    if (option == '9') /* exit option */
    {  gotoxy(1,25);
     cprintf("Do you really want to exit?, Press 'Y' to confirm, anykey to
cancel");
     exit_opt = getch();
     flushall();
     if (exit_opt == 'y' || exit_opt == 'Y')
```

```
          { clrscr();
            refreshscreen();
            drawscreen();
            gotoxy(1,4);
            printf(">> Exit To system <<\n\n");
            exitmenu();
          }
        }
       else /* user presses an invalid key display msg error */
      { gotoxy(1,25);
        cprintf("Error: Invalid option! Select an option between 1 and 9");
        getch();
        flushall(); /* clears buffer */
      }
    }while  (option > '9' || option < '1' );
  }while (option != '`'); /* unlimated loop */
}
```

The function main() display a console menu which has the following options:

- Add Entry
- Delete Entry
- Find room number
- Find phone number
- List all entries
- Display total entries in database
- Sort entries
- Load database from file
- Exit

Each of these menu options calls the appropriate function for performing its designated operation.

```
/*-------------------------------------------------------------------------
      AddEntry Function
      ----------------
      Does not return any values it is used to added valid inputs(only) into
      the database and display the entries which was added.
      * A valid inputs are positive numbers only.
      1. Room no. input with less than or equal to 4 digits only.
      2. Phone no. input with less than or equal to 8 digits only.
      3. Input of Zero for room no. or phone no. inputs is invalid.
--------------------------------------------------------------------------*/
void AddEntry(int r, long int p)
{
      room[i] = r;   /* store r(room) input into db */
      phone[i] = p; /* store r(room) input into db */
      add_count++;  /* keeps track of total entries added. */
```

```
    printf("\nRoom No.  [%-4d]\nPhone No. [%-8ld]\n%d entries
added.",r,p,current_e_add);
    getch();
}
/*-------------------------------------------------------------------------------

    DeleteEntry function
    ____________

    Used to delete entrys in the database.
    Returns 0 if room no. & phone no. was found in the database.
    Returns -1 if room no. & phone no. is not found in the database.

    Note: Auto-Recovery was implemented into this function but was never
    used. room_tmp and phone_tmp arrays contain the deleted data
    which maybe used for recovery.
-------------------------------------------------------------------------------*/
int DeleteEntry(int r, long int p)
{
int k,x,del_found_flag=-1,loop_mov_stop,loop_mov,count_del=0;
char del_me; /* Variable to confirm delete */

   for(k=0; k < add_count; k++)
   {  if (add_count != 0) /* checks if database is not empty */
      {  if (r == room[k] && p == phone[k])
         {  gotoxy(1,8);
            printf("Match Found: \n");
            printf("Room No. [%-4d]\tPhone No. [%-8ld] was found in record No.
[%3d  ]\n",room[k],phone[k],k+1);
            del_found_flag = 0; /* when found, set's del_found_flag=0 */
            gotoxy(1,25);
            cprintf("Delete record [%3d  ]?, Press 'Y' to confirm, anykey to
cancel.",k+1);
            del_me = getch();
            flushall();
            if (del_me == 'y' || del_me == 'Y')
            { room_tmp[tot_del_entry] = room[k]; /* tmp array storage for room
found */
            room[k] = -1; /* marks -1 for deleted */
            phone_tmp[tot_del_entry] = phone[k];
            phone[k] = -1;
            del_entry++; /* counter for deleted entry */
            tot_del_entry++; /* counter for temp storage */
            }
         }
      }
```

```
406     }
407     if (add_count !=0) /* if database is not empty process with delete */
408     {/* keeps looping while move up position is not = to deleted entry */
409         for (x=0; x < del_entry; x++)
410         {   for (k=0; k < add_count; k++)
411           {/* When -1 is found it moves everything by one */
412               if (room[k] == -1 && phone[k] == -1)
413               {  loop_mov_stop=0;
414               loop_mov =0;
415               count_del++;
416               /* loop_mov_stop calculates moves needed */
417               loop_mov_stop = add_count-(k+1);
418               while (loop_mov_stop != loop_mov)
419               {         room[k+loop_mov] = room[(k+1)+loop_mov];
420                         phone[k+loop_mov] = phone[(k+1)+loop_mov];
421                         loop_mov++; /* counter for move */
422               }
423               }
424           }
425         }
426     }
427     /* Calcalates total entry */
428     add_count = add_count - del_entry;
429
430     if (del_found_flag == 0) /* flag is 0 when delete entry input was found */
431     { return(0);  } /* return sucessful */
432     Else
433     { return(-1); } /* return not found */
434 }
```

Let's take a closer look at how the DeleteEntry function works. To make things easier let,
Room =1,2,3,4,5,6,7,8,9,10
Phone=1,2,3,4,5,6,7,8,9,10

Ten entries in the database with the digits from 1 to 10 both having the same values entered. Now if the user requests Room/Phone "4" to be deleted, the delete entry function will find the digit "4" in both Room and Phone matching the user's request.

Find -> is done within a for loop until add_count number is reached, Add_count is the counter for the number of entries added (Line 385). If it finds the digit '4' it asks the user if he/she wants to delete the current entry in the record.
This is what happens when the user selects 'Yes',

1) Copy that current entry to a temp location (Lines 397, 399).
2) Then a '-1' is copied on top of the location where digit '4' was found overwriting it (marking it has been deleted) (Lines 398, 400). Tot_del_entry and del_entry is incremented by one each time this is done (Lines 401,402).

3) Another for loop is nested within the for, used to find '-1's' marked for deleted, it loops for the no. of entries that has been deleted (Lines 409, 412). Calculation of the move up stop position is done on line 417.
4) Then using the while loop (Line 418) everything is moved up by one position. At the end of the while loop (Line 428), the number of records that exist after deletion has been done is calculated.

```
435    /*---------------------------------------------------------------------
436       FindPhone function
437       ------------------
438       Used to search for a phone number in the database.
439
440       Returns 0 if phone no. was found.
441       Returns -1 if phone no. is not found.
442    ---------------------------------------------------------------------*/
443    int FindPhone(long int p)
444    {
445    int k, phone_found_flag= -1;
446       gotoxy(1,8);
447       for(k=0; k < add_count; k++)
448       {  if (add_count != 0) /* if database is not empty then run a search */

449          {  if (k != 0 && (k%15) == 0)
450         {  gotoxy(1,8); /* moves cursor to beginning when screen filled */
451            getch();
452         }
453         if (p == phone[k])
            {  printf("Phone No. [%-8ld] was found in record No. [%3d  ]\tRoom No.
454    [%-4d]\n",phone[k],k+1,room[k]);
455            phone_found++;
456            phone_found_flag= 0;
457         }
458          }
459       }
460       if (phone_found_flag == 0) /* flag is 0 if record was found */
461       { return(0);    } /* return sucessful */
462       else
463       { return(-1); } /* return not found */
464    }
465    /*---------------------------------------------------------------------
466       FindRoom function
467       -----------------
468       Used to search for a Room number in the database.
469
470       Returns 0 if room no. was found.
471       Returns -1 if room no. is not found.
472    ---------------------------------------------------------------------*/
```

```
int FindRoom(int r)
{
int k, room_found_flag=-1;

    gotoxy(1,8);
    for(k=0; k < add_count; k++)
    {  if (add_count != 0) /* if database is not empty then run a search */

        {  if (k != 0 && (k%15) == 0)
       {  gotoxy(1,8); /* moves cursor to beginning when screen filled */
          getch();
       }
       if (r == room[k])
       {  printf("Room No. (%-4d) was found in record No. [%3d  ]\tPhone No.
(%-8ld)\n",room[k],k+1,phone[k]);
          room_found++;
          room_found_flag = 0;
       }
      }
    }

    if (room_found_flag == 0)
    { return(0);  } /* return sucessful */
    else
    { return(-1); } /* return not found */
}
```

The FindRoom and FindPhone function simply match the input parameter to the function with the room and phone array and prints out the values if a match is found.

```
/*------------------------------------------------------------------------
     ListAll Function
     ----------------
     Used for displaying data entered into the database.
     returns -1 if list is empty.
     returns 0 if sucessful (database contains valid entries)
-------------------------------------------------------------------------*/
int ListAll(void)
{
int k;
    gotoxy(1,6);
    for (k=0; k < add_count; k++)
    {
   if (k != 0 && (k%17) == 0)
   {  gotoxy(1,6); /* moves cursor to beginning when screen filled */
      getch();
```

```
        }
        /* double checks - it will not print out delete entries(-1) */
        if (room[k] != -1 && phone[k] != -1)
        {  printf("Room Number [%3d  ]: %-4d\t",k+1,room[k]);
           printf("Phone Number[%3d  ]: %-81d\n",k+1,phone[k]);
        }
    }
    if (add_count == 0)
    {  return(-1); } /* Empty List */
    else
    {  return(0);  } /* Successful */
}
```

The ListAll function iterates through the room and phone array and displays the phone book entries to the user.

```
/*-----------------------------------------------------------------------
    GetTotalEntries function
    ----------------------
    Used to return total entries added to database.
-----------------------------------------------------------------------*/
int GetTotalEntries(void)
{
/* This function is not required as it does nothing but returns the total
entries that have been added.*/

    return(add_count);
}
/*-----------------------------------------------------------------------
    SortAllEntries function
    ----------------------
    Sort is done with the use of bubble sort.
    returns 0 if sort was successful.
    returns -1 if database is empty.
-----------------------------------------------------------------------*/

int SortAllEntries(char sel)
{
int k,room_str_tmp,sortalldone;
long int phone_str_tmp;
    if (add_count !=0) /* if list not empty continue with sort */
    {  do
       { sortalldone=0;
        for (k = 0; k < add_count; k++)
        {  /* sort in ascending order */
           if ((phone[k] > phone[k + 1])&&(sel == 'a' || sel == 'A')&&(k !=
```

```
add_count -1))
            {   phone_str_tmp = phone[k]; /* stores previous array to phone_str_tmp */
              phone[k] = phone[k + 1]; /* copys next array to the previous array before it */
              phone[k + 1] = phone_str_tmp; /* Previous array is copyed to next array */
              /* same process is done here but with room no. */
              room_str_tmp = room[k];
              room[k] = room[k + 1];
              room[k + 1] = room_str_tmp;
              sortalldone =1; /* sets to 1 if sort is done */
            }
            /* same method used here but sorts in decending order */
            if ((phone[k] < phone[k + 1])&&(sel == 'd' || sel == 'D')&&(k != add_count -1))
            {   phone_str_tmp = phone[k];
              phone[k] = phone[k + 1];
              phone[k + 1] = phone_str_tmp;
              room_str_tmp = room[k];
              room[k] = room[k + 1];
              room[k + 1] = room_str_tmp;
              sortalldone =1;
            }
        }
           }while (sortalldone);
      }

      if ((sel == 'a' || sel == 'A')&&add_count !=0)
      {   gotoxy(1,25);
          printf("You have chosen to sort the database in [A]scending order. ");
          return(0);    /* sucessfully sorted */
      }
      else
      if ((sel == 'd' || sel == 'D')&&add_count !=0)
      {  gotoxy(1,25);
         printf("You have chosen to sort the database in [D]ecending order. ");
         return(0);    /* sucesstully sorted */
      }
      else
      if ((sel != 'a' || sel != 'A' || sel != 'd' || sel != 'D')&&add_count !=0)
      {  gotoxy(1,12);
          printf("Invalid option - database was not sorted!");
      }
      else
      { return(-1); } /* list empty */
  }
```

The SortAllEntries uses the bubble sort method for sorting the phone book entries. The bubble sorting method used a temporary variable to swap the values. Sorting is done both in the ascending as well as the descending order. For the ascending order, each time the previous value is greater than the next value, the two values are swaped. For the sescending order, the same principal is used, only when the previous value is less than the next then the value is swapped. This entire process happens within a for loop.

```
/*-------------------------------------------------------------------------
    Chkstrdig(Check string for digits)
    ---------------------------------
    Used to check string inputs, and lenght.
    returning:
    -1 = if string lenght is out of range.
    -2 = if a char is found within the string.
    0 = if successful

    NOTE:
    Addentry specifed that Room allows for 4 digits or less.
    Phone allowing 8 digits or less.
------------------------------------------------------------------------*/
int chkstrdig (char str[], int range)
{
int lenght=0,k;
    lenght = strlen(str); /* get lenght of string */

    if (lenght > range)
    {    return(-1);} /* out of range */
    if (lenght <= range) /* string is in range */
    { for (k=0; k < lenght; k++)
      {    if (isdigit(str[k]) == 0)
        { return(-2); } /* char detected return error msg */
      }
    return(0); /* successful - input string was in range and was digits */
    }
}
/*-------------------------------------------------------------------------
    Load up database from file function
    ---------------------------------
    Used to load a file into the database.
------------------------------------------------------------------------*/
void LoadDB(void)
{
int count,nofilen,dbfilecount=0;
char finphone[80];
```

```
    char finroom[80];
    int error_junk;

    long int l_finphone;
    int i_finroom;

    FILE *f1;
         gotoxy(1,6);
         printf("Enter the filename of the database: ");
         gotoxy(1,7);
         printf("Example: c:\\mydbfile.txt");
         gotoxy(37,6);
         gets(dbload);
         flushall(); /* clears all buffers */
         f1 = fopen (dbload,"r"); /* open file for reading */
         if (f1==NULL)
         {  gotoxy(1,25);
       fprintf(stderr,"There was an error reading your database file!");
       strcpy(dbload, "No database file loaded (RAM MODE!).");
       getch();
       exit;
         }
         else
         {   for (count=0; count < MAXDB; count++)
       {   if (!feof(f1)) /* if not end of file continue to input data */
           { fscanf(f1,"%s\t%s\n",&finroom,&finphone);
             /* saves info to room, phone array */
           error_junk = chkstrdig(finroom,4);
           error_junk = chkstrdig(finphone,8);
            if (error_junk == -1 || error_junk == -2)
            {  printf("Sorry that was an invalid database\n");
               printf("Now working in RAM MODE!");
               getch();
               strcpy(dbload, "No database file loaded (RAM MODE!).");
           break;
         }
             i_finroom = atoi(finroom); /* converts string to int */
             l_finphone = atol(finphone); /* converts string to long int */
             room[count] = i_finroom;
             phone[count] = l_finphone;
             dbfilecount++; /* counts no. of records stored in file */
           }
       }
           if (error_junk ==0)
           {
         gotoxy(1,25);
```

```
679           printf("Database %s, was successfully loaded!",dbload);
680           getch();
681           /* copys no. of records in file into master counter*/
682           add_count = dbfilecount;
683             }
684          }
685          fclose(f1);
686     }
```

The LoadDB function loads the phone book entries from a flat file. The file is opened on line 647 using fopen and the data is loaded into the room and phone arrays (lines 656…675).

```
687     /**********************************************************************

688          MAIN function
689          -------------
690          Menu, ExitMenu, drawscreen and refreshscreen.
691     **********************************************************************/
692     /*--------------------------------------------------------------------
693          Menu function
694          -------------
695          Display valid options on the screen
696     --------------------------------------------------------------------*/
697     char menu(void)
698     {
699     char optrtn;
700          clrscr();
701          window(1,1,80,25); /*Set position and screen mode*/
702          refreshscreen();
703          drawscreen();
704          gotoxy(1,4);
705          printf("[1] - Add entry\n");
706          printf("[2] - Delete entry\n");
707          printf("[3] - Find room number\n");
708          printf("[4] - Find phone number\n");
709          printf("[5] - List all entries\n");
710          printf("[6] - Display total entries in database\n");
711          printf("[7] - Sort entries\n");
712          printf("[8] - Load database from file\n");
713          printf("[9] - Exit");
714          gotoxy(1,25);
715          cprintf("Please select an option between 1 and 9.");
716          gotoxy(1,15);
717          printf("Database loaded: %s",dbload);
718          gotoxy(1,14);
```

```
        printf("Select an option: ");
        optrtn = getch();
        return optrtn;
    }
    /*----------------------------------------------------------------------
       ExitMenu function
       -----------------
       While exiting to system, askes user if he/she wants to save
       database into a file.
    ----------------------------------------------------------------------*/
    void exitmenu(void)
    {   char filename[20],save_opt;
        int k;
        FILE *f1;
        gotoxy(1,6);
        printf("Do You want to Save database before exiting? ");
        gotoxy(1,25);
        cprintf("Press 'Y' to confirm, anykey to cancel.");
        save_opt = getch();
        flushall();
        if (save_opt == 'y' || save_opt == 'Y')
        {  gotoxy(1,8);
       printf("Please Enter the path and filename to save to:");
       gotoxy(1,10);
       printf("Example: c:\\mydbfile.txt");
       gotoxy(48,8); /* move cursor back to line 8 */
       gets(filename);
       flushall();
       f1 = fopen (filename,"a"); /*open file for appending mode */
       if (f1== NULL)
       {  gotoxy(1,12);
          fprintf(stderr, "Error opening file %s.",filename);
          gotoxy(1,25);
          cprintf("Database was not saved!
");
          getch();
          exit;
       }
       else
       {    for (k=0; k < add_count; k++)
            {   fprintf(f1, "%d\t%ld\n",room[k],phone[k]);}
             fclose(f1);
             gotoxy(1,25);
             cprintf("Database was successfully saved in %s",filename);
             getch();
            }
```

```
        }
        else
        {    gotoxy(1,25);
             cprintf("Database was not saved!
");
       getch();
        }
        clrscr();
        gotoxy(23,10);
        printf("Thank you for using this program");
        gotoxy(23,11);
        printf("Coded by: Jude D'souza!");
        gotoxy(23,13);
        printf("Email: shrewdjackal@yahoo.com");
        getch();
        exit(0);
}
/*------------------------------------------------------------------------
     Drawscreen function
     --------------------
     Draws program header.
-----------------------------------------------------------------------*/
void drawscreen(void)
{
        gotoxy(1,1);
         cprintf("-----------------------------------------------------------
------------");
        gotoxy(1,2);
        cprintf("                              *** PHONE BOOK ***
");
        gotoxy(1,3);
         cprintf("-----------------------------------------------------------
------------");
}
/*------------------------------------------------------------------------
     Refreshscreen function
     ---------------------
     used to refresh colour display.
-----------------------------------------------------------------------*/
void refreshscreen(void)
{    clrscr();
        textcolor(WHITE);
        textbackground(BLACK);
        gotoxy(1,25);
        cprintf("
```

```
");
        clrscr();
        textcolor(WHITE);
        textbackground(BLUE);
        gotoxy(1,25);
        cprintf("
");
}

/* EOF */
```

The above functions are used to draw the menu and the exit message on the screen. The ExitMenu function performs the task of saving the data to a flat file before closing the application.

I hope the above case study has been useful to you and will enable you to write applications in C. You could work upon this *Phone book* application and incorporate more features. Try using link lists and binary trees to store the Phone/Room numbers instead of arrays. Remember the saying 'Practice makes perfect'. Happy programming...

Bibliography

Barkakati, N., *Microsoft C Bible*, SAMS, 1990.

Barker, L., *C Tools for Scientists and Engineers*, McGraw-Hill, 1989.

Berry, R. E. and Meekings, B.A.E., *A Book on C*, Macmillan, 1987.

Hancock, L. and Krieger, M., *The C Primer*, McGraw-Hill, 1987.

Hunt, W. J., *The C Toolbox*, Addison-Wesley, 1985.

Hunter, B. H., *Understanding C*, Sybex, 1985.

Kernighan, B. W. and Ritchie, D. M., *The C Programming Language*, Prentice-Hall, 1977.

Kochan, S. G., *Programming in C*, Hyden, 1983.

Miller, L. H. and Quilici, E. A., *C Programming Language: An Applied Perspective*, John Wiley & Sons, 1987.

Purdum, J. J., *C Programming Guide*, Que Corporation, 1985.

Radcliffe, R. A., *Encyclopaedia C*, Sybex, 1990.

Schildt, H., *C Made Easy*, Osborne McGraw-Hill, 1987.

Schildt, H., *Advanced C*, Osborne McGraw-Hill, 1988.

Tim Grady, M., *Turbo C! Programming Principles and Practices*, McGraw-Hill, 1989.

WSI Staff, *C User's Handbook*, Addison-Wesely, 1984.

Wortman, L.A., and Sidebottom, T.O., *The C Programming Tutor*, Prentice-Hall, 1984.

Index